GUMBO FOR THE SOUL
10th Anniversary Edition

THE RECIPE FOR LITERACY IN THE BLACK
COMMUNITY

AN ANTHOLOGY OF INSPIRATIONAL ESSAYS,
POETRY, SAVORY RECIPES AND MORE AIMED AT
SUPPORTING LITERACY

Gumbo for the Soul: 10th Anniversary Celebration Collector's Edition
By Gumbo for the Soul International®

Edited by Gift'd Ink

Book cover and interior design: Designs by SheShe

Photos of Homer Black ©Beverly Black Johnson.

Gumbo for the Soul: 10th Anniversary is available in paperback
via major booksellers and online
www.gumboforthesoul.com

Distributed by Gumbo for the Soul International®
www.gumboforthesoul.com
ISBN-10:
097904796X
ISBN-13:
978-0-9790479-6-1

Produced and Printed in the United States of America

Because of the dynamic nature of the Internet, Web addresses or links contained in this book may have changed since publication and may no longer be valid. The views expressed in this work are solely of the author and do not necessarily reflect the views of the producer or publisher, who hereby disclaims any responsibility for them.
©2013 Gumbo for the Soul International®.

All rights reserved. No part of this book may be used or reproduced by any means, graphic, electronic, or mechanical, including photocopying, recording, taping, or by any information storage retrieval system without the written permission of the publisher except in the case of brief quotations embodied in critical articles and reviews.

A Note From Our Creator, Beverly Black Johnson-

In November 2003, I sat at the computer a blank canvass availing myself to the Lord. "Ok", I announced aloud, "it's me and you." I wanted something from HIM- the source of my creativity. HE answered me in the spirit with, "Gumbo for the Soul." I was off and running with an "inspirational" brand to nurture and grow to fruition. I would be halted soon after by the astounding high school drop-out rates plaguing our nation prompting me to change my focus to literacy, wellness, and education undergirded by spirituality.

Submissions had already been pouring in, so when the focus changed many were in dismay.

I had also sent out a few letters to literary agents. After rejection upon rejection, I decided to self publish. Some agents advised I make *Gumbo* like *Soup*. I would beg to believe God over what man would have me to conform to. I have pressed forward through much adversity to bring my vision to light and life.

My life was also at a personal crossroads. With computer, kids, and clothing in tow, I took a leap of faith towards my freedom and stepped out on my own becoming single again- but not without test and trials. But God...

It does NOT seem like only yesterday since this all began, but in fact, it feels like its been 10 years or more. 10 years of struggle, perseverance, endurance, hope and faith!

I cannot begin to tell you how many challenges I have rose to in my journey to this point. I can tell you I will continue to step up to the plate and give my all to this vision however long it takes me to succeed in seeing *Gumbo* reach the heights I have in my mind's eye.

There are too many generous people to name for sowing their time and talents into my vision. I am eternally grateful to all of you. Thank you Toni Beckham of PR et Cetera, Inc., Synthia SAINT JAMES, Bruce George, Sharon "Shaye" Gray, Lorraine Elzia, and Shawnda Tate. Words can't express all that you have done to make *Gumbo* possible.

Delores "Dee" Stewart, our first editor and Sarah "Rachel" Berry, our first radio show host and my dear sister-girl-friend, you Black Women ROCK, and I know you both Reign-in-Paradise in the spirit of those that love you so. Thank you for being the wind beneath my wings.

Also, thank you to the many contributors of which none of this would be possible.
To my tribe, Khaliid, Keyanna, Eric and Kyeisha, I love you with everything I have.

Last but not least, a very special "Thank You" to the core-contributors: Lorita Childress, Kenya Williams and Linda D. Brown- my home-girl and faithful cheerleader through the years ("Love you Big"- lol). I am eternally grateful for your belief in me and the vision of this compilation through your time, talents and sponsorship. Because of you, this publication was made possible. I love you and God Bless you all. ~bbj

GUMBO FOR THE SOUL:
THE RECIPE FOR LITERACY IN THE BLACK COMMUNITY

AN ANTHOLOGY OF DELICIOUS ESSAYS, POEMS, TESTIMONIALS AND GUMBO RECIPES CONTRIBUTED BY BEST-SELLING AUTHORS, CORPORATE PROFESSIONALS, TV PERSONALITIES, STUDENTS, AND OTHERS WHO ARE DEDICATED TO IMPROVING LITERACY IN THE BLACK COMMUNITY

AN ANTHOLOGY COMPILED BY BEVERLY BLACK JOHNSON

COVER, "WITH HONORS" ©1990 SYNTHIA SAINT JAMES
FOREWORD BY HEATHER COVINGTON
EDITED BY EVE'S LITERARY SERVICES
PUBLICIST: PR ET CETERA, INC.

PENNED BY PROFESSIONALS, PARENTS, STUDENTS
AND SOME OF AMERICA'S MOST PROLIFIC WRITERS
COMPILED BY BEVERLY BLACK JOHNSON
www.gumboforthesoul.com
EDITED BY EVE'S LITERARY SERVICES
www.evesliteraryservice.com
BOOK COVER BY SYNTHIA SAINT JAMES
www.synthiasaintjames.com
PUBLICIST: TONI BECKHAM
PR et Cetera www.pretcetera.com

© 2007 GUMBO FOR THE SOUL PUBLICATIONS
GUMBO FOR THE SOUL:
THE RECIPE FOR LITERACY IN THE BLACK
COMMUNITY

LIBRARY OF CONGRESS

ISBN: 0-9790479-0-0

ISSN 1934-3590

Dedication

This book is dedicated to all the youth of the world. Education is vital to surviving and making it in this ever-changing society. Our contributors have gone to great lengths to convey messages from our own experiences in hopes that one word shared will inspire you to do your best to succeed against all odds!

I thank God for giving me the vision of Gumbo for the Soul.

These works inspire to be a series of thought provoking, hair-raising, anthologies to spark change and raise awareness of humanitarian issues affecting the

Black community.

My deepest gratitude to all of the contributors for your energy. Without your contribution, I stood alone. You came through with so many submissions and so much inspiration and encouragement making this effort what it is.

Thank you sincerely.

Thank you to Synthia Saint James for the adorable book cover that is the perfect fit my heart desired. Without hesitation, you agreed to allow your work to adorn the cover. I am honored and extremely grateful for such an act of kindness.

Toni Beckham of PR et Cetera, publicist for Gumbo for the Soul--I owe everything to you. You held me down through it all. I said I'd never quit and you never quit on me. I can't thank you enough for all of the hard work and energy you've put into giving Gumbo national coverage. A million thanks for putting everything into proper perspective consistently, professionally, and reliably.

Nathasha Brooks-Harris and Davidae "Dee" Stewart, our website' first contributing editors, thank you for your energy and enthusiasm towards education. Your input is priceless.

Sharon Stinson Gray, of Eve's Literary Service, editor for Gumbo

For the Soul anthology and website-you've been sunshine through the storm. Light in times of darkness. What you've put into this vision is immeasurable. I can't thank you enough for all your time and hard work.

Last but not least, to my kids, my family and friends. You've had to listen to Gumbo this and that for years. Nobody else is more inspirational to me than you are.

You've offered support and ideas that is invaluable.

Keyanna, thank you for your poignant pen. Every time you spit a new poem-I had to have it for Gumbo-but none was more on point than Bridgin' the Gap.

Miss Kyeisha, thank you for your creativity as our myspace web stylist. You are a light of hope and inspiration. Never give up on your dreams.

I love you all.

-Beverly Black Johnson

Foreword

When Beverly Johnson announced the birth of the *Gumbo for the Soul* project, I wasted no time tackling my experiences as a teacher in New York City and submitting my heartfelt contribution. I wanted to share my story as a survivor of the elements of my work environment in the South Bronx and the culture shock I experienced as a student teacher on York Avenue in Manhattan's most posh upscale neighborhood then finally settling down in a school in my Northeast Bronx hometown where I reside.

I'll never forget the Tsunami Tragedy several years ago overseas, and before the Katrina Hurricane Disaster in New Orleans when an influx of Albanian youth migrated to New York and many became my students. Also, I will never forget when Albanian parents protested about their children being taken out of the class and placed in a classroom with an Albanian speaking teacher. Of course, I was humbled by the support, and this let me know that even a parent of a different race can recognize when his or her child has a good Black teacher.

Of course, teaching is a labor of love for many Black teachers, and one's greatest reward is witnessing children become competent readers. Many people do not understand the joy that all teachers feel when a child becomes a reader. When I arrive home, I get down on my knees, pray and thank God for giving me the strength to endure the pain and struggle to help facilitate each child's journey as an emergent reader.

When I sent my contribution, I was an angry and bitter woman because I didn't ask to have to deal with drug-ridden neighborhoods, crime, violence and asbestos-filled work environments in the ghettos of New York, but my plight quickly became that of a missionary when I discovered children who no one took the time to try to teach. These were the children, like myself, who would slip through the cracks due to senseless experimentation of our youth with programs made for middle-class suburbia kids sending competent teachers into incompetent mode to deal with the stabs from administration who only recognized new rigorous time schedules, one-sided propaganda and philosophical ideals that stole the creativity of an African American teacher and downtrodden her need to bring out children's natural born talents.

What about the Black child, who did not eat breakfast, was exposed to parents using drugs, witnessed drug deals in front of his or her eyes, had to step over crack pipes in the streets, and developed asthma due to concentrated rats, mice and vermin in the urban ghettos? What about that child?

Furthermore, no one trusted the Black teacher and so tests were changed with bias questions to defray more from entering the system or discourage many who were not tenured into leaving for good. It seemed as if White America enjoyed Bill Cosby's demoralization of Black vernacular or "bad English" and the kids who spoke it already felt incompetent because they could not assimilate to standard language unless someone taught them proper English. I knew just like a broken record, language could not be fixed without dance, art, music and opportunities for children to express themselves and learn from one another. I really did not think anyone would care neither about my struggles, nor about 100+ Black authors' stories, but we would all make the world care with a feast of stories too important to not read.

I researched Beverly's biography and realized that her mission for *Gumbo for The Soul* was greater than just a compiled anthology of some of the greatest writers of the turn of the century, but rather it was an historical account of transitioning writers on the cusp of the millennium, post Harlem Renaissance Era and birth of Generation X; the unheard voices hidden behind works that may have reached the African-American community responsible for 800 billion dollars in annual sales, yet mainstream America only recognizes great writers when they have succumbed to sex, drugs, infidelity, violence and controversial scandals. No, this time 100 or more writers would change the soup's flavor and show the results that occur when you let Black youth-all grown up-express their creativity.

For this reason, every single writer in *Gumbo for the Soul* must be carefully examined for they each tell a story that phenomenally captures the true essence of Black America. Do play Marvin Gaye's song, "What's Goin' On," because this is the mood and era this historical work will take you back to.

Will America reject Black creativity now that the African American writer finally masters society's proper vernacular or keep pimping our urban stories that glamorize crime and gangs and have forced many seasoned, well-versed writers to compose this filth and trash to survive and make a living?

Therefore, why did we bother to assimilate and learn proper English if we keep getting more doors closed in our faces? I will not commit the crime of having children do time as robotic missionaries of America's ideals. I am going to let them dance, shout, read, learn, sing, draw and bring to life the re-birth of African-American sub-culture that has been denied its existence, plus forty acres and a mule by supporting *Gumbo for the Soul*. It will floweth in your veins, intoxicate your ears and get you standing and praising Black writers on mountains of jubilee. Let the rivers of the Euphrates refill and bring back the abundance of great literature with a new African library and its throne, a golden book. If you discover *Gumbo for the Soul* before the world's end due to natural circumstances from Global Warming, a menacing meteorite trying to land on earth, world genocide due to warfare, and toxic fish absorbing the vast pollution of the earth and transferring mercury to humans, I say to you reader, hold on to your authentic voice, write from the heart and stay true to yourself.

Black culture has ascended to more than a minority race in America, but a way of life that can only be captured and remembered through the written word. Rise up my black people, the *Gumbo for the Soul* is ready and fit to be enjoyed by kings and queens of all nationalities who welcome the intellectual rise of Black creativity. Enjoy the flavor while it's here. *Gumbo for the Soul* is a magnificent feast. I can only hope each writer's seasoning is taken more than a grain of salt because even salt leaves everlasting traces; no one can hide this time.

-Heather Covington

GUMBO FO R THE SOUL RAWSISTAZ REVIEW
Date Reviewed: September 27, 2006

GUMBO FOR THE SOUL compiled by Beverly Black Johnson
Gumbo For The Soul Publications, 2007
Paperback, $24.95
ISBN:0979047900
Genre: Non-fiction

RAW Rating: 5 (out of 5)

We can't make it without education

In a collection of essays, poems, recipes and inspirational pieces, GUMBO FOR THE SOUL tells African-Americans exactly what the recipe for a good life is. One of my favorites, "Literacy of History is Crucial," by Ryan Christopher Pinkston, reminds us that without a foundation we have nothing to build upon so it is important that we know our history to avoid repeating the mistakes of the past. "Fear of Being Labeled Smart" by Halima Lee, follows in the same vein. Because we have forgotten our ancestors and their great accomplishments, we have let popular culture befuddle our minds, making us think popularity is more important than academic achievement. Sharon Shaye Gray, in "Boys and Girls," gives a lesson in kindness. If we are in a place of authority, such as the school system, we should be kind to the students. They need it even if they have made a mistake.

"Under the Baobab Tree" by Ja Adams is a great poem pointing out that we weren't always slaves and downtrodden but came from the first people, and we have magnificent ancestors to build on. "Gumbo for the Soul" by Beverly Black Johnson succinctly brings out our stellar history in this country. The inspirational pieces are beautiful stories that let us know God is with us no matter what. The gumbo recipes begged to be tried for dinner.

This collection of writings is inspirational and uplifting. I can't think of a better book to read when depression and a sense of meaningless in this world overtakes your soul. Yes, we face many obstacles in the United States today as descendants of slaves, and some teachers and principals have a low opinion of our ability to achieve, but these stories let you know in no uncertain terms, that we can achieve. We have achieved in the past and we will continue to be a great people regardless of the obstacles thrown in our path. I recommend this book for people of all ages, colors and aspirations. It will change your outlook for sure.

Reviewed by Alice Holman of The RAWSISTAZ Reviewers
http://www.rawsistaz.com

Blurb:
"GUMBO FOR THE SOUL tells African-Americans exactly what the recipe for a good life is. . . it is inspirational, uplifting, and recommended for people of all ages, colors and aspirations. "
- Alice Holman, RAWSISTAZ.com

A Flurry of New Releases, both new and classic

There's never been a better time to read Gwynne Forster

HER SECRET LIFE

(ISBN 13-978-1-58314-771-9) Harlequin, Kimani Romance, July 2006

WHEN YOU DANCE WITH THE DEVIL (ISBN 0-7582-1308-5) Kensington/Dafina Books, August 2006 (Mainstream women's fiction)

MCNEIL'S MATCH, Harlequin, Kimani Arabesque, September, 2006

UNFORGETTABLE PASSION, Harlequin Kimani Arabesque. Collectors Series *(Sealed With A Kiss, Against All Odds, Ecstasy)*. October 2006

AGAINST THE WIND (reissue). Genesis Press, October 2006

DESTINY'S DAUGHTERS, *by Gwynne Forster, Parry "Ebony Satin" Brown, Donna Hill (ISBN 0-7582-1238-0)* mainstream fiction. Anthology. Kensington/Dafina. February 2006

Available at http://www.gwynneforster.com

Fine art is not just about fine art. The visual, musical, performing and literary art created by artists of African descent has long been our method of recording history, conveying thought and evoking change in paradigms and, yes, sometimes it is simply our method of conveying creativity and beauty. The arts have been substantiated and proven to have a direct effect upon the ability of a child to better develop his or her skills in other educational disciplines, from mathematics to psychology.

Charlotte Riley-Webb.
Fine Artist.
Recipient of the 2006 Pollock Krasner Award
www.charlotterileywebb.com

THE MITCHELL LAW GROUP

A PROFESSIONAL CORPORATION

"BE BOLD, LIVE COURAGEOUS, FOR TRUE COURAGE IS WHEN YOU DO THE THINGS <u>THEY</u> SAY YOU CANNOT DO."

S. Raye Mitchell, Esq.
Contributor
&
2006 Nominee for the Prestigious
Wall Street Journal Global Award,
"Top 50 Women to Watch"

****

The Mitchell Law Group, PC

▶ Women Owned   ▶ Harvard Law School/USC MBA

▶ 30 yrs business/legal experience

Built on a Foundation of Creativity, Knowledge, Energy & Commitment.

****

1300 Clay Street Suite 1010 * Oakland, CA, 94612
510.836.2097 (ph)/510.836.2374 (fax)
www.mitchelllawgroup.com

practice areas: intellectual property, entertainment and talent, copyright, civil litigation and business transactions.

KEYANNA BEAN
Rapper, Filmmaker
www.keyanna.com

Currently filming The "Bitch" Documentary, a film intended to address the issues of the hot-button topic of sex and sexism in Hip-Hop. Professors, rappers, producers, youth, and women come together in one film to discuss what's right and wrong about the current state of Hip-Hop and the roles women and sex play in it. Watch Keyanna go behind the scenes as rappers give you a raw and uncut reality behind the music! This film goes there! With appearances by rapper Freeway, Hip-Hop Historian Davey D., producer Traxamillion and more, this film is guaranteed to entertain, offend, address, and inspire.

THE FAMILY WISHES TO CONGRATULATE BEVERLY ON THE SUCCESS OF
GUMBO FOR THE SOUL.

YOU'VE PERSERVERED THROUGH MANY SEASONS IN THE DEVELOPMENT OF THIS PROJECT WHILE GARNERING THE SUPPORT OF THE MANY WONDERFUL AND DEDICATED SUPPORTERS OF THIS WORHTY CAUSE.

WE WATCHED IT ALL UNFOLD AND HAVE CHEERED YOU ON FROM THE SIDELINES.

IT IS WITH GREAT HONOR AND PRIDE THAT WE ACKNOWLEDGE YOUR HARD WORK AND DEDICATION TO SUCH A SELFLESS ENDEAVOR.

CONTINUE TO PURSUE YOUR DREAMS AND LET GOD LIGHT YOUR PATH.

WE LOVE AND APPLAUD YOU.

YOUR FAMILY,
THE NOEL'S, MAXIE'S, BLACK'S, ROSE'S AND WILBON'S.

Sister To Sister: One In The Spirit, Inc.

A Conference of Empowerment for Women of Color in Harlem

Yvonne Singleton Davis
Founder / CEO

Celebrating the Inner Beauty and Spirit of the African American Woman.

Making a Positive Difference in the World "One Sister" at a Time.

151-7 West 136th Street
New York, NY 10030
212. 234.1544

EVEN SINNERS HAVE SOULS
EDITED BY E.N. JOY

Books and authors of books that are categorized as urban, erotic, street, ghetto, gangster, Hip-Hop fiction, or whatever else they are being labeled, are taking hard hits in the industry, especially by these so-called "literary writers". Why is it that whenever black people bring the life they live front and center and turn it into art, society goes crazy? Are we that afraid of and offended by the ghetto to the point where we ridicule those who talk about it? Spite popular belief, everything that comes from the ghetto isn't all bad. There are some good products of the ghetto. It produces great individuals, some even authors. But because of the type of genre that these authors choose to pen, they are stigmatized and rumored unable to create literature without glorifying a trigger happy, drug dealing thug, or a burgundy micro braid wearing, gum poppin', promiscuous gold digger, or a television stealing crack head (in addition to at least two curse words per paragraph).

Even Sinners Have Souls is the book that is going to shatter the myth about urban and street literature and its authors once and for all. Featuring the literary industry's most respected urban, erotic and street lit authors such as Nikki Turner, Noire and Chunichi, each gritty and profound story is told in just as raw and real of a voice as any other urban erotic or urban street story, only these stories omit the use of cursing, offensive slang and explicit sexuality. Instead, readers are lured in by the poignant storylines and themes and the genuine talents and abilities of these prolific authors. Each story has characters who face the same struggles and tragedies that any other character growing up in the hood might endure. But what is phenomenal about these characters is that although they might be living a dangerous and immoral lifestyle, they are not so far gone that they can't acknowledge the power of a higher being and a life changing moment that could alter their lives forever. The end result is nourishing the reading community with a piece of literature that provides a significant upside to a life that otherwise might have been wasted if it had not have been for the mercy and grace of the Creator.

Available on www.amazon.com and www.enjoywrites.com

Table of Contents

"GUMBO FOR THE SOUL THE RECIPE FOR LITERACY IN THE BLACK"

CHAPTER 1 ~SOULFUL GUMBO~ ESSAYS REFLECTING ON EDUCATIONAL AND OCCUPATIONAL EXPERIENCES 30

Pursue Your Dreams:
Dreams Really Do Come True 31
Sisterhood 34
Camping.. 37
'The Best of Times,
the Worst of Times, Mr. Grady' 41
This Too Shall Pass 42
Heritage, 1976 46
So You Really Want to Know What Goes
On Behind the Doors of My Classroom?......... 52
The Path... 56
Outside the Box 59
Our Vision and High Achievement 62
MATHEMATICAL FEMALE 67
Boys and Girls 70
Unexpected 73
Hemispheres: Overcoming Educational
Stereotypes in North and South America 75
An Invitation to the Private Room................... 78
Talking White 83
Blind Eyes 88
The Heartbreak Epidemic................................ 92
An Incredible Journey..................................... 96
Education - What it Really Is 99
NO WAY OUT 101
Quiet Persistence 103
What Do You Want To Be
When You Grow Up? 108
Pressing Towards the Mark............................. 112
"I Can Do All Things. . . ." 114
Persistence 117
Aunt Kathleen 121
I Believe In You 124

TWINKLING from AGES 5 to 105 129
Literacy of History is Crucial 132
Super Sunday: Papa's Big Day 137
The Queen Bee Speaks 140
Think 145
The 3 Laws of the Toddler 148
Discovering Alice 153
Math: My Motivating Enemy 156
The Courage to Reach Our Own 160
The Power of Words 165
BETRAYAL AND THE BULLY 167
OVERCOMING A "SISTER-SLAYER"
IN THE WORKPLACE 172
"Prieta" 177
My Testimony 181
Wild Flowers 187
My Story - Part 1 192
The Question 196
The Fear of Being Labeled Smart 204
Education From The Catbird Seat 208
Lighthouse in the Storm 216
Taking It Day By Day 221
It's Okay to Be Smart 225
Never 229
I WAS BLIND, BUT NOW I SEE 232
AN EDUCATION OF SELF 232

CHAPTER II
~POETIC GUMBO~ 235

I Remember When 244
My Road to PhD 245
Gift To The Earth 248
Heroes 249
In Search of Excellence 250
Fly High 251
Help Me To Heal 252
The Mentor, Strong 253
Imagine That 254
I've Been There 257
The Morehouse Glass of Life 258
I'm Somebody 259
Masks 260
Gumbo for the Soul 261
Levitate 264

Images of Mama 265
ASSUME THE POSITION 267
If   270
Black Butterfly 271
Ode to British Lit 272
You Can Do It! 273
We're Living In a Time 274
Walking That Line! 276
Dumb Questions 278
In Search Of Truth 279
All Me   280
Be A Black Man 281
Monkey See 282
Happy To Be Nappy 283
A Poem for Toni Morrison 284
Mr. Hughes 287
Populacao Magoada!!!
(Wounded Population) 288

CHAPTER III ~SAVORY STEW~ GUMBO RECIPES AND A BIT OF HISTORY 290

A Bit of Gumbo History 291
VeeJay's Gumbo 292
My Family's Gumbo 294
SOUMAS HERITAGE:
CREOLE SEAFOOD GUMBO 297

CHAPTER IV~SPIRITUAL GUMBO~ BLESSINGS AND GIFTS 309

Girl of Grace…Woman of Peace 300
For My Boys 302
No Earthly Father 305
Twenty Year Stew 307
What True Beauty Is! 311
Walker Baptist Institute 313
Just Keep Praying and Pulling 315
Sewing 316
Morning Coffee with Grandpa 319
In The Ruff 322

CONTRIBUTORS.......................... 327

HELPFUL
RESOURCES SECTION 341
Recommended Resources for
Parents and Students 348
How to Become Actively Involved
in Your Child's Education 350
Scholarships for African Americans.................356

"GUMBO FOR THE SOUL HERE'S OUR CHILD~WHERE'S THE VILLAGE"

CHAPTER I~SOULFUL GUMBO~ ESSAYS REFLECTING ON THE VILLAGE 365

What Happened to the Village?......................... 366
Will 370
The State of Motherhood in America 374
The Day I Entered a Group Home................... 378
Never Leaving Home 381
What happened to our village? 384
My Story 388
Headstart 388
Honorable Mention 389
The Village.. 390
Through The Eyes of a Foster Child................. 393
In Our Ghetto.. 399
Every Child's Voice Should Be Heard.............. 401
Do The Math!.. 406
Too Old 408
Through the Eyes of a Child............................. 411
Aunt Louise's Red Pumps 412
A Tribute to Grandparents
Raising Their Grandchildren.............................418

A Diamond in the Rough.................................420
Eva Cara..423
Against the Odds 426
Call Me Ma'am..429
Chapel in Turquoise for the
Children of the Land................................432
Keeping It in the Family..........................434

CHAPTER II
~POETIC GUMBO~ 436

Here's Our Child, Where's The Village? 437
A Myriad of Hands 438
You Talking to Me? 439
Yes, I'm Talking to You......................................441
When Momma and Daddy
Couldn't Be There..443
RESCUE ME 444
Tribute to Foster/Adoptive Parents 446
My Grandma Would 447
Mother Me 449
Mama Cries..450
Children Raising Each Other 451
Where is the Village?..452
Am I Tomorrow's Keeper?..............................453
2,4,6,8 455
Color-Free 456
I Am a Child of God..457
I am a Mother 458
IN PLAIN SIGHT...459
Love Stew-Cooked in a Slow Cooker................461
WE WON'T LEAVE
OUR CHILDREN BEHIND!! 462

RESOURCES 466

CONTRIBUTORS......................... 477

"GUMBO FOR THE SOUL
WOMEN OF HONOR"

~SPECIAL PINK EDITION~

CHAPTER I~SOULFUL GUMBO~ REFELCTIONS ON WOMEN OF HONOR 491

FOREWORD 492

SURVIVOR..494
MWMF (My Women, My Family)...................495
My Aunties!..498
Surviving My Breast Challenge........................503
The Buck Stops Here....................................506
A Whisper of Hope 509
Neecee's Shine...514
Memorial of Janice Carol Tillman 518
I've Got a Hookup 'cuz
God is a Friend of Mine!...............................520
I had Cancer on my Wedding Day 523
Her-Story. Mattie Sanders Carter 525
Commanding Respect 529
The Power of a Mother's Love........................532
QUIET SOLDIERS......................................534
Forever In My Heart: Her Quiet Strength........539
Starr Power Pilates:
Taking Back Your Physical Power...
One Muscle At A Time 543
Annie Pearl's Ballad....................................547

CHAPTER II~POETIC GUMBO~ RHYTHMIC HONOR 553

"I Am" Said So..554
Your Strength 555
Women of Honor Full of Spirit and Light 557
Abundant Love..562
Who Am I? 564
Mama 565
The BIG "C"..566
Woman of Faith 567
Black Women, Tired...................................570

Threshold 572
Mirror of Friendship 573
Wisdom on my Sleeve 575

CONTRIBUTING AUTHORS ... 577

GUMBO FOR THE SOUL MEN OF HONOR ~SPECIAL CANCER AWARENESS EDITION~

FOREWORD 592

LEGACY OF HONOR -
HOMER JOE BLACK, SR. 595
Dear Pa-Pa, ...597
Reflections 598
My Grandfather…The Matriarch 601
Honored Vows 603
Love Heals 604
Man of Honor 608
"MAN OF THE MILLENNIUM"
MICHAEL JOE JACKSON 610
Thumbs Up! 620
Little Big Man 624
We Called Him "Pop" 627
Robert Pinkney:
My Grandfather, My Sage 629
Life with Father 632
LEGAND OF HONOR -
LOWELL W. PERRY SR.: 635
Clocks & Mirrors 640
What My Father Did For Me 643
This One's For My Father 645
There Are Great Men of Honor -
This I Can Attest 648
Taking the Step Out of Stepdad 649
LIFETIME LEGENDARY -
ARCHBISHOP DESMOND TUTU: 654

HELPFUL RESOURCES SECTION 661
ADDITIONAL SERVINGS OF GUMBO ... 664
GUMBO FOR THE SOUL RADIO -
SOUL BROTHER CIRCLE 676
CONTRIBUTING AUTHORS 678
ABOUT THE COMPILERS: 683
ABOUT GUMBO FOR THE SOUL: 685

CHAPTER I
SOULFUL GUMBO
ESSAYS REFLECTING ON EDUCATIONAL AND OCCUPATIONAL EXPERIENCES

"The foundation of our world is the education of our youth"
-Stinson Gray

Pursue Your Dreams:
Dreams Really Do Come True

In 1999, I did as hundreds of serious, knowledge-seeking, support-needing, guidance-hungry Bay Area professional women do annually, I attended the California Professional Black Women's Networking Brunch, which is hosted by the professional women's organization Black Women, INC. Public relations and marketing professional extraordinaire and best-selling author Terrie Williams delivered a motivating keynote address about the unending pursuit of one's dreams. She spoke of having started her entertainment PR, marketing and communications company, the Terrie Williams Agency, ten years earlier, and having acquired her first client, comedian and actor Eddie Murphy. Though inspired by Ms. Williams' most eloquent presentation, I did not buy her "Eddie Murphy story." I chose not to believe that a professional blessing that substantial could be so easy to come by.

That is until ... Later that same year, I went on to establish my own public relations firm PR, et Cetera, Inc. In my company's earliest days, I promoted events for friends and acquaintances without charge to familiarize the public with my work. While involved in one such promotion, I received a phone call from a person who identified herself as a book publicist. She congratulated me on the quality of my work in promoting her client Dr. Julianne Malveaux's upcoming keynote address at a San Jose, California country club. Without pausing to take a breath, Denise Pines proceeded to tell me that she had another influential client who was scheduled to come to the San Francisco Bay Area to promote his new book.

She went on to tell me that she wanted me to represent her

client while in the Bay Area, book his media interviews, and escort him between interview venues and book signing appearances. She informed me of the fee I would receive while apologizing for its nominal amount. *Keep in mind* that I had never received payment for any public relations work before.

After taking a day to "think it over" in my very cool and collected manner, I informed Ms. Pines that I would take the job if the assignment was to last no more than a single day. At that moment, I acquired my very first paying client, Tavis Smiley, author, civic activist, and then host of the widely popular one-hour nightly talk show on national cable station, Black Entertainment Television, "BET Tonight with Tavis Smiley."

When I delivered Mr. Smiley to the Oakland Airport and at the end of that fateful day following 13 interviews, two bookstore signings, and his partaking of a chicken dinner in the back seat of my rented car, he said to me, "This has been the most productive day of my entire book tour." Of course, I smiled with great pride for having impressed Tavis with my skills, professionalism and having arranged interviews with some of the Bay Area's leading radio, television and print media. My company has had the good fortune to represent him and The Smiley Group on several occasions since then.

The credibility and notoriety derived from representing Tavis Smiley enabled me to rapidly transform my entrepreneurial dream into a successful company whose services are highly sought-after by prominent and influential individuals and organizations throughout the San Francisco Bay Area and beyond.

Some years after the experience, I shared this humorous and revealing story with Denise Pines and Terrie Williams. I am unsure if Ms. Williams ever received my letter or email messages because

I've not heard from her. Ms. Pines, who is Director of Business Development for The Smiley Group, Inc., executive producer of Tavis Smiley Presents, Inc., and associate publisher for Smiley Books got a kick out of hearing it, and promised to work again with PR, et Cetera, Inc. *Dreams really do come true!*

- Toni Beckham

10th Anniversary Edition

Sisterhood

They say that it's chance that makes sisters...hearts that make friends. While chance is something that happens without control, explanation, or planning, earning someone's heart is something that is a very purposeful and conscious decision. Not only do we actively make a choice to make a friend, but we also make a cognizant effort to maintain that friendship-through ups and downs, good times and bad, as well as challenges and triumphs. Merriam-Webster Dictionary defines sisterhood as "a community or society of sisters," or the "solidarity of women based on shared conditions, experiences, or concerns." Fortunately for us, as we get older we learn that sisterhood is a journey and not a destination.

We also learn that we are not born understanding what "sisterhood" is, but rather construct what it means to be an integral part of not just one, but several sister-related experiences. For example, we were first introduced to the concept of "sisterhood" when we got together and watched our mothers, aunts, and "play aunts," pull together elaborate meals as we celebrated the Fourth, Memorial Day, Easter, or whatever excuse we needed to eat Aunt Essie's macaroni and cheese, Big Mama's turnip greens, or Cousin Sister's catfish. They were the "sisters" who were there since before we could remember, and who would never let us forget that they "*were there before we were even thought of.*" Like our mothers, they encouraged us, cajoled us, and spanked us when we needed it. It didn't matter how, or if, they were related to us (or our mother) the only thing that mattered...was that we were Family. From this sisterhood experience, we learned the virtues of deference and compassion.

Our second introduction to "sisterhood" was made through the relationships that we formed with our "play cousins" and "play sisters." They were the ones who we couldn't wait to see at church, family gatherings, or birthday parties. We fought like cats and dogs the whole time that we were together-and cried when we had to leave each other-all the while begging to play for "just five more minutes." Moreover, although we didn't see them as often as our real brothers and sisters, time stood still between our visits and we were always able to pick up right where we left off. From this sisterhood experience, we learned the merits of patience and compromise. The third time we experienced sisterhood, was through our "sister friends." They are the girls we met in elementary (or high school), in college (or graduate school), at our first job (or the job we hated), and when we were dating that great guy (or divorcing that jerk).

Through thick and thin waistlines, these were the women-who like our mother's friends, "where there when." These are the sisters, who understand our strengths, as well as our vulnerabilities. We have a natural affinity towards one another, not just because they supported us when we were right, but because they also told us about ourselves when we were wrong. Best of all...these are the "Sisters" who simply love us "just because" it was their choice to do so. From this sisterhood experience, we learned the intrinsic worth of integrity and candor. Therefore, it is no secret or great wonder why so many sage, savvy, talented, and strong women are drawn to magnificent sisterhoods like Delta, AKA, Zeta, or SGRho.

Sororities fulfill our need to connect to "sisters," with common goals, interests, and proclivities. Sisterhoods are an extension of what we already know and a reflection of what we have already experienced.

Through our informal and formal sisterhoods, we model, exchange, and share our education and past experiences with compassion, deference, patience, compromise, integrity, and candor among our Sister Friends, Sorors, and Sisters who may not know that it is impossible to love themselves if they do not love and support other Sisters. It may be that chance creates sisters and hearts that create friendships. The fact that we have sisters is something that definitely happened by chance. And having friends, GOOD FRIENDS, is something that is fashioned by the love we have for ourselves and other sisters. However, it is probably a little bit of both that makes us-regardless of what "sisterhoods" we belong to-SORORS.

-Janeula M. Burt

Camping

I pledge my head to clear thinking
My heart to greater loyalty
My hands to larger service
And my health to better living
For my club, my community, my country and my world
(4-H Club Pledge)

These are the words I lived my life by from ages eight to eighteen, the pledge of the 4-H Club. I know, I know, most people don't realize that there are black people in the 4-H Club. Believe me, they are a special breed. When I heard that Anita Hill was from Kansas, graduated from high school around '68' and was in the 4-H Club, I knew girl friend was alright!

I had little choice in the matter of belonging since my grandmother was the club leader. Our club was called the Rainbow 4-H Club and membership ran from 6 to 15 members depending on how close we were to taking a trip. I belonged to the 4-H club when it was segregated, black clubs and white clubs, before 1964. Believe me for the black members the hay days were before assimilation. After the clubs integrated, black participation dwindled to nothing.

The 4-H Club is like a coed scouts for less money; you don't have to spend a lot for uniforms and gear. The colors are green and white with girls in green and white striped uniforms and guys wearing white shirts and dark pants. They can get a dark green blazer with an emblem if they want. The club is highly flexible fitting into urban or rural areas. The club leaders, both women and men, find people in the community to teach classes or modules in whatever the kids want to learn: sewing, photography, crop rotation, public speaking, cooking, intensive gardening for the city, health, whatever. Club activities emphasize leadership, critical thinking, and discussion and meeting management. The Rainbow Club usually met in my church or my grandma's house.

The 4-H Club had a campsite near Poplar Bluff at Lake Wappapella, MO. After the black and white clubs integrated, I decided to go to camp. Of course as with most of my activities after Jr. High, I was the only black kid there. Now even though I had spent much time doing fieldwork, chopping cotton, corn and soybeans, I really was not an outside person. I didn't like all of those insects, mice, and snakes, but I decided to go camping, Okay!

I got there in the evening and walked to the camp fire where everybody was singing songs and getting ready to square dance. All of the guys were looking around with the "I'm not going to dance with her" look on their faces. Well, one of the male camp advisors, not much older than me, came and took my hand. Of course, I was the instant envy of all the girls because he was a cute college guy and everyone wanted to dance with him. So, I put my head in the air, threw back my shoulders and waited for the call to start.

Fortunately, I could out square dance the lot of them. You see I went to a historically white high school where one quarter each year in P.E. class we learned to square dance. Furthermore, I spent every Saturday evening watching Hee Haw. Yeah, you read it right, Hee Haw. We could only get one TV station in clearly. It was broadcasted from Monkey's Eye Brow, Kentucky and my grandmother insisted on watching that show every Saturday evening. She would be sitting in her chair nodding, but if someone edged close to the TV. to turn it off (*it was a scandal that we were watching Hee Haw*), she would say, "Don't turn that off, I'm watching that!"

Needless to say I found myself giving the white campers a run for their money when the caller sang out:

Let us allemande left on the corner
And a grand ole right and left around the ring
Promenade with your gal, that little gallaponin' gal
When you chop down that old pine tree

After the first call was over they were all impressed, however none but the camp advisor would dance with me. Therefore, while the other girls were feeling pretty persnickety because they had someone to dance with, I got to dance with the camp counselor, a college guy they were all swooning over.

After the campfire was put out, we all went to bed. What a night of terror it was. You see, I scare easily or as they say in the black community, I'm very scary! When I arrived at camp, I was told that one camper had found a snake coiled on their bed when they first opened the cabins---it ruined my whole camp stay! In all my years of fieldwork, I had run into one snake and I met him as I crossed a wheat field to use the bathroom. We moved away from each other as fast as we could. Snakes at camp-I was deathly afraid.

We were housed in cabins, but they were primitive. They were log with a tin roof set on top. You could see between the tops of the walls and the tin roofs. Then, oh, my God, they turned out the lights. The first thing that struck me was the silence. It was deafening; I had to get used to that. I lay there in the dark shaking. For one thing, we could hear the mice run around the top of the walls. I just knew one was going to jump on my face. I asked the counselor to turn on the flashlight a couple of times, no mice. Then as I tried to get settled down I was sure I could hear a snake slithering up the post of my bunk bed. Lord, I was so scared. I catnapped through the night. The next day I was bonkers and my eyes were bloodshot and bleary.

Morning finally came and off to the bathroom we went for showers, which was another trial. I was so scared I would run into a snake in the bathroom that, needless to say, I went as infrequently as possible. When I got home I was smellin' tired, I was rest broken and constipated.

Besides roughing it in the cabins, I also passed another hurdle at camp, the water. I couldn't swim a lick and there were two reasons. I didn't want to get my hair wet and have to get it washed and pressed again, (it was unthinkable to have nappy hair); and in my home town blacks were not allowed to use the city swimming pool---not at any time, not for any reason. Since I was a girl, I could not go out to the creek to swim.

Therefore, I had never been in more water than could fill a number two tin bathtub. However, I was there with all of those white kids and I thought they all knew how to swim so I participated in the boating competition. We put on life jackets, got in a canoe and paddled out to the middle of the lake. The group to complete the task and get back to shore first won the contest. We had to capsize the boat and hang on for so many minutes. After that eternity was up, (I just knew there was a snake in the water nipping at my legs) we had to turn the boat over, get back in and paddle back to shore. And I did it! I did it! I was so proud of myself. I was black and blue on my arms and legs from struggling to get back in the boat (it's hard when you can't swim), but I made it back to shore. 4-H camp had been a success. After all of that, can you believe I went back the next year? How soon we do forget.

-Marquita L. Byrd, PhD

'The Best of Times, the Worst of Times, Mr. Grady'

It was her first day of school, but she was now entering an unknown world. Nandi shuttered, as the big yellow bus approached. The door opened and all she could see was a large white hand that was very different from her darker one. Her eyes never looked up to its owner. Legs shaking, she slowly made it to her seat. One day she nervously lifted her head and was very surprised! Instead of a look of hate and disdain, she had expected, from previously encounters with his race, there were big light-blue eyes that seemed to sparkle and a smile which made her feel like the sweet little girl she was.

He would often stop at a store so we could buy candy and chips. Sometimes he would surprise us with giant red apples from his store. Each one was nestled in colorful tissue type paper and appeared as if it was selected for someone special. Many years later, she worked as a paraprofessional with the local school system. The teacher I worked with treated me kindly and with respect. Most of the others just looked away when I walked by.

To my surprise, while we were talking one day, I found out that her father was my friend, my childhood bus driver; proving the apple never falls far from the tree. During the following years of my life, many doors were closed because of my color. Thanks to Mr. Grady, there would always be someone there to open them. One person can always make a difference.

'It was the worst of times; it was the best of times'

-Betty 'Nandi' Cantrell

10th Anniversary Edition

This Too Shall Pass

Whoever said, "A journey of a thousand miles begins with a single step" wasn't lying! My journey began in 1997 when I barely graduated from high school with a 2.5 grade point average. I thought that I can do what I want to do 'cause I'm 18 and grown, thank you very much. I stepped onto the campus of Xavier University of Louisiana in New Orleans, very much against the will and wallets of my family.

Suddenly I found myself 3000 miles away from the fast paced, high fashion, 'Bloods' versus 'Crips' world of Pasadena Unified, walking slowly and wide eyed into a whole new world. To my left was the third generation 'Xavierites', making moves to blaze the same paths as their parents before them. To my right were the biology premedical students, chemistry premedical students and pharmacy majors already planning which medical schools to apply to, even though they were freshman! I was amazed. All around me where people, black people my age who were focused and goal oriented, people who had their eyes on the prize and were not stopping until they reached the Promised Land. Instantly, I began to feel a tremendous personal pressure to stop making excuses and recall what little education I received in High School and become a part of the academic 'in crowd'.

Early, I discovered that I loved my English classes. I tore through the required readings like a mad woman soaking in every word as though I was a brand new sponge and it was a puddle of fresh soapy water. Suddenly I found myself writing and rewriting draft after draft, not stopping until I was satisfied with the final product. When I got my first A, I couldn't wait to go home and call my mom and tell her how excited I was that I was succeeding in college.

Yet despite all of my excitement and joy in my freshman lit

classes, this was not the only subject I was required to take. I had to take science, math, history and religion classes, all of which I could have cared less about. I tried though, I really did. I recruited one of my fellow classmates to become my math and science tutor to help me pull away from the blatant F's I was receiving in these classes, and though I did technically try to fix the problem, my "tutor" eventually became my boyfriend and I wound up failing those classes anyway. I left Xavier with a cumulative 1.9 grade point average; my stellar grades in English were the sole reason I didn't fail completely. Nevertheless, failing at Xavier was only the beginning because I still had to go back to California and face mom.

By returning home, my life dramatically changed. I was told clearly that the only amenities that would be provided for me would be my room and board, and only under the expectation that I was to get a job and get back into school. I knew that even if I didn't want to this, I was lucky because this was all that was being asked of me.

With the weight of Mom's disappointment resting heavily on my shoulders, I got my first part time job as a recreation leader with the city. My once carefree afternoons were spent chasing eight year olds around a basketball court after school. The only school I knew I could get into was a Junior College down the street, but only if I was willing to start completely over. Adding insult to injury, I had to wait a semester before I enrolled because I had to save up enough money to pay for the fees and tuition.

However, getting to class this time wasn't as hard because skipping class meant that I would be wasting the money I worked hard to save in order to make this school thing happen. I was not wasting my 450 dollars! This time, I began to seriously pay attention in class and I found myself staying up late to study, and eventually my grades started to reflect my efforts. Something inside of me clicked and I began to believe that I could actually be good at this. Soon, school became my first priority and before I knew it, I had earned my Associates Degree in only two-year's time.

For a year and a half after my graduation, I worked in a clothing store as an Assistant Manager. Day after day, I went to work and dealt with managers who felt that it was their job to let me know exactly how unimportant I was to the company and how easily I could be replaced. Dealing with customers was the fun part of the job, but going to work and dealing with an upper management that you knew you could out wit on any task, easily became my motivation for wanting more. I knew that I had to get back to college somehow and get my degree, because I was not going to spend the rest of my life feeling disposable.

I went back to my Junior College and got an application for the University of California system and every day for a month and a half, I devoted my precious free time to completing this application. With the UC's there was only one application to fill out and you had to pay for each campus you were interested in. It took more than a month for me to get everything completed, but I felt a tremendous sense of pride when I finally was able to mail that application off. I went to work with a brand new attitude, because I knew that no matter what happened it was only temporary. I was about to start my life.

I applied to five University of California campuses. The rules were to apply to a school that you know you would be able to get into (Santa Barbara and San Diego), apply to a school you think you have a good shot of getting into (Davis and UCLA) and apply to one school that you know you most likely won't get into (Berkeley). Berkeley was always the school that you only ever heard of people being rejected from. No one ever actually got into Berkeley. I knew that my GPA was not a 4.0 and I was nowhere near that, but I had nothing to lose. My Grandmother always told me, never tell yourself no, let them tell you no--that way you'll know for sure. Therefore, I applied.

A few months later my first letter came from UC Davis letting me know that they were pleased to admit me into their College of Letters and Science for the fall semester. I was so excited. I knew that no matter what I was going to be in school for the fall. Shortly after Davis, I received letters from Santa Barbara and San Diego both welcoming me onto their campus for the fall semester. News from Berkeley came next. By this time, I was all set to go to Davis, but I wanted to hear from Berkeley out of curiosity.

On the specified day, I went to the special website for applicants and was told to come back in an hour to check the results. I was going to be in another class by that time, (I had picked up a class or two at my Junior College to fill my idle time) so I called my mom to see if she could check it for me. Once I got her to calm down (I hadn't told her I was applying to Berkeley, because again, I knew I wasn't going to get in) I gave her the information and she checked the site. She called me and left me a message, but of course, as luck would have it, my phone died. I went into a professor's office and called her back, and my tearful mother told me that I had been accepted to Berkeley. Something about hearing those words brought tears to my own eyes and I broke down right there in my professor's office. I couldn't believe it.

All of the challenges I faced were completely worth it and after they were over, I realized what the lesson was about perseverance. We all go through hard times, but it is the ability to look at the greater goal, set priorities and barrel through those hard times that determines the people who have what it takes to be successful in life. There were times when I couldn't see the possibilities of my dreams becoming reality. There were times when I felt a cloud of mediocrity settling over me and had it not been for my family pushing me and standing behind me, I probably would not have made it. Nevertheless, as I sat at my graduation from Berkeley two years later, I knew now without a doubt that I had the determination and strength to get through anything.

-Brandelyn N. Castine

10th Anniversary Edition

Heritage, 1976

Roasting hot dogs. Sun-baked asphalt on the parking lot. Briny breezes. A welcoming rosewood sign painted with cartoon pelicans: FOLLY BEACH & FISHING PIER.

The smells and sights usually spawned a smile on my round face. A subdued smile, of course—I was twelve, and, like my boys, mimicked the fierce, quiet cool and roughneck swagger of favored film stars like Jim Brown and Richard Roundtree. But today, as I peered from the open passenger side window of my father's huge, idling Monte Carlo, there was no smile, subdued or otherwise. Today, all I could muster was a pained grimace.

Behind the wheel, my father was yawning and stretching like a giant, contented tomcat. I said to myself, Hey, I wanna be one of these gulls so I can fly away from this damn beach. Oh yes, I figured my father was as oblivious to my pensive pose as he was to the heat. Daddy was a big man who drove a big hot car, and he'd sweat gallons like all big men. The moisture had already beaded on his great shaven head, and soaked through his white dress shirt. At least he'd allowed himself to slough his suit jacket, tug his tie away from his meaty neck and roll his shirtsleeves up where forearms were thicker than my thighs. He didn't allow me an equal measure of comfort. Oh no, I groused inwardly how unfair it was to remain trussed in a hot suit jacket my mother purchased at Dillards. My feet sweltered in shiny black Oxfords from Aunt Tobi. My collar was buttoned tight and his tie remained knotted. And all Daddy could do was yawn and stretch while I suffered!

Then I felt my father's hand on my shoulder. Heavier than usual. Maybe Daddy wasn't oblivious at all. He was smiling, nodding.

"'Sup, son," he said, softly. "This is your big day."

When I mumbled a response, my sister Kimmie, age six, giggled from the back seat and busted me good. "Chris' scared, Daddy!" she squealed. She started bouncing on the seat like a little brown rabbit, with her braids splaying with each joyful rise. "Axe him whyyyyyyyyyy!"

"Shut up Kimmie!" I snapped back. "Monkey-head!"

One stern look from Daddy cut off the shouting and the bouncing. With Kimmie stilled and me quiet, Daddy hit the power door unlock button and motioned with his head. My chest sank. Sure, I was scared—who wants to be punked on some beach? He attended West Ashley Junior High School. Down on the beach were North Charleston Junior High kids. The adults would joke that this was just a quaint little "pee-wee rivalry," but my friends would never forgive me if I backed down to North Charleston taunts.

"Daddy, I'm wearin' a suit and this stupid tie," I complained.

"Hold your head up. Walk long strides, like me. What you're doing is important, and you should never back down from teaching folks why it's important, and who you are, understand? You show folks some heart, they'll come running to learn. Trust me."

"Naw, not today…Daddy…I don't wanna…" I mumbled back.

"I tole you he scared, Daddy!" Kimmie squeaked. "Let me do it!"

I lifted my head. "Hey if she wantsta …" I waved a small crème-colored envelope in the air. Daddy's look quieted me once more. "Daddy, do I gotta take that, too?" I was pointing to a single red rose, fragrant and moist, set on the back seat beside Kimmie.

My father leaned close to me, so close I could smell his woodsy cologne and the hint of coffee on his breath as he whispered, "You're almost thirteen. Same age as me when I did it, same age as your grandfather and his father—way back to that night." He paused, frustrated with me, yet loving, proud. "Listen…remember what Pa-Pa said this morning in the church, at your cousin's Christening? We do this on July 16, when the oldest boy in the family is twelve years old. We do this because no one else will." Daddy then looked over his shoulder at Kimmie . "Hand your brother the rose, baby," he said. "Be mindful of the thorns. See—

something that draws blood, something that hurts, like thorns, always goes hand-in-hand with something as pretty as a blossom. Never forget that. Heart's not about being 'hard,' or showing off, son. Heart's about responsibility. Caring. Taking up the banner."

I climbed out of the car, rose and envelope in hand. I trudged, achingly slow, onto the sandy path winding through the dunes. Balloons tied to volleyball nets marked West Ashley territory. Squinting in the harsh sun, I saw only adult women unfolding beach chairs, popping open coolers. A few pot-bellied men in baseball caps were tending grills. Then I saw the sign: WEST ASHLEY JUNIOR HIGH SCHOOL P.T.A. SUMMER BEACH BASH. I swallowed hard, halted.

The adults stared at me. Daddy's ire was something I could risk now, for sure! Family disgrace, too…this was stupid! Who cares about some boy— dead almost a whole century? Nobody talks about him on TV. No Commodores or Al Green tribute to him. No comic books dedicated to him. I pivoted away from the breakers, ready to run for the car.

Before I could escape, a young female voice mocked, "Hmm, whatchew like a Jehovah's Witness or somethin', vexing people on the beach?"

Another voice, a boy's, jested, "Naw, he th'ice cream man!"

The music hit my ears—the Commodores of course, "Slippery When Wet." More voices, distant laughs, girls' squeals in the surf. Too late. I turned slowly. Standing before me was a girl too young to be wearing that bikini, and a boy wearing a droopy Atlanta Hawks tank jersey. The boy's gym shorts bore a North Charleston logo.

The girl spoke first, popping her gum and tossing back her braids. "This ain't your school's party. Uh-huh…DeVon—this DeVon right here—he say he know you west Ashley. An' why you dressed up like some white boy?"

I muttered back, searching my shoes, "Y'all… I gotta go."

The boy blocked my path. "She ask you a question, cuz. This

whole big-ass beach and you gotta roll up here—on us? Dressed stoo-pid? Ha! You touched…you crazy."

My boys, or my heroes like Shaft or Slaughter or Priest would say drop that envelope and that stupid flower. Puff out that chest and back that niggah off. Yes, two twelve year olds posturing. Calling each other "nigger." But my father's fortifying words seeped back into my soul before anything started.

"I-I gotta…got something to do. It's important. An' you shouldn't pick at what…what you don't understand."

Arms waving, DeVon cried, "Hold up…what'd you say? I could jump in your eye right here, yella niggah. But my father and uncle be right over on me! You lucky today, cuz."

Some kids spied the confrontation; they called or whistled to their cohorts. Bodies peeled off the patch of hot sand that had been their dance floor. Some emerged from the ocean to see what was going on. The adults—eating, gossiping, tanning—didn't even notice. DeVon's reinforcements arrived. The North Charleston kids were arrayed in a half-moon in front of me. Just looking me up and down. Murmuring jokes to each other. I felt three inches tall.

Lips aquiver and heart pounding against my sternum, I stepped right up to the biggest boy in front of me. The crowd hushed; the boy knuckled up. Neither he nor I flinched until I whispered, "I'm here…'cause no one else comes."

Laughter exploded from every mouth. Even the adults took note and chortled, thinking it was just the kids having fun. DeVon snickered to the big boy, "See, all them West Ashley fools either soft or crazy. He crazy, so leave him be. I be jonesin' fo' some hot dogs…"

I could have walked to the shore, done my deed. Yeah, let them go eat hot dogs, and I can get out of that stupid tie, and toss the tight shoes now filled with hot sand. Just like it would have been easier for another twelve year old, on that very beach, long ago, to turn-tail and run. I drew a heavy breath, blew it out…

"No," I said. Sharp. Resolute. Defying the easy way. Defying ignorance. "I want y'all to come with me…see why I'm here." I pushed through the group and started walking to foamy shore. Nonplussed, shrugging, even shocked, the kids watched, and then silently, followed.

When I reached the wet sand left by a retreating wave, I knelt in my dress khakis, dug out a little hole. A wave rushed me, soaked me. Some kids laughed and I didn't care. When that wave ebbed, I placed the envelope in the sand, buried it, then tossed the rose into the sea. I faced the perplexed group and said, "A long time ago…this boy, he came here, and was scared. He was my age, and he saw his friends die."

"Some crackers jump him?" One boy asked.

"No. But he saw a lot of blood. And he did a brave thing when the others were scared. What he did saved a lot of folks. Made them free. But…" I looked up at the frolicking gulls, "…but he didn't want anybody to thank him."

"Who was he?" a girl asked.

"Someone like…us."

I wiped the wet sand from my hands, and then walked back toward the dunes; this time, in wide strides, like my father's. Head up. Smiling. Oh no, not subdued. And the scent of roasting hot dogs, sun-baked parking lot asphalt and briny breezes filled my nostrils, making me smile. Back on the beach, the kids gathered around the spot where I'd buried the envelope. It was now just a wet dimple in the sand. DeVon scooped out some handfuls until he reached paper. He removed the envelope, and then handed it to one of the girls.

"Whaffaw you give it to me?" She shoved it back at DeVon.

DeVon stammered, "Might be somethin'…I dunno…somethin'…" DeVon opened the soggy flap. Inside was a card.

All it said was THANK YOU.

DeVon yelled to one of his friends, "G'won up there and ask that boy to come back! We wanna know what happened here!"

I came back to a group of new friends. I spoke words I would later write down so I wouldn't forget them.

And so I finished school and moved away from South Carolina. I went to Princeton University, and then law school, worked, and became an author. Somewhere in that grand procession, I refined the prose scribbled when I was turning thirteen, for that day when my child will come to Folly Beach. These are the words they will hear:

In the bloody nightmare called the American Civil War, African American volunteers—some free men of color, some escaped or freed slaves—flocked to Readville, near Boston, where the first black regiment in the Union Army, the 54th Massachusetts Colored Infantry, established a training camp. On the night of July 16, 1863, Jupiter Chambers, an orphan from Bedford, Massachusetts, Drummer Boy of B Company, charged in the first wave of the assault on Battery Wagner, Folly Island, South Carolina. He was only twelve years old. When he saw the battalion color-bearer fall from the parapet, he dropped his drumsticks and seized the banner, waving it, exhorting B Company forward. Columns of them were leveled by Confederate rifle file, canister rounds. Many hesitated, afraid, but when they saw the scrawny drummer boy waving the bloody colors, they stormed the walls, shouting, cheering. Hundreds lay dead or wounded after the assault. Nevertheless, Jupiter was untouched. To honor his fallen brothers he decided to remain in Charleston as company drummer. But once news of his valor reached President Lincoln and Secretary of War Stanton, the War Department sent him on a tour to recruit black men for the Army. This infusion of brave, determined troops doomed the South to defeat. Jupiter returned to Charleston after the war. He married and had four children. He died in 1909, still fighting for his people from the pulpit of his tiny clapboard church on James Island.

Moreover, he never, ever asked to be thanked. Therefore, we say "Thank You," because no one else does.

-Christopher Chambers

10th Anniversary Edition

So You Really Want to Know What Goes On Behind the Doors of My Classroom?

When you care for children's education as much as I do as a teacher, you religiously guard against any comments about what goes on in today's classrooms from people who have never been around a class full of youth for 180 days a year and successfully taught more than perhaps their own children out of selfishness how to read, or truly understand there is more to teaching youth than the mandated curriculum or force fed knowledge in an attempt to prepare youth to become independent citizens.

I say to these people, you are no different from the militia groups of the Congo raping women of their dignity and pride. You are no different from Hitler who wished for one superior race. You are no different from the gangs who fight to defend their own, but kill their brother of the same culture because he is from a different gang. You are no different from the brainwashed Black police officer who sees blue and not a brother on the street in need of help. You are responsible for the rebirth of institutionalized slavery that steals the creativity of youth, imparts that some textbooks' core knowledge is more valuable than their own, and bewitches you to only nurture and care for children from your own womb.

Now is the time for you to step into your own conscious to unlearn what you have been taught, and learn what you have always known, 'Children of today are gifted, intelligent, capable and need every mom's support, not just their own. It is YOU who stand in their way. I am talking to parents, teachers, administrators, school staff, and the community.

You are the parent who glorifies your own child, but never say hello to the other children in my classroom. You are the teacher who wants supplies for your own classroom, but never thought to volunteer to obtain supplies for the children of my classroom. You are the administrator who has become desensitized to the needs of staff to know you care about them and their well-being. You are the school staff who have conversations of laughter about youth YOU label as behavioral problems, but never knew their pain, hurt and suffering from daily living conditions. You are the community who calls the kids animals for destroying your property on the way home instead of developing a rapport with youth on a daily basis with a simple, Hello that spells respect. Don't turn your back or flip the page, YOU know I am talking about YOU.

Allow me to expound on my childhood to help you understand why I believe my premonition that humankind proves you lack respect for today's youth, their experiences, and especially if you cannot stay focused to read on. If you stop now, my point is validated, and mission is accomplished....

From the first day, a teacher enters a classroom full of children; one has to establish trust and an everlasting rapport that is built on respect and core values. I won't let you pry into my classroom, a mysterious place to know how I teach the youth to read because like I said, it is too valuable and a formula I only share with the youth and real parents and teachers who care. Don't waste my time. I am not trying to impress YOU.

If you really care about all youth, you begin by helping all children and not just your own or the children you favor. I am too angry right now to relate to the selfish reader who just wants to know how to impart success to children, but has never volunteered to visit my classroom and help the youth or better yet, help anyone else's child. Do not close your eyes on the number one cause for failure among children in America. A parent can nurture a child with love, care, respect and understanding, but if the formula of molding a successful child does not resonate to their surroundings, and other parents and teachers counteract a child's feeling of success, the formula fails.

I say to parents and teachers who have shunned other people's children, and including their own, you should be ashamed of yourself. How dare you want information you care nothing about or will never use. If I am wrong, than I will let the world know I was out of mind when I wrote this journal entry. YOU are fake, and don't really care about what goes on in my classroom because you don't care about the youth!

I implore teachers and parents to make a difference in as many children's lives as possible. When they know you care, their reading, math and writing excel. What I have experienced is sort of like a stepping stone process all children must rise above. I take all of the hard knocks when they first enter school from their fits, defiance, and unwillingness to communicate and get along with others. Many learn to change for the better, and go on to be Valedictorians, gain acceptance into gifted programs and earn awards. I take pride in creating that fire in the youth to succeed.

If you really want to know, sincerely, what goes on behind the closed doors of my classroom, I will give one clue. I respect all of my students, treat them equally, am constantly aware that I am their role model for half of their day and 180 days a year and the children return the respect by READING and most of all understanding that education is worth it. It may take one week to the whole year, but my children read. This mission of mine is personal. I have long gone astray from wearing fashion, glitter and jewels in the classroom, but was amazed when a little girl, who is a preteen now, contacted me from one of my classes to tell me that she wants to be a teacher, model, fashion designer and make-up artist.

Overall, the day the children begin to read one-by-one is magical. The more respect you give, the more they read. That's what goes on and I make no apologies for following this formula of facilitating a respectful community. If you have a problem with my formula, get in my classroom and fix it or save your complaints, ridicule of teachers, applied principles of teaching children to read, and favoritism over kids who act like your own.

I am from the Bronx, and although have long since living in the ghettos obtained a home; please know I am still in the Bronx, and always will stick up for the kids. They are not like YOU! They are children. If I misjudged you, understand why. I am an adult. This mission is perSOULnal and to refute my judgment, offer to really support the youth whom I teach or just continue being YOU and don't get in my way. I have children to teach. They need me. Someone who is an adult, but understands her soul because within me is an inner-child I never let go of. It stirs in me like Gumbo for the SOUL.

-Heather Covington

The Path

The African American youth of today need to realize and understand that education is a necessity if you are to survive and sustain a comfortable lifestyle. Our youth cannot afford to be complacent with minimum wage jobs while other minorities are stepping up their game and are obtaining the higher paying jobs while African Americans are left behind.

Our youth must stay on the path of higher learning. Education is as essential to our youth's development as the air that we breathe. Our youth must acknowledge education as one of the keys of life that will lead them toward the path of success and financial stability.

As I have gone through life's journey, I have experienced my ups and downs. At conception, my path was laid before me. The path was not always straight. Sometimes it curved and sloped. Often I stumbled and fell. Nevertheless, with God's grace I got back up and continued on my way.

As I reflect, I wish I could turn back the hands of time, particularly when I was a freshman in high school. That's about the time when I thought I knew everything and no one could tell me anything different. To read a book for enjoyment was not even on my agenda. I barely read the books that I needed to complete my homework. Like they say if I knew then what I know now I would be further ahead.

If I could go back in time, I would have developed a thirst for knowledge and education. I would have read every book that I could get my hands on. I have come to realize my greatest failure in life was detouring from the path of education and not graduating from college. My detours led me to my first marriage, two wonderful children, and subsequently a divorce.

I firmly believe if I had received my college diploma that my path would have widened and the opportunities that crossed my path would have been greater. I am certain, had I chosen to stay on course I would be further along in my career. I am convinced that when my path started to whine down hills and valleys, if I had obtained my diploma I would have been prepared, and better equipped to take better care of my children and myself.

I truly believe that had I stayed on the academic path, I could have been a Forensic Scientist, a CSI Investigator, a Doctor, or even a Senator. The world was literally at my feet. I had every opportunity afforded to me by my parents. I didn't even take advantage of the private schools that they sent me to. I could have been anything in the world I wanted to be if I had just stayed focused and educated myself to the fullest.

Instead, today, I am a Purchasing Agent who can't become a Director of Purchasing because I don't have the one requirement to get me to the next level; the one thing that is holding me back is the fact that I don't have a college degree! My potential to significantly increase my finances has come to a standstill all because I don't have that one piece of paper, which certifies me as educated!

As you walk your path, know that you will need God to direct you and often times carry you. Know that the devil will try to destroy you and throw you down a mountain. Don't be discouraged! Remember God has not given you the spirit of fear but He has given you a strong mind to overcome all of your obstacles. Stay prayerful and focused and your path will be filled with all of your heart's desires.

Education is one of the keys to unlocking a future filled with great promises and opportunities. Don't let it pass you by. Don't go down the wrong path.

>
> Enlighten, enhance, and embrace your mind and spirit
> Diligently and dutifully seek all of the knowledge you can obtain
> Ultimately, utilize your intellect so that you can rise
> Cultivate a love for school and books
> Acquire and aspire a thirst for learning
> Transcend and achieve all of your dreams.
> Empower yourself and embark on your path.
> Equipped to conquer the world.

-Lorita Kelsey Childress

Outside the Box

Our mother used to walk us downtown for library books, and to shop. Our family didn't own a car, and we lived within a long walk from downtown, so the walk up Swan Street was a weekend ritual, one which resulted in Willa Mae's three kids all developing a love of reading. White folks at the Buffalo Public Library got used to seeing three little black inner-city kids, accompanied by their mom, carrying stacks of books through the library corridors, checking them out, and lugging them home.

Our mother, who never finished high school, going only as far as the 11th grade, was a voracious reader, and she wanted her kids to develop the same love of learning and books. She named one of my sisters, Daphne, after Daphne du Maurier, the famous French female novelist. How's that for a black woman thinking outside the box? Most of the people in library probably couldn't imagine that she read novels, to say nothing of French novels in translation.

As black folk, it is important we instill in our young people the ability and sensitivity to think outside, and live outside, the box. By "living outside the box," I mean fathom and function, and even dare to dream in such a way that we transcend those societal expectations and limitations ascribed to us based on our race or class. One of my childhood friends, now deceased, lived a life, which exemplified this kind of thinking.

Donald Smith, known by his friends as "Angel," died a hero. He told local drug dealers in Buffalo, NY to get that mess off his block, and they gunned him down.

On a trip back home to Buffalo, I hear about my old friend's murder from Bubs and Donnie, two other old neighborhood friends. Angel's death is recorded in the local paper with the headline, "Wave of Killings takes Life of Hero Dedicated to Others," because in 1994, "he jumped into a water-filled construction hole to help save the life of a disturbed man who had dived into the hole." The news article doesn't mention Donald's heroism in the hood, which is what led to his shooting. According the paper, he was "an innocent victim of random street violence." But he wasn't. As Bubs and Donnie, former next-door neighbors of Angel, tell me the real deal, I fight back disbelief and rage.

"They shot Angel, because he told them to take those drugs off his block. Angel was still rough, man. He wasn't scared of them. He didn't back down from no one." Bubs works as a prison guard, a job he secured after the factory where he'd worked

closed down. He's been there long enough, over fifteen years, which he works in the prison arsenal. We eat chicken wings and pizza and drink sodas as we talk.

"Angel was still strong. Stayed in shape by walking all the time, or rode that bike. He wasn't scared of no one." Donnie adds, "He was just walking to the store, and they ambushed him. Shot him in the head. Bleeding, he still made it to a neighbor's porch. Some other neighbors said the people peeped out their curtains at him on the porch, but wouldn't open the door, wouldn't let him in. He bled to death on that porch."

"By the time the paramedics arrived, he was dead, man," Bubs adds. I think of the movie The Untouchables, the scene where Sean Connery crawls across the floor bleeding, dying. And I picture our friend Angel stumbling to the house, crawling to the door, ringing the doorbell, and his blood leaving its mark on their porch.

Donald "Angel" Smith left his mark on my life in a different way. He was a member of the "Cambridge Street Boys," along with Donnie, Bubs, Cobbs, Rodney and myself, although I lived three streets over, on Stevens Street. We played street football, shoveling the snow during the winter in Buffalo, so we could run and catch. We competed at football, basketball and even staged Monopoly tournaments. We pooled our money to buy cheap wine, which we all shared: Ripple and Mad Dog.

But the thing about Donald, aka Angel, which stands out is he lived and moved outside the box. My friend Donald was a fencer. No, I don't mean that he mended fences, or that he jumped fences, although we did a few in our ramblings through the neighborhood. No, what I mean is that in an age, the 1960's and '70's, when black boys were only supposed to play basketball, football, and perhaps run track, he competed in the sport of fencing. He would get off the bus and walk down Cambridge Street toward home wearing his fencing gear; a big black kid, well over 6 feet tall, wearing his fencing jacket and pants, and carrying his foil. Sometimes he wore his fencing mask. Angel seemed to revel in doing something that none of the rest of us did, and we respected him for it, asking questions of him, and watching him demonstrate various fencing stances. For a black kid back then just to ride the city buses, or walk down a (ghetto) street dressed in fencing garb took a certain kind of courage, which Angel, singularly among us, possessed: the courage to live outside the box.

The news article on Angel's death ends with a statement from his last employer, "Donald was a big, tall guy, and very well read. He seemed to know a little bit about everything."

To which I say, "Amen."

Angel's heroism, like my mother's steadfast commitment to our weekly library treks, is an example of living outside the box that will remain with me always. As a people, we must remember that no "boxes" can hold us, our spirits, our wills, our minds. Moreover, through words and examples, we must teach our young people to think outside the box. We must show them that they possess the spiritual and intellectual wherewithal to "live and move and have their being," outside any boxes and any limitations.

-Frank E. Dobson Jr.

10th Anniversary Edition

Our Vision and High Achievement

I believe history is written in dark ink upon our minds and emotions causing us to think and act in ways that are mysterious and beyond our immediate understanding. I believe becoming a Black parent can open a Pandora's Box filled with stories, nightmares and images borne of our past in this society.

THE DARK SIDE OF PARENTING

I sense that fear has obscured the joys of parenthood in many Black families. I also believe that such fear may taint the joy of childhood for our little boys and girls. This happens in many subtle ways that, in the end, I believe contributes to how children act, what they do, and ultimately what they learn.

Until a few years ago, whenever I looked at my child, I saw through eyes that continually assessed the future. If she failed to speak well, learn well, and develop all the habits that reflect "good raising", then I had my work cut out for me. When teachers informed me of a failed test, the implication was that I, too, had failed. If her hair stood wild and frizzy all over her head, I wondered what people would think? Was it my job to catch that before we left the house? If somebody singled her out as spoiled, or a kid with an attitude, then I had enabled these "violations" and sent her out into the world to be judged. In my mind was a long checklist of conditions that could go wrong for my Black child. Neglecting to meet these criteria could result in: no options for college, nobody to help or hire her, or her being singled out or suspected of wrongdoing; then her being in the wrong place at the wrong time could lead to wrongful accusations and false arrest; or her record or reputation being marred early on-- dooming her to a future of God knows what?

Parenting with fear in my heart opened up a dark world of infinite images of what I did not want to happen to my child. I spent my time trying-- from sun up until sun down-- to fix whatever might be broken, or construed as broken, before I sent her into the world. I certainly didn't want the world to have to fix her for me.

Then I wondered if children who are parented with so much fear might miss the luxury of growing fully into who they are. I'm beginning to think those who are over-managed and watched too closely for signs of trouble might end up angry, rebellious or maybe, insecure. I think it might hinder natural, healthy exploration and investigation. Too much interference might keep them from learning as freely and broadly as they would without the sense of someone looking constantly over their shoulders. Would inclinations to seek and find and questions be managed right out of them? Have we all witnessed the warnings not to come home dirty, lose our bows, or run down the sidewalk?

Have we heard the "no's" to playing in the good clothes, walking in the rain, or cutting up magazines? Yet, are these all the precursors to learning and living out the ideas and questions that blossom in their minds?

I don't suggest that children run wild and undisciplined. I'm suggesting that the curiosity not be judged as "bad" or "hard-headed". It's important to recognize the milky-eyed beauty, the round-cheeked innocence, and the health in unbridled energy. When they are clumsy, dirty-faced, or noisy, we must not look too far beyond that moment. We can see that dirty face as a testimony to discovery of his environment. We can see the lost bows as evidence that there was so much joy brewing in her soul that she had no time to think of her hair. We must lose some of the fear that their appearance will ultimately lead to unfavorable glances from a stranger. We must not lose sleep worrying that perpetually untied laces will be interpreted as a gross motor problem. Neither must we link the natural urge to run as somehow related to those two failed spelling tests last week. We have to dig down beyond our history and regain our trust that if they are healthy and happy, with some tweaking here and there, they'll grow into their potential.

Everything I've read along spiritual lines says that what we focus on increases or expands. When my daughter started school, for a while I focused more on shortcomings than strengths. From the time she entered preschool, teachers and administrators have kept me continually aware of where she fits on one scale or another-- developmental checklists and readiness scales in preschool and early childhood. Then, there were standardized tests scores and academic proficiency levels thereafter. From August until June of every year, the temperature of our parent-child relationship could be measured according to missing homework assignments, lost worksheets, forgotten tests, and grades. Sometimes there was cause for a celebration. Frequently a failure of one kind or another followed, warranting unpleasant consequences.

After third grade, I could not shape her personality and behaviors in ways that led to the approval of *all of* the systems in which she navigated. A natural artist will not always be a perfect student. A talkative individual with a tendency to learn through verbal discourse will not fit easily into quiet classrooms dominated by silent reading and independent seatwork. In time, the demands of managing, instructing, constructing, and taking responsibility for every aspect of a human being became so overwhelming that anger and resentment became the constant companions of love and acceptance. The continuous pressure to "make" someone into something different is not a natural process.

THE LIGHT COMES IN

Out of the blue one day, I had a conversation with a doctor. She made a comment that liberated me from the notion of parenting in response to societal injustices. "Parents can't allow school work be the most important part of their relationship and interactions," she said and continued, "that's not why we become parents."

It was a simple statement. Momentarily, it allowed me to glimpse a corner of freedom--of breathing room, to do it differently. The feelings and memories that informed my role as "mother" came to me like the weaving of a tale. I was instantly in touch with the legacy of my parenting paradigm.

The soul memories of our people's need for good education are relevant in order to pull ourselves up by our bootstraps. The link between education and survival that lives in my mind is like blood vessels supplying nourishment to my daily purpose and activities. The constant awareness of our operating at a deficit from the minute we are thrust into the world with having to come up with plans that earn us fair treatment and inclusion.

And just like that, I had a shift in consciousness.

Education is certainly important. As a former educator and current developer of educational programs, I recognize the need for equity, achievement and preparation for the society in which we live. However, love and acceptance are more important. Before we were slaves, we were people with sound, strong relationships unaffected by determinants such as test scores, intelligence scales, or classroom placements. Our recent history cannot be allowed to rewrite our human nature. No matter what standards are used to judge us within society's institutions, we must be aware of a more important standard within our homes. Children need parents who care about their spirits more than their grades. We must be mindful of providing loving discipline, structure, and setting sound boundaries and high expectations across the board. I also believe that a parent should be the kindest mirror into which a child looks every day so that they are inspired to meet those expectations.

If we scrutinize our children from the vantage point of a critical, imbalanced and often cruel society, how will they learn to love themselves? If we correct with the negative vision of an indicting dominant culture in our mind, where do children get their messages of strong internal resources, motivation, and spiritual perfection?

Unconditional love has been documented as a precursor to resilience and better academic outcomes. If we focus on test scores and social norms as primary indicators of successful parenting, then we overlook the rich opportunity to support the growing spirit of a whole person embarking on a life-long journey. If children don't find the best of themselves in the words and eyes of their families and culture, we might actually contribute to the sense of alienation that leads to failure. Then will many ultimately seek validation outside themselves and their homes in order to feel special and wonderful? Is that the very thing that leads to drug use, delinquency, school drop out, and a lack of achievement?

    How ironic!

-Angela Epps

MATHEMATICAL FEMALE

As a youngster, I bought into the boy/girl hype. You know the theory that girls do well in English but poorly in Math and vice versa for boys. I was a trusting person, who usually believed what my authority figures told me. In elementary school, everything went smoothly until we got to the Fractions. I struggled with common denominators and mixed numbers but didn't worry too much. I'd been getting straights A's since kindergarten and usually overcame whatever might stump me initially. My teachers were patient and kind, going over it with me as many times as it took for me to get it right. I went into junior high school confident in my abilities.

However, in junior high, the math skills test placed me in Remedial Math. I couldn't believe it! Nevertheless, my counselor assured me it was normal--he stated females generally excel in the humanities (English, Foreign Languages, and Sociology) but don't do so well in Mathematics. Oh, I thought, so it's not really me, it's a gender thing. I accepted what the counselor said that day and resigned myself to poor grades in that subject. After all, why would this adult lie to a kid?

The fact is that the counselor didn't lie; he honestly believed what he said. He was just telling me something he had been told and probably had no evil intent. However, his statement simply wasn't true. Saying most girls are bad in Math is like saying most Black people smoke crack. It's a stereotype that is based on someone else's perceptions about females but it is not rooted in fact. There are no inherent gender characteristics that can be attributed to education, including mathematic ability.

I made it into college only taking geometry and tested into remedial math again. At this point, I had adjusted mentally to honor classes in English and needing tutors for Math. Yet college was a lot harder than high school. Can I just say - STATISTICS? The first time I took that class, I cried everyday when we got our homework back. I simply could not understand the basic concepts that would allow me to pass a test. My tutor tried his best but to no avail. My Statistics teacher could only threw up his hands up at my stubborn insistence with failing every single test.

I took Statistics twice more while getting my Bachelor's Degree in Sociology; the third time the instructor took pity on me and let me pass with a "D".

A few years after college, I was hanging out with a good friend who had known me since 7th grade. She said, "Hey Tish, what's (so and so's) phone number?"

I was confused because that came out the blue and answered, "How do I know?"

She replied, "Come on, you know everybody's phone number by heart! You always have, ever since I've known you."

I thought about it for a second and realized how right she was. Not only did I know the number she had just asked for, but I knew ALL our friends numbers! I knew the phone number to the local drugstore. I knew the number to the DMV. As a matter of fact, I knew the addresses too. I didn't really want to believe it at first; numbers were the bane of my educational existence! I was supposed to be bad in Math. But if that was true, how could I remember any set of numbers I saw or heard? I just couldn't deny my weird little talent as my friend tested me on random numbers and I remembered every single one of them--weeks and even months later.

It took some years but I finally realized how I cheated myself by believing what my junior high school teacher told me. I wasted all that time not applying myself in Math because I let someone else tell me what I could and could not do. I allowed a negative perception of myself to impact my early education. Now, my special talent has given me confidence in my Mathematics abilities. I CAN DO ANYTHING I WANT TO DO! That is a fact. Math problems no longer mystify me because I know I am capable of figuring them out. I can instantly memorize any set of numbers I come across. I can quickly calculate the sales tax of any purchase to the penny, and I have memorized the sales tax of every state. I am a leasing agent for an internet software company, and I calculate the funding amounts for each new client. I give current customers' account balances, figure payoffs and refigure the debt amounts for the collection files. I would have never trusted myself with computing such important numbers before my epiphany, but now I do so flawlessly. Most importantly, I immediately challenge anyone who tells me I can't do something. I am a woman, and I'm GOOD in math.

-Tatisha Jackson

10th Anniversary Edition

Boys and Girls

Journal Entry. Monday May 22, 2006

She was waiting patiently at my door this morning.

Valentina is one of my 'A' students. She's always on time with her assignments, eager to participate in our lectures and she's a wonderful spirit around the others. Like clockwork, she's here early.. *a bit early*, I ponder as she approaches me before I reach the classroom door.

"Ms. Gray, I won't be able to take the high school assessment tests this week."

"Why, Valentina, what's up? These tests are very important."

Valentina is a petite flower with flawless dark chocolate skin and big young eyes that are aglow with the wonderment of the world and all that encompasses a golden future. At that moment, I was a tad baffled at her urgency.

"I gotta tell you something. Really important something. But, you gotta promise not to give me THAT look, Ms. Gray. It's already hard enough telling you this but I can't take that look. It's like you don't yell at us, just give us that LOOK."

My stomach turns a bit..the anticipation is proverbial and I notice Valentina has broken her eye contact with me. She glances down and fiddles with nothing but something to seem 'busy'. My soul silently screeches. Lord, she's only fifteen.

"*Valentina..what's going on…*"

Reluctantly, I paused..fighting my inner self to even blurt these words out but I do.. it's such familiar terrain for me as an educator of 7 years...so I continue. This time, I gently tap her chin to indicate that I seek eye contact and I touch her soft hands-- in an effort to let her know things will be just fine.

"*Are you pregnant Valentina?*"

A long silence. Then, it emerges, so virginal and pure--a solitary tear from this young flower of a girl. Her eyes are heavy with pain, regret and most of all fear of rejection.

"*Yes, um.. I am..my mom told me the other day and um.. today, I have morning sickness and um.. well, I don't even know if I plan to have it but..*"

"*Hush now,*" I whisper to Valentina and give her a tight squeeze. In a mellow and comforting tone, I tell her…'*mistakes happen*' then I smile.

Valentina gazes up at me with her pleading eyes... begging me for guidance. But, I feel powerless as she continues.

"*The boy doesn't know. See, he's going to school here and we just um, kicked it. Anyway, Ma says I have to get rid of it but..um..*"

Her words trail off to that other world—a fluency of familiarity from others like herself—as she contends to her version of this harsh reality—another young girl pregnant. Another young couple engaging in unprotected sex. Grown folks' business.

I listened to Valentina then wrote her a pass to the office for dismissal.

10th Anniversary Edition

-Sharon 'Shaye' Gray

Unexpected

Starting a new job is difficult enough. Couple that with a new location and new co-workers and you will find that it isn't easy being the new kid (or in my case the new teacher) on the block. Immediately you think, wow! I'll be meeting new people and discovering new personalities (young and old); this could truly be exciting! And just when you've psyched yourself into believing you'll be meeting exciting friendly people, you're thrown a curve-ball.

The first day of work on my new job was challenging to say the least. My job is described as a Paraprofessional who works in the "Learning Center" with academically and behaviorally challenged elementary students. My duties include pulling students from their classrooms and bringing them to my class where I enforce learning skills such as reading, spelling, and math concepts. "A wonderful job, I thought." That is until I showed up at several classrooms to pull each student. I was more than surprised when I received scowls, huffs, puffs, and hands raised high in protest by those who obviously didn't want me there; by those who perhaps felt they didn't need or want my help. "Ouch! That really hurt," I thought. I know children sometimes become uneasy with change and meeting a new teacher, but this reaction caught me totally off guard, and who would believe that these little ones would not accept me? After all, I was only trying to be helpful. I only wanted to reinforce what they were already being taught, or lacking in, and besides that's what my job description says I should do. I thought to myself, "how could this be happening?" "How could they not want my services?" I had done this kind of work for many years and was proficient at it.

Well, instead of displaying major attitude by huffing and puffing or scowling and throwing my hands up in the air, I decided to keep my head up, to keep smiling and going to those classrooms everyday in spite of the negative reception. Nevertheless, when it became almost unbearable for me to handle, I decided to speak with my supervisor, and do you know what she did? Neither did she place the children in detention, make them write lines on the board, nor did she discuss it with their parents. Moreover, would you like to know why? Because it wasn't the children who behaved this way, it was the teachers!

Although I was hurt by this incident, I couldn't quit the position because I refused to succumb to adversity, and I knew that my love was greater for those children then my disdain for those teachers who behaved that way.

So, I guess the moral of this story is, try not to let the unexpected take you off course, instead, if possible find a positive way to deal with it especially if it's something you love doing or you know without a doubt that it is your calling.

-Linda Jai

Hemispheres: Overcoming Educational Stereotypes in North and South America

One afternoon, my girlfriend and I were discussing Oprah's interview of Senator Barack Obama. They had discussed the race card and the fact that people may attribute their success to them being an exceptional African American politician or media professional as opposed to being simply put...exceptional. We talked about how much diverse talent exists in our community—a unique blend of thoughts, ideals, philosophies and outlooks on life jumbled together to make a savory stew or gumbo. It was at this time I started to tell Lisa about my experiences with being labeled by our own people in both the northern and southern hemispheres. I come from a family that always thirsted for education. Having attended Benjamin Banneker SHS in Washington, DC, a nationally renowned all-academic magnet school, I was surrounded by overachievers. In fact, the school mascot name was Achievers. Washington, DC has one of the most affluent pockets of educated African Americans in the United States. Entrepreneurs, artists, economists, writers, doctors, lawyers and such, surrounded me. That was normal to me.

The severity of the lack of respect for education did not become as real to me until I volunteered at a neighborhood academic enrichment after school program as a freshman in college. The children hailed from the historic Shaw neighborhood and ranged from 6 to 14 years of age. The students often referred to me as "Black Barbie" as if I was black...but not really black. At first glance, one would think that the children were referring to a particular aesthetic quality. At the time, I wore my hair in locks, so I did not look like the proverbial Black Barbie. One afternoon the students explained what they really meant. The fact that I did not split verbs and enunciated was anathema to them. I tried to stress the importance of literacy to them. I explained to them that the need to take their education seriously so they would have the opportunity to attend the college of their choice. At the very least, they would need to finish high school. It felt like my words were falling on deaf ears. The students came to the center for shelter to receive assistance with homework completion. They were fine with that—but there was an underlying issue that was keeping them from achieving more. In their neighborhood, it was not cool to "sound white" or strive academically. Six months later, I experienced a similar feeling as I was in the Palenques of Colombia, ex-slave maroon settlements, explaining to the villagers that I, too, was Black. They called me La Gringa Negra...because I spoke perfect Castellano, the grammatical name for Spanish. As the kids hung on the "corner" in the middle of the jungle with their tennis shoes on and caps turned backwards...looking like your average young brother in Any Urban City, USA, I talked to them about the importance of pursuing their own educations. It blew their minds that I was there on an exchange from another country...and that people of African descent even had access to such resources. I wanted the Palenqueros to know that even if their employment opportunities were limited, they should take pride in their heritage while embracing the formalities of the Spanish language. Before attending law school, I took time to teach Spanish in the DC Public School system...as one attempt to give back to the community. This time I was faced with a double dilemma. Classes full of students who not only could not read English...they had no idea of how they would learn Spanish.

I had returned to Black Barbie status and was now faced with actually motivating my students to step past their hurts and insecurities and find the joy in learning. It was amazing how students were more concerned with maintaining their hard reputations...as if being recognized for their academic achievements would adversely affect them outside of the classroom. The sad thing is…it did. I allowed many students to eat lunch with me in the classroom so they could get extra time in with me without being taunted by their schoolmates. They embraced new ideas and tried to speak properly while spending safe time sequestered in my classroom. Hours later…they would not sound the same as they walked down the corridors and talked with their fellow classmates. The common denominator from all three experiences…that young people of African descent were not always equating their survival with their education and ability to effectively communicate in the general population. Society—or at least educated African Americans must take the time to volunteer with the younger generation so they understand and appreciate how to overcome societal limitations through educational advancement. There should not be a stigma attached to a young girl or boy who works hard in school and takes the time to formulate and enunciate his or her thoughts. I believe that often times the simple act of sharing one's own story or testimony would be enough to spark the flame of excellence in young people today. I am encouraging you to take time to speak in front of an audience of students at your church or house of worship, your local elementary, junior and senior high schools, and neighborhood organizations. Our children need to see us. We don't have to be on a national or international media platform like Oprah or Senator Obama to make a difference. The difference starts with us.

-Niambi Jarvis

10th Anniversary Edition

An Invitation to the Private Room

I can visualize the paper, bleeding with red correction marks and questions of understanding: "What? Your wording is awkward?" My paper had disappeared under the red sea of criticism from Mr. Bennett my eleventh grade advanced English teacher. That was his name, Mr. Bennett. The name draws a clear picture of me sitting in the front seat of the second-to-last row, next to the mid-wall-to ceiling windows, with bare shrubs lining the wall outside. The class was in C hall, two classrooms from the end of the hall. The classroom that now holds and symbolizes all of my fears and negative thoughts about being a writer. A classroom filled with the words that follow the thought of his name: IT IS A SHAME YOUR WRITING IS SO POOR WHEN YOU ARE SO SMART ORALLY. These words ring in my head every time I am asked about my school experience. A young girl with a mother addicted to drugs, who ended up being the sole provider for her two younger brothers at the age of 19; also a veteran English teacher and an editor of an African American newsmagazine. The questions were a search for understanding of how I became successful and what teachers must to do to make sure students are successful. The interrogators wanted to know: *What are we doing wrong?* Immediately Mr. Bennett is the only person I see. I relive the moment with Mr. Bennett sitting on his stool with his arms draped over the podium, only the top of his striped shirt and the sides of his belt and beige trousers show. He rubs his hand along his prickly haired lips and his salt and peppered chin. His words float out, riding a stale coffee smell. Thirty other students watched the words that pierced the air to crush my spirit. Those same thirty students who would later wondered why I, one of three black girls in our group that has been together since seventh grade, am not in their senior English class.

My mind drifted to that first day of school. Those students

believe I am absent until I show up in the first ever calculus class to be offered at the high school, which was back in my rightful place with the advanced students. They crowd my desk and implore me to explain where I've been all day. I look at them while vulnerability cloaking my response, and shrug my shoulders. Didn't they hear Mr. Bennett two weeks before school ended as he called each student up to give them his recommendation for senior year? Didn't they see the words from his mouth, dark brown from all the coffee that coated them? Didn't they feel the sting of the words like fresh cut onions make my eyes water? "You are a very smart student but your writing isn't up to my standards. I don't believe you can be successful in advanced English next year. I am recommending you for regular 12th grade English." I rode BART home from school that day to the place I called home, a shelter in San Leandro feeling that I had been dumped by the side of the road. I had been kicked out of the smart kids club and not by my peers who were always impressed by my ability to achieve despite my circumstances, but by my teacher who was certain that success was not in my future. I thought to tell my mother about Mr. Bennett, as I knew other students had. They would immediately voice openly that they were going to tell their parents. The next day they would share the conversation and how the teacher's unjust act had been righted immediately by a stern phone call to the counselor or principal. I rehearsed what I would tell my mom and how I would share my same story of victory over the malice of Mr. Bennett. My story never came.

I entered the shelter and the balancing act began. The balancing act consisted of protecting my belongings from new residents, looking after my two younger brothers, and praying that my mother would make it back to the shelter before curfew so that my brothers and I wouldn't have to hide in our room, unable to come out for dinner because being in the shelter without your mother was cause for the shelter workers to call Child Protective Services, so instead I sat in regular 12th grade English. Helping my new and mostly black peers with the Shakespeare that baffled them and the modifiers they couldn't describe, I made friends quickly. We traded languages. They taught me the language to socialize with those I had been separated from for the past five years, and I gave them the answers to questions nobody cared if they learned and told them of subjects no one thought they would even master or needed to know for where they were going in life. This was English class. Days turned into weeks and weeks into the end of the first quarter and that's when my life changed. Mrs. Pickell called me into her back room. The back room was Mrs. Pickell's personal space and it was more than just her desk area, it was her private room where she held her secrets of teaching. No student went into the teacher's back room except prized teacher's assistants and there were few of them. Mrs. Pickell stood over me, her tall, thin, frail and aged frame fitted her always overly excited voice, but she was calm and her eyes focused on me with such intensity that I was sure I was in trouble for helping my peers who often used me as their primary resource. "What are you doing in my class? You obviously don't belong."

I laid my hands along my legs and gripped the seam of my jeans, my chest tightened and I began to arrange my curse words. I would not be hurt again by a teacher. She looked at me, took a second glance at her grade book, turned her back and began to slide her hands along the spines of books that filled her bookcase. My eyes followed as if her hand were the pointer used during eye exams. She turned toward me and extended to me a small paperback book. "I can see that you are very smart and you must be bored in my class. Here is a book I'd like you to read. The author is African American and the story is about a young girl. I believe you will enjoy this book. Don't worry about the class work I already know you can do it. I'll give you alternate assignments." I glared at the book. The title "Marked by Fire" and the illustrated flames matched the glow in my eyes. I waited unsurely. Mrs. Pickell smiled and extended her arm farther out. "I don't know much about the author or the book but I am confident that you will have no problem interpreting the theme of the book. When you finish, I have several more and then you can always go to the library and begin to check out books of other authors." Mrs. Pickell pointed to the empty chair in her back room as she passed by me, placing the book in my hand before walking out into the classroom, leaving me standing in her private room. I sat and opened page one. In Mrs. Pickell's class, I would read my first Toni Morrison, Alice Walker, and Joyce Carol Thomas novels.

By the end of the school year, I began to declare to friends that I would be a writer. I recalled the first day that I dared to dream of being a writer. My ninth grade teacher Ms. Carrai commented to me, "I wrote that essay question just for you because you are a gifted writer." Mr. Bennett had wiped out the words of Ms. Carrai, but Mrs. Pickell gave them back with tools to sharpen them. I spent the next 10 years writing through my pain and happiness but never confident enough to share my writing. At age 29, I encountered another Mr. Bennett. The words you aren't good enough shook my stable foundation. I left teaching, a marriage and began living alone for the first time in my life. Instantly all the painful experiences of my past surfaced and with them the few but powerful moments of being told I was smart enough to survive everything. I thought back to Mrs. Pickell and found a private room of my own. I sat at my small glass table for two and filled out an application to be a writer of a local magazine. Sixty days later, I opened the CityFlight Newsmagazine and read my name under contributing writer. I flipped to my article and read the words that came from my inner being. The printed words turning into a bright thick red, yellow, blu By the end of the school year, I began to declare to friends that I would be a writer. I recalled the first day that I dared to dream of being a writer. My ninth grade teacher Ms. Carrai commented to me, "I wrote that essay question just for you because you are a gifted writer." Mr. Bennett had wiped out the words of Ms. Carrai, but Mrs. Pickell gave them back with tools to sharpen them. I spent the next 10 years writing through my pain and happiness but never confident enough to share my writing. At age 29, I encountered another Mr. Bennett. The words you aren't good enough shook my stable foundation. I left teaching, a marriage and began living alone for the first time in my life. Instantly all the painful experiences of my past surfaced and with them the few but powerful moments of being told I was smart enough to survive everything. I thought back to Mrs. Pickell and found a private room of my own. I sat at my small glass table for two and filled out an application to be a writer of a local magazine. Sixty days later, I opened the CityFlight Newsmagazine and read my name under contributing writer. I flipped to my article and read the words that came from my inner being. The printed words turning into a bright thick red, yellow, blue, pink, and green rainbow guided the way to the pot of gold, success.

-Lanette Jimerson

Talking White

When I first saw Barack Obama give his historic speech during the 2004 Democratic National Convention, I watched with interest. Here was an articulate black man speaking with such fervor and bravery about issues that affected us all as a country. However, when he said the words, "children can't achieve unless we raise their expectations and turn off the television sets and eradicate the slander that says a black youth with a book is acting white," I nearly jumped out of my seat!

His statement brought me back to the days when I was constantly ridiculed for trying to be white.

My parents, both of whom were serving in the U.S. Air Force, separated when I was eight years old. We were living in Italy, and after the separation, my mother sent my sister and me to New Orleans to live with our grandmother. This was our first taste of attending a predominantly African-American school, so, right from the start, we were at a disadvantage in the eyes of our peers. We spoke differently, acted differently, and in some ways, even thought differently. We weren't any better or worse than the kids, we went to school with—just different.

So different that we were often accused of "talking white." Our speech, coupled by the fact that we had moved there from another country, gained us automatic teasing. This teasing became so bad that many times I went home near tears. I was tired of being ribbed for the way I talked, reading too fast, and even the way I dressed. From a third grader's point of view, it wasn't an easy life.

My family tried to encourage me to hold my head up and try to strike back when I was teased, but it wasn't easy. I wasn't as versed in the snappy comebacks as my peers. To make things worse, I wasn't a great dancer and didn't know how to double Dutch. There was hardly anything or subject that I could really connect with anyone on. I was a bookworm.

My sister was only four at the time, so it was easier for her to eventually fit in. She was young enough to blend in, and eventually cultivated some great friendships. I also made friends, but the way I spoke was so much ingrained in me, that I couldn't hide it if I wanted to! Oh, I tried to assimilate by speaking the way my friends were, but it brought even more teasing. Even one of my friends commented one day, "Look, the Italy Girl is trying to talk black now."

Can you imagine how hard that was? Here I was, finally going to school with people who looked like me, and I was being rejected. I wanted to fit in, but my attempts were being ridiculed. I felt that I just couldn't win!

Eventually, as I got older, I finally learned to accept that I spoke differently and even began to enjoy it. I guess I finally realized that the way I spoke was a part of me and no matter how much I tried to hide it, it just wasn't going anywhere. Thanks to my family's encouragement, I began enjoying the admiration some people gave me for speaking "proper" English. I was the smart girl. I even began laughing with my peers when they shot their "talking white" jokes at me.

Those jokes went on throughout my teenaged years, even after we moved back with my mother in Texas. We went back to attending predominantly white schools with other military kids. The "talking white" comments continued to an extent, but by this time, it didn't hurt so much. I still wasn't the most popular girl in school, and like most teenagers, I was struggling to find myself. However, fortunately, or maybe unfortunately, the way I talked was the least of my problems.

To many, I was the unattractive semi-nerdy girl. I was still a bookworm, but that attribute may have been thrust upon me because I couldn't *buy* a boyfriend! I tried fitting in the best way I could, but I guess my speech didn't always cooperate. Some of my black schoolmates, usually those who had actually grown up in Texas, still saw me as acting white. Some were pretty bold in their opinions. One day, while I working in the school library, a black schoolmate, who probably thought she was being friendly, asked me directly, "Rhonda, why do you talk like a white girl?"

I shrugged my shoulders, trying to think of an answer that she would accept. I knew she wasn't trying to hear anything deep so I simply said, "I don't know. I guess it's because I spent most of my life around white people."

It wasn't the best answer, but it shut her up.

The stigma of trying to be white didn't end there. Even some of my boyfriends questioned the way I spoke. I still laugh when thinking back to one guy I dated when I was sixteen. I called him one night and his brother answered the phone. After asking for him, I heard him ask my boyfriend if I was white. I laughed and later asked my boyfriend why he thought someone with a voice as deep as mine would sound white. He laughed and told me it wasn't my voice, but the way I "talked." He then proceeded to teach me how to say, "What's up cuz" the "right" way!

Unfortunately, not everyone in my situation had learned to accept the ribbing. One night, while attending a party, a young lady whom I had befriended had left in tears because of a disagreement she'd had with someone. I don't remember the argument, but I do remember her voicing her frustration over teasing she'd received over the years.

"People always rib me because I talk white or act white. I can't help how I talk!" she sobbed as we stood around her, trying to console her.

I wondered what that had to do with what had happened that night, but I realized that whatever the incident, it was merely a catalyst to her vocalizing the pain she felt over feeling that she had been rejected on every front. Before that night, I had never noticed that she spoke differently, but that may have been because I spoke the same way. The only difference was that I had finally learned to live with how I spoke. I didn't care what others had to say about it—I took pride in my "proper speech."

Today, that young lady is doing well for herself. I hear she has a nice job and is now married with children and still lives in Texas. I'm not sure how she got over those feelings of persecution that resulted from her "talking white," but I thank God that she did. So many children who experienced the same thing weren't so lucky. So many children are hiding their intelligence and speaking in slang just so they can fit in! As a result, we're watching more mothers on the news professing how smart their children were, and wondering how they could have gotten caught up with the wrong people. Even the not-so-extreme cases are in danger. They might not be on the wrong side of the law, but their parents have suffered the displeasure of watching their grades slide lower and lower all in the name of "fitting in."

How sad is that?

Is the only way to prove our so-called blackness to hide our values and education? Do our children have to skip school or visit detention twice a week just to prove they're "down?" I hope not, but this may be the case if they're not given a sense of self at a young age. I was blessed with a family who gave me just that. I wasn't the most self-assured person in the world, but I was blessed with a mother and grandmother who would kick me in the butt if I brought home anything less than a B or said anything less than what was thought of as my level of speech. In short, my family did as Senator Obama urged all parents do—they encourage me and granted high expectations.

Today, I'm rearing my own child. She will be starting kindergarten soon, and already, I'm working to ensure that she expects nothing but the best in life. I don't have to push her—she just has an amazing drive. Failure brings her nothing but frustration. She's already learning to read and has a vocabulary unlike many children her age. The funny thing is that I sometimes laugh when I hear her speak. She sounds like the same white girl I was accused of being when I was a child. But, you know what? I wouldn't have it any other way. Because if acting white means getting the most out of life, then so be it.

-Rhonda M. Lawson

10th Anniversary Edition

Blind Eyes

Ignorance.

An untamed disease knows no bound while tainting any mind devoid of knowledge to combat it. Black, white, young, old, male, female--it doesn't matter. If you know its power and influence, then at some point in your life, it probably infected you, too. Its virus may even flow through your veins still, leeching off your ability to "see" beyond your own two eyes.

No one is immune. Not even me.

It took a long leap into adulthood to split open my narrow-minded ways. As a 33-year-old man, I can now look back into my stained memory lane and pinpoint several bouts of ignorance--but for some reason, one trivial moment sticks out.

It was 1986 and during my freshman year in High school. As I'd done almost everyday in study hall, I'd crack open my Government textbook and prop my head on the palm of my hand.

Not really studying, though. Nope. Shoot, you'd think I used that precious classroom time wisely, the way a sharp 15-year-old should, right? Maybe finishing my Accounting Fundamentals homework or researching for my Science project?

Uh-uh. Not young James.

A page with a White House picture faced me, but learning where Ronald Reagan laid his head at night couldn't keep my attention. Not enough interest for my taste, anyway. An open page was just a front.

Since the school year began, I hardly strayed from my study hall routine once sleep molecules kicked in: Open a book, angle my head down with my palm or fist pressed against my cheek--and "read." Each day, teachers would swap duties as study hall "babysitters," so only those with eagle eyes caught my act.

The teacher would enforce classroom silence--which only

granted peace to exercise my eyes. Yeah, I exercised them, all right. Let's just say the back of my eyelids held my attention way better than some house on Pennsylvania Avenue.

Bill, a 16-year-old young man I'd known since childhood--but didn't really consider a buddy--was sitting across from me near the front row. Before my escape to dreamland, Bill reached under his desk for a textbook. I didn't think much of it--until I noticed "Trigonometry" on the cover.

He opened the book and jotted notes on a white pad. My eyebrows flew open and mouth was the shape of a donut. What the...?

Bill? In an advanced Math Class? Impossible.

Why my shocked reaction, you ask?

Simple. I had learned blacks couldn't excel in higher learning.

Like I said, <u>ignorance</u>.

Television, movies, magazines, books ... they all warped a negative view of my own--and I didn't even know it. When a ubiquitous media spreads cancerous propaganda about a group of people almost daily; its virus can poison young minds. Even those in the same skin.

And Bill and I shared the same skin.

Graphic images had painted a less-than-human picture of dark-skinned folks, which polluted my under-developed brain. In my youth, I had developed a sort of latent prejudice.

Toward black folks.

And believe it or not, I had many black friends. Still didn't matter. We all sailed on a "slave" ship bound to sink.

According to stereotypical mumbo-jumbo, I'd absorbed for years--including nonsense from fellow students, friends, and, believe it or not, <u>adults</u>--anyone "cursed" with dark melanin fell far behind in one basic necessity: intelligence.

Young James believed that mess, too. What I'd read and heard had conned me into soaking in false truths that proliferated self-hate.

That's right--<u>self-hate</u>.

What else do you call it when your programmed mind breeds doubt, hostility, and suspicion toward people who <u>look</u> like you?

Except for The Cosby Show and a sprinkle of black TV personalities, mug shots, drugs, murders and shirt-less black men with cuffs behind their backs ruled the nightly news. The TV spoon-fed false advertisement to a billion people around the world: Only a bottom-of-the-barrel black society existed in America.

Didn't show many brothers in suits and ties calling shots, either--unless you count Jesse Jackson. Even in sports like the NFL, we had almost every position on lock--<u>except</u> quarterback and head coach. Pretty obvious, right? Can have an HNIC in a role that required analytical skill? Scientific research "proved" blacks could never obtain a luxury such as high aptitude and/or on-your-toes intellect.

Remember, the Bell Curve for black folks slanted further down than the so-called "Lilly White." Yup, and part of me believed it. I was a young black teenager with blind eyes and deep-seated thoughts--hardly any different from some old white racist.

Hate. Toward <u>my own</u>. For men and women--my brothers and sisters--in the same skin.

Nothing is sadder.

As an adult, I sometimes question myself whenever I see my young "peeps" today: Why the roughneck hostility toward each other? Where'd the distrust come from? Why does a young brother who speaks "proper" English equate to acting white?

Part of me understands. I saw the same things growing up. I'd already confessed to the blanket of ignorance wrapped around my head.

But I grabbed that blanket and yanked it away. Now, I know my folks stand on equal ground with everyone else. Want proof? Just check out the 20-plus black quarterbacks in today's NFL. Got a few HNICs regulating million-dollar players, too.

Yeah, that scientific research about black folks' brainpower

Gumbo For The Soul
definitely holds water today.
What do <u>you</u> think?

-James Lewis

10th Anniversary Edition

The Heartbreak Epidemic

Heartbreak held my classroom hostage.

My students weren't focused, unable to understand and connect with the lesson. The young but *grown* boys and girls were diverted by a treacherous "love bug" that was hovering throughout the building. Faces expressed a desperate pain, confusion, disappointment, and a lack of self-worth.

Because of the genuine connection, I shared with my students, based on a sincere and mutual *keep it real* allegiance, I knew that their distraction would eventually affect them academically.

Therefore, one day I sat in the classroom and just listened. It turns out that many of my students, at the tender ages of 12 and 13, would open up and share very personal stories of loving someone who didn't love them back; ending in familiar statements as…

"Ms. Mackey, he don't love me!"

"Ms. Mackey, she cheated on me!"

"Ms. Mackey, she disrespected me!"

My primary concern as their teacher was to effectively prepare my students for the real world. And in doing so it was critical for me to once again revert their attention toward learning. They needed help and I had to give it to them in a nippy fashion. I knew the only way my students would "bounce back" was to know that even *I* had experienced love, infidelity, and disrespect; therefore, understanding that they certainly didn't need me to tell them that what they were experiencing was just "puppy love," and that they should promptly get over it.

Ironically, we were studying poetry at the time, and this would be the cure I would use to heal my students.

By this time, following Bloom's Taxonomy, we were at the evaluation process in the unit. The students were working on a poetry project that consisted of several components, which would of course conclude in their composing a polished, original poem, which weighed heavily on presentation and authenticity.

Poetry time! Students one by one (with or without their poems) took to the podium. And one by one my heartsick students expressed meticulous and assertive verses about love, success, ambition, poverty, crime, mistakes, drugs, gangs, etc. A captive audience of their peers, families, and my fellow teachers looked on, amazed and in awe of the raw, creative passion in their words and presentations. An outburst of tears, claps, laughs, and sighs filled the room as students walked to and from the podium leaving the audience hungry for more.

Our emcee followed the program and introduced me.

"Now, we will be hearing a poem by Ms. Mackey."

Nervousness covered me at the sound of all the chants from *"You go Ms. Mackey"* to *"That's my teacher!"* I knew that not only had my students mastered the understanding of poetry, but also they were also eager to hear me *keep it real*. I had purposefully prepared a poem specifically for my students. Therefore, whatever I was going to do had to be done through this poem. I scanned the audience carefully looking into the eyes of my students…hoping to seize their hearts, souls, and most importantly their minds, and spoke these words…

The Disease That Almost Killed Me!
There wasn't a cure for my infection,
Neither a pill nor a shot could give me a day's satisfaction.
It caught me off guard as I thought I stood protected from the heinous disease.
It all started from the painless question, "May I have your number please?"
The melody of the words as they left his tongue swept me off my feet,
While my heart and soul tapped to his beat.
The lonely days and nights, I gasped for air that was succumbed by the heat.
I lay down but could not sleep because of the painstaking aches I experienced while I slept.
Laying in bed, talking to friends, eating heaps of food, and isolating myself

from the real world were all the things I tried to distract me from my promised emotional death.

As the months passed by, my pain worsened by the mere thought of his shadow, which only appeared as a ghost.

My mind and soul fought with my head trying to keep the soul intact, which was already lost.

Searching for a remedy, I read a book for the nourishment I needed to maintain a fragile heart.

But neither the author nor his words could soothe my pain that profoundly confused me like a piece of priceless, unexplainable art.

Bewildered by what tortured my inner soul,
life had begun to soak the only bristle of air I prayed as I knelt.

Scribbling in a journal, staring at the invisible, and begging the guardian angel to not turn the other cheek were all the things I tried to distract me from my promised emotional death.

One year proceeded another year; I lived with this fatal disease by hope of mere chance that I would receive the love that I was giving.

How did I know that I was blindly visualizing that it was love I was feeling when I said that he was forgiven?

A misunderstanding, a misconception, and especially a mismatch should've been all the diagnoses that put me into remission.

Vividly, I remember looking in every direction except up wishing to find a cure to terminate the causes of unfelt love and hopeless promises from his contagious passion.

Becoming feeble by the second when I thought of the lies I fell for, I shook the doubt and vowed to myself that I wouldn't believe the next time.

See, I was a good woman - I cooked, cleaned, and worked...never once asking him for a dime.

Loving myself, Believing in myself, and Understanding myself were all the things that I had not only tried but they ALSO kept me from my promised emotional death.

I noticed the same students who expressed pain, confusion,

disappointment, and low self-esteem, now bared a face of pleasure, understanding, satisfaction, and genuine self-worth. I knew that my cure honestly healed my students.

I received numerous letters from students thanking me for my honesty. Nevertheless, one particular student came by my classroom before leaving school that day.

"Ms. Mackey, if that happened to you and you found a way to make it, I know I can make it and move on," he said, his eyes beaming with confidence.

For the benefit of my students, it was best that I gain their attention realistically instead of idealistically. Needless to say, for the duration of the school year my students overcame the obstacle that could've taken a toll on their academics. I wanted to show my students that despite my role as a teacher, I am also a human in the real world who shares even their rawest, most desperate emotions.

-Anna M. Mackey

10th Anniversary Edition

An Incredible Journey

I am Dwana Makeba, Artist Representative for Sweet Honey in the Rock. Sweet Honey in the Rock is a GRAMMY award winning acapella group that travels all around the world. It's a dream job but before I tell you how I landed it, I must give you some background. On February 14, 1971I was born in New Orleans, Louisiana to Ricardo Stevenson and Mary Harvey. Both of my parents came from lower economic backgrounds. My mother lived in the Desire Housing Project and my father lived in the Lower 9th Ward.

My mother wed at the age of 16 and had me at 19. Shortly after I was born, my parents divorced and my mother moved to California where, 34 years later she still lives there. Even though my parents divorced, their love for me never ceased. In fact, they both remarried and I have strong positive relations with their spouses. My mother and father gave and continue to give me a lot of love. Each of them went on to have two boys and a girl. I don't make distinctions so when asked I always respond by acknowledging my four brothers and two sisters. One vivid memory I have of my childhood was my education. My mother emphasized math, science and reading while growing up. I would participate in spelling bees and science fairs but my true love was reading. I loved reading books because they could take you to places you may not visit otherwise.

I took a long route getting my education. When I graduated from high school, I joined the Army. I served a six-year term and then I went to Junior College. After attending Los Angeles Community College, I went to Mohler Beauty School in New Orleans and then on to Southern University. In 1996, I received a Bachelor's degree in English from Southern University at New

Orleans and went on to receive a Master's degree in Africana Women's Studies from Clark Atlanta University in 2000.

While in college, I volunteered for the New Orleans Jazz and Heritage festival. After one year, I was hired to be the Congo Square Assistant. I worked that job throughout my undergraduate experience and learned a lot about organizing people--a skill I initially became familiar with while I was in the military. Working at the Jazz Fest enabled me to appreciate the culture, food, and items from people throughout the Diaspora. The producer I worked for asked me if I was interested in a project he was working on in Atlanta. I jumped at opportunity to travel to Atlanta. The project was the National Black Arts Festival and the year was 1996 when the Olympics was going on in Atlanta. I had an excellent summer. While I was working at the Olympics, my supervisor watched me. I didn't know this was going on. He made a recommendation to Harry Belafonte that I would be great to travel as the Assistant Tour Manager. I must say that Mr. "B", as I affectionately refer to him, gave me the opportunity of a lifetime. I learned on the job. The actual tour manager was Steve Jones who now works for the Apollo Foundation in NY. We traveled to Canada, the Caribbean and all throughout the US. One of the greatest lessons I learned from that experience is that in order to take care of everybody else you must take care of yourself first.

I learned to drink enough water and to get rest when I could. After living in NY and touring in 1996, I returned to college for my Master's degree. I graduated in May of 2000 and in August of 2000, I began my career with Sweet Honey in the Rock.

This time I was the Road Manager. Bernice Johnson Reagon, the founder of Sweet Honey in the Rock gave me a call and asked if I would be able to join the ladies for a series of three weekends. I said yes. The job would be organizing airline, hotel, ground transportation and other details related to the groups tour schedule. It would mean taking care of women old enough to be my mother.

Four years later, Dr. Reagon retired from the Sweet Honey, but I continue to live by her words of wisdom. With two new members of the ensemble, Sweet Honey lives on. We are continuing to spread the words and work of our ancestors. I am thankful to be on this journey.

-Dwana Makeba

Education - What it Really Is

Recently, I was introduced to one of UrbGriots editors Rashid Fai'Sal, who like myself, felt that the educational system in Detroit and most urban areas was atrocious. With only one out of every ten Black children meeting requirements to move forward and succeed in today's society, actually shows how we have failed in educating our current and the next generation.

As Mr. Fai'Sal and I continued talking about the destruction of an adequate education for African Americans, we agreed that it did not just happen, that it was conceived out of the lack of unity. The unity of parents, schools and churches had always been the cornerstone of a Black child's education. In today's society, this triangle no longer exists. Without it, a Black child raised in an urban environment is destined to become dysfunctional as an illiterate in a community. When a child does not understand even the basics of reading, writing and arithmetic, the child embraces failure.

Whose fault is it? The question serves no purpose at this juncture. It is what I call a "done deed." Parents have already abandoned their responsibility of parental guidance. Public schools have ceased to articulate their purpose while churches have become obsolete. The question asked now should be "How do we fix it?" I say to start with the triangle and beginning with the parents.

A child's first encounter with structure begins at home. Parents of today must relearn raising a child. Home is where a child takes his or her early steps toward becoming whole. It is where parents design a child's road to follow. They would construct the road to lead the child to a life of achievement in the community and society, which include setting the success bar higher than it was set for parents, to go beyond in learning, sharing, and passing on any knowledge leaving behind legacies.

Next, schools should work with parents in formulating a

package that will guarantee a child's ability to attain goals. As they do so, schools should welcome new ideology that requires adjustments and redevelopments to its principle convictions for existence. It is only then that the schools can complete their mission of educating children. Lastly is the church. Religious institutions have too long been invisible to an urban child. As the third leg of the stool of which a child stands on, the church must voice its philosophy. The church is the unifying arm of the triangle. It is through the church that parents and schools combine their strength to nullify all that endangers a child's accomplishments. Having been a substitute teacher for the past two years, I have seen first-hand the results of division. Backstabbing, name-calling and clique bounding have not only been between the children. My belief is the reestablished unity of the three institutions would affirm what an education really is . . . a child succeeding in a society that produces well rounded, intellectually astute and undoubtedly moral individuals.

-Sylvia McClain

NO WAY OUT

"You have arthritis." As the doctor said those words, I thought that my life was over. At the age of 13, this is a very shocking and devastating thing to hear. A million questions raced through my mind about the ways my life would change. Am I going to be able to walk? Will I be able to complete my 8th grade year? Can I still have fun? At that moment, I knew the answers to all my questions: God. I decided right then that I would use my faith to conquer my disease. My life would be a lot different but no less significant. Since that day, I use the Lord as my guiding light to take each day one step at a time.

Many mornings I woke up in agonizing pain with my knee and feet so swollen that I was left immobile. One such day I was in extreme pain, but I needed to go to school to take a test. Since I am in college now, I know that every little bit of effort counts toward my future goals of becoming a journalist. I would not let my disease enslave me so I got up, got dressed, grabbed my backpack and caught my two buses to school. The process took longer than usual but nonetheless I made it to school. During the exam, I was trying to concentrate on the right answers but at the same time feeling the throbbing of my knee. When I got my "A," I knew that my effort had not been in vain. I had applied myself and in the end, I emerged successful.

In my life, however, my grades not only counted, but also working with and tutoring 8th grade students for a standardized test made the difference. This not only requires a weekly preparation of lessons but also an hour of fidgety kids who would rather be anywhere on a Saturday than at a school. When I do not feel at my best, it does not suffice to tell my tutees that we will just skip lessons and rest. I have made a commitment to them to give my all. I take a couple of deep breaths and keep on with our lesson. This takes a lot of effort and dedication but it is worth it when I hear their enthusiastic voices telling me that their scores have improved.

However, I would not be able to pursue my education or work with students if I did not have the love and support of my family and boyfriend. When there are times that I encounter feelings of helplessness and despair, I know I can depend on them. With their love, I was able to cope with confinement in a wheelchair for six months and through their encouragement, I knew that I would walk again. Their love has caused me to work harder so they can be proud of me and know that their investment in me was worth their sacrifice. If they were not here for me, I truly do not believe I would have had the strength to keep on going.

Coping with arthritis has given me a whole new insight into life. It has shown me there will always be obstacles in my life that cannot be avoided, but they must be met head on while trusting in the Lord, leaning on my family and excelling in academics. Although arthritis is a major component of my being it is not my whole life and cannot define me.

This essay was not written to be a poor-me-sob story, but hopefully an inspiration to someone who is facing an obstacle and feels there is no way out and no one who knows how you feel. I am here to tell you as long as you have blood running through your veins, you must trek on. Never stop living your life; you only have one. In the immortal words of Mahatma Gandhi, "Live as if you were to die tomorrow. Learn as if you were to live forever."

-Tamara McCullough

Quiet Persistence

The child did not like to go to the school.
The child did not like to pay attention in the school.
The problems seem to persist for years.
The child never said why she did not like school.
The mother never asked, but waited.   *Quiet Persistence.*

The school called the mother.
"You need to send your child to school." They said.
"There is something wrong with your child." They said.
"We need to put her in a special program." They said.
The mother said nothing.   *Quiet Persistence.*

The mother was a small, quiet woman.
Raised in an era when she could not talk back to 'them'.
But she could not say yes to 'them,' it was not right.
She said nothing.   *Quiet Persistence.*

The child still refused to attend school.
The school called again.
The mother said nothing.   *Quiet Persistence.*

A new year, a new school, the same question.
"Why won't you send your child to school?"
The mother said nothing.
They were frustrated and hoping to prove something wrong with the child,
They asked another question.
"Can we test her?"
The mother said nothing.   *Quiet Persistence.*

The test was done.

The results were in.

The school called.

"Well, we see your child is very *special*." They said.

"Your child, the one who would not come to school,"

"Your child, the one who would not pay attention when she came,"

"Her scores are not normal." They said.

"Well, we have to put her in the *special advanced accelerated programs*." They said.

Quiet Persistence.

The mother said nothing, but she smiled.

She had won; she had saved her child.

The child smiled, she saw how the quiet persistence of a small black woman changed her life forever.

That child is I. I grew up in a two-parent household--my grandmother and my mother. We were so poor; I now say we had to borrow money to be poor. My great-great-grandmother was born into slavery and never attended school. My wonderful grandmother (we called her "Gra") finished the 4th grade in southern Texas. My sweet, gentle mother finished the 8th grade in the projects of Houston, Texas.

I had the worst attendance record in the first six years of my education. I never like school because I was not challenged and easily bored. They never asked me what I liked and didn't like about school. I loved to read but they never let me read. I loved math but they never let me do math. I loved working independently; they always made me follow "the program set for the class." It just was not going to work.

After the test in the 6th grade in Los Angeles Unified School District in the early 70's, I was placed in the *Gifted Children's Program*. The program allowed each student to set his or her own pace. I read everything and when I finished the assigned work, I read some more. I won perfect attendance awards from the 6th grade until I left for college. I won math trophies and leadership awards. When they stopped looking for what was *wrong* with me and found out what was *right* with me, so I thrived. When I *stopped listening* to what was wrong with me and *started loving* what was right with me, I thrived.

My mother had a host of personal challenges in her life. It was all she could do to survive and care for herself. But the one fight she silently undertook, saved me from a path of neglect, and abandonment by a system that simply failed to see a talented child lost in the process.

The payoff for her efforts? After entering the *Gifted Program*, I surpassed junior high school work and was doing high school level work 2 years before I attended high school. When I arrived in high school, I was all but complete with my high school requirements. They were "running out of stuff for me." I had advanced placement credits for college before I advanced to college.

Then, I entered the University of Southern California in 1976 on early admissions. I was to complete my college work and apply for a high school diploma. I never looked back to the LA Unified School District and to this day, I do not believe that I have a high school diploma.

So what you say? I graduated undergraduate with honors. I believe *Magna Cum Laude*. I immediately entered the Master of Business Administration Program at the USC Marshall of Business on a full academic fellowship in 1980. I graduated and for ten years, worked my way up in management in high profile companies such as General Mills, RJR/Nabisco, Gillette, and the Colgate Company.

In 1991, I was "boarded" with the confines of corporate America and quit my job to go to Harvard Law School. In 1994, I graduated from Harvard Law School with honor grads in most of my classes.

I am the Managing Principal of my own firm, The Mitchell Law Group, PC. We are a full service and compete with some of the largest law firms in the bay area. I have provided legal services for such industry leaders as Carol H. Williams Advertising, Coors Brewing Company, Diamond Radio, Inc, and the Peralta Community College District. We have represented individuals in disputes with major corporations such as Bank of America, Wells Fargo Bank, the Disney Company, the Estate of Tupac Shakur, Visa International, Comcast, Main Street Main (TGI Friday's Franchises in California), and a host of others.

Even though I do not rock climb, my journey through this life is like rock climbing. I stay focused on the moment and the good space around me. I take some chances on some moves and make deliberate moves on others. All actions are purposeful. All actions, even movement to the side and a few steps backwards, are to move me up the rock. I do not look down to see how far I have come. It might be too easy to get frightened and fear falling back. I do not look up to see the finish line, because the top is an ever-moving target and my life is full of too many good things ahead to ask the question "when will I reach the top?" I hope never to reach "the top." I just want to keep moving up. Each day I look around, give thanks at how far I have come and ask for grace when I realize how far I can still go. Despite it all, I still stay focused on my next few moves and the good space around me.

Separate from the financial and business success, I believe in God and his blessings. I believe that God always has a blessing and deliverance, no matter what the circumstances. For me, it was the quiet persistence of a small black woman who could not let them "track me" but did not know how to set me on the right track. Her refusal to let them track me into underachieving and limiting programs saved me from preset limitations and low expectations. Because of her quiet strength, and my belief that all things are possible through God and our Lord Jesus Christ, my life is rich with friends, personal and professional success, hope and above all, excitement for continued spiritual growth and development. My spiritual relationship with God is my only safety harness and my only anchors in my climb up and over the rock.

That's my story of love and respect for a simple, small black woman who was too fragile and gentle for a tough world and is captured in my simple poem called *Quiet Persistence*.

-S. Raye Mitchell

10th Anniversary Edition

What Do You Want To Be When You Grow Up?

Have you ever thought about what you want to be when you grow up and you're grown? Well, I've been there and done that! Before I had kids, I was trying to do all kinds of things. I worked in a bank and didn't like it; I was always afraid that someone would rob me. Then I worked for a mortgage company, but I got tired of someone always telling me what to do. Then I worked for several temporary agencies so I could work when I wanted to work and travel with my husband when I wanted to, but I was left with no medical benefits. Then I got my license to become a manicurist, but I got tired of waiting for customers to come get their nails done in order for me to get paid. I just couldn't seem to find anything that would make me happy.

Finally, my husband started telling me, why don't you just stick to one thing and do something long enough to get to like it. I thought about what he said and reflected introspectively about my life, but I didn't know what I want to do, which is why I keep doing several things! That was when I realized I was doing so many different things and not concentrating on one thing long enough to figure out what I really wanted to do with my life.

Finally, it took a talk show to change my entire life. I was watching the Sally Jesse Rafael show--some of you may not even remember that show. Anyway, as I watched the guest for the day, romance writer Judith Kranz speak, she said a few simple words that changed my entire life. She said, "You'll never know what you can create, until you put your mind to it." After hearing that simple phrase, I begin to think. Judith had been talking about what it took her to become a successful writer and what motivated her to what was in her heart. It was a simple as just putting your mind to it and doing it. I thought, I like to write, let me write a story. Then I thought, but if I write a story, I want to write something that will make me some money, because I didn't want to just do something and not be paid.

So I began to think, what could I write? Right away, I thought about SEX! Then, I begin writing my first story, which resulted in a steamy romance titled "No Words Were Spoken." After I completed the story, I shared it with several family and friends. Their overwhelming and positive responses assured me I was on the right track. In fact, their response confirmed that I was on the track inspired by God. I remember letting my Aunt Ivy read my story and after she was done, she told me she needed to go home to spend time with her husband. Then, when I read my story to my husband, he, too, became very excited and asked me whom I had been with! After their reactions, I knew I was on a roll and there was no looking back for me when it came to being a creative writer.

However, after reading Terry McMillan's book, 'Waiting to Exhale,' I was further encouraged to write with an added ethic culture and sassy flair. Terry's book made me laugh. I could really relate to the characters. This was something new for me, because often black characters were not greatly portrayed in print, or in a positive and entertaining way. I knew then, I could conformably write what was on my heart. I knew about by

being an African-American woman and about African-American people seeking acceptance by the public, both black and white.

Since that talk show, I have been on the right path and I'm assured everyday I pick up a pen to write, or get on my computer that being a writer is what I'm suppose to be when I grow up! Now, I wake up everyday and want to write; I want to create.

In 1993, my first story was published in the Precinct Reporter. I wrote a story called "Mean Moms". I always thought my mom was mean when I was a kid, but after I grew up and started my own family, I realized she was only protecting me from the craziness of the world.

10th Anniversary Edition

Since my first published story, I have more than 200 bylines in the United States and Canada. I have written stories and interviewed celebrities like, B2K, Laila Ali, Sugar Shane Mosely, Boney James, Jaheim, Take 6, Lisa "Left Eye" Lopez, Marilyn McCoo & Billy Davis, Jr., Patti LaBelle, Eric Jerome Dickey, and NAACP Chairman Kweisi Mfume to name a few. I have also worn the hat of publisher, by publishing my own magazine titled "Mini Romances," which was a magazine designed to allow a voice for new and unpublished writers. Then, I wanted more, so I began writing books and screenplays. Moreover, just when I was having fun, I became discouraged and began second guessing myself and my God-given talent, because I received several rejection letters from publishers. Then thoughts of encouragement came to me and reminded me that several people like my work and I enjoy doing what I'm doing. This was the first career I had ever done in my life that I really felt good about. It was the first thing I thought about when I woke up, and it was the first thing I couldn't wait to do each day. I knew my talent was something God had inspired me to do. I remembered what my husband had preached to me so many times to just stick to something for awhile and don't give up so easily.

I decided I wasn't going to allow anyone to block my dreams, block my blessings, or discourage me from writing by not accepting my work, so I set higher goals for myself and in 2001, I published my first book, *Momma, Please Forgive Me!* Entertainers like Vivica A. Fox, James Ingram, Patrice Rushen, and actor TC Carson have endorsed my book. *Momma, Please Forgive Me* addresses domestic violence, which was a subject I was faced with in my family as a child by watching my mother be abused by my stepfather. This situation was so strong in my heart that my husband and me vowed to never allow violence to destroy our relationship, and now we've been married for more than 20 years. Due to the overwhelming response to my book and how I self-published my book, I got tired of giving people names of other writers' books they could buy to become self-published, so I wrote my own. It's called, *How to Self*

Publish Your Novel on a Shoestring Budget -In 10 Easy Steps. You see, I like to do things simply and easily. Later, I published my second book, *Mind Games*, which is the sequel to *Momma, Please Forgive Me!* It's a mystery book, laced with romance--the same kind of romance my husband wondered about with my first short story.

Now, I am happy to say I have many fans that enjoy my books and constantly request to read more. At the age of forty-something, I have learned if you follow your heart and stick to your dreams you can find happiness and become something special

once you grow up, even if growing up means having a full blown household filled with teenage kids, a husband, dogs, cats, birds and fish. Growing up can come at anytime; just keep striving until you find your desire. I want to encourage people that you, too, can discover who you want to be when you grow up by just listening to your heart and following your dreams. I truly believe my dreams are just the beginning. I'm constantly setting higher goals, after reaching the realistic goals I previously set for myself. I truly believe the sky is our only limit, so never give up on yourself or your dreams, even if others give up on you! Thank you!

-Toi Moore

10th Anniversary Edition

Pressing Towards the Mark

"All of your life you are told the things you cannot do. All of your life they will say you're not good enough or strong enough or talented enough; they will say you're the wrong height or the wrong type to play this or be this or achieve this. The will tell you no, a thousand times no, until all of the no's become meaningless. All of your life they will tell you no, quite firmly and very quickly. And you will tell them yes" -- Nick Ad

Since I was a child, people have tried to put limitations on me. At the age of 3 1/2 I was diagnosed with epilepsy. During my battle with this neurological disorder, doctors told me I probably wouldn't be able to drive and there was a possibility that I wouldn't grow out of it. By the time I reached forth grade, I had been on numerous anti-seizure medications and was told by educators that I had a learning disability and speech impediment. Shortly afterward, I was placed in special education classes. I struggled with my reading and writing and was insecure as a result. I was afraid of failure and of humiliation. However, I was determined and motivated to learn. Within the special educational system, I felt under-challenged and unsatisfied. I felt that God had a better plan for my life and so I began asking Him to open my mind and give me understanding.

God was faithful and did exactly that. In my eleventh grade year with aspirations of becoming a doctor, I convinced my opposing counselor to give me a medical assistant class. My medical assistant teacher, Mrs. Reon Glenn, saw that I had potential and encouraged me to participate in a speech competition within HOSA, Health Occupations Students of America, and a national student health organization. Prior to this, I was reluctant to speak before people, but I accepted the challenge and found great success. I advanced to nationals and made top ten in the nation. The following year I advanced to the nationals and this time I took first place. I graduated with honors and president of my class. Today, I am seizure free and I am studying print journalism at Henry Ford Community College in Dearborn, MI. In addition, I am a published poet, a writer for the New Citizens Press, and a youth motivational speaker. Although I've come a long way, I'm still pressing toward the mark. "God doesn't call the qualified. He qualifies the called."

-Robin Morris

10th Anniversary Edition

"I Can Do All Things. . . ."

My paternal grandmother embedded my appreciation for education in me. She was an educator in the Charlton County schools of Folkston, GA. One of the first black women to teach in the school system, my "Granny" was very much the disciplinarian and believed in hard work. When my parents divorced, my siblings and I lived with our father and Granny on the farm for years. It all started there. I remember being told that I was going to college before I knew what college was. I liked learning and reading. Now that I think about, I didn't have a choice.

In high school, I became pregnant at age 16 and gave birth at age 17. I was very popular and had good grades but book smarts don't always cut it. I very much wanted to finish high school, so after having my son on December 19, 1987, I went back to school with the other kids after Christmas break. It was a bit soon but I wanted my diploma badly.

Finishing high school was tougher than I thought it would be. I was still tired from the emotional and physical trauma of childbirth and many nights I fell asleep with a book in one hand and my baby boy in the other. However, in June of 1988 I graduated from high school.

I entered junior college during the fall of 1988 and dropped out in spring of 1989 when I found out I was pregnant with my second child. I was devastated. I felt like a failure. I was trying to accomplish my dreams and my Granny's dreams for me, and failed miserably so I thought.

Waycross, GA 1992. I was living in the projects with two small children. Shooting, drug dealing, prostitution—all was there. I started back to college a year before, after dropping out for two years with my daughter. Going back to school was hard after being out for so long. I prayed about returning to school and received confirmation to do so.

School was difficult, so much so, I considered changing from my Computer Science major to keep from having to take all four Calculus classes. I simply did not have time to study for the subject. I was a work study student, potty-training my daughter, cooking, cleaning my apartment, laundry, Bible Study, choir practice and church service twice on Sundays.

I walked to school on most days. It didn't matter the weather. Rain, sleet, heat and cold were not going to keep me from class. Different instructors and classmates started to notice me on the side of the road and started offering rides to and from class. I was very thankful for that. Especially, when I had to take a night class. Walking alongside Corridor Z/Hwy 82 with 18-wheelers and such at night was not the best of times. I used to be so afraid of stepping on a snake or something in the dark, but I just prayed and kept going.

The last two quarters were the toughest. The critical moment came the very last quarter--the fifth straight quarter. I woke up one morning exhausted. I had absolutely nothing else to give. I cried until I shook and my throat grew sore. I felt like giving up as if I could go no more. I had to work, I had tests and other obligations that day but I just laid there until I couldn't cry anymore. What was I going to do? With much prayer and crying out to God for help, I got up and finished my day. I got up and finished my Associates Degree in Science during the summer of 1992 with a write-up in the local paper acknowledging my perseverance to finish my degree.

After Waycross College, I wanted my four-year degree but decided against it because it was so hard to get my two-year degree. One of my older sisters stepped in and convinced me to carry on while she kept the children. I found myself at Georgia Southern University during the fall of 1992. Hard times crept in again when I didn't fill out my financial aid and housing applications in time, a cousin who lived in Hinesville, GA, about 45 minutes from the university, offered to let me live with her and her family. That didn't work for very long because I couldn't afford the gas money for the commute. I eventually found myself with no money and no place to stay. I bummed a place to sleep at a different friend's house every night. I called home asking for money but everybody had his or her own financial trials. About a week and a half of living off friends and a box of crackers and Little Debbie cakes, I finally heard of an emergency loan the school would give to students. I thought I'd try it. After being rejected the first time, I went back the same day for the same loan and was approved by a different loan officer. God is so good. I put a deposit and first month's rent on an apartment, bought linens for my bed and groceries to gladly cook and eat!

Not knowing much about university life, I had to learn the hard way about deadlines and such. I also learned if you have to work, you want to secure a job before starting school. I had been out of work for eight months before getting on at the local Taco Bell. I had a car then and was behind in my payments. My credit union was talking about repossession. I took off one summer quarter to work at the paper bag plant at home to try to catch up. I was too far behind. I called different family members again and this time three siblings and their spouses agreed to bring my car loan up-to-date and continue making the payments until I graduate. What a blessing that was! To this day, even after thanking them several times, I don't think they understand how much they helped me during those last few quarters at Georgia Southern University. It is only my hope that I will be able to repay them in some way.

Graduate I did on December 11, 2004. Both of my parents, siblings, and my children attended. It was a very special moment for my family and me. I am the youngest of 15 siblings and the very first to graduate with a college degree. "I can do all things through Christ Jesus who strengthens me."

We all have our stories of trying times and triumph. I do believe the common thread in the success stories is the desire of the individual. Take that desire and put it in motion, even if you don't see how you'll make it. Do what you can, and allow God to do the rest.

-Felecia Kennedy

Persistence

"HIYAHHH!"

I ran around the house doing death-defying drop kicks and power punches, emulating martial arts legend Bruce Lee. My scrawny eight-year-old arms crisscrossed as I used invisible nun chucks to fight make-believe enemies, evil villains, and bad guys who threatened the livelihood of law-abiding citizens. Being a martial arts superhero was definitely the life for me. I'd travel all over the world fighting crime in America, Europe, Asia, Africa, and sometimes outer space. I just had to make sure I was home before dark or my mother would be upset.

"Yaaaah!"

"Michael, stop running in the house!" My mother yelled."

"Heeyah! HAAA!"

"I said stop running before you break something, boy!"

"Ma, I wanna take karate lessons."

"No."

"I wanna be like Bruce Lee, pleeeease lemme take karate."

"Is your room clean?" she asked, knowing that would keep me out of her hair for a while. Her peace and quiet would only last a few minutes, just long enough for me to stuff everything under the bed or in the closet.

For the next few weeks, I continued my routine of watching karate on television, practicing everything I saw. I couldn't take it anymore; I had to take karate at any cost. So, I decided to do what any intelligent kid would do—I begged until my mother finally said 'yes'.

When I held my brand new white belt the night before the first class, my chest inflated along with my ego. I knew for sure, that in one or two classes, I'd be just like Bruce Lee! In the first class, we did a series of stretching exercises. My eight-year-old body was contorted in unimaginable ways. *You want me to put my leg where? Bend over and touch what?* I questioned the instructor in my head. *Bruce Lee never did this stuff—it hurts too much.*

"Down...one." The instructor barked as we did push-ups on our fingertips. "...Down, two."

The popping, cracking, and snapping of my finger joints combined with the groaning and moaning of my fellow classmates rang out in a miserable chorus. It seemed as though 'ten' would never come. When it did, we collectively sighed, lying flat on our stomachs like exhausted sea lions.

"TEN MORE!" the instructor yelled—two of the most dreaded words ever.

"Ugghhh," we groaned.

When the class ended, I bowed to the instructor, bowed to my classmates, and headed outside to meet my mother. We weren't allowed to show weakness in the class—that's why I waited until I was in the car to cry!

"Mama, I don't wanna go back, please don't make me go baaaaack."

Having my mother laugh after I cried for sympathy wasn't the greatest feeling. She quickly dismissed my antics and said, "You begged me to let you take karate. You're going back!" I cried harder. The next day, I cried all the way up to the entrance of the building before wiping away my tears, and putting on my serious 'karate tough guy' face. *Today we'd learn how to do triple back flips,* I told myself. To my dismay, I experienced the same routine as the day before-- stretches, exercises, and pain! I cried again after class. Again, my mother gave me the 'I'm ignoring you' treatment.' At that point, I knew I had to get my act together.

As the weeks passed, I began enjoying the classes. My body was used to the exercises and I quickly became one of the top students in the class. I would even stay after my class ended to watch the advanced classes. I was eager to practice their moves when I got home. In order to advance to the next belt, I had to pass a test that consisted of reciting martial arts code of conduct passages, demonstrating different forms of karate, and finally breaking two wooden boards. I knew memorizing the passages would be easy, but breaking boards worried me. Even with my newly found confidence, I knew there was no way I could break a solid board. I'm only eight so how in the world can I break a board? I asked myself every single day leading up to the test.

When test day arrived, I felt I was ready. I had the sidekick and roundhouse kick down to a perfect science. My mother told said that even if I didn't break the boards, it was okay, as long as I did my best. However, after all of the pain I endured, I wanted to pass the test no matter what!

The instructor gripped the board tightly and told me to kick it when I was ready. My heart bounced in my chest, doing some karate of its own. I got in my stance and tried not to think about how embarrassed I'd be if the board didn't break. Focusing my eyes on the board, I tightened my fists, and took two deep breaths.

"Hiyaaaaaah!" I yelled, kicking the board with everything I had. To my surprise, it snapped in half! I wanted to jump for joy but I had to show discipline and restraint. Therefore, I bowed to the instructor before calmly walking away as if breaking boards was an everyday occurrence for me. The crowd clapped and I knew my mother was softly saying to herself, 'that's my, baby!'

There was one more board to break and I would advance to a yellow belt. The instructor signaled me to break the next board. Still running off the adrenaline from my last kick, I spun around with a solid roundhouse kick that landed with a dull thud. I heard my heel hit the board but I didn't hear the broken wood sound I expected. The butterflies I had been feeling in my stomach now felt like lead marbles. My world was temporarily shattered. I think I even stopped breathing for a few seconds. With envy, I looked to my right at a boy who actually broke his board. I felt even worse.

"Try again..." My instructor urged.

To my left was a girl who also had difficulty breaking her board. I hoped she wouldn't break hers before me. I didn't want to be the last one.

"HAAAA!" I kicked the board again. It didn't break.

The instructor asked his assistant to exchange the board for another. Yeah, that's why it didn't break, it was a bad board, I rationalized to myself. The new board didn't break either. My shoulders slumped as I backed away to gather myself. I just knew everyone was looking at me—the exact thing I wanted to avoid. I was too embarrassed to glance in the crowd for my mother because I'd have to look across all of the staring eyes to find her. I did however glance over at the girl next to me. I drowned out the applause she received when she broke her board. Now, I was alone. The embarrassment was almost enough to bring tears to my eyes. But, I couldn't let the other students see me cry—they'd never let me live it down. *Wuss boy, sissy, crybaby,* I could already hear their squeaky voices.

With nothing to lose, I regained my focus. I had to break that board. It was the only thing standing in the way of my next belt and me. I tightened my fist and executed a perfect roundhouse kick, hitting the board dead center and splitting it in half. Watching the broken pieces fall to the ground made me feel invincible again. Now I would get my yellow belt!

Today, my mother still teases me about the days I used to cry after every karate class. I'm glad she refused to let me quit because I learned the importance of persistence and hard work. Life is full of "boards" that must be broken in order to achieve a goal. They may not break on the first try, and maybe not the second, but through persistence, success will eventually come.

-Michael T. Owens

Aunt Kathleen

God is truly amazing! Over forty years ago, my mother received a special gift of love in the offer by her aunt to temporarily adopt me as a means to help with the expenses of raising four young children. Aunt Kathleen was in fact my mother's paternal grandaunt. She lived on the beautiful island of Nassau in the Bahamas.

Each year Aunt Kathleen would visit our family in Miami Florida. Primarily this was her vacation, but for my siblings and me, it was a time when we learned much of our family legacy of hard work and intelligence. Aunt Kathleen was the keeper of the family's history and she insisted on sharing it with us, making it clear that we were to share it as well.

At seven years old, while living in the Bahamas in a small, but adequate home, Aunt Kathleen with her elementary school education began to sow the potent seeds of confidence into my life. There were no doubts in my mind about my potential nor were there doubts in my mind about the expectation that was place on my being someone purposed for great things.

Years later I would wonder how she knew exactly what to say or do to motivate me and stimulate my curiosity for life and for knowledge. As I reflect on growing up and the daily interactions with Aunt Kathleen, her words about the importance of acquiring an education seem fresh in my mind. She always talked about breaking the cycle of poverty and literacy. Although, she would express this message in many different ways, it was always understood that she intended for me to have more education than she received and to reach a greater level of professional success than she had.

Aunt Kathleen encouraged me to read daily. She insisted on my weekly bible study with her. In hindsight, I discovered that she would ask me to read only the scripture that she had memorized, therefore, she would know how well I was reading, and most importantly, she could correct me if I pronounced a word incorrectly. Her corrections would be gentle, but always letting me know that she would only tell me a word once, because she expected me to remember it after being corrected.

Going to the library was a privilege in my neighborhood. It was time taken away from my domestic responsibilities; therefore, when I was allowed to spend time there, it was meaningful and appreciated. Telling Aunt Kathleen about the stories I read was an exciting time for both of us. She would pretend she was not excited about hearing about the books I was reading, but I knew it brought her joy. Her ways were just as transparent to me as mine were to her. We studied each other equally.

Many of my days in college were spent thinking about my dear aunt Kathleen and wondering how she would have felt to witness my years of being a college student. Her death occurred in my freshman year while I was in Boston Massachusetts at Emerson College. Her spirit remained a strong force in my life and served as motivation for me to push pass my comfort level on many occasions. It wasn't until years after her death that I confronted the devastating effect losing her had on my life. I discontinued my schooling and began a career as a Flight Attendant, where I remained for almost seventeen years.

The thirst for living a whole and complete life with the certainty that I had fulfilled all of my dreams and aspirations that Aunt Kathleen instilled in me, was the catalyst for my return back to college. I completed my undergraduate degree and master's degree within eight years while working and managing a family with two small children. Today, I am beyond the halfway mark for earning a PhD. My goal for completion is before I turn age 50.

Education has changed my life in such a positive way. I am most proud of the fact that my teenage children can witness the dedication and commitment I have made to acquire an education. Our home is filled with books on all subjects. We travel extensively for the purpose of seeing and understanding the world we live in. I have obtained the same wisdom and understanding about life as my dear aunt Kathleen did. I have offered my children no other option but to become literate and educated. "People can take many things away from you, but what is in your head cannot be taken away" (Kathleen Marshall).

-Barbara Perkins

10th Anniversary Edition

I Believe In You

I was blessed with the opportunity to teach this summer. I say, "Blessed" because God is an awesome, on time God. For weeks this past spring, the newspapers reported about a third grade crisis happening in New York City. One Wednesday morning, on my way to work, while reading the newspaper on the ferry I said to myself, "I wish I could do something." Ahhhhh, be careful of what you wish for. God is listening!! That night there was a message on my answering machine from one of the largest arts in education organizations in the New York City tri-state area. The message said I had been referred to them, and asked if I was available to teach second and third graders who failed. If so, I was to call back, get finger printed by Friday and report to work on Tuesday.

At the time, I was attending Marymount Manhattan College for an Arts in Education Certificate. For several years I had contemplated leaving the corporate world to pursue my first love - teaching. I had not completed the program yet! And normally, an audition was required for this Arts in Education organization to even be considered for a contract!! But you know something? God has His own timetable. God has His own audition. God has His own certificate program. I was blessed to teach. At the end of the residency, a written evaluation was required. The question was asked, "What were the most successful aspects of the program in my classroom? Discuss them and make recommendations." This is how I responded.

I would have to answer by way of an introduction of myself and then discuss my two successes. My son was a problem child. We spent ten years, off and on, in therapy. My son sat outside of the principal's office more than he was in class. He was constantly under suspension and fighting. Daily, I received telephone calls from his teachers about his attitude and behavior.

My son graduated (barely) with a 67 average. He was admitted to Shaw University in Raleigh, North Carolina on probation. A miracle!! There is a God! And there was the National Urban League Upward Bound Program. He completed his first semester with a 3.79 GPA Shaw University gave him a financial award for academic excellence in his second semester. In his fourth semester he earned a 4.0 GPA while taking nine classes and seventeen credit hours. He has since made the Dean's List every semester for the past four years.

In 2002-2003, he received the award for Outstanding Student Honoree in Mathematics Education. In 2003-2004, he was the recipient of a United Negro College Fund Scholarship. Also, he was inducted into Alpha Chi, a national honor society for juniors and seniors in the upper 10% of their class. And he was elected the president of the local chapter of Alpha Chi.

For the past year, he has been student teaching in an alternative high school in North Carolina. This school has already offered him a job on graduation. In May 2004, the United Negro College Fund called with a job offer in New York City.

About a month ago, my son called me at 2:00 a.m. to thank me for not putting him out of the house. Huh? He explained that he and his friends were up trading "war stories" about growing up. After listening to the various stories, he realized that he was blessed and needed to call me right away.

"Mom, thanks for believing in me."

Soooooo...my gifts that I bring to my teaching are:

Twelve years of "on the job training" and patience

Learning and understanding what makes a problem child "tick"

Creativity, respect and LISTENING SKILLS

Teaching Agenda

Marymount Manhattan College teaches that you must have an academic agenda as well as your own personal teaching agenda. Respect is my "hidden" teaching agenda. I assign two students to act as rotating monitors to hold up a respect sign when the class or someone gets out of order. The monitors have to explain why the situation or behavior was not respectful. Occasionally, the other students would add to the explanation. Respect became the operative and "magic" word.

Success One

Nehemiah was a special education student. I don't believe in "labels." The system tried to label my son as a special education student. I looked at Nehemiah and saw my son. Nehemiah was "behavior and attitude" challenged. Daily, he entered the classroom fighting, pushing and being totally disruptive. When he came to class on the last day, I took a deep breath and said a silent prayer – "Let the time that I have spent with the kids not have been in vain." I should have known that God was listening.

Now God, religion and touching are no no's in the classroom.

"Nehemiah !!! Do you know where your name comes from?"

He answered, "The Bible."

"Do you know that Nehemiah was a leader?" Nehemiah slowly made his way to sit in the story circle on the floor. He had never done this before.

"Class – can anyone describe a leader? What does a leader do? How does a leader act? Why does a leader have to act a certain way? AND the magic word – does a leader have to be respectful?" I wrote the responses on the board and proceeded to teach with a minimum of disruption.

I gave out stickers at the end of each class for good behavior and respect. The children line up by size and I call out each name. Cooperatively and enthusiastically the children will vote yes or no. If they vote no, they will explain. Nehemiah would always get in line, knowing that his behavior precluded any sticker!

When his turn came this time, there was silence.

"Guys – no vote?"

Finally, one girl responded, "Well he wasn't good, good. But he wasn't as bad as he usually is." All the other kids agreed.

I looked at Nehemiah and said, "Do you know what this means? YOU get a sticker!" A collective class cheer went up. There were smiles everywhere!

As Nehemiah was standing in line for dismissal, I touched him on his shoulder and I asked, "Who are you?"

He responded with a look I will never forget – a mix of wonderment, WOW and a big smile, "I am a leader!"

Success Two

Tyrell was also "behavior" challenged. I had given the children a writing exercise, which was met with a few groans from Tyrell.

"What did you like most about my classes?"

Tyrell was very resistant and angry. I then changed the instructions and stated that they could either write and/or draw. More frowns and anger! He made several attempts to try to spell.

"Tyrell, if you don't want to write then draw something! It's okay." I said.

Several of the children asked for spelling assistance as they completed the assignment. Except Tyrell. All the children handed in the assignment. Except Tyrell. After class, I had to look for his paper in the desk where he had been sitting. To my surprise, he had drawn himself and me smiling and holding hands.

Not to be dissuaded, I attempted a similar assignment two classes later.

"What is your favorite color, TV program, song, food and after school past time?"

The second time around, I was more proactive in giving spelling assistance to the children. Tyrell had responded that he liked wrestling.

"Tyrell would you like help in spelling 'wrestling'?"

"Yes." he said.

This went on for several questions. At story time, Tyrell who NEVER sits still, sat next to me and tried to read along with me as I pointed to the words. He struggled, but he was confident and comfortable - I could hear my son saying, "Thanks, mom for believing in me."

You know there is a song we sing in church – *God looked beyond my faults and saw my needs.* It not only takes a village to raise a child, but it takes a commitment from each one of us to look beyond and see the need of each child to become all that they can be. They need to believe in themselves. My son, the Nehemiahs and the Tyrells need to know that there is someone who cares and believes in them. I challenge you all today to hear them and answer their call.

-Joyce Parr

TWINKLING from AGES 5 to 105

In 2001, my family lived in East Cleveland, Ohio. Our city and school district were said to be among the worst in the country. But I felt our community had a lot to be proud of. I wanted my children to feel proud of where they lived. My deep prayer was that their public school would seem like a great private school. I did not know how this would happen, but I believed it could. That school year, my first child enrolled in Chambers Elementary. Since then, many wonderful programs have come to her school and to the district. I also discovered programs that were already in place.

The Step Up program offers young students monthly learning workshops, fun educational field trips, a free computer and college scholarships. There are Japanese and Spanish language classes, drama, art, piano, chorus, dance, math and computer classes, a bridge construction contest and other extra activities. One of these activities is the East Cleveland Suzuki Strings Program.

Dr. Shinichi Suzuki (1898-1998) was a Japanese violinist and teacher. He believed "every child can learn." It was his belief that children develop well if they are taught well by their parents or other people in their lives. He wanted to help all children become their happiest and best. He created Talent Education—a way to teach children of all ages. In the 1940's he founded the Talent Education Research Institute in Japan. Talent Education is Dr. Suzuki's teaching method based on the way children learn to speak their native languages. They learn by hearing the people around them repeat words. Suzuki music students learn to play music by first listening to songs repeatedly played on an instrument.

Suzuki music caregivers must go to their children's weekly private lessons. They must also learn to play the instrument so they can teach their children everyday at home. In the winter of 2001, the Suzuki Strings program in East Cleveland began with 21 kindergarten students at Chambers Elementary. Families were asked to pay a small fee each year to take part in the program.

My three children each began playing violin in the program. After learning many early skills, they received their own violins. Like all Suzuki music students, the first song they learned to play was "Twinkle, Twinkle Little Star." Like the other parents, grandparents, aunts and uncles that signed up for violin, my husband and I learned to play "Twinkle", too.

Our children have three teachers—Michele Higa George, M. Diane Slone and Calista Koh. Michele Higa George and Diane Slone studied Talent Education with Dr. Suzuki in Japan. Calista Koh studied music education with Michele Higa George at the Cleveland Institute of Music (CIM).

Chambers music teacher Jeanne Lyons, school principal Cheryl King, and Eleanor Holt from CIM worked with the violin teachers. Together they all made the new program come to life. Diane Slone moved from Chicago, Illinois to the Cleveland area to begin the program. Later, Kim Kidd became the Chambers school principal. She supported the violin program, Chambers students, parents and teachers and the East Cleveland community.

Older brothers and sisters of the first Chambers violin students could not play in the school's Suzuki program. They were in higher grades when the program began; violin students had to start as kindergarteners. Many of the older children felt sad about not playing the instrument. Michele Higa George wanted to help them. So in 2005, she began teaching the older children cello—a larger instrument in the violin family.

Today the East Cleveland Rainbow Suzuki Strings travel across the United States to play with professional musicians. Soon they will travel overseas. Like millions of Suzuki students worldwide who are learning music, math and other subjects, they show how well Talent Education works.

There are not many American families in inner city neighborhoods whose children take Suzuki music lessons. The lessons are usually expensive. But I am very thankful for Diane Slone, Michele George, Calista Koh, Jeanne Lyons, Cheryl King, Eleanor Holt and Kim Kidd. They gave the people of East Cleveland one more reason to feel very proud of their city. They helped Dr. Suzuki's belief in the promise of every child live on.

-M. LaVora Perry

10th Anniversary Edition
Literacy of History is Crucial

Without a foundation, there is nothing to build upon and there is nowhere to go; as Black people, our foundation is our history. The only thing you can build upon history is future, hopefully without repeating it. We must learn our history so that we can develop worthwhile objectives and efforts to make life better for ourselves. When we think about our objectives as a people, we cannot help but ponder about all who have made life as miserable and dreadful as they possibly could for our people. But we must keep in mind that holding grudges and internalizing anger can decrease our physical and mental health. Therefore, our objective must be to forgive, but never to forget.

Unfortunately, much of the Black community seems to have forgotten where we have come from and how long we have fought and struggled to get where we are. We must remember that only 300 years ago, Willie Lynch wrote his conspiracy to keep the Black people separate amongst themselves. And 300 years later, we are separate amongst ourselves for unnecessary reasons. Some of the easterners hate the westerners, while some of the northerners hate the southerners. Some of the upper and middle-class citizens hate the lower-class citizens and vice versa; but what we don't realize is that these minor characteristics are the only things that separate us and are neither intelligent nor right. It is vital that we cherish our community's ethnic identity, because this is all we will ever be guaranteed.

Our heritage is the backbone of this country, our enslaved labor and subjection to discrimination is what built many of the major empires of this nation. We are only 50 years past the desegregation of schools and we are only 30 years past the mass public use of the word, "nigger," as a derogatory term toward blacks. Many of our people only hear about Martin Luther King, Jr., and other "famous" black heroes. I am convinced that certain black leaders are publicly recognized by society for two reasons: 1) Due to the fact that such civil rights leaders made incredible contributions to our struggle; and 2) To silence the Black community from wanting more. We deserve more than what we have, and unless we learn our history, we will never make progress. Only 35 years have passed since our people were taken to jail for randomly frivolous reasons, and it is still happening due to a system set up for us to become criminals and failures. We are only 35 years passed being assaulted by people whose job it was to protect public safety. I am referring to the firemen who hosed us down with brute force and the policemen who unleashed attack dogs on us. We also cannot forget Malcolm X who was a great example of going from ignorance to intelligence in his quest for equality. He was adamant that white people were devils and treated all black people the same until he went on his pilgrimage to the Middle East. When he returned, he began to change his method of approaching the racial tension in the United States. And for that reason he was a threat to the militant of the Black Americans as well as the conspirators of the White Americans; the result was his assassination.

We still face the unspoken prejudices of society today; instead of using words and violent acts, jobs and opportunities are becoming increasingly slim through educational and governmental conspiracy. Our ancestry shows us that we were taken and used as slaves and after we were set free, we were isolated and we assimilated into accepting an identity of being unsuccessful and unable. And for those of us who refused to accept this, we created our own businesses and opportunities. We created our own organizations to ensure that we had our own economical resources and successes. This era of the early 1900's is known as the Black Renaissance. But what the history books won't say, if they even mention the era at all, is that this era and these mass structures and economical resources were destroyed by bombings. There is only one possible way that such a deed could have possibly been executed as successfully as it was, and that was through an intense conspiracy by people who were determined to not allow an economical up-rise of African-Americans.

It has not even been 100 years since we were allowed, as a whole, to vote in public elections. We were the object of scrutiny and illegal recreation by J. Edgar Hoover, when he was in control of the (FBI) Federal Bureau of Investigation. We were the pawns by which many white men built their law enforcement careers, by means of conspiracy.

Through our culture's experiences we have an ancestral scar; it is our heritage, our history, our past. We must make the decision whether or not we wish for this scar to be recognized as an ugly symbol, or as a beauty mark. I am quite confident that most, if not all, black people would prefer the second of those two choices. Our heritage is what makes us so beautiful as a people; it is what separates us from the rest of the world. We are still hated and we are still the victims of prejudice on a daily basis.

As a people, we are a numerical minority, in terms of civilian population. But quite confusingly, we are the undisputed and unquestionable numerical majority in terms of prison population. There is definitely something wrong with this picture, a picture that has been painted by the prejudiced people of this nation. When we became free from slavery, organizations such as the Ku Klux Klan were formed. Our properties were taken, and we were deprived of what we were duly owed, 40 acres and a mule. We were deprived of the educational resources we deserved and we still are deprived; we were deprived of our constitutional rights. Worst of all, we were deprived and stripped of our human rights. This was able to happen because there was prejudice and evil people supervising the law, they created resources and they created the law. Although prejudice is still heavily apparent today, there are those who want nothing more than equality, and those people are not to be marginalized or unjustly put into a category based on their skin color, for that is what we do not want for ourselves. Some progress has been made over the years.

With this progress taken into consideration, we are still not where we should be, we are allowing drugs to take over our communities. We have gone from physical slavery to pharmaceutical slavery. The drugs that are the real bestsellers in the urban residential areas are not for injury or disease; they are for getting a "high" and chasing the breeze to get us further and further away from reality. We have been labeled as consumers and workers, seemingly with no additional purpose. This is untrue, because we are the original people and we are the original children. It is because of this that we must live life in a daily remembrance of how we got to where we are. We made it here through sweat, blood, and countless hours of protest to racial injustice, and unless we recognize it and develop a desire to never let it happen in the future, it will continue to occur.

Our journey has not been made for us to end up with our young people spending so much time trying to fit into popular urban culture, that they do not have plans for their own lives about who and what they want to become as adults; this is a conspiracy. Our journey has not been made for our young people to be able to memorize the most popular songs on the radio (Rap, R&B, Pop, Latin Pop), but do not know how to spell, read, and comprehend. I know teenagers who would rather watch music videos than read, because they say that reading takes too much work. And this is why parents need to stop spoiling and befriending their children and start instilling in them strong work ethic. This is also why we see many of our people working at the bottom of the industrial and corporate employment chain. They sat and watched music videos instead of studying; they were dancing and having sex instead of thinking about their future. Then when people end up working as receptionists, valets, and fast food clerks, they have a problem with racism. No, no, no, get a work ethic, learn your history, and then complain when you are actually doing something to make a change.

We cannot afford to relax and kick back; our population is at its highest rate of decline in this country. Our heritage is our key to the future and success; we must honor it, know it, and most of all, use it. Our literacy of our history is our power.

-Ryan Christopher Pinkston

Super Sunday: Papa's Big Day

It was on a second Sunday, Youth Sunday, at the St. John Missionary Baptist Church in 1968. This was a morning of great anticipation at the Prince household, even though everybody was trying to act as normal as possible. You could tell that Papa was a bit on the nervous side, but Mama was just being her usual Sunday morning self. She was the organizer, rushing people, making sure everything was in order and ready to get to church on time. My cousin Debby and I knew better than to even halfway look as if we wanted to take our sweet time, because Mama was not patient on Sunday morning. She always had that look as if she were daring us to say something just so she could pull an ear off our heads. If we even appeared to have the, "Don't rush me attitude," we would know it was coming. Without exception after the ear pulling was the lecture: "THAT'S 'CAUSE I KNOW YOUR GONNA ACT UP IN CHURCH, AND IF YOU DO, I'M GONNA PUT SUMPIN' ON YOU AGIN." On Sunday mornings we were on our best behavior!

Breakfast was the usual staples: grits, with bacon from the big box of bacon scraps. (Oh, how I loved those scraps, because you could often get some GIANT pieces!) Also included were Mama's homemade biscuits, scrambled eggs, and my favorite, chocolate milk. By the time we had finished breakfast it was about 9:25 a.m. Debby and I had to make our way down to the church because Sunday school started at 9:30 a.m. It only took us five minutes to make our way down to the church, but we dare not be late, especially today.

Well, we got through Sunday school, but the anticipation was killing both Debby and me! I was supposed to sing with the youth choir that morning, but opted not to, since singing with the choir meant that I would have had to march in with the choir. That in turn meant I would have to miss the devotion service because the choir marched in after the devotional service was finished. The devotional was what all the excitement in the Prince household was about. As usual, Sister Payne began to play the piano while the people were finding their seats; as the music played, I looked over to see if my grandmother had made her way to her usual seat. She always sat where the mothers of the church (the Mothers' board) had their own section. Sure enough, Mama was there, and she looked up just in time to catch my eye. As usual, she had to give me that last stare. You know the look that has the words written in it: "I-better-not-look-up-and-catch-you-chewing-gum-in- church-because-I-know--how-you-are." Sure enough, Mary Prince knew me quite well because I had just slipped a stick of Juicy Fruit in my mouth. I closed my mouth and tried hard to remember not to let her see me chew. I was relieved as the music stopped and the youth ushers closed the doors to the vestibule where the stragglers and the youth choir were.

Then came the moment the Prince family had been waiting for. Papa Prince made his way to the front of the church and stood next to the collection table by the pulpit. He looked out at the crowd of about 150 sitting in the main sanctuary and upstairs in the balcony, the other 40 or so still standing in the vestibule. He then opened his Bible and turned to the book of John, even though I don't remember the exact chapter or verse. However, I do remember the first words uttered from his mouth: these precious words were, "Verily, verily I say unto you ..." Then Papa was on his way, and the crowd sat spellbound until he wrapped up his message.

For me this was Papa's (and my) Super Sunday. I likened this moment to the way a coach would feel with one second left on the clock in the biggest game of his or her life. It was the equivalent of someone kicking a fifty-four yard field goal in that last second to win the game. I listened as Chester Prince, Sr. poured out the sweetest words I'd ever heard. ..."MAY GOD ADD A BLESSING

TO THE READING OF HIS WORD." My throat was choked with emotion as I thought about Uncle Roger's pastor, Elder Hicks, who had been giving my Papa reading lessons every Tuesday for the past three years. In addition, my time spent learning to read at Liberation Saturday had allowed me to be able to tutor him every day after school. But I had to admit that there had been times when I bellyached about it because I wanted to go outside to play basketball with my friend James Gray.

As he finished, Papa walked back to his seat slowly but proudly. Unlike today's modern suits, which are permanent press, in those days one had to be very careful to not wrinkle the tail of the suit coat, or ruin the crease of the trousers, so the picture of Papa still lingers in my mind as I remember his final act. He flipped his coattail up and tugged at the knees of his favorite brown pants as he took his seat. You could hear the congregation buzzing.

"LORD, I DIDN'T KNOW DEAC COULD READ!"

The music began to play as the whispering continued. Then the doors were opened to the vestibule, and the youth choir made its way into the main sanctuary. Looking back, I realize that in those precious moments Liberation Saturday had reached more than one generation of the Prince family.

- Joe Prince

10th Anniversary Edition

The Queen Bee Speaks

The third grade spelling bee was the first time I can remember speaking in front of a group at school, although I had been reciting speeches at church since I was three years old. At that time, I thought I was smart for my age. In first grade, I remember being selected as one of the students to help my classmates with reading. And it was my first grade teacher who recommended my mother take me out of that particular school system because it lacked the resources to challenge me academically.

So, by third grade, I was attending my second elementary school. There were roughly twenty-five of us on stage at the beginning of the spelling bee. Both of my parents worked, so they could not attend. The competition covered words from our textbook, starting alphabetically. My friend and one of the few Black students participating, Katrina, got up to spell "buggy". Her mother, who had come to see her, had just stood up to take her picture. Katrina had lean arm muscles, especially for a third grader. Perhaps it was a prelude to the athlete she would become.

"B-U-G-G-I-E," she said.

"I'm sorry that is not correct," replied the proctor.

Katrina sat down before her mother had a chance to take her picture. The spelling bee continued until lunchtime. Since we were in the cafeteria, we had to take a break and clear the room. After lunch, we came back and the spelling bee had been reduced to two people, me and a girl named Deborah. She was a skinny White girl with dark hair.

Then it happened. The proctor asked Deborah to spell "journey".

"J-O-U-R-N-Y"

"I'm sorry that is not correct," the proctor said. I looked down front on the floor. There were at least five Black students sitting in a row, displaying bright Kool-Aid smiles. I saw one guy hold his fist up as if to say, "Yes!" I smiled. I knew how to spell "journey". I was going to win the trophy.

Then, from nowhere, one of the White third grade teachers, Ms. Smith, stood up in the back of the audience and said, "She spelled the word correctly." She had bright blond hair and she was a hefty woman.

The proctor turned around to acknowledge her. There was some discussion about the fact that Deborah left the "E" out of the word and then she was given a chance to spell it again. The proctor reluctantly made the decision, as Ms. Smith would not sit down until she did. She spelled it right the second time.

We reached the words that started with the letter K. I was given the word, "kitten." I never thought the feline infant would be my downfall. I spelled it "K-I-T-T-I-N". In my mind, I questioned whether I was supposed to use an "I" or an "E", but I chose the wrong one. And this time, no one stood up. No one questioned whether I had indeed spelled the word correctly. How could I have been so dumb? Me, the person who excelled so much that I was helping my peers with work, actually misspelled "kitten." I looked down front at the faces that thirty minutes earlier had been smiling at me. Downcast eyes and trodden shoulders filled the space. Silence gripped the cafeteria. Regret welled in my mouth. But I didn't get a second chance. Deborah spelled "kitten" correctly and won the spelling bee.

That afternoon at recess, I saw Deborah with the trophy. If Ms. Smith hadn't stood up, I would have won. But there was no one to stand up for me. By late afternoon, none of the parents remained. When I told my mother that night about the word I misspelled, she couldn't' believe it.

Losing the spelling bee began my quest for my own prize. Though I was embarrassed after and started to question my intelligence for a while, by fifth grade, I was back in front of the student body. I was attending a different elementary school because of redistricting, and I tried a different challenge. I entered an oratorical contest. We had to write a speech on the topic, "Leaders who have made a difference." I remember talking about Martin Luther King Jr., along with two other leaders. The winner, Kristin Garbarino, wrote a speech on Benjamin Franklin. I placed fourth, so I didn't win a trophy. Still, I had a taste for victory. It was just an appetizer and I yearned for the full course.

In sixth grade I entered the same contest. The topic that year was "Inventions that have improved the quality of life." I chose to write about the computer. I remember as they announced the top places, my heart pounded like a Djembe drum at a West African festival. My armpits became wet as a tourist on the Maid of the Midst in Niagara Falls. To say I was nervous is an understatement. Then, I heard Kristin's name announced as the second place winner. "What? I didn't place at all? How could that be? I know I was better than some of those other students. I don't understand it." At some point, that internal monologue was interrupted by the announcement of the first place winner, Angela Ray. I came in first place!! Finally, I got the trophy. It was my first one. Three years after the "kitten" fiasco, I brought home the prize. I couldn't stop smiling.

Both Kristin and I advanced to the district competition. This time Kristin placed first and I placed second. Those wins qualified both of us for the state competition where sadly, neither of us placed.

Elementary school was only the beginning of my trophy collecting as I was completely driven by the quest. Plus the competition between Kristin and I was motivating. We were friends and we had all of the same classes. And, we were both in the gifted and talented program. When we got to junior high, we both were competing in forensics, again trading places at times winning the ultimate prize.

Then, in ninth grade, because of redistricting by the school system, I was sent to a different junior high. While I was reunited with my old friend from third grade, Katrina, who by this time was a star athlete, Kristin was no longer around. In fact, she moved out of the area completely. The oratorical contest from elementary school had a competition my ninth grade year and I entered it again. Not only did I win first place, but I also made it all the way to the national competition. My picture was in the paper. I got calls and letters from all kinds of officials in my hometown and I was even named the person of the week by one of the radio stations. The success was wonderful, though a little bittersweet without Kristin.

Naturally in college, I majored in speech communication. I entered an oratorical contest three times while there and never won. I didn't stop though. I couldn't stop. Fortunately, I had a track record that reminded me I was an accomplished orator. Plus, other performance outlets helped keep my confidence boosted.

During my junior year in college, I was walking across campus and I saw a familiar face. That wasn't unusual with the size of the school and the fact that I bumped into people I knew all the time. But this was a face I hadn't seen in a while. She had long, long blonde hair. We stared at each other for a minute. After a while, I realized it was Kristin. I hadn't seen her in over 6 years. We hugged and though we didn't have much time to fully catch up, we did talk briefly.

Perhaps I never got over losing the third grade spelling bee. I think that's a good thing. If I had won that day, maybe I would have become complacent. On the other hand, I could have easily given up when I was eight years old and decided that racism was too much for me to deal with. After all, why else would a White teacher stand up and say that the proctor was wrong when everyone else in the room knew better. Sometimes I think that I chose to fight. Then other times, I think the fight chose me. I lost the first round and that loss wasn't fair. But in that loss, I learned much more than I could have ever won. Despite the racism I experienced, I learned to befriend and respect another White student and truly enjoy our friendly competition. Plus it was a White teacher who recognized my potential and recommended me for the gifted and talented

10th Anniversary Edition

program. And, my almost "lifelong" quest for trophies enabled me to develop my talent as a speaker. I may not have won the spelling bee, but the spelling bee ultimately made me a winner.

-Angela Ray

Think

A dialogue with high school students after reading the poem "We Real Cool" by Gwendolyn Brooks.

"So," asked the teacher, "what is considered 'cool' to kids your age?"

Hands went up in the air and the teacher called on a few students for their input. One said, "Being popular." Another said, "Having freedom and a late curfew." Soon, others gave their input. Throughout the discussion, there was laughter of agreement and concurrence. Some students even exchanged high-fives. The teacher encouraged the discussion and wrote the responses on the chalkboard as follows:

1. Being popular and well liked
2. Freedom and late curfew
3. Stylish name-brand clothes
4. Attention from the opposite sex
5. Not appearing to be too intelligent
6. Hanging out late
7. Being at all of the cool parties
8. Social drinking
9. Smoking cigarettes and sometimes marijuana
10. Not being a "virgin."

The teacher stopped the list at ten despite the few hands still hovering in the air. She went on to ask the students a second question: "What will be considered 'cool' to you in ten years – when you're almost thirty?" Again hands shot in the air and the teacher documented the answers on the board as follows:

1. Having a luxury car
2. Successful career
3. Nice home
4. Married
5. Children
6. Financial stability
7. Investments
8. College degree (s)
9. Traveling
10. Attractive appearance

The teacher instructed the students to copy down both lists, side-by-side, on a piece of notebook paper. The students followed her instructions and then just sat at their desks. She could tell that they were trying to figure out the point she was trying to make. Instead of engaging the students in the usual lecture, to which they had grown numb, she decided to guide them toward making their own connection

"So, what happens when you hang out late?"

"You don't get your homework done," said one student.

"You're too tired to work the next day," another responded.

"How about the whole "sex" thing? What happens if you decide to become sexually active?"

"You could get pregnant," a voice chimed in.

"Or even get a disease and die," another cautious voice replied.

The teacher encouraged the students to continue their

discussion, complimenting them on their honesty and insight. She also made a mental note of the contradictory nature of their current statements as compared to the sentiments they had expressed while compiling list one. They spent nearly the rest of class discussing the ill effects of the behaviors on list one. The students were eager to provide personal examples of cousins, friends, and even parents who had fallen victim to the aforementioned pitfalls. The teacher watched as the students became more and more emotionally involved in the discussion and waited until their emotions reached the virtual apex when she stopped them and posed her third and final question.

"So, if you decide to do what is considered cool to you now, will you be cool in ten years?" Silence fell across the room and then the bell rang. The teacher erased both lists from the board and filled the now empty space with the statement that would guide the next day's lesson: "The common sense of life is often so difficult to grasp."

-Arnitria Karen Shaw

10th Anniversary Edition

The 3 Laws of the Toddler

Is life too boring? Look to the toddler. Feeling stuck and don't know what to do next? Look to the toddler. Stressed out and cannot find relief? Look to the toddler. I look to mine.

Long ago, my daughter, who is now approaching five years of age, made the connection between performance and rewards; the most prevalent of the rewards being a treat--candy, cake, chocolate milk, anything sweet and sugary. More recently, she has also begun to recognize boredom and unhappiness and the need to avoid them. She will abandon a toy for greener pastures as soon as the thought of boredom enters her young mind. And she has always approached each and every day with the wisdom that the possibilities for happiness are endless. There have been countless Saturdays where she's requested to do more activities than there are hours in the waking day--at least in my waking day.

Now, I don't expect these revelations to knock anyone for a loop creating a flood of letters from the nation's top gifted and talented programs for children. I have been around enough toddlers over the years to realize this is not particularly unique behavior. These children are simply following natural human instinct; learned behaviors designed to please the soul and make life enjoyable. And I have recently acknowledged my own repression of those behaviors in most of my adult years.

I am not a professional psychologist, psychiatrist, or psychic-- not sure there is such a thing as an amateur psychic; you either are or you aren't. But I was awakened to something recently. While helping raise a child and experiencing major personal life changes at the same time I realized that when life has you by the neck and is squeezing tighter everyday, look to the 3 Laws of the Toddler:

1. Never be afraid to ask for what you deserve.

2. Always do what you enjoy.

3. Firmly believe that anything is possible.

Sound corny? A little contrived like an iRobot rip off? Still not impressed? Well read on because Law #3 is in effect.

Law #1: Never be afraid to ask for what you deserve.

"Daddy, I ate all of my broccoli. Can I have my treat now?"

"That's 'May I have my treat now.' May I ..."

"May I have my treat nooowwwww."

"No whining sweetheart."

"Sorry Daddy."

"Did you give me a happy plate?"

"Yes. I ate all my chicken and broccoli. And I even ate the rice I don't like and you didn't even have to tell me to."

"Good job sweetie. You deserve a treat."

    I frequently have this conversation, or some derivation thereof, after dinner with my sensei daughter (she who is teaching me the way of the toddler). It is a wonderful example of her embracing Law #1. It is my objective as her parent to not simply provide nutrition, but to enlighten her on the benefits of regular, balanced meals and healthy snacks and drinks. However, until she reaches that enlightened state, she gets rewarded for obeying the rules with a treat. And she never fails to remind me when she is due that treat. I made a commitment and she trusts I will follow through.

    I have steadily climbed the corporate ladder during ten years in the Information Technology profession. I have had five wonderful managers and one horrific one. I even ran my own semi-successful business with two other partners for three years. And yet, when it has come time for me to request what I am due, whether it be salary, commission, SkyMiles, or long distance calling cards, I freeze. I get scared. It could be a fear of rejection, or of being branded ungrateful, or of finding my view of my worth false. What is clear, however, is that at some point in my life, I stopped embracing Law #1.

As luck would have it, I had my annual review at work soon after I discovered the 3 Laws. The annual review is universal. I'm willing to bet even the lunchtime fry cook at Happy Burger is regularly reviewed on the overall quality of his frying. It is a moment for confidence and self-assuredness. I was to use that time to express how I not only met my objectives for the year, but how I excelled at my duties under difficult conditions and am deserving of an extraordinary treat; a nice big bonus payment.

It was my first chance to put my sensei daughter's teachings into action. And I was nervous, but I pushed through. The jury is still out on my results, but they are not the point of my sharing. What is important is I was not afraid to ask for what I deserve. I may not get it, but I will never wonder what could have been. And that makes me happy.

Law #2: Always do what you enjoy.

"Daddy, can I paint?"
"Sure sweetie. But I thought you were playing with your Play Doh."
"I was, but I don't want to anymore."
"You're bored? Well you have to clean up the Play Doh first."
"Okaaaaay."

You have heard it before. Perhaps it was your college career placement counselor trying to help you choose a career. Or maybe it was Hippie Joe who always found a way to strike up conversations about the true path to happiness. Or it might have been a parent, sometime after a long grueling day at work, crying out to you with warnings on the dangers of drugs, unprotected sex, and having a job you hate. Regardless the source, the message was the same, "Always do what you enjoy."

But you must look to the toddler to see Law #2 in action. My sensei daughter shows me everyday. She is very meticulous in her methods of play requiring many props and an ample amount of set up time. Yet, she will abandon the toys in a heartbeat once she is bored. And she accepts the pain of cleaning up as the necessary evil it is. Anything is better than having to play with boring toys.

Of course this is a very extreme example. No adult would be advised to swap jobs, relationships, cities, or whatever bores them as many times a day as a child does toys. But to paraphrase my mother, if you are doing something that makes you unhappy, stop doing it. And that's the foundation of Law #2. It is impossible to find happiness in life if you are always doing something that makes you unhappy. Separate yourself from the source, clean up the mess, and set up some other toys. You will be happier in the end. I am.

Rule #3: Firmly believe that anything is possible.

"Daddy, can we go to the park?"
"Not today sweetie. It's raining outside."
"I know what we can do. We can get some rubber raincoats and some rubber boots and then we won't get wet."

My sensei daughter does not acknowledge limitations as easily as the more mature ones of her species. She would rather offer alternatives and solutions. There is always a way. It is a lesson we teach our kids to embrace but often do not follow ourselves. Fortunately for me, I have held tight to Law #3 all my life, long before I knew it as Law #3.

Its presence was first manifested when I was 23 and fresh out of college. I had more escaped than graduated. To this day I still have nightmares of having one more final to take in a class I neither attended nor read about. My mother was kind enough to host me during the 8 months I searched for a job. I never thought I would move back home after college, especially considering how I excelled at all my prior education. But it was what it was. And all I could do was look forward to each new day and the possibilities the sunrise brought.

I finally found a job thanks to a friend, who knew a friend, who knew a manager willing to ignore my academic performance and focus on the content of the young man he interviewed. In the months prior to that, I worked at a non-paying internship that laid the groundwork for my starting a business 2 years later.

I have had many more affirmations of the power of Law #3 since then, but none were stronger or more pertinent to my happiness than that first time. I believe I can accomplish anything, and that makes me happy.

As mentioned before, the 3 Laws of the Toddler are not the product of a trained and certified psychological professional. They resulted from the random musings and ponderings of a man reawakened to the beauty of life. Take from this what you will. Regardless of what it is, I will be happy. Isn't that the point?

-Zuri A. Stanback

Discovering Alice

My friends and I stood around outside on a warm summer evening as the streetlights began to flicker indicating that they would be fully lit in a matter of seconds. To my grandmother, this meant that she should be hearing me running up the front porch steps right away. It was a rule in our house that I had to be at the house when the streetlights came on. Without fail I made it to the top of the porch by the time the lights were at they're brightest. This night was no different, but I could see that something was wrong all over my grandmother's face. I put my basketball on the floor and sat down on the couch near my grandmother's recliner. She told me that one of her many friends had phoned to let her know that I'd been skipping school and running the streets with my boyfriend. My mother worked late most nights, so my grandmother served as the disciplinarian in the household. I'd been busted by one of her "spies" as I called them. There was no need to lie to my grandmother, because it seemed that she always knew when I was lying. I tried anyhow, to no avail, and was sent to my room without permission to get on the phone or even watch television. I was devastated to have my phone privileges taken away. This meant no calling my boyfriend.

Though it wasn't that long ago, no one had personal cell phones to use whenever they pleased. Back then, I used to use "grandma's phone". I stomped up the stairs until I reached the bedroom that I shared with my mother and flopped down on my twin bed near the slightly opened window. It was Friday night, and since I couldn't talk on the phone, I was bored senseless. And what do teenage girls who share a room with their mothers do when they're bored? They go through they're mother's things. I looked in the drawers, rambled through old shoeboxes, read papers in envelopes and found nothing that peaked my interest or told me anything that I didn't already know. I dropped to my knees and began looking under my mom's twin bed on the opposite wall of the room. I saw a long box sitting against the wall hidden by rows of shoes and other things. I stretched my body under the bed until I had a good enough grip to slide it toward me. I pulled the heavy box until I had it in the open space between our beds. The box was covered in dust as I removed the lid to discover neatly organized books. I read books from time to time, but only the young girl blossoming titles from Judy Blume or Nancy Drew and the Hardy Boy mysteries. Lately, I'd read nothing but *Right On* magazine to keep up with my favorites stars. At 14 years old and going on twenty, I felt that I was much more mature than what those books had to offer me. I wanted something that I could identify with and to read about people who were just like me. I fingered through the tabs grazing over the titles on the spines of the books. I read the names of the books aloud, but low enough for my grandmother not to hear me downstairs. There was *Native Son, Malcolm X, Invisible Man, Roots, Kindred* and a bunch of others. I'd never heard of any of these titles, but for some strange reason I was interested and needed to find out more.

I lifted one of the books out of the box and opened the first page letting my eyes flow over the words. It was *The Color Purple* written by Alice Walker and then and there I was immediately sucked in by the raw use of words describing Celie in the throws of having her father's baby in a worn shed as she screamed in pain. I lifted my eyes from the yellowish worn paper in amazement. My heart was beating fast as I read on. I wondered to myself as to why my mother was hiding these books under her bed away from me. Did she think that I was too young? Instead of lingering on that, I continued to read about Celie and the series of women and men that shaped her life as she grew into a woman. Before I knew it, I'd read far enough into the novel to know that the man Celie thought was her father really wasn't. I was happier for Celie than she was.

The hours flew by quickly as I remained buried in the world of Celie, Nettie and Mister until I was reading the very last line of the book. I let out a deep cleansing breath as I closed the paperback. I had never read a book like this and didn't realize how much power they possessed. The story had moved me and suddenly all of the cattiness and drama in my own life didn't seem to compare to that of Celie's life. My world had been turned upside down by Alice Walker and the wonderful characters she wrote of. Night after night thereafter, I didn't have to be sent to my room, I went there on my own to read from the collection of books hidden under my mother's bed. It didn't take her long to find out about what I'd been doing after getting careless about replacing the box as I had found it. I'd expected the worst, but being the wonderful woman she is, my mother gave me the box of books and told me to learn as much as I could from the great stories she'd collected over the years. By the end of the summer of 1986, I'd read the entire box of books. It is to this date the best gift I'd ever received. And, I never skipped school again after that either.

-Sybil Barkley-Staples

10th Anniversary Edition

Math: My Motivating Enemy

"Life has meaning only in the struggle. Triumph or defeat is in the hands of the Gods. So let us celebrate the struggle." ~ Swahili Warrior Song

Math is not my friend. I get the basics – addition, subtraction, multiplication, and division. I love fractions. But there are some essentials from the math textbooks of life that are not in my long-term memory. If you say certain phrases to me, my brain simply does not compute.

Sure I could blame it on some teachers. Mr. Krupman's inadequacies were a big factor in how poorly I did in algebra. The truth is that I was too busy trying to be cool to listen to a teacher who had zero control over any of his classes.

Mrs. Mennigen's idiosyncrasies surely were to blame for me not doing well in geometry past the first quarter. I was too busy kicking it with my girls in class. Mr. Thomas had a rough time trying to control my last period Algebra II class and we never let him forget it. My grades reflected it.

Fast forward to my arrival as a freshman at Wittenberg University in Springfield, Ohio in September 1993, where I had to sit down to take the math entrance exam. To this day, all I know is that I failed. I attributed my failure to a lot of different factors, including never having a graphing calculator.

I took my failure with stride. A whole bunch of my friends failed the test. We reveled in our failure together.

I was told in order to take my college math course; I would need to pass the first eight chapters of intermediate algebra. I had two options. I could teach myself the eight chapters and go to the math workshop for the tests or I could take the semester long course but not receive any college credit.

Who had the time to do either? Especially me. Math's number one public enemy. Fight the power!

Freshman year went by and the only contact I had with math was balancing my checkbook. I failed at that too.

Sophomore year came and by then I had declared my majors. I still had not worked on my math.

End of sophomore year, I met with Dr. Zembar, my psychology advisor, to schedule my courses. She asked me when I was going to take psychology statistics. I told her I needed to pass the prerequisite math course. She asked me had I been working on it. I told her the truth, but I assured her I would work on the math.

She was not very encouraging. She made me want to change advisors that day. I complained to all of my friends who were psych majors like me. Some of us shared Dr. Zembar as an advisor. They had all told me how tough she could be. They were right.

That day I left her office, feeling for the first time like maybe I was not good enough and that she was not on my side. I had to prove her wrong. Sure I had got an A in her seminar class, but I needed to do more than that. Everyone who is a psychology major should get A's in the seminar classes.

After our conversation, I went and bought the math book to begin to teach myself math. Do you know how stupid that idea was?

I started with chapter one. I could handle chapter one. I did chapter one. I passed the test on my first try. I can do this.

I did chapters two and three. I even had one of my girlfriends doing it with me. We studied together. She kept me motivated to do the math.

I got up to chapter four. Chapter four was very much like a hurdle to me. I had never been a runner before and I had always admired those who ran the hurdles because in my eyes they appeared to be difficult to get over. Much like chapter four.

The first three chapters were akin to running, or a review of running. I learned a few new concepts with those chapters but essentially it was a review. I mastered what I should have already known. But this time because I was the teacher and the student, I grasped the material much better than when my teachers had taught the same thing. For free.

Chapter four brought me to the math workshop almost everyday. Fellow students tutored me. Even the director of the workshop tutored me. Her dog was my classmate. I think he got chapter four better than I did.

I finally surrendered the spring semester of my junior year. I signed up for the no credit, remedial math class. I went to that class everyday it met. I had to complete the first three chapters again. I was the only girl in that class. There were seven of us. There was no hiding in the class. I had to come prepared every class session. I did it. I passed.

Summer came and I decided to take my statistics class in eight weeks versus sixteen. I might be math challenged, but I am not crazy. I wish I could say that I excelled in psych stats. Dr. Eimer was the teacher. Pretty cool person. I went to class every morning. While in class, I seemed to have an understanding of what was being taught. But when I left the class, my understanding of the lesson seemed to leave as well. I wrote down all the steps. I would go to work right after class and do my homework. I would not understand anything. I would call Dr. Eimer so much that he grew to expect my calls. The math workshop was on a modified schedule during the summer so I went straight to the man himself.

Right before the last exam, Dr. Eimer told me I would need to get a C on the test just to get a D in the class. Are you kidding me? I mean I came to class everyday. I understood it in class. I did my homework. I wanted to cry.

I got a C in psych stats. I danced all around campus that day. A C had never meant so much to me in my life. I was too broke to send Dr. Eimer a dozen roses. Maybe if I had washed his car from day one, I would have got a B.

I continued on with my last two years of college because of my two majors and education minor. During that time, I took two more courses with Dr. Zembar. Plus as my advisor, she had to oversee my internship/independent study. I had to work my butt off for every A I received from her.

My last two years in college, I served as the student representative for the sexual harassment board. Dr. Zembar was the faculty head of the sexual harassment board during my fifth year. We had one case together that year. It was a hard case that dealt with a homosexual student. I spent a lot of time with her that fall which increased my respect and understanding of Dr. Zembar.

That spring, I had to complete my student teaching and write a thesis for Dr. Zembar on sexual abuse in homosexual relationships. I thought that she was trying to punish me for my verdict on the sexual harassment case from the previous fall. Not only that, but writing for her was intimidating. Dr. Zembar was tough when it came to research. I requested every book I could find on the subject. In 1998, there were four books. I read them all. I took thorough notes on my reading and I worked very hard on that paper. It paid off because I received an A on my thesis.

I had applied to teach with the Columbus Public Schools. Both of my advisors wrote my recommendation letters. Dr. Zembar wrote a two-page recommendation and gave me a copy of the recommendation as I left her office one day.

When I read Dr. Zembar's letter, I knew then that our five years together had paid off. I read it as I walked down the steps of Zimmerman Hall. I smiled at a lot of her comments. But it was not until I read, "If I had to have one person teach my daughter, it would be Carla Sarratt," that I cried.

I came to college totally unprepared for the rigorous academics that Wittenberg demanded. I knew it the day I stepped foot in my first class. I could have allowed myself to give up and go to another school. I could have, but I knew that there was greatness within me. I thrived at Wittenberg. I came to Wittenberg to further my education and make a difference, for my family, my community, and myself. Wittenberg gave me the necessary skills as they prepared me to be a leader and to handle adversity. My adversity in the classroom prepared me for life after Wittenberg. Wittenberg prepared me to succeed and pass the torch.

-Carla R. Sarratt

10th Anniversary Edition

The Courage to Reach Our Own

Two weeks into the school year, I sat in the first staff meeting barely conscious of Principal Cooley's discourse. I looked around at the room-full of teachers. The sum of all their experiences totaled more than 100 years of expertise. Every single one of them was a veteran at teaching children. Their self-assurance reminded me of my inadequacies. Their academic jargon took on so much more weight because they had been in the trenches for so long. I could feel them sizing me up, questioning my very existence in their territory, "What can she offer?" "Will she last?"

While the principal lectured, like everyone else, I stared at her attentively. But, I only heard her voice and not her words. My thoughts drifted to a conversation I had with my husband after my second day of teaching at Excelsior Preparatory.

"I cannot do this. It's way above me."

"You always handle pressure well."

"You don't understand. These kids are disrespectful, loud, they have no interest in academics, and foul language is a natural part of their vocabulary. I'm not getting through to them at all."

"I'm sure you'll find a way."

"You're not listening. I want to quit. Yesterday a teacher expressed her sympathy because I was given the *worst* class in the school."

"They're that bad?"

"Yes, and I'm going to resign."

"Give it two more weeks, honey," my husband counseled. I knew that as a Minister he was going to pray about it. My mind, however, was set. I had already told God that this was it.

Principal Cooley, looked straight at me, "So Mrs. Richards, do you agree or disagree? I did not get your vote."

Clueless about what she was saying I looked around the room

for help.

"Do you agree that we should turn in a copy of our weekly lesson plans to the Principal?" Mrs. Brown the kindergarten teacher, bless her heart, came to my rescue.

"Yes." I whispered, and the vote was carried. My hands were folded over the daily planner that contained my letter of resignation. Once again, I tried battling the feelings of defeat that had crowded my mind for the past weeks. I felt like a total failure. I was an educator with a graduate degree, had taught at the college level for some years, had traveled extensively, could speak four languages, yet, I had been incapable of handling twenty-five sixth graders. I had always considered myself a progressive woman and had taken pride in my professional accomplishments. Yet, for the first time in my life I had to admit failure.

Principal Cooley began to read general recommendations from the school's Board of Trustees for the new school year. I drowned her out again. I was not interested in what she had to say. After the meeting I was saying good-bye. My thoughts drifted again.

"That's so stupid, Yo!" Dayjon had yelled. "Why you gonna call my Mom 'cause I didn't bring some stupid books to school!" More than a question his retort was a threat. He slammed his fist on my desk and stared down at me maliciously.

I stood up from behind my desk to face him at eye level. I felt my body growing warm. *"How dare a twelve-year-old threaten me like this?"* Most of the time I felt as if it were a competition to see who was really in charge; the kids constantly tested my wits, as if they were appraising if I was up to the challenge.

I tried to sound just as threatening. "You do not come into this classroom bringing a book bag of expensive sneakers. That is not going to get you an education. As long as I am your teacher you respect yourself, your classmates and me, by coming into this classroom ready to acquire an education!" I wanted my words to spell *"beat down"* to him. The class became deadly silent.

Dayjon, one of the school's notorious bullies, was famous for his outbursts. I had sensed early on that most teachers feared his temper. Dayjon did not hold my stare; instead he knocked some books from my desk unto the floor. Cursing under his breath, he walked to his seat. Disappointed, I thought that I had squelched his previous outburst. I battled between ignoring his action, or having him rectify it.

I choose the latter. I placed my hands on my hips and mustered the meanest face and the firmest voice that I possibly could, and fired back, "NaNaNaNaNaNaNa!" It broke the ice.

The kids giggled, "How did she do that?"

"Dayjon, you will pick my books up and put them back on my desk. When you are through, you will apologize for cursing, and then, you may take your seat. I'm sure you don't want me to add this little performance to my conversation with your mother."

"No," he grumbled, picked the books up, placed them on the desk, and took his seat.

"You forgot to apologize for the cursing," I reminded him, arms folded across my chest, face still in mean mode.

He rolled his eyes. One of the girls groaned, "Shoot, she don't let nothing pass her."

"Sorry." Dayjon grumbled loud enough, and I proceeded to teach.

Principal Cooley, was still talking, "I am happy to report that most parents are extremely pleased with the new sixth grade teacher. They like that she is firm and has the children strongly engaged in academics. There has been a refreshing turn around in that group...."

She was talking about *my* sixth grade class. I managed a half-smile as some senior teachers nodded their approval. Yet, scenes of the previous day flashed before my eyes. I had asked the class to take out their English textbooks. They had all slammed the books on their desks in protest. They had done the same thing the first two days of school, and I had attributed it to 'vacation blues'. They were doing the same thing after two weeks. Startled, I questioned their reaction.

"You give us too much work, we are tired," Malrika complained, arms defiantly folded across her chest.

Others added: "You don't have to finish the textbook, you know?"

"Why can't we just chill sometimes?"

"Why don't you give us multiple-choice work? That's easier. You make us write too much."

"You make us read too much."

"Yeah, this stuff is whack, yo!" Dayjon proclaimed.

Dashicka added more support to their complaints, "You give too much homework. We never got homework before."

"Why we have to learn this stuff, anyway?" Germaine put in.

"Why can't you just take us to the park like we did last year?" Someone yelled from the back. The whole class clapped their approval to this suggestion.

I didn't get it. Was I really being too serious about their education? But, wasn't I supposed to teach them? Wasn't it part of my responsibility to prepare them for future academic challenges?

Thinking quickly, I counterattacked, "The day of tomorrow when you go to that interview to get into college or to get that job, and you don't have the skills to compete, are you going to tell them that your sixth grade teacher took you to the park instead of teaching you how to read, write and think? Do you think they will then have pity on you and give you the job?" No one replied, but they were convinced enough to open their textbooks.

The staff meeting finally ended, and I remained in my seat. *How was I going to hand this letter to the principal?* I now felt, in a way, accountable. There were people depending on me. I shoved the letter back in the planner upset at myself. My cowardice bothered me. Why was I so concerned about them?

Principal Cooley turned to me, "Mrs. Richards, you said before the meeting that you needed to speak to me."

"Hmmm," I stumbled for something to save me from my predicament. "I was wondering when the Spanish textbooks would be arriving." I lied.

"Oh. In the next two weeks." She smiled, strangely, as if she knew. "We'll see you tomorrow, then?"

I nodded. Yet, I still wanted to run away. I feared failure. I felt unfit for the challenge. These kids needed someone who was willing to reach them, by whatever means possible. They needed someone who would not give up on them as so many others had already done. They needed someone who could look past the impossibilities of their tough facades to see their possibilities. I was sure that I could not be the one. I opened the planner and stared at my letter of resignation. As I lifted it, quoted on the page were it had lain, were Eleanor Roosevelt's words: "You gain strength, courage, and confidence by every experience in which you really stop to look fear in the face. You must do the thing which you think you cannot do."

-Norka Blackman-Richards

The Power of Words

I love quotes. I love reading new quotes and hearing people use them. I have a room in my house (I call it my blue room) where I keep several books with many wonderful quotes from people all over the world. There's something infectious about the power of the words we say. Just a simple expression can bring both destruction and victory to people.

We are all familiar with the quote, "Sticks and stones may break my bones, but words will never hurt me!" WRONG…Words do hurt people. But, I try to remain encouraged, believing that we all can get pass the hurt that some words bring. I've tried to live my life through a simple, yet positive premise, which says, "And this too shall pass." It transcends all disbelief and encourages me to keep life in perspective.

Last week I was talking to a young girl about what she wanted to do with her life. She continued to spout out disbelief about her decisions to pursue her dreams. Each word that came out of her mouth screamed uncertainty. My insides were yelling out "Stop doubting yourself!!!" Suddenly, I pulled back and responded with a passage from one of my favorite books to read, the Bible. I said to her, "As water reflects a face, so a man's heart reflects the man." Simply put, I told her that the negative words that she continues to speak about herself will eventually reflect who she truly is. I don't know if it made a difference, but I at least planted the seed.

During my time on *Survivor* and post-*Survivor*, there were many good and bad words spoken about me on the Internet and by others. Some of the comments I wouldn't care to read again and others made me feel rather special. But through it all, I realized that everything has a price. Me going on *Survivor* had a price, both for my family and for me. I prepared myself mentally to look at each comment as both constructive and therapeutic. In every instance

10th Anniversary Edition

the price I had to pay came in many forms from effort, to energy, to money and time. I had to consider what it was all worth to me. Some results were positive while others were negative, but I never let the power of those words endanger my well being and hinder my pursuit for excellence. A Chinese proverb says, "The gem cannot be polished without friction...nor you perfected without trails." Post-*Survivor* proved that all things are possible regardless to what others think. Remaining positive and staying focus is the key to overcoming the words of others.

Remember this, "Sticks and stones may try and break my bones, but words will only encourage me." You control the power of words, don't let them control you.

-Vecepia Towery Robinson

BETRAYAL AND THE BULLY

In the 1950's we lived in the South Bronx. Even then it was not exactly the best place to raise children. City housing projects were going up around us. Two-family homes like ours, across from the majestic turrets of Morris High School, were being razed and replaced by cold, imposing obelisks. Towering over us, they seemed to invade the sense of community of our block of neat, yet worn, brick row houses—our Jackson Avenue. The stoops that jutted out from each building were endless spiraling staircases to castles in the imaginings of the young schoolgirl that I was.

Almost fifty years later I still have vivid memories of people on the block. The O'Garas resided next door. The DeZelles, our landlords, lived below us and sometimes let us play in their backyard—that oasis of grass and greenery in a world of pavement and asphalt. Neighbors would often comment to my parents that they took such good care of all four of us kids—Mario Jr., two years my senior, Rick and Tony, my younger brothers and me, Bonita. My father dubbed me "Bonnie Braids" after the Dick Tracy cartoon character found every Sunday in the New York Daily News. I was very proud of the comparison and my long shiny black braids. As the grown-ups congregated on the stoops and sidewalks, the activities of we kids spilled out into the street. My brothers and I, along with our friends, played all the city kids' games—stoopball, stickball, skelly, ring-a-leevio, kick the can and double-dutch.

My parents decided to take Mario and me out of P.S. 63, our local school, which fell short of providing us with the academic environment they deemed suitable. We were slated to attend school "outside of the district," a common practice then for the upwardly mobile. I'm sure Rick and Tony would follow in our footsteps when they were old enough. Using the address of friends in a better area, 1062 Teller Avenue, they enrolled us at P.S. 53. With bus passes I hand, we embarked upon a journey to a better education.

That's where I met Wymona Craft, who was called "Mona" by her friends and family. She was brown-skinned, much plumper than my ninety-five pounds, and wore round tortoise-shell eyeglasses. It was the glasses that endowed her with an intellectual aura that attracted me to her. Mona's coarse, kinky hair was always super-neat with bright color barrettes and bow ribbons that held her braids in place. She and I both wore plaid dresses with Peter Pan collars and bows that tied in the back, very much the style for schoolgirls at that time.

In my estimation, Mona was a very talented artist--always sketching people of no particular color in profile with her own distinctive style. Their faces looked very much like the brackets in an English class outline used to group similar ideas together. She drew a single upturned comma for the mouth. I, too, could draw well, but preferred and tried to mimic Mona's style. Mona lived around the corner from us on Home Street. Often Mario and I would meet her at the bus stop to head off to school each morning. She, like us, had to keep the secret of a bogus address. We had to walk up a precipitous hill, which pitched our bodies forward at a sixty-degree angle, from the bus stop to get to P.S. 53. Every morning we would mill about the playground until the din of the cowbell summoned us into the building. Not all those responding to the bell, however, were obedient lambs like Mona and me. Very few children of color attended our school and even at such a young age I was aware that the white teachers marveled at the abilities of pupils like Mario, Mona and me. Mona and I excelled in Mrs. Margolis' class and were classmates again and best friends by the time we moved up to the next grade.

We frequently visited one another's homes, drawing together and working on our stamp collections. I was an egg cream* with extra chocolate syrup when I was with Mona. After dismissal from school, I usually met Mario at the bottom of the hill. He would walk me across the wide traffic laden street to the bus stop for the ride home—my mother's strict instructions to us both. I was looking forward to going into Edelman's Bakery on the corner where we waited for the bus. Mario and I sometimes bought a special treat there—black and whites** for our ride home. On this particular afternoon, Mona and I were chatting and laughing together right outside the mammoth red steel doors where we exited the school building daily. Clutching our school bags heavy with loose-leaf binders and books, a group of four hard-looking girls with mean eyes encircled us. They were "colored," too. We knew them by sight only and always tried to avoid them on the playground during recess. As city kids, we had to fend for ourselves. We never even thought about telling the teachers if someone was bothering us.

The one who appeared to be the ringleader terrified me as she yanked my pigtails causing my bow ribbons to come undone. She shouted right up close to my face, "You think you're somethin' special, you skinny Puerto Rican-- with your good hair and your prissy hair bows. You think you're cute 'because you get good grades and all!" In those days anyone of Hispanic descent was called Puerto Rican. My mother was West Indian and my father was Honduran. As this queen of intimidation waited for me to say something, I stood mute and totally vulnerable. She released my hair after giving my braids several more hard tugs. I winced and whispered, "Ouch." Internal tremors rocked any resolve I might have had. She glared her venom directly into my eyes and shoved me down on the rough surface of the sidewalk. I was mortified. Getting back up, I checked my knees; no skin was broken. Then she and the others started in on Mona.

Again, the same girl was the spokesperson, "And you, Four-eyes, with that nappy hair—what do you have to say?"

She pulled off one of Mona's hair barrettes and slammed it down to the ground. Mona, more courageous than I, replied, "Leave me alone! I didn't do anything to you!" She kneeled to retrieve her barrette. They just laughed as her voice trembled and cracked. Whirling in a pivot of power, the leader of the pack refocused her fury on me.

"Ain't this nappy-headed girl your friend? Ain't she another one of Miss McClain's teachers' pets?"

Not wanting to, yet still—I denied Mona. I felt just like Judas that I had learned about in Sunday school at Trinity Church down the street from our house. "No; she's just a girl in my class—that's all. My brother is waiting down the bottom of the hill. I gotta go!"

The words seemed to come from somewhere inside of me that I had no familiarity with. I began to run down the hill, barely holding on to my heavy book bag, propelled by the gravitational pull of the steep incline. I did not look back even once to see if Mona escaped their menacing wrath. Out of breath, I crossed the street with Mario. I said nothing to him about what had occurred at the top of the hill. I checked my knees again and retied my hair ribbons.

Mario said, "What happened to you?"

"Oh, I tripped when I was coming down the hill."

"Where's Mona?"

"I don't know: I didn't see her when the bell rang. She can always catch the next bus."

"Well, if you're all right, let's get our black and whites!" Wanting to get to a safe place far away from those girls and from Mona, I replied, "No, the bus is coming right now!" I was never so glad to see a New York City bus as it pulled up almost on cue.

The next day, I was relieved that Mona was not at the bus stop. I avoided her in class. Luckily, we did not sit side by side. But after much hesitation, I finally mustered up enough pitiful courage to go over to her desk.

"Mona, are you okay?" All she said was, "I'm fine." She went right back to the exercises in her arithmetic workbook.

From then on, when we did arrive at the bus stop at the same time, our interaction never went further than, "Hi" or "Hello."

I told Mario that we just weren't best friends any more. In my shame and embarrassment, I never told anyone that I had abandoned Mona—not even my mother. At the end of that school year, my family packed up and moved to Long Island. I didn't even go over to Mona's house to let her know. To this day, I still miss Mona.

Footnotes: *egg cream: a New York City soda fountain drink of seltzer water, milk and chocolate syrup.

** Black and Whites: cake-like cookies with half vanilla and half chocolate glaze on top.

Unlike the experiences of the students in this story, you can do something about bullying and other problems with your peers. Tell a teacher, a guidance counselor and, of course, your parents. You are not "punks" or "nerds" for seeking help from adults. Take advantage of the Conflict Resolution Program in your school. Ask your guidance counselor about starting up such a program if none exists. Go online for innumerable websites about such programs. There are peaceful and positive ways to solve problems so that everyone comes up a winner! Always take pride in getting good grades and doing your very best in your school studies. Others may be jealous of your achievements. Remain steadfast on your course that will lead you to college and a successful future! Try this writing exercise: Write a letter to the narrator, Mona or to the bully. Tell how you would handle the situation differently with the help of a Conflict Resolution Program.

-By Bonita Sanabria

10th Anniversary Edition

OVERCOMING A "SISTER-SLAYER" IN THE WORKPLACE

One of the greatest aspects of growing up in my African American family, was having a loving mother whose strong faith in God, taught my sister and I, how to persevere in times of difficulty. It was that strong faith that empowered me to overcome the malicious actions of a "sister-slayer" in the workplace. One who deliberately closed the door in my face when there was an opportunity for my advancement.

During this juncture in time, I had worked in education for fifteen years, receiving annual satisfactory ratings for my exemplary job performance as a teacher. I've always been a conscientious employee, never abused my time, and commanded the respect of those with whom I worked. It was through my excellent instructional delivery, and interpersonal communication with parents, community members, and especially children, that I was able to address and adjust to the myriad styles and competencies of an audience. More importantly, however, my students had always experienced success in scoring at or above grade level on their reading assessments, and I had managed to earn the love and respect of the children.

I taught all of my students from the very core of my being. My commitment to the children came first; and they knew the sincerity of that commitment. My contributions to education included serving for fourteen years as the faculty adviser for the school yearbook, working as coordinator of the programs for the Arista Honor Society and Graduation, which afforded me the opportunity to engage and meet high-powered politicians and community leaders as guest speakers for the school. The major highlights of my career though, included being selected as one of three teachers featured on a past documentary of WABC TV's Like It Is, is my spring 2000 nomination for the Walt Disney American Teacher Award, and the four years that I was listed in Who's Who Among Americas Teachers; where the best teachers in America are nominated for induction by the best students of the same.

When our new public school commander-in-chief, the "sister-slayer," showed up, it was due to the unexpected departure of our previous administrator. Upon her arrival, she had succumbed to falling under the spell of Saul Slacker, a Caucasian assistant principal who was preparing to retire; and the one I was destined to replace. He was a gossipy man who admittedly "hated veteran teachers," such as myself, because they were not afraid of him or his crude tactics of intimidation. Principal Brazen hung on to his every word; and those whom he disliked, she disliked them even more. She was introduced to her staff through his vindictive voice, and those anecdotes included information about my credentials, which were laced with two Master degrees; one in Language and Literacy, the second in Administration & Supervision; as well as a license to work as a public school administrator. My credentials and experience in the system, was believed by many, to exceed what she had to qualify her as a principal; the lead educator of the school.

Having received the approval to advance from the previous administration, and earning the trust of my students and their parents, I was ready and more than qualified to assume the role of assistant principal, once it had become available.

Despite the fact that this new principal was a very attractive African American female, she had some issues, and was apparently haunted by a sea of insecurities, which therefore, caused her to feel threatened by other strong African American women in the workplace. And that's the reason why she despised my very existence. I was an educated, strong, confident, African American female, who had absolutely no trouble holding her own. As soon as I came to realize the "sister-slayer" was intimidated by my overall demeanor, I discovered that she was in the process of plotting what she thought was going to be my professional demise.

I was serving in the capacity of dean of students, when it had become common knowledge to everyone on staff that I was going to assume the position of the outgoing Saul Slacker. However, to begin executing her plan to obstruct my advancement, the "sister-slayer" called me into her office, exactly one day before school was scheduled to close. She proceeded to inform me that "Mr. Slacker would indeed be retiring, but had not yet submitted his papers." Therefore, she continued to say, I can not offer you anything at this time," snatching the hope I had of advancing my career that following September. I heard the thump of my heart hit its floor, but I knew she was misrepresenting the truth. How can one plan to retire and not submit the necessary paperwork to do so? In conjunction with this fabricated story, she told me of her decision to return me to the classroom, even though I was one of the most effective deans she had in the school. Clearly, this was a move purposely orchestrated to hinder any further progress in that school.

Mr. Slacker retired as planned in June of 2003, but by August of that same year, he had expired, never to enjoy the benefits reaped from the fruits of his labor. The principal, dictated to from his grave, ultimately gave the position to which I aspired, to an aloof, Caucasian male, from outside of the school. I never expected to be everyone's choice, but I did expect fairness.

It was my belief in God, my unshakable faith, and the fact that "I can do all things through Christ who strengthens me," that sustained me and allowed me to persevere in the face of adversity. Within two short years, without ever taking the time to get to know me for herself, this principal tried her best to break me down and kill my spirit, as she had done to so many others before me. But I was determined to maintain my self-respect, my dignity, and everything else my mother had taught me. And in the words of that old Negro Spiritual, I was just like the tree planted by the water, I would not be moved. You see, at a very early age, I was taught to understand that many of the stumbling blocks that people deliberately place in your path can sometimes turn out to be blessings in disguise. And this was my disguised blessing.

As the motivational speaker, Willie Jolly says, a setback is nothing but a setup for a comeback. I knew that I was on the comeback trail, and there was something greater that lied ahead. So, I kept my eyes on the prize. I flipped the switch, and reversed that meant-for-evil situation, and became inspired to turn that obstacle into a stepping-stone, and was blessed in completing a three-year old manuscript, which led to the publication of my first book <u>Teachers Under Siege</u> (ISBN#1-4184-2748-9). I am still not an assistant principal, but because of Principal Brazen, that's the school's loss.

I continue to educate, and was proffered the opportunity to work in a position that allows me the freedom of movement. I am once again, out of the classroom, and trusted with the responsibility and autonomy to determine my own schedule; and have been blessed to be free of the high levels of stress that one can experience in an administrative position. I have also founded Sister To Sister: One In The Spirit Productions, a sponsor of women's conferences in New York City. We continue to flourish, and have now begun to shift our focus to explore the dynamics of how women interact with other women in the workplace; and how women come to view other women in such negative ways. It is my goal, through this powerful "sister" organization, to help eradicate this type of thinking with hopes to change these competitive, catty mindsets and behaviors that women seem to direct toward other women in business.

My hope for all African American youth is to look deep within their soul and summon the courage necessary to stand up to the ills of adversity. As African Americans, we have a rich legacy that was passed down to us from courageous men and women like Harriet Tubman, Frederick Douglass, Mary McLeod Bethune, Martin Luther King, Jr., and Rosa Parks, all of whom were victorious over the monumental measures of adversity experienced in their own lives. I urge you to strive for excellence, and get a quality education, and understand that many in our heritage died without ever

10th Anniversary Edition

experiencing the joy of reading a book. They died, determined that you and I would have the right to a better life. Finally, just like school, life will administer a series of blows or tests. It will test us in our personal and family relationships; it will also test us on our jobs. But remember this, without the life test, you will never be able to have a life testimony.

-Yvonne Singleton Davis

"Prieta"

My name is Kara, derived from the Italian and Spanish "cara", meaning beautiful, dear and face respectively. Me. Born, raised, noted, and recognized for a beautiful, dear face. Maybe had those that I encountered in the Dominican Republic had been privy to this information, I would not have been renamed. Maldita [1], not Karita [2]. Haitiana [3], not hermana [4]. "fea [5]" not "bonita" [6] marked the deepened contour of my brazened cheekbones, and the deliberate slope and shape of my nose and mouth, "sucia" [7] described the type, texture, condition, and state of my African hair, and "prieta" [8], a unanimously violent response to the exposure of the blackened color of my skin. My identity, lost in translation…

My initial premise for moving to the Dominican Republic was to work on an international education project, whereas its ambitious, if not quixotic, mission is aimed at exposing Dominican primary and secondary school students to the contributions that Africans have made to their culture and humanity. I later learned, however, the life that I lived on this small-island nation was an unexpected journey—a sojourn. My sojourn. A brick-hard introductory lesson into identity, self-love, self-discovery, survival, and black womanhood.

Living in the Dominican Republic as a dark-skinned, African-American woman was an exercise in and insight into the psychology of human conditioning. The endemic repercussions of a five hundred year old slave and colonial state continue to have functional, practical roles in contemporary Dominican society. They define expectations, determine privilege, and dictate one's access to humanity. With blatant, overt acts of discrimination, subtle social cues, and symbolic reminders, I, too, became a subject in this real-life Pavlovian cultural experiment; I learned the worth and value of black women; what I expected for myself, of myself, and from those that looked like me.

I did not expect to be addressed with a formal Usted [9]. I was elated to see a black woman in print or on screen in a position of authority. It was considered a good day if no one tried to touch my hair, hips, breasts, buttocks, or thighs. I witnessed black women clean, carry, wash, fold, pull, push...ache, yearn, and desire in screaming silence.

When I walked down the streets and heard pelts of "fea" and "sucia", I owned the insults, because without looking up or around, I knew that they were directed towards me. I owned my position and subconsciously apologized for offending their sensibilities. The locks that I once cultivated with pride seemed... not so beautiful. Transformed. Dingy, Inappropriate. Unbecoming. Soon I could not distinguish between the voices in the streets and the ones in my head that were telling me to keep them covered.

In my quiet, solemn moments of clarity, the begging question of who I was in the absence of love and support and in the presence of proactive hate and looming, imminent danger lingered. In essence, I had to answer: Who was I when no one was watching? What were my non-negotiables? Were my identity politics a matter of cultural convenience or personal conviction?

Pulling from a spiritual reserve and an ideological space that rooted me in Afrocentricity, I took back my humanity and stood alone. I became my own best friend by revealing and accepting my insecurities and frailties to my ancestors and myself. I made a choice. I refused to deny my heritage by succumbing to the society's perverse preoccupation with, and rancid idolatry of European paradigms and standards of beauty. I had covered my head for too long and would not permit myself to do it any longer. Displaying my locks became conscious, confrontational, deliberate political daily statements of my commitment, loyalty, and love of my beautiful, beautiful, beautiful blackness. My legacy.

Dr. Carter G. Woodson's *The Miseducation of the Negro*, Marcus Garvey's *The Philosophy and Opinions of Marcus Garvey*, Nelson

Mandela's speech *Our Greatest Fear*, several Rastafari newsletters from my mother country Antigua, and a handful of love letters shed light, reason, and continued impetus for my passion and drive for a self-loving, Black-affirming space for those of African-descent. From Dominicans, I demanded my place in their cultural landscape, --a landscape entrenched in and saturated with African cuisine, folklore, religion, and nuance. To this end, I mastered their colonizer's tongue and I retorted with dagger-like speed and precision at the slightest hint of injustice and racial bigotry.

It's only in hindsight and with body of water and a calendar year between us, that I have been able to put my experience in its psychosocial context. That is, I cannot, with all fairness, harbor feelings of hatred and venom for those that subjected me to abject rejection and marginalization. Because like overexposure to the sun, overexposure to prolific, pounding, subsuming self-hate, damages one. Chronically. Irreparably. It damages egos; it damages hope, and it rewrites history.

I, like they, am at the mercy of human persuasion and slight-of-hand agendas. What separated us was the power of choice. I had the privilege of options. For as much commercial support and media endorsement that African-American women obviously uncomfortable with their Africanisms received, I, as a black woman in search of self, could identify historic, symbolic, and present-day representations, although not with the same ease of black folk embracing all things that made them black. Tools of education, travel, critical thinking, and introspection guided me to an Afrocentric, intellectual, and cultural cipher dedicated to the empowerment and fortification of black mental hygiene and political presence.

I left the Dominican Republic in 2003. That was over a year ago. And here I am, on the cusp of my 25th birthday, speaking to you from a very special place. It smells is strong, intense, and sweet. I cannot accurately pinpoint its location. All I know is that it's housed within. I am a woman of African descent. A beautiful black one.

[1] Maldita; a curse word

[2] Karita; In Spanish, ending a person's name with the diminutive – ita, -ito denotes endearment

[3] Haitiana: Superficially, this means a woman from Haiti. However, in the Dominican context, Haitiana is used as a pejorative.

[4] Hermana; sister

[5] Fea; ugly; unattractive

[6] Bonita; beautiful

[7] Sucia; dirty

[8] Prieta; Black woman; often used as a pejorative.

[9] Usted; In the Spanish language system, there are two forms of stating the third-person, singular. Tu, which denotes familiarity and Usted, which denotes distance, formality, and respect.

-By Kara Stevens

My Testimony

Many of my years have been spent in the hospital visiting family and friends. I was exposed to terminal illness and death at an early age…from my uncle and to my grandmother. I've always felt my calling is to help others, particularly the dying. Never did I think I would end up at death's door.

From about 1996 until 1998, I was experiencing episodes where my nose would burn like I was sniffing ammonia. Dizziness, confusion, and flashbacks of my childhood would follow this sensation and then everything would rush to my head. I would have a massive headache for about an hour. This occurred about 10 times in the three-year period. My insurance company kept diagnosing it as a migraine. I would later learn I was actually having olfactory seizures.

It was the late summer of 1998 and I had just begun my final course, organic chemistry, before applying to medical school. I had undergone a traumatic event in my life and experienced the worst of these seizures while at work preparing to leave for class. I passed out and the owner of the company I worked for rushed me to my insurance company's aftercare facility. I was once again diagnosed with a migraine. I stayed home from work and class for a week. During this time I went to the doctor and demanded a referral for an MRI. She said I really didn't need it because I just had a migraine but she would give me a referral anyway. I went for the test the following week and was told that the results would be ready in 8-10 business days. My primary care physician called me the NEXT day at work and told me they had found an aneurysm and I needed to go out-of-network to Georgetown University Hospital to see the head of cerebrovascular surgery.

While reviewing my MRI results, Dr. Kevin McGrail found an arteriovenus malformation (AVM) the size of a plum on the left temporal lobe of my brain. An AVM is a cluster of abnormally connecting arteries and veins. Instead of the arteries branching into arterioles, capillaries where the oxygen exchange occurs, venules, and then veins... the high-pressured arteries went directly to the low-pressured veins. It looked sort of like a sudden tangle at the end of a piece of string. Within this cluster were aneurysms. This portion of my brain had to be removed otherwise coma, paralysis or death was probable. Before removing it, they needed to see what would be affected. They performed what's called a WADA test. During this test, both sides of my brain were put to sleep one side at a time. I was then asked to do certain things. When the medication reached my left temporal lobe I was unable to speak. I was trying to say, "Red Ball" but my speech was severely slurred....VERY SCARY!!! They concluded that the AVM needed to be reduced as much as possible before the major surgery. This would minimize the chances of losing my speech and suffering paralysis on the right side.

For a year, I was under the care of the head neuro-radiologist there at Georgetown. He was part of Dr. McGrail's team. His goal was to shrink the AVM down to the size of a grape. Then Dr. McGrail would do the major surgery. I underwent procedures called embolizations. A catheter was inserted into my femoral artery via the groin (ouch!!).

It was then fed up my leg, through my heart and up into my brain. Glue was released into the tangle blocking blood flow and causing the AVM to shrink. I was then put on stroke watch for two days and then released. This procedure had not been approved by the FDA at the time and was completely experimental so I had to sign lots of forms. I had to go through this every 6-8 weeks for almost a year. According to my mother, the last embolization was terrible. She could hear me screaming from the waiting room. The nurse came out to talk to her and felt terrible. His head was down because he didn't want to tell her that they pulled the catheter out without giving me more anesthesia and I FELT IT BEING REMOVED!

After the series of embolizations, it was time for the BIG surgery. Dr. McGrail informed me that this was a very risky surgery. He said it was in the top 10% of the most dangerous surgeries. My option would've been to do a radiation treatment and wait a year to see if it worked. In the meantime I would be at a high risk of having a stroke and going into a coma. I prayed about it and called the surgeon. I let him know I wanted to go forward with the surgery.

The night before the surgery, my family held a huge prayer service for me. I really learned who my true friends are throughout this whole ordeal. I had never seen people pray like they did that evening. Individuals prayed, circles of people prayed, circles of women prayed, circles of men prayed, all kinds of combinations prayed. I was then anointed. I must admit, Pastor Preston offered to anoint me when I was first diagnosed but I refused. I had always associated anointing with death. I was quite mistaken. It was a wonderful experience. After the service, I was at peace and ready to die if necessary.

I arrived at the hospital the next morning…you know how insurance companies are today…you have to check in just before MAJOR surgery…can you imagine? Once I was registered, we were taken into a room for final instruction. They also made a second attempt to get me to sign a permission form for a blood transfusion. This is because a week prior to the surgery during my prep exam I refused to sign. A friend had offered to donate blood to me but I found out it needed to be drawn a month in advance. I had no intention of having a stranger's blood transfused into my body. For every reason they gave me to sign, I had a reason why I shouldn't sign. Reluctantly, I signed.

Dr. McGrail figured I would be in intensive care for a day and out of the hospital in a week. Unfortunately, this did not happen. The surgery lasted 9 hours, longer than initially expected. It's a good thing I signed those blood transfusion papers because as soon as Dr. McGrail opened my skull and began the surgery, I began to hemorrhage. I needed two blood transfusions immediately. If I had not signed the papers I would've died before they got to do the surgery. Once I came through the surgery, my forehead began to swell from excessive blood building up in my head. At one point I'm told I was getting ready to go into cardiac arrest. My mother had left the hospital already. Dr. McGrail called and asked for permission to put a hole in the right side of my skull in order to insert a tube to drain the blood. They had just tried to save a man down the hall with the same procedure but he died. The draining was a very slow process so Dr. McGrail ordered an operating room and was going to perform additional surgery. This operation would result in me having to wear an external tube for the rest of my life for drainage. Dr. McGrail and my mother discussed this and he agreed to give me a few more days.

Mom didn't want me to have to go around the rest of my life with a tube coming out of my head. Thank goodness the first procedure for draining my brain worked and I didn't need to go through any additional surgery. The swelling from the surgery pushed on my optic nerve. This caused my left eye to move over to the side of my head. My glasses had to be taped and my eye gradually returned to its correct anatomical position. I was in ICU on a respirator for 3 ½ weeks. I also developed pneumonia from lying immobile in the bed for so long.

After my month's stay at Georgetown, I was transported by ambulance to INOVA Mount Vernon Hospital for rehabilitation. My mother says I was initially scheduled to be at this facility for 1-3 months. Those of you who know me know that I wasn't having that. No way! I was in a pre-coma state while at Georgetown so I don't remember a thing. But I sure do remember the rehab hospital. I wanted to leave so badly. They were needle happy there. There were 36 needle scars on my wrists alone. I also had to get injections in my STOMACH twice a day.....EXTREMELY PAINFUL! I can remember holding the nurse's hand with the needle and pleading with her not to do it. Anyway, I stayed for only one week after talking the doctor into releasing me to go home where I recuperated for another month or so. During this time, I had a rigorous schedule of outpatient physical, occupational and speech therapy.

Prayer really is powerful. People all over the world were praying for me. My mother received calls from people who had heard about the surgery at prayer meeting and couldn't believe I was going through all of this. WGTS was kind enough to stop their radio station broadcast and pray during the surgery.

The entire experience was a miracle/blessing because I am just fine. My speech was not affected as expected. My short-term memory was definitely affected. Initially I would forget information within 5 minutes. My memory has improved drastically however. You don't know what you have until it's gone. I'm realizing that I once had PHENOMINAL memory. Now it's like that of a normal person I suppose.

Due to my loss of short-term memory after the surgery, I decided not to attend medical school where I had always hoped to become an orthopedic surgeon. There was just no way would I be able to retain all of the information and skills required for the medical profession.

The Lord has blessed me with my current position. I am the Residency Program Coordinator for podiatry and orthopedic surgery at one of the top trauma hospitals in the Washington metropolitan area. Although I will probably never practice orthopedic surgery, I am grateful that I can live vicariously through my residents.

Today, I continue to help others through volunteering for several organizations. I have a degree in psychology. After my near death experience, I decided to use my counseling skills by volunteering for the Hospices of the National Capital Area. I counsel the terminally ill along with their family members, helping them prepare for death. On the first Saturday of each month, I feed the homeless with my Homeless Ministries team at church. In order to assist in encouraging young black students to read, I volunteer for an organization called *In2Books*. I read books with 5th graders in DC public schools. We email each other about the books we're reading together. The goal is to get them interested in reading. Finally, I am

10th Anniversary Edition
the proofreader for an African American web magazine called *Alluring Looks*.

-Kimberly Etherith-Spence

Wild Flowers

"Class--class, may I please have your attention?" Ms. Wilber said. "I'd like to introduce Mr. Roxsiden and Mr. And Mr. Britt. They're here from the School Board to make observations and recommendations."

Mr. Britt, a scratchy-faced, lean white man, looked at the room of unruly teenagers and said smugly, "We're considering closing this school. The violence has been noted for years, and the test scores have gotten progressively worse."

"But first," interjected Mr. Roxsiden, "we'd like to interview students and teachers to ascertain the justification of pumping more tax dollars into this facility."

Ms. Wilber looked across the room at Romeo, who was drawing a sketch on the back of his literature paper, at Nate who was turned toward the back of the room engaged in a conversation with another student, and at Moneeka who seemed lost in thought. What could I do to impress upon them the importance of an education, she thought.

"We'll need volunteers to participate in the study. There's a short questionnaire and an informal interview," Mr. Roxsiden said.

"Please don't come down to clown or waste our time," Mr. Britt said with disgust.

"We have so many other important things we can be doing." It was apparent to all in the classroom that Mr. Britt had no love for Champion Middle.

As the two men turned toward the door, the room once again came to life. Moneeka pulled out a nail file and thought about how she desperately needed a fill-in. Nate nudged Romeo, laughing and teasing him for staring at Moneeka. Two girls at a table near the window were flipping the pages of an Essence magazine.

Ms. Wilber walked over to the window. Across the street she

could see the vast wasteland, with the boarded windows of some of the abandoned units in the projects. Not to mention the liquor store down the block, with its steady stream of patrons. Champion Middle used to be such a nice place, she thought. But that was before the iron bars had to cover the first floor windows to protect the computer room from vandals. Ah, yes, and possibly even before the padlocks and door bells were attached to the main entrance.

"Class, before you're dismissed for music, I'd like for you to be thinking about what Mr. Britt and Mr. Roxsiden said." She looked from student to student trying to establish eye contact--trying to see if any of them even cared.

"I'll go down there, Ms. Wilber. I'm--uh, well, I'm a slow-learner but...."

Suddenly, thunderous laughter spewed forth as Evan stood near his desk. He smiled, and giant dimples swallowed his jaws.

"Man, we don't want your retarded butt going down there representing." It was Romeo leading the charge, with other hecklers bringing up the rear.

The ebony-colored boy with smooth silky skin refused to be dismissed. "Ms. Wilber, I know I'm slow but ain't nobody else saying nothing about going down there."

The students were still laughing and pointing, despite Ms. Wilber's attempts to restore order.

"I'll go with him!" Moneeka said, as she rose from her seat and walked over to Evan. "When did they say we'd have to participate, Ms. Wilber?"

"They didn't says, but I would imagine that it will be between now and Friday. That's when the School Board will be hearing recommendations. I'm so happy that you two have chosen to represent your school. Now, you all have about ten minutes before the bell, why don't you look over that English handout on your desks. There'll be a quiz right after lunch."

Moneeka looked down at the paper on her desk. For some reason the prepositions, interjections, conjunctions, and other parts of speech, didn't seem important now. What had she gotten herself into--and how could she face Mr. Britt, and Mr. Roxsiden.

"Aren't you going to music, Moneeka?" Evan asked.

"Oh--oh, yes, I didn't hear the bell. Thanks for bringing me back to earth. And, by the way, Evan, don't ever say you're a slow learner. Don't ever say that!"

"OK."

"Now let's go."

All through music and gym, Moneeka wondered how she'd present herself to Mr. Britt and Mr. Roxsiden on Friday. Although she was an "A" student it was difficult for her to stay motivated. She lived in an impoverished area which was crime-ridden, to say the very least. Most of her classmates had serious issues and behavioral problems. The one thing they all had in common was their love for Champion Middle School, which was a source of pride for teachers and community leaders as well. After all it was Champion Middle that boasted having the most professional alumni in the city. There was even a "Wall of Champions," in the main corridor. Pictures of some of Columbus, Ohio's most prestigious citizens hung there.

On Friday, Moneeka took care in dressing for school--she wanted to look her very best. She tried on a pair of Levi's with an orange T-shirt, naw. Next, she put on her DKNY dress with matching slippers. Still not quite right. Aha! There's my Reebok nylon-jogging suit with the hooded jacket. She put it on, then kneeled beside her bed and retrieved her Reebok Classics. Now let me plug-in the curlers, crimp my ponytail, and I'm out of here. She turned to look in the mirror one last time. Dang I'm cute, she thought. She was 5' 5" tall and weighed 110 pounds. Flawless skin, well maybe not flawless she admitted, but smooth none-the-less. Yes, chocolate and smooth, like a Hershey Bar. Her light brown eyes, and thick dark brown hair provided a stunning contrast. She smiled exposing a beautiful set of pearly whites. Yes, I'm cute she concluded.

Moneeka entered the library quietly, tiptoeing behind the carrels in search of Evan. She saw him near the back of the room, along the wall. "It's time to go see Mr. Britt and Mr. Roxsiden," she whispered in his ear.

"I'm looking up some stuff...hey you look good girl!"

"Thanks. You don't look bad yourself. You are working that Phatfarm outfit my brotha." She smiled into his dark brown eyes, marveling at how attractive he was. A little small for a boy, he was only 120 pounds on a 5'3" frame. But, he had those gigantic dimples, and a smile that would melt a 'Slushy', if he stood too close. AND...he was a great dresser.

"You're right Moneeka, let's go get it over with."

Mr. Britt and Mr. Roxsiden were seated in the Conference Room on the third floor. They didn't look up to acknowledge the students when they arrived. Instead the concentrated on scrawled notes and written reports on the long wooden table where they sat. "Come, have a seat, Mr. Roxsiden said, motioning to Moneeka and Evan.

"Evan, I see here that you have a learning disability." It was Mr. Britt going for blood.

"I don't learn too good, if that's what you mean. Sometimes I think I'm stupid like everybody says, but other times I believe if I keep trying and don't give up, I'll get it."

"Do you get help from your parents, teachers or friends?" It was Mr. Britt this time.

"I don't get no help at home, but uh, my teachers work with me. And Moneeka, she helps me in study hall."

"Do your parents understand the importance of an education?" Mr. Roxsiden asked.

Moneeka sprang to her feet and grabbed Evan by the arm, starting toward the door. She knew she had to get him out of there fast! If there was one thing you didn't do to a black child, it was to insinuate negativity on the part of their parents. Old pinched-nosed Roxsiden was wading treacherous waters.

"Wait young lady...please, both of you come back," pleaded

Mr. Britt.

Moneeka turned and looked at the men. "Let me tell you two something," she started, oblivious to the tears streaming down her face. "I've been working on a presentation since Tuesday, but it's not even important now. I would like to say a few things if you don't mind. "Evan is a shining example to me. Although he tested below normal on standardized tests, he still does his best. The other students tease and ridicule him but that doesn't deter him. He still does his best! He was disowned by his father and abandoned by his mother."

"C'mon Moneeka," Evan said. "Let's just leave."

"No, no I'm not ready to leave now. Look, Evan is really an inspiration. He's the true spirit of Champion Middle School. You see, we're in a high crime area. We're not expected to succeed. The community has changed, there's not a lot of support for civic causes. We're not like the heroes on the *Wall of Champions*. But, Evan is special...he's like the wild flowers that bloom all along the open fields, near the highways. Without any care they just magically appear each spring. That's what Evan is, something beautiful which appears and blossoms in the most unimaginable place." Moneeka rubbed the back of her hand across her face, swiping tears that were now flowing freeing.

"Great presentation, young lady, and to you also young man," Mr. Roxsiden said. "We haven't been perfectly honest with you two. We are compiling data for the board, but we're also getting information for "School Spirit," an event scheduled for this fall."

"And I apologize to you both," Mr. Britt added. "We just needed to capture your true sentiments. You kids have a great school here...come downstairs with us, we'd like to take your picture beside the *Wall of Champions*.

-Delores Thornton

10th Anniversary Edition

My Story - Part 1

What is success?

An attainment of material wealth? An event that accomplishes its intended purpose? A state of fame or prosperity? A series of achievements?

Success is all these things, by definition. However, a pimp can be successful, by definition; a drug dealer can be successful, by definition; a con-artist can be successful, by definition -- because their successes are defined by the physical -- the car they drive; the house they live in; the amount of money they have accumulated in bank accounts; the power that they exercise over others...

In truth, however, material wealth and accolades are the very things that have great potential to surpass or even destroy an individual, especially if that is the stick used to measure their self-worth. If a pimp or a drug dealer or a con-artist were to lose all of their material gains, recovery would be tremendously difficult because they failed to capitalize on their God-given talents or other fruitful opportunities that may have been available to them throughout the course of their lives for the betterment of the greater good. I measure my triumphs by the depths in which I believe in myself.

I consistently challenge and compete with my former self, striving to be a better individual than I was yesterday, knowing that I am a work in progress and am limitless. It is great to know that I am equipped with, or have available to me, the tools of knowledge, strength and determination. Therefore, I am a successful person -- not by definition, but by faith. "Faith is the substance of things hoped for, the evidence of things not seen." (Hebrews 11:1.)

I have abandoned or lost countless material possessions in the midst of the higher and lower moments of life, but I was able to rise in the knowing that I possess something so tenacious that it cannot be taken away or stripped from me. That is dignity. Dignity is a self-esteem and respect that can only be attained through integrity, humility and commitment. Dignity is what allows a person to ask the self -- not "Why me?", but "Why not me?" We are all blessed with the power of choice. I made it a point to consistently choose to do the right thing according to my morals and values.

For me, that meant choosing to be honest and compassionate with myself and all people, and humbling myself enough to take a lowly position in order to benefit the greater good for all or, at least, the majority. Education is extremely helpful and important because it teaches a person how to think, reason, consider, reflect, imagine and, more importantly, believe to expand the mind and elevate the level of consciousness. It was said to me that, if you wanna get out the ghetto, you gotta think bigger than the neighborhood! That's real talk! However, knowledge comes through all types of sources -- not just a book or classroom instruction. Some must learn and acquire through life's lessons because, unfortunately, extended education in America is a privilege and not a right. A silver spoon was merely a piece of tableware in my house, but I never used that as an excuse to be angry with the world or keep myself down.

My mother made me fully aware that gifts do not come from man, but from above; and I understood that the only thing that stands between me and my dreams is me. Girded within this armor of wisdom, I never had an issue working for minimum wage, sometimes less, which I did for a lot of years from the age of 11, because a) it was an honest living; b) I was assisting my mother who already had three jobs because she refused to be categorized as just another welfare statistic; and c) in the long run, I gained knowledge and invaluable work experience that no one can ever take away from me. I learned the importance of punctuality since I had people depending on me; I learned how to be detail-oriented and trustworthy by counting money and balancing a cash register ledger; I learned organizational skills by sorting mail and filing; I learned discretion by being entrusted with important documents; I learned customer service skills and patience by answering telephones and assisting irate customers; I learned the power of teamwork when there were deadlines to meet; I learned discipline and professionalism by not losing my head when things did not necessarily go the way I would have liked them to. Therefore, working for $3.35, per hour, made me a success by far.

Moreover, I believe that so long as I do my best and toil with reverence, then the dreams that I am chasing will turn around and chase me. It is true that we reap what we sow, so it is imperative that we exercise discernment when planting our seeds. Seeds take root and grow. I took the time to figure out what I wanted to see take root and grow in my life. What kind of karma did I want to create? A man will be rewarded according to his deeds. Yes, that's what my mama told me, and Jesus told her. So, I believe it! Keep in mind, however, the rewards may not appear over night, so nothing done is so in vain, but things hoped for will definitely manifest at the divinely appointed time. I believe that because my intentions were always focused on doing what is right and being of service to others, a certain Angel entered into my life. This Angel was disguised as a person, a friend and mentor sent for the purposes of taking me off the horizontal path and placing me on a vertical one of professional growth. This person saw something in me that I failed to see in myself. This person noticed something right in all the wrong I thought I may have done. This person had the ability to change my life and shape my future into something my mind conceived, which was within my grasp but not completely within my reach. This person sought to find the leader in me, when all the while I was acting merely as a follower. This Angel called himself Joe. Joe saw that I possessed a certain quality that God had given him the power to assist me in cultivating.

He took me under his wing and taught me all that I would need to know to lead a staff of 33 in a prestigious Manhattan law firm, with no college education or supervisory experience. And whatever Joe could not teach me himself, he made possible through outside sources by sending me to management seminars, technical demonstrations and classes to strengthen my talents and professional skills. Oftentimes, he would just throw me in the Board room full of people having two or three degrees under their belts, using words that I could only understand by relating it to the context of their sentences -- having full confidence in me -- knowing that if I could not fly, I would grow wings and soar. Hence, the term -- "Just wing it!" Today, I have since relocated to California from the East Coast, and am a successful Legal Secretary, Administrative Confidential Employee, for the County of Santa Clara, Office of the County Counsel.

I never did attend college, but I do make more money than some college graduates and am able to maintain a comfortable lifestyle. This is because I am reaping the benefits of the seeds which I have sewn in the past - the seed of dignity, by working with integrity and humility; and the seed of commitment, by staying consistent in my employment, having been working in the legal field since the age of 17, starting as a file clerk/receptionist working my way up, over the years, to a Secretarial Supervisor.

However, every person has within them a divine discontent that is designed to say, "Hey, don't stop there!" Thus, I know it is never too late to be the person I always wanted to be, and the possibilities are endless. So, at the age of 34, and a single parent myself, I am now studying to take and pass three College Level Examination Program ("CLEP") tests, which will afford me the opportunity to sit for the Law School Admission Test ("LSAT"), and upon obtaining an acceptable score, I plan to attend the Lincoln Law School of San Jose, a California Bar Examiners approved law school, in the Fall.

If I work hard, study diligently, and remain committed to my goals, which I intend to do, after completing the four years of the requisite evening classes, I will be eligible to take the California Bar examination. By the age of 39, which is still young by the way, I will be a licensed, practicing California attorney, and who knows what comes next . . . a Judge at 50?

-Cassaundra M. Foster

The Question

10th Anniversary Edition

> A teacher affects eternity; he can never tell where his influence stops.
> -Henry Adams (1838 - 1918), *the Education of Henry Adams*

For most of my life I was able to "coast" my way through school. I usually made B's and C's with little effort. I was content with just sliding through and never gave much thought as to what would occur after high school. After graduation, my initial plan was to make money so I found a manual laborer job packing meat at a local meat distributor. I quickly found out that the hours were long and hard. The factory was kept just above freezing and for most of the day; I remained wet from the steam emanating from the huge ovens, which baked hams and sausages before they were packed for shipping. It was a cold miserable job with only one consolation - it paid well.

After a summer of misery, I decided that perhaps going to college would not be so bad after all. I hurried home to inform my mother of my decision and as expected, she seemed pleased and drove me to the local community college to register for my first semester of classes. While standing in the long lines waiting to see the registrar, I began wondering about my future and for the first time seriously began thinking about what I wanted to do with the rest of my life. Paging through the brochure, examining all of the courses and fields of studies listed, and my mind began to wander as I envisioned myself in any number of jobs. Suddenly, in the middle of my daydream; I realized that I was next in line to meet with a counselor. Because I was unsure as to what major endeavor I wanted to pursue, the counselor suggested that I enroll in the "liberal arts" program. I agreed and my first class curriculum consisted of Intro to Computers, College Algebra, Intro Sociology, and English Lit 101.

After an expensive trip to the bookstore to purchase my books, with a rejuvenated attitude carrying my new enrollment packet under arm, I journeyed home happy in the knowledge that this was a positive step towards embarking into my future. Strangely enough, I didn't sleep that night. I began to wonder if I had made the right decision. I started second guessing myself and even began to think about canceling my classes and returning my books.

After a night of tossing and turning I made a decision that I would go to classes for one week and if I didn't like it, I would withdraw from school and return to work. The night before my first class was to begin, uncertainty set in with a vengeance once more causing me a restless night with much tossing and turning. I began wondering "would I fit in? Would I be able to do the work?"

Before long it was morning, I was both nervous and excited intermittently, as I walked to class. I arrived in class and much like in high school; I chose a seat in the back of the room. The classroom filled quickly and because I was attending a community college, the class was mixed with a diverse bunch of students. Some of the students appeared to be in their thirties and had returned to school, some were single moms, there were some foreign students and then there were also 18-21 year old kids like me there. I still felt a little uneasy, but now I was more excited that I was actually attending my first college class.

The Instructor came in; she wore glasses and her hair was in a bun. I immediately took note that she had a beautiful smile. For some reason, maybe it was the way she carried herself, she had a warm loving glow about her, which immediately reminded me of my mother. I began to relax.

She wrote her name on the board, Dr. Vivian B. Ford. Just as quickly, the smile was replaced with a no-nonsense litany as she began to lay down the laws of her classroom. You 'could not be late" she exclaimed "lateness will not be tolerated; work assignments must be completed on time". Dr. Ford began to explain her absence policy when I suddenly remembered why I didn't like school – 'it was all of the rules"! I actually began wondering about the hassle of withdrawing from my classes.

As I tuned back into Dr Ford's lecture, she wrote on the chalkboard "I Can't " in big letters and explained that these words 'will not" be allowed in her classroom.

The first exercise Dr. Ford gave us was to have each student stand up and say his/her name. There were about twenty students in the room so one by one, we all stood and stated our names. After the last person was done, Dr Ford asked for a volunteer. A girl sitting in the front of the class raised her hand and was selected by Dr Ford. The girl was then asked to recite everyone's name in the class. I began to snicker because I didn't think that she would be able to recite everyone's name. Much to my chagrin, Dr. Ford heard me snicker and asked me to recite everyone's name. I stood up feeling a little embarrassed, and with a nervous smile on my face, I began to recite the few names that I could recall.

At some point, I came across a student's name who I didn't remember and I began to say "I can't remember" but suddenly my eyes focused on the words "I can't", which were written on the 'words not allowed" list on the board. So thinking fast, I wittily proclaimed "I can not remember everyone's name". The class laughed and I thought I was really smart because I had found a way around the "I can't" rule. The class continued, I received my course itinerary and before long the class was dismissed.

On my way out, Dr. Ford informed me that she wanted to see me in her office. I had a sinking feeling in my gut as I said "okay" and proceeded to her office. I sat in Dr. Ford's office for what seemed an eternity but was actually only about ten minutes. Looking back, I remember gazing at all of the books on the shelves and at her degrees hanging on the walls. As I anticipated how much trouble I was in, Dr. Ford appeared at the door. She sat down, took out a piece of paper, scribbled something down on it and handed the paper to me. She simply looked at me and told me to read the note later then dismissed me. I remember that I left Dr. Ford's office feeling relieved at the time but I was curious about the paper.

Since I had another class I had to hurry to, I forgot about the paper until later. After dinner that night, I suddenly remembered the paper, which I dug it out of my pocket. On that note was a simple question Dr. Ford had written which changed my life forever:

"Why do you choose to be mediocre? When you are not."

That thought-provoking note inspired me to apply myself and I made the Dean's list that semester. Dr. Ford really inspired me in many ways that day. She was the first person of color I had ever met with a PhD.

Ultimately, Dr. Ford became a close family friend and as she was then, she continues to be a role model for me. Every now and then when I am tempted to give less then 100% in any effort, I am always reminded of that note tucked safely in my wallet.

-Courtney Gale

10th Anniversary Edition

The Dangerous Curve of the Slippery Slope

"Alright. I want to discuss this matter from the perspective of the material we covered yesterday. This topic permeates a variety of issues. Let's talk about how this theory plays out with some programs." Uh, oh. I sense a sharp detour ahead and can smell the faint stench of glossy statistics. I will be one happy person when I walk across that stage. "Take Head Start for example. We our spending millions on these programs with the hopes of change, but what can we really expect?" Oh, boy. Here we go again for the millionth time. If I don't look at him, maybe he will look the other way and move towards the windows. Just look down at the paper and pretend to be taking notes.

"We can not alter or modify our genetic make up." Is it getting warm in here?

If I take off my sweater, it may get his attention and he will move towards me and look into my eyes. Hide the truth. Just sit still. Maybe it is not so hot in here. I wish I could stand up and tell the people who are seeking a reaction from me to stop staring because they're wasting their time.

"Some people have difficulty accepting scientific data."

Science? Science? So science, professor, makes it alright. What about reality in the face of s-c-i-e-n-c-e.? What kinda science is this? This science is not for me. "According to the Bell Curve.." Man, class won't be over for another thirty minutes. My ears are ringing. I don't care about your bells, his bells or anyone else's for that matter.

As a young student fresh into my twenties, I spent several wasted weeks as an academic hostage within the lofty world of one memorable professor's kingdom. I was one of a tiny few number of blacks who had the misfortune to grace his domain. This particular professor relished any and every opportunity to discuss the now infamous, debunked Bell Curve theory of intelligence as it relates to minorities. The Bell Curve espouses, essentially, that blacks achieved lower scores when compared to whites on standardize intelligence tests and these differences are primarily a function of genetics. While I am not an acclaimed research scholar, even at that age, intuitively and based on my numerous personal experiences with the population advocates of this theory sought to denigrate, I knew the truth of the matter.

Proponents of this science joyfully welcomed every opportunity to eradicate or marginalize any social responsibility for the conditions, academic or economic of particular groups. For some, this theory also offered a convenient -scientifically supported- option to curtail any efforts to level the playing field. If one accepts that environmental variables have little or no influence on potential achievement then necessarily, enrichment or social programs are doomed to failure and those minorities who exceed beyond their genetic limitations are rare exceptions to the general rule.

Because this particular professor spent an inordinate amount of his lecture time on this theory without providing a reasonable counterbalance, I was suspicious of his desire to have us accept his assertions as gospel.

What about the basic tenants of higher education, namely, to encourage debate, free thought, and dialogue? Had he provided balance, perhaps his lectures would have had the appearance of some level of legitimacy. To justify the need to once again cover this theory in nauseating detail, he would comically struggled to establish a fictional bridge between this topic and what should have been the subject of the day with some artificial glue of logic.

The mere presence of blacks in the classroom, combined with the dictates of academic integrity and psychological sensitivity demanded alternative viewpoints. If there were at least five or seven blacks in this large class, would he have been so carefree and academically negligent in his teachings? Probably not or perhaps. I expected more from someone whose mission at that time appeared to be rooted in advocacy as opposed to education.

Despite my youth, I was not a blank slate and had enough sense not to allow these "lectures" to influence me to leave college, toss my books into the some trash bin and head for the nearest cotton-picking, pancake- mixing employment opportunity. I had an uncompromising belief in my abilities and knew not to allow another person dictate my level of expectation or restrict my dreams.

Likewise, I appreciated the peril of embracing corrosive fiction that is the genesis of debilitating stereotypes and the danger of allowing small increments of this philosophy to permeate my conscious. To do so, would have placed me on a hazardous slippery slope toward a path of destruction. This path would have forced me to abdicate any responsibility for my life plans. I knew that social conditions can have a marked impact on intellectual development. Where did I draw the strength to combat the constant exposure of negativity as a result of this particular classroom experience? I relied heavily on the positive experiences derived from my other courses and my personal experiences outside of college. I was attentive enough to recognize that our society's history is replete with examples of how racial minorities have achieved beyond their immediate surroundings and expectations.

I also had enough of a spiritual based to appreciate the limitations of man. The IQ is a man-made construct that must yield to the limitations of its creator. Efforts to identify or categorize pure predicts of intelligence will always fail because human beings are ill-equipped to ascertain the exact formula for determining how multifaceted experiences specifically influence an individual. Determination and desire can ruin any elaborate, intricate, well-researched, purportedly empirical predictor of ability.

People should use their past experiences as a tool for addressing strengths and weaknesses and seek to improve in those areas necessary for achieving a particular goal. It is and has always been dangerous for racial minorities, women and the economically disadvantaged to embrace, without question, someone else's prescription for achievement. Intelligence tests measure the performance of an individual at that particular point in time based on a multitude of variables-including whether the test taker had a bad breakfast, had any food at all that day or if personal experiences impede one's ability to formulate and produce an appropriate response to a particular task.

The IQ provides the assessor with a picture of that person on that particular day, beyond that, and barring extremes that reflect pathology, it is not and should not have been used as an absolute, irrefutable predictor of future accomplishments. People should seek to have faith in what they intrinsically know to be their abilities. Young people should combine this understanding with their interests, develop educational plans to enhance their knowledge and utilize this formula for success. In doing so, one can avoid the dangerous, slippery slope of prejudice and bias such that when sophisticated, muted barks of negativity seeks to insult one's intelligence the subconscious voice will cry -Whatever, professor.

-Laverne Lewis Gaskins

10th Anniversary Edition

The Fear of Being Labeled Smart

Some people consider their four years of high school to be the best time of their life. For me, high school was simply a means to an end, a stepping-stone on my way to college. I honestly can't remember a lot of things that occurred during those four years that didn't pertain to academics. However, I do clearly recall the social stigma that was associated with success as well as the barriers that prevented many from realizing their full potential.

When I began attending James Logan high school in Union City, California, my level of comprehension far surpassed the coursework I received, so much so that I was soon placed in honors curriculum. When that transition took place, it was literally as if I had left one world and entered a new one as the images around me changed drastically. For instance, before my acceptance into the honors society, I was surrounded by gang violence, drug use, and teenage pregnancy. I will never forget the astonishment that came over me at the age of fourteen as I sat next to an eight-month pregnant classmate of the same age. I felt a similar sense of shock when I was asked by one of my fellow classmates to simply exchange, a packet of marijuana for cash in his absence. Situations that I had once saw only on television, were now taking place right in front of me. Despite my negative surroundings, I actually received a lot of respect from my fellow classmates who admired my hard work and achievements. I honestly didn't consider my accomplishments as proof of intellectual superiority given that I was able to befriend a lot of my peers and therefore gain insight into some of the reasons why they were not also excelling academically.

Unfortunately, many of them were either from broken or dysfunctional homes and did not receive the support and encouragement that is often necessary for one to succeed. I believe that everyone is blessed with the ability to accomplish great things, but without the proper motivation and cultivation of one's personal gifts and talents, that ability can and will cease to exist. Ironically, many of my peers in the honors society who had been fortunate enough to escape adverse conditions and had been granted the opportunity to cultivate their talents and intellect, did not fully appreciate the position they were in. I found that many of my African-American peers in particular would down play their achievements as to not be considered an overachiever or worse, the teacher's pet.

Although they would exhibit their exemplary skills inside the classroom, outside they chose to present quite a different image. For instance, rather than utilize the same impressive vocabulary spoken around teachers, excessive profanity was the preferred method of communication when interacting with friends. Thus, instead of sharing their knowledge with others, they chose to hide it as if it were something to be ashamed of. Fear of being labeled smart, was practically synonymous with the fear of being labeled, White-washed. I remember being teased and ridiculed by members of the African-American Student Association (AASA), who felt that I wasn't down, or Black enough, simply because I chose to speak proper English. Even some of my African-American honors society counterparts failed to accept and support me because I didn't adhere to the unspoken, keep it in the classroom, policy they had chosen to follow. Unfortunately, it seems that the youth of today have forgotten about what it means to be African-American.

The strong sense of pride, determination, and achievement that our ancestors tried so desperately to instill in us has somehow become lost in society's current definition of victory. Examples of greatness such as W.E.B. DuBois, Madame C.J. Walker, and Martin Luther King, Jr. have been thrust into the shadows as rappers, actors, and sports figures have now become the new prototypes for success. Because of this, many now see money, material possessions, and the lavish lifestyles of celebrities as signs of achievement instead of the mere attainment of personal goals. Consequently, intelligence is rarely toted as a valuable tool for building a successful future.

Being smart isn't considered a cool thing, which is why many youth turn to alternative methods for gaining fame and respect. Things such as dating, clothes and other material possessions take precedence over academic excellence as many try to emulate the images of success that they see on television.

The desire for popularity and social acceptance therefore overpowers the desire for academic achievement. Many become so overwhelmed by pressures to fit in that they either try desperately to hide the fact that they are smart, or give up aspiring to be smart altogether. Although the fear of being labeled smart, did not cause me to stop striving for success, it did cause me to withdraw from my peers. I turned down an invitation to join the AASA because I didn't want to be scrutinized or criticized for who I was. Looking back on that situation, I wish I had been courageous enough to stand up against the immature and misguided beliefs of my peers.

Why couldn't I have held my head up high and explained to them that my Blackness wasn't defined by how many slang terms I used, nor was my dialect a symbol of White-washing? I didn't and still don't understand why many have chosen to associate ignorance and negativity with the concept of Blackness. It wasn't until I entered college that I began to feel comfortable interacting with my African-American peers on a social level. That is because I was no longer criticized by them for being considered smart or expressing my intelligence. I believe that is because most people who attend college understand the struggle and determination it takes to get there. Far too many of us had witnessed an unfortunate number of our high school classmates drop out or be held back due to the fact that they didn't have the grades to advance to the next level. Being labeled smart suddenly became cool because it became evident that hard work was the only means to a successful end. This is a hard concept for many youth to grasp because it is often difficult for them to realize that there exists a world beyond high school and that what makes one appear cool today, will be of little or no significance tomorrow. As a society, we must demonstrate to the youth of today that true success is not defined by outer appearances, but rather the satisfaction and sense of achievement one gains from accomplishing their goals.

Although there is nothing wrong with the pursuit of money and material possessions, academic excellence should be toted as a viable means of attaining these things. Being a rapper, an actor, or an athlete is cool, but so is being a scientist, a lawyer, or a teacher. We must therefore place more emphasis on the benefits one can reap from performing well academically in order to change society's concept of coolness. African-American children in particular need to be reminded of their ancestors, many of whom were intelligent inventors and scholars who made great sacrifices so that they too could see their dreams come to fruition. By helping the youth realize their talents and encouraging them to believe in their dreams, the fear of being labeled smart will begin to fade, and we'll see an entire generation of youth prosper.

-Halima Lee

10th Anniversary Edition

Education From The Catbird Seat

As a student growing up in the New York City public school system in the turbulent 1960's and 1970's, my educational experience was non-eventful. My parents had just bought a home in an all-white area so that I would have a shot at quality education because the neighborhood, from which we'd moved, had begun to deteriorate by the day. The big things then were young people shooting heroin and attending "pot parties," and my dad did what he could to ensure that his little girl wouldn't partake of either!

The move to the new area was ordinary—except for a few of the white neighbors who circulated a petition for the others to sign demanding that we sell our home. My parents got wind of it, and their attempts were quelled very quickly.

When it came to school, that went well because my mother was prepared for everything the officials could throw at her. All of the documentation was in order; she informed them that I would be bringing a homemade lunch to school everyday, and that I had a good father who worked. Whatever myths they had about children of color were squashed within minutes. After that, my parents made every meeting, performance, and parent-teacher's conference—so they knew that I wasn't the student to mess with. In fact, my mother was up there so regularly keeping them in check that they offered her a job!

All of my relatives on my father's side were educators, so that was the song my father sang most often to me: become a teacher because it's secure and I'd get a pension. Of course, *none* of that mattered to me. To my way of thinking, I was a maverick, and the last thing I wanted to do was teach! I defied him and insisted that I wanted to become a writer.

However, I did it his way and took enough classes to enable me to fall back on teaching if times got rough, but I changed my major back to journalism because that, I felt, was my true calling. Little did I know that some years later, I'd wind up teaching in the New York City public school system.

I taught on all levels: elementary school, middle school, and high school, but it was my experience in elementary school that was most memorable. I'd heard about an opening in a school up in the South Bronx. A friend of mine worked there, and she told him about me, and he called me for an interview. It went well, and when he read my writing and editing background on my resume, he told me that he would rather give me an "out-of-classroom" position instead of my having a regular class all day. He asked me if I would set up a Writing Lab for the top upper grade students and filter in the slower students. Of course, I jumped at that chance, thinking what a great opportunity to do something meaningful. However, I had absolutely no idea what I was in for. It wasn't as easy as getting the program operational and teaching the students.

The first tip-off should have been when he told me not to expect much out of the children because they weren't very bright and they had lots of issues. I guess that I didn't pay any attention to that because those words were negative, and I didn't want to greet my new students with any preconceived notions about them—especially bad ones. Also, he told me that many of them didn't speak English well and were bilingual. On and on he went about why the children were destined to fail. I politely shook my head or told him I understood, but I really didn't. Those were children of his nationality, and as the head of that school, he set the tone for the teachers and them. He was supposed to be a role model and mentor for the students, I thought.

Certainly, my uncle who had been a principal for many years was that and more, I remembered. If the principal of that school didn't believe in the students, who would?

Still, much of what he said went over my head because I believed that if the children functioned at the bottom of the district, there was a reason. I didn't believe the fault was theirs, but it had to do with either poor administration or being constantly told they couldn't do any better--or both. I was young and idealistic and full of positive thinking—thanks to parents who told me that I could do anything I set my mind to. In my mind, so could those children—if only they had someone to challenge them.

As it was, they had to deal with problems that children shouldn't have to even know about. After nightfall, warring drug dealers would have shootouts that would leave holes the size of baseballs in my blackboards. One student wrote compelling compositions about how his brother was involved in the underworld of drugs, guns, and bootleg everything, and his enemies frequently burst in their home in the wee hours of the morning to find him. He wrote that his brother escaped to a passageway hidden under the floor. He said that he'd lie in bed and shake and cry until it was over. Behaviorally, he was a terror and after reading that, I understood why! Another student was homeless and slept in a car every night until school began each morning. Their issues were endless, and many of them had grown up far before their time.

Before I went into the newly created Writing Lab, I prayed and asked for guidance, strength, and wisdom because I wasn't sure that it was only the kids who would get an education. Instinctively, I felt they'd teach me a thing or two! And they did. They were receptive to my teaching them the writing process. They worked hard, behaved, and cranked out wonderful poems, raps, short stories, and essays.

Several of my co-workers were envious that I was brand-new to the school and had an "easy" assignment, but what they didn't know, is that I saw fifty-one kids a day, and I was exhausted by three o'clock. Not only was I reading their writings, but they were telling me what was going on in their lives through their pieces, and some of them came to me for advice. Some of what I heard should have been reported to the child welfare authorities, because many of their lives were endangered and teachers were mandated reporters. However, my hands were tied because we were forbidden to report anything –as bad as it was. We were forced to take a "see and don't see" attitude. I begged to differ with the nay Sayers: my job may have looked cushy, but it was <u>far</u> from easy.

On the flip side, it was rewarding because the students achieved the impossible. They performed at a level that no one had expected. I remember that on my first day, I laid down the ground rules and let them know that we were going to work hard and that misbehavior would be dealt with–not tolerated. I also let them know that we'd be doing some interesting things together, and that they would do it well.

I'll never forget the one boy who asked me why was I so sure they would do well when everyone else (their past and other teachers) told them that neither they were nothing and would never amount to anything, nor could they do anything right.

That was the beginning of my speech about positive thinking and how in real life, there were some people who always expected others to fail for various reasons, but they'd have to fight twice as hard to win. He cocked his head to the side, deep in thought, and he said, "I like you Ms. Brooks, I want to win." I told him that he was already a winner, and that only <u>winners</u> could participate in the writing lab.

From that day on, the students were given pep talks on excelling and how to be the best at whatever they set out to do. They came into the Writing Lab with a new zeal and they wrote with passion. Every lesson had some type of theme or historical references that would make them appreciate their various Hispanic cultures or those of others. It was easy to see positive changes in their thinking and great improvement in their writing skills.

Their confidence was at an all-time high, so I felt it was time to put it to the test. I asked them if they would like to write something for the upcoming Bronx Boroughwide and Citywide Writing Contests. Everyone said yes, so each of the five classes worked diligently on their submissions—writing, rewriting, editing, and revising them several times until they were as clean as possible. They wished each other luck, and their submissions were sent in.

They were forgotten and we went on with other writings and

reviewing how to write essays so they'd ace the upcoming citywide writing test. By that time, I had acquired several new students whose parents heard about the success of the Writing Lab and they demanded that their children be placed in it. They blended in well with my multi-hued students, and we kept on working.

One day, I got summoned to the Main Office. The secretary handed me a letter saying that not one—but eleven of my students—had won the Bronx Boroughwide Writing Contest! One of the eleven took the top award and won the Citywide Writing Award as well. She was to receive her award in a special ceremony from then-Mayor David I. Dinkins at City Hall. To say that I was outdone and totally shocked was an understatement!

I asked a friend to read that letter and tell me what it said. I thought my eyes deceived me. She did and they hadn't.

Elated, I couldn't wait to tell the students and congratulate them on a job well done. Approximately one fifth of my students had won awards. The word of their success spread around the school like proverbial wildfire. Some people wished us congratulations, and some gave us the screw face. I told the students to expect anything because there would be some unhappy people, so that led to a short discussion about jealousy. But I told them to be proud of what they accomplished because they had done the work and that it was in them all the time. The problem was that no one had ever demanded their best or challenged them to do anything other than achieve the bare minimum as they'd done for years.

Word of their wins brought the brass from the District office to meet them and me and bring deliver their kudos in person. They went on to say how that level of achievement had never been done and that that district was thought of as one of the lowest performing ones academically. They were beside themselves with joy. Such an achievement called for a party—a celebration of the finest kind, so I sprang for a cake, food, music, sparkling cider, and the works. The students were worth the expense and I wanted them to have the best. I wanted them to see that yes, they could achieve beyond their wildest imaginations—if they worked hard—which they had. We took photos and invited their parents, the District Office bigwigs, and the principal to share in their celebration.

It was quite an emotional day for all, but as the teacher, I couldn't show but so much.

I had to keep them in check for fear that tears of joy would have been my undoing in the future whenever I had to discipline them. Many times, students use emotions against the teachers and they pay for having shown them the rest of the school year when the students disrespect them or won't listen to their authority. For that reason, I couldn't risk what I had already built up.

The students accepted their awards, and the one student with the double win, got dressed up in her new fancy clothes, and went to City Hall--where she met the mayor and accepted her award. I had planned to go with her (since I'd been personally invited) to cheer her on, but the principal commandeered my invitation and went! He went because he wanted to network and meet the mayor and "stick his chest out" as if he'd worked with her and the others to achieve winning the awards. I was ballistic about that because his motives were less than honorable and were selfish in nature, but it wasn't about me. It was about the children who had been lost for so long because of his low opinion of them and his doubting they could do anything right. I was happy that they had a better opinion of themselves and that they didn't have to be ashamed because they lived in many of the projects in the area. They had an increased self-esteem and it began to spill over into other parts of their lives. *That* was what I wanted for them, so as far as I was concerned, their participation in the Writing Lab was a success.

Those same students went on to rock the school singing in the gospel choir we created. They were acting in an original musical for Black History Month and the music teacher refused to rehearse the songs with them because he hadn't initiated the project. They were very upset, because he voiced his negativity about their "trying to sing" blah blah blah. I called them together and told them to ignore that noise.

I asked them if they wanted to sing and they said yes, so I told them they would.

We all came in early the next day, and like in Brooklyn Boroughwide Chorus, I tested their voices, put them in their proper vocal group, and rehearsed their parts with them. We worked before and after school for several weeks until they had the songs and the harmony perfect.

One of my friends there knew a pianist, and she had him to come in a few times so they'd have a piano to rehearse with, since they'd only sung acappella. As the day of the play approached, they knew they were ready and I told them "to break a leg" and to sing the roof off that school because we had a point to prove.

That day came, and those children did indeed rock the house. They sang as if their lives depended on that performance. They tried to sing the roof off the building. The result of all their hard work earned them a rousing standing ovation and positive words from the District muckety-mucks who'd attended at our invitations. Again, the principal beamed with pride because his school was standing out yet again. The staff stood in disbelief that the kids sang like that. Many congratulated them; others didn't. They just stood on the fringes finger-pointing and saying bad things. The music teacher looked sheepish and made a smart comment. I told him that I wasn't going to deny those kids a chance to perform onstage because *he* wouldn't rehearse them—that there was more than one way to skin a cat. So I found it!

The moral of that experience is that children are like sponges. They will soak up what we adults give them—good or bad. If we tell and show them that they are beautiful, worthy, and can excel at whatever they do, they will believe it. They will do it.

I am proud to say that in the case of my students, they needed some serious reprogramming about their level of academic achievement and how to change it from the negative to the positive.. They performed better than they ever had on the Writing Test, and they finally believed that they didn't have to let life's circumstances or poverty keep them down. They knew that they were intelligent and could perform at the highest level academically. They had proven everyone wrong and had shown them that they had what it took to excel.

For me, that was what it was all about!

-Nathasha Brooks-Harris

10ᵗʰ Anniversary Edition

Lighthouse in the Storm

Mrs. Wilkerson, Junior High School Guidance Counselor

Every adult who has achieved some level of success in life is indebted to someone who has inspired, encouraged and believed in them. My parents and other family members were among those who inspired me. But Mrs. Wilkerson, my junior high school guidance counselor, inspired me in ways I never realized until decades later. I want to share how Mrs. Wilkerson inspired me, what it has meant to me, and how, like a lighthouse shining on a stormy sea, her encouragement guided me on my life journey.

During my junior high school years, the uncertainty, drama, and insecurity of puberty was further complicated by the apprehension of no longer walking down to the corner to school, as I had done all through elementary school. Now I would have to walk a few miles into uncharted, unfamiliar neighborhoods to reach my new school destination, Garfield Junior High School (since renamed Martin Luther King Junior High.)

The place was Berkeley, California, circa 1964. Teachers, mostly women, still dressed in suits, pearls and high heels; all adults were respectfully called Mr., Miss or Mrs.; and all adults in authority still commanded respect. I arrived at Garfield Junior High School as a shy, obedient, and academically excellent student.

During the fifth and sixth grades at my elementary school, Franklin Elementary School, an experimental academic tracking program had placed me in the highest track, the trapezoids. The academic tracking program was, in part, preparation for the citywide integration program that would have students from all over the city integrated into one school for ninth grade, and rezoned into other junior high schools in the seventh and eighth grades. I was diverted from my working class neighborhood junior high school, Burbank-- which was to become the new ninth grade-only school, to the seventh-eighth grade school in a predominantly white middle class neighborhood, Garfield. In preparation for the experience of junior high, in addition to the academic tracking in the fifth and sixth grades, we had to change classrooms and teachers in periods of study. Presumably, this early practice in changing classrooms and teachers would get us used to changing classes in junior high, and give us additional mental and emotional capacity for dealing with the school racial integration that was to come in the seventh grade. The assistance and support of a guidance counselor was to help us make a smooth transition to a more integrated school.

In every year of elementary school, I received good grades, good citizenship marks, and wanted to be just like my teacher. As it happened, I had female teachers from kindergarten through sixth grade, and I even had teachers of color, including Chinese, Hawaiian and Latino. But I never had an African American teacher.

The ultra-liberal reputation Berkeley has enjoyed over the years as a college town in the shadows of U.C. Berkeley, did not rebuke the harsh realities of a society that resisted the progress that the Civil Rights movement sought to redress. I recalled vividly being spat on, called the "n" word, and being chased down the street on my way to and from my piano lessons. A sense of dread sat with me as I graduated from elementary school, and knew that the relative safety of my own neighborhood could be taken away at any moment. After all of the classroom preparation for the differences I would face in the new junior high school in an unfamiliar neighborhood, imagine my surprise to be assigned to a black guidance counselor, and a woman at that! Mrs. Wilkerson was the first black female authority figure I ever interacted with outside of my family. In those pre-Black Power, Black Pride days, I idolized everything about her. As if she could sense my adoration, she took me under her wing and made me feel as though I was a special person assigned to her, and who she needed to treat with extraordinary care.

Immaculately dressed, Mrs. Wilkerson stood out in her Kaldor knit suits; Doris Day plain black pumps; perfectly coifed, Jackie Kennedy style flip hairdo with every straightened hair in place;

conservative, black-rimmed reading glasses; minimal and tasteful makeup on her smooth, medium-brown skin; short, plain and manicured nails; and her ever-present cigarette. All of these attributes combined perfectly to exude an air of authority and supremacy that I both admired and feared. None of the perverted school relationships of today, bereft with pedophiles, child abusers and the like, figured into the picture of student-teacher or student-counselor relationships back then. Relationships were formal and adequately at a distance. I never knew anything about Mrs. Wilkerson, not even her first name, and there was no need for me to talk to her outside of her office. I knew and she knew that her role was to guide my educational journey, and my role was to follow her lead.

I came to her office as the consummate bookworm who always received good grades, worked hard, liked school, and as a reader and not a talker, I never stood out as someone who could be considered leadership material. Some of my classmates called me sidity, and I obsessed over the thought that this was a word that was derived by combining my name (Sidalia) and my family nickname (Ditty.) As is often the case, shyness gets misinterpreted as aloofness, a superior attitude or a sedate persona. One of my first conversations with Mrs. Wilkerson was about being called this name, and she assured me that the word had nothing to do with me, and that I should not worry about what other people said about me.

From our conversations, what Mrs. Wilkerson learned about me was that I loved to read, I was a great writer, and good in math, but I did not speak up in class. As one of six children, I had been raised to speak only when spoken to, and that children should be seen not heard. She knew and understood how I came to be so shy. She figured that in large families you have to learn to speak loud at times to be heard, so I had the capacity to speak up in public. She viewed the task of helping me overcome my shyness and fear of public speaking as her personal challenge.

In seventh grade, I did well academically, and I excelled in sports without even trying. During physical education class, my performance in the "President's Council on Fitness" testing, I jumped so far in the long jump, and sprinted so fast that I matched or beat school records. As a result I was invited to participate on the school's track team, as well as a private track club. This early success led Mrs. Wilkerson to give me high praise for performing well and for possessing innate, natural abilities in track. Upon joining the track team I developed through practice and coaching, and became an even better athlete.

Mrs. Wilkerson encouraged my love of reading and recommended books to read. Then, going into the eight grade, Mrs. Wilkerson decided that I needed a new challenge because I needed to keep growing. She asked me to do the unthinkable – join the after school drama club, and perform in a play. She praised my sports participation, and noted that I was getting good grades, but she advised me that my success in life would not be complete unless I learned to speak up with confidence and give people a reason to notice me. She explained in a way, which made sense to me that overcoming my fear of public speaking and trying something that I did not already do as effortlessly as I had done in track and field events would help me learn a great lesson: you never know what you can do until you try. When I tried to explain that I had played violin in the orchestra in elementary school, she acknowledged that performance, but she told me that it was a group performance, not an individual one.

Reluctantly I went to my first drama club meeting with such a feeling of fear and trepidation that I almost turned around and walked out as soon as I entered the auditorium. Not only did I recognize that other students in the club had already performed in school drama productions, but I was the only black student in the room. The spring semester production was to be Shakespeare's "Twelfth Night." At this point in my life, I had never read any Shakespeare plays or sonnets that I understood, and I remembered the one Shakespeare play that I had seen as a movie, "A Midsummer Night's Dream," was totally incomprehensible and boring.

After the initial meetings and auditions, I landed the role of Malvolio, the supporting role of the steward to the Countess Olivia, one of the main characters. Not only would I have to learn the Elizabethan English of Shakespeare, but to add insult to injury, I was going to play the role of a man! The Elizabethan English was as challenging, if not more so, than understanding the King James' version of the Bible. With Mrs. Wilkerson's encouragement to study the words, practice the acting, and keep working until it was done, I persevered and pulled off two performances.

What did I learn from Mrs. Wilkerson? Practice makes perfect. Feel the fear and do it any way. There's nothing wrong with being different. Persistence pays off. Always find ways to stretch and grow. It is not that my parents did not teach me the same values, or want the same successes for me in life. But when someone outside of your family believes in you, supports you, and encourages you to do more, it may be just the extra guiding light to see you through.

-Sidalia G. Reel

Taking It Day By Day

An African-American Women's Experience as A Peace Corps Volunteer In

Namibia, Southern Africa

"Namibia, Southern Africa, the land of contrasts." This popular tourist slogan popped out at me as I read up on the new country that I would call my home for the next 2 years. Mainly referring to the dryness of the Namib Desert and rolling Kavango mountains of green located right next to each other, Namibia truly does live up to her name. Gaining independence only 15 years ago, the stark contrasts also refer to the remnants of the apartheid system and the new hope of freedom. As a Peace Corps PACE (Parents and Communities for Education) volunteer and grade 8 English teacher in the rural town of Omuthiya, I am spending two years in a place where people live in tin shacks next to wealthy game parks, where the rich and beautiful landscape often hides the fact that 20% of the population in Namibia's northern regions are infected with HIV/AIDS and in the midst of all of this negativity, each day my students in my grade 8 English class make me feel like I am truly making a difference in their lives.

After finishing college, I was not quite sure of my next move. I wanted to use my economics degree for something better than sitting in a corporate office and I started looking into community service organizations. This is when the Peace Corps found me. While considering my next move after college, a good friend of mine had just finished her service in Malawi and described it as the best and most challenging experience of her life. After hearing about her experiences as a HIV/AIDS community worker, I believed that I was up for the challenge. Needless to say, my decision to join the Peace Corps received a mixed reaction from my family and friends. Leaving home for two years to volunteer in a foreign land and uncertain circumstances, my parents especially, tried to talk me out of it. But when my invitation to serve in Namibia came in the mail, I knew that this would be an opportunity of a lifetime.

Like many young African Americans, I shared in the grandiose notions of returning home to the "motherland". Setting foot in the capital of Windhoek, Namibia after a 23-hour flight was the most exhilarating experience of my life. My first thought was of how amazing beautiful Namibia was. Arriving at sunset, the palm trees stood in sharp contrast to the purple-blossomed trees and red and orange skyline. I could see all the way to the surrounding green mountains without one tall building blocking my view. At that moment, I knew that I had returned to the place of original creation.

My permanent site is positioned north about 8 hours from the capital city. As we drove through the extravagance and wealth of the capital to my new home in the rural town of Omuthiya, the true reason why we were called to serve in this developing country was revealed.

Namibia, known for her contrasts, disclosed a beautiful landscape filled with people that lived in desperate situations. All along the roads, people lived in homes that were made from tin siding, living 15 people to a small shack. Many homes lacked running water and children are required to walk up to 20 kilometers to carry water back home to their families from the well. But worst of all, the devastation of HIV/AIDS has left many children as heads of their households, begging on the street in rags for food to feed their families. It was at this point, I truly had a feel for the Peace Corps slogan "The toughest job you will ever love". For it was the hardest thing to see such poverty and despair in the midst of such a beautiful landscape.

As a PACE volunteer / English teacher, I have a multi-tasked job of being a grade 8 English teacher, a teacher trainer as well as a consultant on community development projects. Trying to navigate my job through my elementary knowledge of the Bantu-dialect of Oshindonga and lack of resources have proved challenging. Each day one must learn how to share scarce resources with the other teachers and students. In many instances, we are without the proper number of books for the students and lack adequate space to accommodate the ever-increasing population of students that arrive at the school's gate each year.

But the most disheartening part of my job is the lack of motivation or hopelessness that I see in some of the students. Most students are the first generation of children to be educated in their families.

Before independence under the apartheid system, it was illegal for the black population to be educated after grade 8. Coupled with the stifling unemployment and lack of opportunity, most students do not see the importance of education. The extraordinarily high pregnancy and HIV/AIDS rate among the youth speaks to their inability to see any other way out of their poverty.

Nevertheless, for the many hardened students there are, they are always a handful of students that make me feel like I am truly making a difference. These students are the ones that know that getting a good education and passing with high marks are their only way to escape from this debilitating life of poverty. Just the other day, a neighborhood girl proudly showed me her passing marks and revealed her goal to me of becoming a teacher. Her pride and confidence in her ability put a smile on my face and in my heart.

It is moments like this when I know that I was sent here for a purpose bigger than just to teach and do a few development projects. On days when my heart smiles with pride over the children's accomplishments through adversity, I know that God has sent me here to truly make a difference, not in the entirety of Namibia, but in the lives of the children I teach who will grow up strong and confident becoming the leaders of tomorrow and build a nation that we ALL can call "home".

I am unsure of how the rest of my time in Namibia will play out.

The school year is beginning again and I will be faced with new challenges as well as familiar ones. But I am confident not only in my abilities, but also in my students' determination to make their lives better. When I first arrived in Namibia, I talked with former volunteers to find out their secrets for success in the midst of the challenges, and the best advice that I received was to take things day to day. They advised not to try to save the whole world rather make small accomplishments total into large ones in the end. So now, I take everything day to day and hope that the sum of those days will result into something great.

-Jennifer Jackson

It's Okay to Be Smart

In the whole world, you know there are billion boys and girls who are young, gifted and black, and that's a fact! Nina Simone, Weldon Irvine, Jr., 1969.

As a child, I was labeled "smart" and placed in the top or honors level classes, accordingly. I was also in the Special Progress (SP) class, a program in New York City Schools for gifted children, which condensed and accelerated and the 7th, 8th, and 9th grade curriculums into 2 years. It just so happened that I was usually one of a handful of African-Americans in these classes. In addition, I was most often the only one who came from the "*pre-integration*" predominantly white side of the street.

As a result, I was teased, picked on, and downright chastised at times - no, not by the White children in my class, but by my very own brothahs and sistahs in other classes. They thought that I couldn't possibly be truly black, because I was an honor student, I didn't cut class or play hooky, and I completed my assignments on time. Oh, and I also happened to be in those "smart" classes with those white kids. While all forms of racism are appalling, I am repeatedly disheartened by the taunts and accusations posed upon our gifted African-American children - by our own people. Sure, most good students, no matter their race or ethnicity, are ridiculed - they're called nerds, geeks, or eggheads.

The mere fact that intellect is downplayed at all is reprehensible in and of itself. However, when doing your homework, showing up for all classes, and getting an A on your algebra final makes you unblack, then it's just downright absurd. Sure, this is not necessarily the opinion of every black person out there, but we need to acknowledge the fact that it's still prevalent within our community. Yes, folks, our babies are still being made to feel "not black enough" because they "talk propah," and are considered "whitey-fied," because they scored high on their SATs and are going to a good college. Equating intelligence with being white is, in my humble opinion, much like equating light skin with beauty. We all know that neither is a factual tenet, yet these myths live on and on.

What's even worse is that those brave enough to challenge the myth, by using their brains, talent, or skills, are accused of crossing over into Caucasian-land. Why is it that so many of our bright, young princes and princesses are not embraced but instead, outcast, ostracized or overlooked because they opt to spend some of their free time reading, instead of aimless mall-cruising or shaking their booties in "da clubs?" Some would argue that a sad blend of poor self-esteem and jealousy are responsible for the behavior of their tormenters. I would agree to a certain extent, but it goes way beyond that. Centuries of brainwashing have convinced many-a-black-folk that he or she is inherently ignorant and that those who do use their brains are to be punished. Beginning with the white slave owners, the message has been sent throughout history, that African-Americans are of inferior intelligence to other races - especially Caucasians - and therefore thinking and learning were unnecessary. Slaves were not permitted to learn to read or write - those who did were, literally, risking their lives.

One of the largest slave revolts in colonial America was the Stono Rebellion of 1739 in South Carolina. That event, led by a slave named Jemmy resulted, not only in the deaths of several - both black and white, but also paved the way for the "Negro Act", which outlawed, among other freedoms, a slave's right to read. While this legislation began in South Carolina, the Negro Act became the model for slave laws throughout the colonies.

Obviously, reading posed a threat - a threat of knowledge that these white colonists saw as a key to intellectual power that they did not want in the hands of the enslaved Africans. Sadly, we continue to perpetuate the shackling of the gifted within our own communities - long after the slave owners set the tone. I fear that we are in the throes of an era of self-inflicted intellectual slavery.

And in so doing, we are placing ourselves in a most vulnerable space - one in which, new social beliefs, theories, and terms that clearly mock and attack the dignity of African-Americans will continue to arise. For example, ask yourself...how did "Ebonics" move from the urban slang of today's generation (and every generation had its own - bebop, jive, etc.) to a controversial vernacular worthy of scholarly debate? Back in the seventies I had the pleasure of interviewing a popular NYC radio DJ", who told me about the requests that she received from white station executives, to "tone down" her educated vocabulary to her predominantly urban African-American audience. Insulted and angered that once again her people were being assumed ignorant, she adamantly informed the execs, and that if any of her people did not understand her words "then let them learn from me." While her words have stayed with me throughout all of these years, I still, on occasion find myself editing the 4+ syllable words that come out of my mouth, when speaking to my own people.

No, not because I am a snob, but because I spent so many years being chastised for my intelligence, that I fear that "proper speech and big words will make folks think that I am "trying to act white." It has taken me years to confront the Intelligence = White stereotypical formula that was infused into my spirit by my schoolmates, so many years ago. So where did this all lead me? I have had my share of both successes and failures. But most important, I have finally learned to take pride in my intellect.

I cannot pinpoint one major event in my life that kept me from drowning in a sea of unused brain matter. It was more the never-ending, gnawing hunger for knowledge, information, and insight that made me realize that an empty head was as bad as an empty stomach, and I was not about to starve myself to death. It's true that I write these words from the heart and out of my own personal experience, but I write not to complain about being a bright, black child in an environment that challenged the value of that notion. I write these words to share, testify and tell my brilliant young black men and women - it's okay to be smart. In fact, cherish it, embrace it, and for heaven's sake use it. Keeping your nose in a book is no longer a privilege that is only provided to white people, as it was during our ancestor's lifetimes. It's your right, your freedom and your obligation to use the brain that God gave you.

For those who fight to dumb you down, or make you feel that your level of blackness drops with each IQ point over the average, just stand proud and remind them what the United Negro College Fund has been telling us for years: "*A mind is a terrible thing to waste.*"

"Thank you sister Judy"

That summer day in the playground, you infuriated me. My friends were having fun. You wouldn't let me. Until I completed that book about animals and their babies, you kept me there. I didn't care about the cubs, the lambs, the fawns or the foals. But you made me sit there. Determined that I read before I begin school, YOU MADE ME READ THAT DARN BOOK COVER TO COVER!

Okay, so maybe it wasn't so bad, after all. I began to enjoy it. Went on to win spelling bees, Words became my best friends I get the answers right when I watch *Jeopardy* on TV. I should go on that show. Got a scholarship to college. For the full four years. Now I read and I write, and hope that others will read my words. You taught me, my sister Judy, and for that, I thank you.

-Ruth B. Utley

Never

"You have destroyed your life! You will never go to college now. You have ruined your chances of achieving your goals."

Ms. Turner, my guidance counselor, yelled on and on. Her face was distorted and I thought "I better get out of here." I calmly walked to her door and said "Thank you for your time." I didn't know what else to say.

As I walked down the hall I thought maybe she was using discouragement as a way to encourage. It seemed strange, but I had seen and heard stranger things. My life had not been difficult, at least not as I saw it. Yes, I knew the story. My mother and father separated when I was five or six years old. My mother eventually moved to Virginia for better job opportunities and my grandmother (the Boss) thought it best that I stay with her in North Carolina. She felt she could provide a better environment. I was happy with summer and holiday stays in Virginia. I had the best of both worlds; I didn't have to leave my friends and still had my mama. I grew up with my grandmother, uncle and sister.

My sister is ten years older. I had all of my needs and wants met and was happy with my family arrangement. My grandmother was a hard worker and good businesswoman, so financially we did well. However; my grandmother believed in showing her love with material things. She wasn't a hugger or kisser and I was affectionate. This was not good at times when I needed a hug or kiss. As I became older I overheard the adults talking about my mother's health. I knew she wasn't well sometimes, but she never looked "sick" to me. One day my mother told my grandmother she needed a kidney. I wasn't quite sure how important a kidney was, but I offered to give her mine. She smiled and said "Little Papoose, I've lived my life and yours is just beginning. I wouldn't take your kidney."

I said, "O.K., but let me know if you change your mind." and gave her a big hug.

My mother died when I was 15 years old. Things became more difficult for me. I was comfortable with my father not being an active parent (at all), but I didn't know how to deal with not having my mother. It never bothered me when other kids asked "Where's your mom?" I would tell them where she was, in Virginia. Now I had to say, "She's dead." That was difficult for me. It was so final.

Everyone was nice to me and comforting, but it still felt strange. One day I met someone and he became not only my comforter, but my refuge. Too much of a refuge. We became a couple, later became parents and them became "uncoupled." The day Ms. Turner spoke those words to me, I told her I was pregnant. After leaving her office I walked down the hall and was puzzled. Puzzled about how she meant the words and why she spoke them. I ran into Mrs. Dunn. Mrs. Dunn (as was everyone) was use to me smiling. Mrs. Dunn asked, "Why aren't you sunny today?"

I told what happened and about Ms. Turner's comments. She smiled and said, "You can do whatever you want. You can go to college and you will go to college. If you want to be an attorney, you will be one. Nothing or no one can stop you. They never can."

Over the years I've often thought about Ms. Turner's comments for years I would become angry.

I also thought of Mrs. Dunn's comments and used them to succeed. I also thought of my mother. She wanted me to go to college to become a nurse. That was her dream, to become a nurse. She would say a "real nurse". She worked as a home care attendant and died before fulfilling her dream.

I completed my high school education and graduated from college with a B.A. in Administration of Justice and Public Administration. I decided not to go to law school, but that's another story.

I am a Virginia Supreme Court Mediator, Certified Substance Abuse Counselor and Juvenile Probation Officer. Ms. Turner sentenced me to a life of "never", but I overturned Ms. Turner's sentence. I did succeed and now I encourage other young people to do the same; no matter what their situation, circumstance, mistake(s) or obstacles. No matter what you do; what mistakes you make; you can succeed in reaching your educational goals. Whenever I hear 'never', I think 'never quit'. Don't let anyone "sentence" you.

-Felisicia Williams

10th Anniversary Edition

I WAS BLIND, BUT NOW I SEE
AN EDUCATION OF SELF

A few mornings ago, I met a seemingly good-natured woman. Having seen her from a distance on a variety of occasions for many, many years, I never made an attempt to interact. In observing her doing any number of things, I often picture a woman from an African village with the basket atop her head. This particular woman held her head always somewhat bowed, as though her basket were heavy with all her troubles, worries and stress. This particular morning, however, there was something different. She seemed at ease. I guess she'd put her basket down.

Upon making eye contact, I smiled. She smiled back. There was warmth about her. Her eyes smiled today. We exchanged morning pleasantries. I made mention of her haircut, it was becoming. She smiled, reaching up to touch her hair, saying it was new. We fell into a comfortable silence. Then this woman, who I had known for all of two minutes, looked me directly in the eye and said "You are a beautiful, deserving, powerful woman. You are hugely successful and I love you!"

So, now I'm standing there thinking, "Where did that come from? Does she know something I don't?"

While inside, the questions were bouncing around like kids in an astro jump, outside my smile is wrapping around my head, much like the earth spins on its axis. I was both delighted to have met and intrigued by this woman.
Upon reflecting on that special meeting, I began to wonder how it was that this woman could say to me, what I had been secretly,

faintly whispering within for so long. Then, was the question of truth.

Is what she said true?

After further thought and deeper reflection, the answer was (to quote Usher, Little John and Ludacris) "Y-E-A-H!" Our creator had a whole world to put together. You know luminous stars to hang and intricacies to unfold. As such, there was no time to create a nobody. Each of us was very purposely, brilliantly and wonderfully fashioned, to include the gifts weaved into the very fibers of our being. I realized that I met this woman on the way to discovering my gift and purpose. Along the way, I have concluded that I want a J-O-Y, not a J-O-B. And, to have the former, I must share my predestined gift. Through an intrepid utterance, the seed planted in my flowering spirit was watered and the volume on the song inside has been turned up. I am a beautiful, deserving, powerful, successful woman!

Since our first meeting that morning, the divine diva and I hang out all the time. We've developed quite the friendship, through our times spent talking and sharing. Sometimes we listen to music, reflect on various thoughts and events, take walks and sometimes we just sit and enjoy the quiet. We do all sorts of things, this lovely lady and me. I am ever blessed by our closeness.

For whatever reason, sometimes we lose our way and have a hard time getting back on track. Sadly, some of us just give up on ourselves all together. It is my belief that if we spend some time thinking about and, or, remember why we are here, we'll run smack dab into the truism that we all have gifts and we cheat the world by not sharing them.

I was blind, but now I see the gift within and beauty that is me!

10th Anniversary Edition

Oh, by the way, the woman I met...was me! I met myself in the mirror that morning and am so happy to have made my acquaintance.

-Kenya G. Williams

CHAPTER II
~POETIC GUMBO~

"Born of African descent,
I'm predisposed to greatness"

~Beverly Black Johnson

Above and Beyond

Trying to reach the top anyway that I can
Wanting so much to be more than I am
Tooth and nail I struggle as I plan to succeed
Being more than is expected being all that I can be
The potential and qualities to stand out in the crowd
Never been a failure and won't be called one now
I'm moving up slow every bit counts
I'll show this here world what I'm all about
The greater things in life I will achieve
Just keep on looking Watch, you'll see
I'll rise above and start to soar
And while in fight my new wings form
The top is where I'm destined to get
Once there, I won't be removed from it
By any means necessary won't settle for less
Believe that if you never believe anything else
I won't get lost in the crevice of life
Nor will I let time just pass me by
As I look up the distance is far
I'll be there in no time I'm trying so hard
Just when it seems it's far out of reach
God reminds me it's closer than I think

-Kenya D. Acy

Under the Baobab Tree

Come my Children sit with me
Underneath the baobab tree
Listen as I tell a story of generations old,
The tale of Beautiful Africa as I've been told.
My name is Raawiya. It means storyteller, you see.
So, come now and sit with me under the baobab tree.
My story is of Beautiful Africa, the birthplace of all life.
A vast continent of many countries, kingdoms and men of strife.

Africa, the mother of the earth
Where Queens and great women gave birth
To kings, fierce warriors. and wisest of the wise.
Who in battle claimed their Africa as their prize.
As each kingdom established itself
Recognized by its prosperity and wealth,
The people prospered and together grew strong
As they worked to live in peace and in dance and in song.
There were marriages and unions that led to strong bonds
Among the people of Africa's countries and beyond.
Lead by the children of their queens and kings,
Songs of victory and vast conquest they did sing.
Its warriors, the most feared.
Against foreign invasion persevered.
Successful they were until a new invader emerged
Those north of the land of the sun converged
Upon Beautiful Africa like locust on a host
Stealing souls from the motherland only to boast.
Bound with chains on their Ankles and chains at their hands,
Stolen from Beautiful Africa, taken to strange and distant lands.
In the belly of a ship feeling lost, forgotten, and alone.

Sold away from their families so far away from home.

A people lost amongst empty faces.

A child beyond its mother's embraces.

A frighten culture; will they survive?

Those left behind, struggle, determined to thrive.

Hold your head high, do not be throttled by the sail.

Your children, strong by tradition, will prevail.

Beautiful Africa, rich in all tribal glory

Underneath the baobab tree, we will forever retell your story.

The place were all life began

And Sun first shined upon the face of man.

All creatures great and small; the plants, the butterfly;

Man placed as physical master over all.

Through the children of man, life continues its rebirth.

Mankind, the greatest of all to inherit the earth.

Through the watchful eyes of the spirits,

The storyteller tells us to beware.

We are the earth's keepers.

It has been entrusted in our care.

It all began with Beautiful Africa,

a vast land spirited and free.

Underneath the baobab tree.

-Ja Adams

Knew It Was Time

When my first child was born, I knew it was time
To lay down my games and educate my mind
The first thing I did was move in with my grandmother
Her faith and religious believes to me were like no one other
She gave my baby and me a room a place to sleep, a place to groom
She cooked everyday so that we could eat
She would have done anything for me to get on my feet
I registered for College and went everyday
My mission was to learn how to make my own way
As time went on, I began to date
A very nice guy with whom I could communicate
He took me places and made me feel good
Soon he wanted to marry me and move from the hood
I married him and we began our lives
Took classes at night, worked dayshift to survive
Promotions and more babies started to come
Soon there was no time for classes, not even one
Years later with job cutbacks and downsizing trends
I found myself divorced and no way to meet ends
I sat down and thought about what I should do
What were my options now and what was my next move
My life had moved faster than I once thought it would
The education I missed would have helped then I understood I raised my sons and went back to school a little at a time I saw my children graduate and then I finally got mine
A Master's degree the first in my family to do it; my grandmother's faith and my determination I know pushed me through it

H. Renay Anderson

Bridgin' the Gap

To my young generation of black angels and faces
Who weren't here yet to see the racist plays, the "Black Faces"
The "Mammies", "Step 'N Fetchits" and the straight blatant hatred
No blacks hangin' out of trees, swayin' in the breeze
So it's hard to see our appreciation.
We're not livin' in that, so bridgin' the gap is necessary to merge this separation
"Ya'll don't respect us!" "Well, ya'll don't understand us!"
Is it just age or miscommunication?
We depend on *you* to teach what they don't teach us in school
But, let me holla at my young generation
Cuz with a whole new set of issues we facin'
We receivin' a different education.
We know what happened in the hood
But not what happened in Rosewood
And we know about 50 Cent
But not John Carlos and Tommy Smith
And we know all about Tip Drill
But we don't know about Emmett Till
And we faithfully read Vibe
But never heard of Richard Wright?!
I *challenge* us to spark change
To break out of these mental chains!
Tupac said he wouldn't change the world
But guaranteed he'd spark the brain.
That's us, that's our generation, that's me
On behalf of those in the struggle slain
The Huey Newtons, Fred Hamptons, Bobby Huttons
Malcolm Xs, Harriet Tubmans and Dr. Kings.

Gumbo For The Soul

We don't *have* to use the restroom in outhouses
Or drink from "Colored Only" fountains
We don't *have* to go to the back of the bus
Or look down when we respond to whites with "Yes, Suh."
We don't *have* to go to the back of the restaurant
Like animals to pick up our food
And it's damn near not a factor to us
To hang out of a noose.
(Yells) YOUNG PEOPLE!!
Raise your hand if you ever got blasted
Into a concrete wall with a fire hose.
How bout beat to your knees with black eyes and bloody nose
Tryna receive the right to vote?
Don't it almost sound unheard of?!

Oh, but this was cold-hearted reality to our old and departed
And I bet they'd turn straight circles in their grave
To see us right black where we started.
How hard did those before us fight?
Too numerous and hard to know.
Yeah, we've come a long way, but don't stop now!
Cuz we still got so far to go.
We don't need the baton to carry it on
Pick it up if you don't feel like they passed it!
Cuz I can see the underlyin' factors
And I'm finally startin to grow out this relaxer.
We in a state of emergency, LOOK AT STATISTICS
Pay attention to the aids epidemic.
1 out of every 4 black males will go to jail
1..2..3..YOU go to jail, 1..2..3..YOU, you in jail
Till' a fourth of this population's missin'.
UPLIFTMENT, PERSERVERENCE, MOTIVATION, EDUCATION
EMPOWERMENT for my young generation!!
But don't think for a second I'mma close this up

Without hollerin' at the older generation.
To my older generation, first of all, we respect you
We thank you and we honor you today
And we want you to know that Hip-Hop is a culture
Not a means for self-destruction or hate.
Now, I admit that just like every culture or system
It gets imitated and infiltrated
But not every artist you hear is real Hip-Hop
Some are just whack rappers that made it.
CIVIL RIGHTS GENERATION!!
Raise your hand if you can claim
That you and most of your friends
Never met or knew their fathers.
That there was so much drugs and violence
On your way to school
That you almost didn't bother?
Don't it almost sound unheard of?!
Oh, but this is cold-hearted reality
To your grandsons and daughters.
And it reflects in our music, think about it
The lack of mentors and role models.
Hip-Hop is *our* voice, *our* movement, we claim it
We're proud cuz it's something we created.
It's the voice of the streets, the underdog, the oppressed
And it became a universal language.

Jesus Walks, Keep Your Head Up, Ghetto Gospel, Hope
These are songs with immeasurable influence.
And it hurts us to hear you generalize it as ignorant
If you don't truly listen to the music.
Don't shake your head at me disapprovingly
Instead of sittin' me down and schoolin' me
Don't blame *my* generation for N-I-Double G-A

Like *we* the first black people to use it.

Never Ignorant about Getting Goals Accomplished

That's what Tupac meant when he used it.

So before you give up on us, rest assured.

WE STILL PRESSIN' ON WITH THE BLACK MOVEMENT.

-Keyanna Celina Bean

10th Anniversary Edition

I Remember When

One quarter bought a lot of candy from the corner store.
the word technology didn't describe so many different things.
quilts were hand sewn from scrap pieces of cloth.
there were only five channels on the television.
the TV would go off at a certain time each night.
doctors made house calls. votes were properly counted.
leaders fought for justice. children had daily chores in addition to their schoolwork.
children were seen and not heard. children had to be home before the street lights came on.
a paddle was the first thing you saw when you entered a classroom.
everyone took out time to pray in school. there were more schools than jails.
I can even remember when: families prayed for one another.
parents welcomed a neighbor's information about their child, and disciplined them accordingly.
parents knew the value of an education. parents cooked meals for their family daily.
as a society, we honored elders, teachers, and those in authority.
respect didn't even have to be earned! there were no cell phones or pagers not even call waiting.
you would see husbands in the same room with their wives on a TV program but they slept in separate beds.
divorce only happened in Hollywood.
Life began with Love!
What do you remember? and when?

-Elder GiGi Brown

My Road to PhD

When I was young school was cool
The work was easy and I was on the honor roll
One of the popular girls and a cheerleader to boot it was all-good until
I transferred to Catholic High School life changed in the 10th grade
School became torture surrounded by rich white kids,
Nuns and priest telling me what to do trying to find my way, forcing people to see the black in me
Setting up every protest, I was labeled a political activist Black Sunshine Day at OU
Hope filled wishes grew I felt freedom on campus
And that was the day I knew I had to go to college
What did I need to do? I eagerly prepared for the ACT
One of top students in my class Over 350 Community Service hours
Had a job at the mall, Spanish club, Debate team you know I did it all
College applications, financial aid, and scholarships my parents were excited as they asked are you ready to go?
I packed a box every week marked off the days on the calendar
The preparation was so neat Graduation day from high school was MAGNIFICENT!
My family showed up and showed out! The pride on their faces got my all scared
The future was bright but was my mind right? My first night on campus
My roommate and I went out drinking and partying all night
We knew everyone on the yard we thought we were hard
Our circle of friends was large nine young ladies, all in charge
I spent most of that year in a haze Going to class wasn't even on the page

When my grades came that when I knew I kicked it to hard and didn't know what to do
By sophomore year Nine become five
Their GPA's too low, money all gone but my dad was there to make sure I knew
That college wasn't free and that I really really needed a degree
Life slapped me in the face my man was a trip and friends weren't true
I had to get my head in my books who could I talk to?
Project Threshold – Saved me they taught me how to study
How to talk to professors showed me to use the services on campus
They activated my spirit and I grew My Junior year flew by, senior year too
Who would have thought in four short years I would be through?
That's right – College Grad Bachelor's Degree in Public Administration
My sorors, family, friends were so proud Then I decided to stay around
Can you believe it? Graduate School Time passed so fast
One year became two it was time to walk again, but with a Masters Degree
Now what to do? Stuck in the book mode
Guaranteed a job in Housing Free place to live
I continued to attend classes and before you know
Another degree, and I was good to go by now I was teaching
Students that looked like me how great it feels to have a college degree
Now it's 18 years later I'm still in school
Teaching, Advising, and telling my story that you too can reach
Your crown and glory
Just stay strong, persistent, and have courage
Work hard, set goals and know your limitations
Go to class always and study hard
College is doable if you allow God to be in charge

Believe in yourself just as I do
Graduation is worth it
Now do what you do.

-Monique Miles Bruner

10th Anniversary Edition
Gift To The Earth

I AM
A woman of confidence,
Believing in myself.

I AM
A woman of courage,
Accepting any challenge.

I AM
A woman of strength,
Enduring life's hardships

I AM
A woman of spirit
Defying all obstacles.

I AM
A woman of vision,
Knowing my destiny.

I AM
A woman of dignity
Worthy of your respect.

I AM
The Black Woman--
A GIFT TO THE EARTH.

-Sylvia L. Green-Chatman

Heroes

wounded, blooded heads unbowed.
distorted, frustrated dreams deferred.
hopelessly wondering searching for the light soaring, reaching past the night.
laughing in the darkness, crying in the rain, silent screams against yesterday's pain.
mothers, fathers, sisters, brothers marching, standing sitting and praying.
washing others clothes, floors, youngins teaching, reaching preaching another day's a commin'.
harsh words, from a heart broken by another son/daughter loved one gone too soon too quick too late to say good bye.
standing up from bended knees, singing "Sweet Chariot, let me be" got too much work, too much dreams, too much tomorrow yet to see.
Grandma, Grandpa, mom, dad brotherman and auntee.
Cotton picking hands,
bleeding in the sands,
corn bread baking in the pans,
BB playing on the way,
College,
sharecropping,
survival,
damnation,
love, hate, and papa with his brand new bag.
We shall over come, by any means necessary,
we will earn it, burn it, and make it ours,
we have no permanent friends, or enemies but our agenda is holy,
strange fruit adorns those funny southern trees, blood lines,
sacred ties to Africa calls us to stand up and be heroes.

-Rodney Coates

10th Anniversary Edition

In Search of Excellence

Who I am
and what I can be is not easy for me to see
I am life, I am magic
I am the future here in the present
My destiny is the key
My persistence will unlock the door to a path of excellence
The journey I must travel to find my true self
My talents
My passions
How will I recognize them?
I must listen to the inner calling
I must yield to the yearning of my soul
Manifest the rhythm in my mind and make my thoughts tangible
I must search for excellence
But my self-esteem may be fragile
and like a seed it needs to be nurtured and cultivated
in order for me to blossom and grow strong
I need your love and compassion
to help me believe I am majestically and infinitely bound
I need to believe not only can I fly
But that I will soar confidently with excellence
I am a gift from the womb
I am the spirit of a child

-Lynette A. Daniels

Gumbo For The Soul
Fly High

The greatest feeling,
The highest freedom,
Is to fly, fly above all else,
To not be bound by what
Has weighed you to the ground.
So fly, and fly high
Achieve your highest aspirations,
And most intimate dreams,
Fly on the wings of knowledge,
Fly on the wings of wisdom,
And soar on the winds of opportunity.
Fly, and fly high,
Never again to be earthly bound.
Not chained by low expectations,
Or hindered by other's opinion.
Set yourself free.
Fly, and fly high,
And rise, to a better place.
My sister, fly on wings of compassion,
My brother, fly on wings of forgiveness,
My people, fly on wings of love,
Believe in yourselves,
Fly past what has held you back,
Spread your wings,
Be free, fly, Fly high

-Pierre Etienne

10th Anniversary Edition

Help Me To Heal

Lord make me an instrument of your healing
Help me to mend those who can't bend
To ease the pain and relieve the strain
of earth and man born Ills
Lead me to devise a plan with the wise
of ways to make health whole
Remove all the scold from those who would mold
all life into bandages and pills
Give me sound ideas; banish all the fears
of failure and error and pride
My mission, Lord, let me not hide
let me walk with a sure stride
Toward the goal of healing with head, heart, and hands
I continue searching and dealing
With words that spark courses from light to dark
Thank you Lord for this mission; it reverses lack of Ambition
Help me to no harm cause as I venture without pause
On this battleground of broken beings.

-Charlotte Sista C. Ferrell

The Mentor, Strong

The Mentor, master of technique,
makes sounds with his keys seem so sensual.
The Mentor's notes seem to flow so gently.
He's got no time to waste, for nothing is done in haste,
for all his life is spent learning, teaching, and reaching.

Who can sing the Mentor's song?
His hands caressing keys so softly,
gently blended with words so strong,
teaching music is where he belongs.

Sometimes in teaching he becomes tired and drained,
burdened and depressed from the tremendous strain.
For, his tasks are many, but never completed in haste.
He takes a break but not for long,
for in being a Mentor, his heart lies strong.

Some call him astounding, others great sounding.
Some call him adorable, others enjoyable.
I've found nothing about him deplorable.
I call him amazing, admirable, and truly beloved.
The Mentor, strong--this is the Mentor's song.

-Mary Bains-Fort

10th Anniversary Edition

A True Friend

A true friend is a treasure whose love and support cannot be measured.
A true friend can give you correction without the fear of rejection.
A true friend will be ecstatic about your successes and encourage you through your failures.
A true friend is loyal and will not honor your disloyalty.
A true friend rejoices with you through the good times and mourns with you through the difficult times.
A true friend won't envy, covet or become jealous.
A true friend marvels at your originality, your grace and your poise.
A true friend will pray for you even when they are down and out.
A true friend is family regardless of their DNA.
A true friend is one of God's Angels who will be there when you are old and gray.
And when it's time to leave this earth, a true friend will weep. They will always keep you close in their heart, take comfort you are with The Lord and they will cherish the laughter, the precious memories and the love you shared.
A true friend is a treasure whose love and support cannot be measured.

-Lorita Kelsey Childress 9/5/13

Imagine That

Imagine what your life would be like, if no one took education seriously.

Imagine if this world didn't have any libraries. Where would we go for information about our past? Imagine the world without books.

Imagine if no one was able to write those words to go in the books, there would be nothing but a library filled with books with blank pages. But I forgot, there aren't any libraries.

Imagine if our forefathers didn't know how to write. Would there have been a Declaration of Independence? Probably not.

Imagine if none of us knew how to read or write. Our history would be lost to those from the past. Imagine life without numbers and formulas. There would be no airplanes or cars because there would be no one with the knowledge to build them. There would be more sickness and death because no one would have the foresight to experiment and come up with medicine to save us.

Imagine if there were no telephones, communication the way we know it today wouldn't exist. Imagine a world without the Internet superhighway. How would we communicate with others across the world?

Imagine if George Washington Carver refused to teach himself how to read and write. Would we be enjoying the fruits of his labor such as adding mayonnaise to our favorite sandwich or keeping our meat tenderized before cooking it?

Imagine if Nathaniel Alexander hadn't used his education and imagination, we would be sitting on the floor instead of a folding chair.

Imagine if your central heater didn't exist, that would have meant Alice Parker didn't take her education seriously and apply her reading, writing and math skills to develop what we now take for granted.

Imagine a life without all of the amenities and luxuries we enjoy. IMAGINE THAT.

-Shelia M Goss

I've Been There

I'm younger, yeah But I've been there.
To the corn fields, to the pea patches,
To the row after row of sugar cane.
Yes, I've been there. I know the street light curfew... Wait...
There was no leaving my house playing with the neighbors in the city.
Just tossing the ball over the fence, back and forth, back and forth.
Yeah, I've been there. Clean plate club. Wash the dishes, clean the kitchen, only thirty minutes of TV club. I've been there.
Pot Liquour. Castor Oil. Yellow Root Tea.
I've been there. And sometimes.... I wish... I could go back.
Let your gift make room for you!

-Tasha Grier

10th Anniversary Edition

The Morehouse Glass of Life

A Morehouse Man can do anything
In Chapel, Doctor Benjamin Mays remarked, "One day the glass of life is always half-filled and never half-empty."
Morehouse men can accomplish anything for the betterment of black folks and graduates still believe these ringing words of "Buck Benny" hollowing in their ears today.
Essentially, there is always a bit of good in everything one does in life no matter how bad or evil it may seem---there is always hope at the end of the rainbow. There is always room for that positive dream.
It's not ego-tripping to toot your own horn. If you don't believe in yourself, who will?
You must be your own publicist for no one will know who you are unless you blow your own horn--blow loudly with a soft, harmonious tonality.
And when the glass of life becomes full, you will believe that you can do anything your heart and mind dream of achieving.
The glass of life is always half-filled and never half-empty.

-Michael Henderson

I'm Somebody

I'm a descendant of former slaves,
But my history doesn't stop here:
My history is infinite you can look through books,
My history is everywhere
I discovered the North Pole and created Washington, DC
Check the record books I'm there.
I can do more than play basketball
And the majority of inventions, I created them all
From the elevator to the printing press,
So I did more than some history books suggest.
I took a trip to outer space,
And I settled in every place
Known to man
I build this country with my bare hands.
I'm the first black during slavery to receive my PH. D
I created my own education institution for people like me,
While Christopher Columbus was trying to discover America to make history
I already made that discovery.
God doesn't make nobodies,
So I'm somebody.

-Benjamin Hicks

Masks

Our portrayal of life versus
what we know to be real,
false facades we exhibit while
suppressing and keeping our
innermost self concealed. Self-
inflicted wounds resulting from
empty characters we portray,
slowly killing our dreams laying
them to rest in shallow graves.
Consumed in destitute souls, no
tranquil thoughts we know, phobias
that have mastery over our minds, that
don't allow our inner child, our inner
spirit to grow. Passed from generation to
generation, maintaining blinders that keep
the truth from view, searching for happiness
and purpose in life in all the meaningless and
frivolous things that we do. Yet happiness has
always been here, you lost it when you fell out of
love with you, for beneath the darkness of the mask
is the revealing guiding light that is truly you.
Self-inflicted wounds resulting from
empty characters we portray,
slowly killing our dreams laying
them to rest in shallow graves.

-Che' Hill

Gumbo for the Soul

I am a savory blend of many things
originally born an African, an extension of those beaten, stripped,
and in 1619 brought here on a Dutch slave ship.
Torn from the bosom of the motherland,
ostracized and renamed American.
I am a savory blend of the free blacks that fought with the Minutemen
In the initial Revolutionary War, My people bare the battle scars.

A savory blend of Benjamin Banneker, with a blessed pen
Created the first Almanac, that took more than a notion.
Like Richard Allen who in 1794, founded the Bethel African Methodist Church
personifying spiritual God fearing women and men.
By faith and God, my destiny is predetermined.
Take 1829, when David Walker created a pamphlet, An Appeal to the Colored People of the World, at the time, this work, was the first of its kind.
Or in the same year the creation of the first National Negro Convention.
I am a savory blend of all I've mentioned.
I am a savory blend of the men and women that took over the slave ship, Amistad, and won their freedom, now our freedom, sometimes taken for granted.

I am a savory blend of Sojourner Truth, Harriet Tubman and strong black women, like Rosa Parks, Mary McLeod Bethune and Barbara Jordan... Blended with Ella Fitzgerald and Lena Horne, gifted to sing and those that pressed towards the mark like Susan L. Taylor and Coretta Scott King. Spirited to succeed like Madam C.J. Walker and Oprah Winfrey just to name a few, poetically influenced like Maya Angelou.

A blend of the time between 1922 and 1929, the Harlem Renaissance.

A blend of strong men, like James Stone, the first black to enlist to fight for the Union and Edward G. Walker and Charles L. Mitchell, who, in 1866, sat on the American Legislature of Massachusetts.

I am a savory blend of many more men from the late 18 and 1900's, Booker T. Washington, W.E.B. Du Bois, Carter G. Woodson, A. Philip Randolph and Jesse Owens.

Their great achievements are no mystery, products of our heritage that made history.

I'm predisposed to greatness, hell bent on makin' it.

A savory blend of many firsts from men like Jackie Robinson, Ralph J. Bunche, Thomas Bradley, Kenneth Gibson and Maynard H. Jackson.

Then we all know of the many men who gave their lives fightin', marching, preachin', Malcom X and Martin, were always teachin'while some still carry the torch like Al Sharpton, Barack Obama and Jesse L. Jackson.

There are too many to mention of our heritage that comprise this beautiful blend and there are some of which don't bear the same color of our skin. But they too contributed to that of which we benefited.

All that I am goes back to them, the heroes of the past and the torchbearers of the present.

I am a savory blend of many things, a protégé of my Aunt Catherine with Bigmama's soul stirred in. I won't stop til I win. And then I'll start something back up again, like Gumbo for The Soul, supporting education.

Gumbo For The Soul

I am a savory blend of generations, those that came before and the ones followin'.

-Beverly Black Johnson

Levitate

Levitate your mind
from negativity
Levitate your actions
to productive proclivity
Levitate your wishes
until they accomplish dreams
Levitate your brothers and sisters
beyond what they currently seem
We can all move beyond our plateau state
if we just choose to levitate.

-Lorraine Elzia

Images of Mama

"Mama may have. Papa may have but God bless the child that's got his own."
--Billie Holiday

Images of Mama
From childhood daze
Wrap me in the warmth
Of memories set ablaze
She played jazz in the mornings
And sang HOT
Over the stove
Her voice seasoned with
That heartbreak that only Mama knows
But them notes smelled good
Dipped in sunrise-- Browned-just-right
& the rhythm of her blues
Calmed us every night
Images of Mama's
Tears beneath life's fists
My soul held the bruises
Her heart felt The HITS
Still she sang
& painted through the daytime
Then prayed to God for Light
She poured poetry over supper
Then my mama cried into the night
Images of Mama
Growing sweeter still
My veins hum with a sadness
That makes my blood chill
She laughed when the sun rose

But wasn't nothin funny
Cause they never gave her love
& she wouldn't beg for money
But ole B.B. blew Through crispy morning air
& Smokey cruised with us
Without a single care...
Yeah...yeah...yeah
    Images of Mama
Feed and help me see
This life...this love...
The "music" burns
Images of me
I now laugh at the sunrise
& again Not all for "joy"
I try to cook-up sustenance
Shine Light into this void
But jazz still smells gooood
Come God's morning light & there's a touch of rhythm
To my own blues In the night

-Lisa Bartley-Lacey

ASSUME THE POSITION

Assume the position
From the moment you emerged
Cryin' as though you already knew
That you might be exchanging
One temporary confinement
For another.
Being black, being male
Totally out of your control
But you came anyway…

Assume the position
That being black and poor
And stayin' in the "hood"
While your mamma's prayin'
And she should
Though she done all she would
Not knowing that she could
Question
Why you were left back and put in that "special class"…
when you could read the cereal boxes at age two.
But you…

Assume the position
Peering out of half-lidded eyes
As you stand on the corner cutting class with the guys
For the fifth time
One week into the semester
Pants hung low
For reasons you don't know
Ask James…he's out on probation this time.

Assume the position
You with indignant stares
Why, how would they dare
Pull you out of the lineup
Flying friendly first class
To stand spread eagle.
And we smile.
'cause it's you this time
being defiled while profiled
But… you assumed your position.

Assume the position
That conspiracy's real,
Reparation won't heal
And they aren't gonna give it to you anyway.
'Least not without a fight.
No forty acres
But sixty percent of those back on the plantation
Look like you.

Assume the position
That you are the smarter
With knowledge it's harder
To put you in that cage
they keep building for you
While they sell you to the highest bidder
As cheap labor.

Assume the position
That before things get right
You must change your fight
To a level playground.
With zero tolerance for those who make excuses

For the deliberate lack of knowledge.
Ignore - ance is not bliss.

Assume the position
That the choice is yours
To get down on all fours
Or stand on two feet
Be a man - not my "nigga"
'Cause you become his
Every moment you allow him to
Define you.

-E. Joyce Moore

10th Anniversary Edition

If

If there were no dream
Where would I be....?
Would I be Black,
I wonder... Would I be free?
If there were no dream
What would I feel....Would I still be human?
walk city streets, breathe country air?
Would I know I'm African?

-Gwendolyn Brown-Massey

Black Butterfly

Why don't you fly?
It's okay to spread your wings
Don't be afraid to show the world what you have to offer
Remember the courage of our founding fathers in spite of racism and indifference
Sometimes the sky will be gray and the situation will seem grim
This is where from self doubt you must suspend
To free your body you must free your soul
Believe in yourself despite what you are told
Welcome the promise as your dreams unfold
Take healthy initiatives to achieve your goals
When you are down don't forget to get back up
It's your attitude, not adversity, that leaves you feeling stuck
Challenge the powers that be with intelligence
By embracing your own independent thinking
Develop your recipe for success
The ingredients can be a little bit of this and that
You can succeed against all odds
I identify with your persistence and feel the tenacity of your spirit
This is a message from one to another Black Butterfly
Let's uplift each other as we embark on our journey in the sky

-Alicia M. Morgan

Ode to British Lit

Ode to British lit and a vow to thee,
Not to let a prejudice professor get the best of me.

While studying Browning and not a hint of Hughes,
I felt I was climbing the crystal stairs with the British lit blues.

Molare and Shakespeare, two greats that didn't mean much to me,
For I wanted to read James Baldwin and Lorraine Hansberry.

My grade was in jeopardy and my dignity as well.
I didn't want to lower my GPA and I refused to fail.

Hence went forth the pressure and the rolling up the sleeve.
I read Chaucer, Dickens, and Keates and I studied to achieve.

I aced my exams and exceed my white counterparts,
But the professor didn't have love for blacks in his heart.

So, he lowered my grade and made me try harder.
But in the end, it made me tough it made me smarter.

Ode to British lit and my adversity.
I kept my head up for success was owed to me.

-Vickie L. Williams-Morris

You Can Do It!

You can do it!
Just put your mind to it!
Anything you want is within your reach
Just listen to your elders and learn what we teach!
Although it may seem difficult at times
All you have to do is make up your mind
Trust the Lord and follow Him
And every obstacle will grow dim.
Remember we are praying and cheering you on
It'll happen before you know it, it won't be long!
You can be anything you want to be
Just study hard and you will see
In the end, when your story is told
It will surely say that you have reached your goal!
I BELIEVE IN YOU!

-Rolanda Pyle

10th Anniversary Edition

We're Living In a Time

We're living in a time
When education is practically free
And things should be quite
Uncomplicated and easy
Yet there are many struggles
And set backs to bare
Some come unrecognizable
Making education a game not always fair
The journey to succeed is challenging
For those who want to achieve
Yet at some point - in yourself
You have to believe
I stand here today
Still with an educational thirst
For I'm from a family line where higher ed was achieved by many
But in my other line I am the first
Don't deny yourself the riches
Education can bring
As a child of color
Working twice as hard is the thing
There may be bumps in the road
Things to knock you down
But have the strength to stand right up
And keep reaching for higher ground
They'll tell you that your disadvantages
Are from the culture that you're in
But don't ever let them limit you
Because of the color of your skin
Whenever you feel defeated
Remember the struggle of the past

Gumbo For The Soul

When our forefathers persevered on
In order for our liberties to last
Follow their beat
As it flows through your mind
Know that education's a gift
Each experience one-of-a-kind

If you feel lost
There's always another day
To begin again
And chart a new way
Stand proud my sisters and brothers
For the future is all yours
Have faith in your power
To achieve so much more
And like me you'll be standing
With that educational thirst
'Cause I'm one of my family's many
But more importantly I am one of the first.

-Pamela S. Rivers

10th Anniversary Edition

Walking That Line!

"As long as you get an education…"
"As long as you stay in school…"
"We'll do our best to support you…"
"But don't go actin' no fool…"
I complied with half of dad's request
Then I took an alternative route…
I acted that fool really thinking
That I knew what life was all about.
My studies grew non-productive
The company I kept…no support…
I knew I had to make a change
My dorm life I had to abort.
I knew I needed to begin again
I knew I needed to change…
I started at a new school
My goals, I rearranged.
I thought I was ready to buckle down
Study and become a success…
Again, I stumbled and found myself
In yet, another mess.
Still, determined to make it
I picked up and moved again…
This time in a positive setting
Without bad influences who called themselves friends.
Employed and carrying a full load of classes
I struggled with one thing in mind…
To focus and accomplish goals I'd set for myself
Beginning with walking that line!
More bumps in the road tried to "trip me up"
But, nothing was going to stop me now…

Gumbo For The Soul

My grades, alas, began to improve
Uplifted, was my declining morale
They said mom and dad practically held their breath
'Til they saw me let go of my pride…
Convinced their youngest would make it now
'Cause they knew God was at my side.
Joyous was I for that precious moment
Walking that line to get my degree…
This young Black woman fought hard to achieve
And, I made it, you can, too…you'll see.

-Kathie Strother-Scholl

10th Anniversary Edition

Dumb Questions

good morning
today you will be tested on *Romeo and Juliet*
be sure to read directions carefully
answer the essay question fully and completely
all books are away
are there any questions?
the smell of brains sizzling snatches the stuffy air
the sounds of souls searching inside themselves for answers
an eerie sullen silence settles across the atmosphere
suddenly …
"hey, miss
I don't get it
I was reading this last night
why would they put the picture of Juliet stabbing herself
after it happened?"
Gulps, giggles, grins, gyrating bodies
launch a laughter that laces the room
"That's so stupid," someone says.
"Boy, you're dumb."
But I realize
that there <u>really</u> is no such thing as a silly question
because silly questions are the stuff
that learning is made from

-Simone M. Shields

In Search Of Truth

I Searched and Searched For Truth Each Day
But So Many Obstacles Stood In My Way
I Searched and Searched But I Could Not See
That The Truth I Desired Was Inside of Me
Why Did I Search for Something I Already Possessed?
Surely This Is An Issue I Must Address
In My Search for Truth
I Often Found Empty Spaces
Simply Because I Was Searching
In All the Wrong Places
In My Search for Truth
I Finally Looked Inside My Soul
And Suddenly I Found a Truth As Good As Gold

-Glenda Staten

All Me

All Me
Right down to the curve of my hips
The stride in my step
The words coming from my lips
The things I accept
The bounce of my hair
The essential stares
Right down to my legs
The backside curve
The essential nerve
The chocolate complexion
Right down to my fingertips
The faith I have
The delight I share
All Me

-Nicole Marie Stevenson

Be A Black Man

Be a black man, if you can.
Walk one mile in his shoes.
Seek within, take time and spend
Life from his point of view.
Do the work, try twice as hard
Watch promotions passing by.
Though still oppressed,
Black Man, be blessed
Keep your visions to the sky.
The day will come when you shall reign
As the royalty you are.
Grasp your hardships, bear your pain
Let not your life be scarred.
The wicked, the heartless, the cowards all know
Your strength lies in your mind.
Stand tall my brothers, as you grow.
All will be yours in time.

-Rene Camper-Stewart

Monkey See

I watched her
I watched her as the gray patch of hair stared me in the eyes
As she
Engrossed
And entertained by this close friend
I wondered
I knew she knew I was there
But
She didn't look up
I wondered what was so delicious
Between those pages
That she greedily partook of
I wondered
I wondered why
Why
She read
She had 10's of 50's of books
As my small hands thumbed
The smooth pages of one
Feet on the table scooted down in the chair
I read

-Anna K. Stone

Happy To Be Nappy

Twists, locks and braids;
our individual freedom of speech Why is "Corporate America" tripping?
What are they trying to teach?
Our hair is natural; wavy, tight, or straight
Whom are you trying to desecrate?
Why the need for the great debate?
Our purpose is to reach and educate,
the African-American experience is something you just cannot relate
Brought from our homeland in shackles and shame
We lost our true identity responding to your unfamiliar name
Now you want to snicker and grin whenever we enter a room
Our persona, our aura is overpowering, too much to be consumed
Educated, classy, oh we got it going on
We are a people of dignity empowered by grace
Releasing the chains of the past, moving upwards to a higher place.

Delores Thomas

10th Anniversary Edition

A Poem for Toni Morrison

(For Toni, at her book signing in Washington, D.C.)

we are educated women
black women
traveling women
who come in droves
seeking truth-tales
about the stories
of our own lives
can't you see
the narrative in my eyes
dark and black
as coal
i bear witness
even though my spirit
sometimes lags behind
tired
overburdened
overworked
underpaid
i still travel
to toni morrison's book signing
with this thought
(indisputable)
in the back of my mind:

it's not about the book.

it's about
a community of women

giving order
to the sense of disarray
in their own lives
crafting culture
in a world devoid of spirit
that seeks to keep women mute
and objectified
toni gathers the women
lower-class
middle-class
academic
motherless
childless women
whose secrets—honey hush!
have never lied
a true anthropologist
a zora of her own time
whose down home blues
speak rivers
about you and i
toni gathers the women
and we her audience
sit noble and erect
in the pews
of the church
where she has come
to testify and to signify
clutching the great book—
her next book
from behind a podium
where her words
will protrude
from her lips
every cell in her body
we laugh

10th Anniversary Edition

clap
shout hallelujah
or amen
whenever toni
keeps it plain
knowing full well
that 'Sula' is auntie laura
and in many ways us too—
a tree without roots
trying to love herself whole
and recreate herself anew.
toni teaches us that there is a god
inside me and you like the god
inside pecola breedlove who pecola never knew—
her rich legacy of struggle and culture of resistance;
her connection to the past
and other sistuh-seekers
in the village
who have vowed
to never forget;
who have come to this book signing to re-member.

-Jamie Walker

Mr. Hughes

I've never been to Harlem
But renaissance I know
As a boy I'd write a hymn
The words: I let them flow
Did you grab rhymes out of the air?
Or did they come to you?
The United States was made aware
You speak of rivers too
I see your face on stamps and posters
And on website banners
Some poets don't use drink coasters
Teach them stanza manners
What is a dream deferred?
Ambition put on hold
What is the spoken word?
A poetic pot of gold
I thank you, Mr. Hughes
Your work has taught me
Different styles we use
to write our poetry
I salute you, Mr. Hughes
Because there is no other
Harlem montage lit my fuse
You're like a big brother
I salute you, Mr. Hughes
True poets stand and fight
Harlem montage lit my fuse
And to this day, I write

-Michael Webster

Populacao Magoada!!! (Wounded Population)

A Nossa Onha Tem Que Ser Lavada (Our Honor Needs to be Restored)
In an over-served room that serves an underserved population
My brotha speak of pain, struggle, a deep sense of weariness
That doesn't even belong to him ...
It... doesn't... even... belong... to... him ...
"Why?" I asked.
Because I have to be strong,
More capable,
Most intelligent
I have to show them ....
"Why?"
Because our ancestors struggled,
Bled
Acquiesced to live
fought to die ...
So I have to!!! Cracked out through his tears.
So I have to ...I have to.

I shook my head slowly and said in a feathered voice, "No you don't ..."
My voice found, I said again, "No you don't. Don't you see the ancients did all that so you <u>don't</u> have to.
Don't you realize that - all over the world for many hundreds of years before you and I were thought of – the ancients toiled, strained and died in mass graves, fought, ran and hid under b***s*** (literally), screamed, held tongues and had their tongues cut out, lived half lives, died too young and killed their own seed to prevent it from seeing a world like the one they subsisted in ...
So we don't have to ...

Don't you see – our great, grand ancestors gain no joy in watching us repeat their work. They do not smile as we suffer stepping backward into shoes they've already filled.

Haven't they suffered enough by force? Haven't we suffered enough by choice?

Don't you hear the ancestral drum play every time a black child graduates high school?

Don't you feel the Natives dancing – beating the earth in rhythm with their tired feet – every time a Latina girl gets a job?

Don't you hear those old Jewish ancestors singing and snapping their fingers every time one of their children buys a home for his family?

I hear the drums of joy

Feel the drums of joy beating in my chest

The air I breathe is filled with the *poeira* …the dust of dancing ancestors

The songs I sing are songs of light, love unconditional and freedom – they are the songs of sage smoke mixed with juju combined with communion wine all poured into a yarmulke and sipped through a bamboo straw while sitting in lotus pose …

Isn't it time our wounds of old …so old and so tired …were cleaned… bandaged… treated …healed?

Isn't it time our honor was restored… {*Não que e hora de lavar a nossa onha …*}

Isn't it high time we lived for the light in our ancestor's smiles?

-Erica Y. Woods

CHAPTER III

SAVORY STEW
GUMBO RECIPES AND A BIT OF HISTORY

"One day, I want to be able to point to any spot on the globe and say, "I've been there."

~Kyeisha Johnson

A Bit of Gumbo History

Gumbo is derived from various Bantu dialects (Southern & Central Africa) and terms for okra (i.e. quingumbo, grugombo, gumbo, gombo, ngombo gomboaud, ngumbo, ochinggombo). The word is one of very few African language words brought over by slaves which have entered the English language. Some of the others are goober or goober pea (peanut) also of Bantu dialect origin, Yam from West Africa, and cooter (turtle) of Bantu and Mandingo origin.

Today, gumbo is, generally, a southern U.S. regional term for stew-like dishes with meat or seafood, tomatoes and sweet bell peppers, but more specifically it is a Créole dish whose characteristic ingredients are okra and filé powder (although some gumbos do not have okra, and are thickened only with filé powder after it's removed from the heat). Okra has a mucilaginous quality, which thickens and gives body to the gumbo. Some folks say, *"if it ain't got okra, it ain't gumbo!"*

Créole Gumbo is a stew-like dish made with brown roux, okra, filé powder, onions, green peppers, tomatoes and seafood, chicken and/or meat. Gumbo has an incomparably rich flavor and texture, and derives from the cooking traditions of the French, Spanish, Indian and African residents of the area. Ingredients can vary widely (there are literally hundreds of different gumbos). Seafood (especially shrimp) is common to many gumbos, and there is a special *gumbo z'herbes* (or *gumbo maigre*) made with herbs and greens (usually seven or more) such as collard greens, mustard greens, and spinach, which was traditionally served on Good Friday. Gumbo should never be over spiced; it should have a subtle flavor. Gumbo is always served with rice.

VeeJay's Gumbo

Ingredients:

2-3 Large Cooking Spoons of Vegetable Oil
2-3 Large Cooking Spoons of All Purpose Flour
1 Med size Onion, chopped
1 Small-med size Bell Pepper cut in small pieces
1 Tablespoon Parsley (fresh or flakes)
Smoked Turkey Necks cut in chunks - for smoked flavor (optional)
1 Lb of your favorite Smoke Sausage cut in bite size pieces (pork, beef or turkey)
1 Lb Andouille cut in bite size pieces
4-6 Skinless/boneless chicken breasts (cut in pieces)
8-12 Chicken wings (split, cleaned and seasoned to taste)
2 lb Fresh shrimp (peeled, deveined and seasoned to taste)
Oysters - Fresh or Canned (optional)
4-6 Medium - Large Crabs (fresh or boiled, cleaned and split in half)
1 Pack of Dried Shrimp (optional)
1 Can Mushroom stems and pieces (optional)
1 Tablespoon Gumbo file'
Salt and Pepper (red) to taste
Accent seasoning to taste
Garlic Powder to taste

Using a 20 qt Stockpot, fill pt halfway with tap water. Add cleaned crabs and boil on medium heat for 30 minutes. **Combine 2-3 cooking spoons of oil to 2-3 cooking spoons of flour and cook on low-medium flour to make roux, stirring constantly until desired color is obtained. Add to crab stock and stir until mixed thoroughly. Fill pot ¾ full and let boil for 30 minutes. Add turkey necks, onion, bell pepper and parsley flakes to stock and continue to boil. After 30 minutes, add Andouille, smoke sausage and continue to boil. After

30 minutes, add chicken pieces, dried shrimp, gumbo file', mushroom pieces and continue to boil for 30 minutes. Add shrimp. Bring to boil and taste before adding any more and salt and pepper to stock. Remove from heat and skim off excess oil on top. Serve hot over cooked rice.

After removing from heat, let cool while stirring occasionally to bring the temperature down evenly. Refrigerate when completely cool. *Note - As mixture boils down, you can replenish the water, keeping the pot filled near capacity while boiling. Never cover pot completely while boiling. Use seasonings listed above to season meats before adding to stock. **Additional Note - To cut down on the oil in the roux, you may opt to use instant roux available from your favorite grocer. I use Tony Chachere's Instant Roux mix, although there are other brands on the market. Prepare according to canned directions.

Variations: You can add okra that has been pre-fried/or baked to remove the slime to this dish. To remove slime, cook okra on a low fire in oil, stirring occasionally to keep from sticking. A quicker, easier way to remove the slime is to spray a baking pan with Pam and place the cut okra in the oven on 325 - 350 degrees, stirring occasionally until the slime is gone (usually 1-2 hours depending on amount). Add to stock before you add the chicken.

You can also change this recipe according to your taste buds. You can use only seafood (shrimp, crab/crabmeat and oysters) for a Seafood Gumbo, or omit the seafood and use your favorite meats (sausage and chicken) or whatever meats your taste buds call for. Down south, I've known people to use Hog Chitterlings and Wild meats (deer, rabbit, coon, just to name a few). A popular saying in the south is, "A gumbo can consist of everything but the kitchen sink." Unused gumbo may be frozen for up to 6 months.

-Vanessa A. Johnson

10th Anniversary Edition
My Family's Gumbo

Gumbo is a very popular Louisiana dish, a kind of soup. There must be a million variations on how to make it. Every person who makes it thinks theirs is better than the next. I have seen people arguing over what is the best way to make this dish. Just like life, everyone has some input on what would make the next person's life better. Some people want more sausage, more shrimp or no shrimp. Some want crab or oysters. Some prefer more spice, more file. One thing they all have in common is a Roux (Roo). Roux is the gravy base and the foundation of this dish. It gives the soup flavor and is what makes you get that second bowl. Everyone has a Roux in his or her life. Someone who influenced every step they took, and in some way gave their life direction. Mother was my Roux.

Laissez les Bon Temps Rouler

3 lbs. snow crab, cleaned and washed
15 chicken wings, washed and cleaned
1 lb. chicken gizzards, chopped fine
4 lbs. diced smoked sausage (Hillshire Farms).
 Fry lightly to remove some fat
3 lbs large shrimp, peeled and deveined
4 packs dried shrimp
2 lbs. baby shrimp
4 stalks of cleaned and diced celery
3 diced onions
3 packs of onion soup mix
2 cans of okra; preferably "Trappeys" brand. Drain off liquid and fry in ¼ cup of oil. This removes the slime
Gumbo file (ground sassafras leaves)
Lawry's seasoning salt
Black pepper
Celery salt

Prepared rice

Roux:
1 cup of vegetable oil
1 cup of flour

If you prefer a thicker soup, add more flour. Heat the oil over medium heat. Sprinkle flour over grease while constantly stirring, so as not to scorch, based on your preference. I prefer a nut brown or caramel color. Some people like a darker roux. You can always taste as you go along. Set aside.

Gumbo:

Use a large stockpot. Fill half way with water and set on high to boil. You can divide ingredients into 2 or 3 smaller pots. I prefer this method, because it takes awhile to get the water to boil. It will also decrease the chance of your Gumbo sticking to the bottom. There is nothing worse than a burnt pot of Gumbo.

"Chile just thinking about it makes me want to cry." Gumbo is something that every time it's made, it just gets better as you add or take away ingredients to tailor to your taste, much like a fine suit of clothes. Other variations have bell pepper, tomato puree, oysters, crawfish, rabbit, turkey or chicken, parsley, green onion and garlic. I could fill this book up with various ways to prepare this dish. Do not be afraid to experiment.

Add gizzards, onion, celery, onion soup mix, dried shrimp and sausage. When it reaches a rapid boil, reduce flame to low and cook for an additional 20 minutes. Add Roux and stir. Add chicken, crab legs, okra, black pepper, seasoning and celery salt. Be very careful with celery salt, it can overpower the other flavors. Add 1 teaspoon to entire pot. You can always go back and add more. Boil for 35 to 40 minutes. Add shrimp and boil 5 minutes more. Remove from heat add 1 teaspoon of gumbo file to each pot.

Serve in a bowl over rice.

Sprinkle file to taste. Do not be afraid to get your fingers dirty. Also, do not forget to suck the gravy out of the crab legs before you open them up.

-Kim Robinson

SOUMAS HERITAGE: CREOLE SEAFOOD GUMBO

Make a roux with 1-cup flour and 1-cup oil set aside to use later. Place shrimp shells/crawfish claws, and liquid from oysters in a stockpot. Cover with water, with fresh vegetable seasonings. Bring to a boil, set aside (this will be your water/seafood stock)

4-5 washed crabs and claws cut
1-2 lbs. of fresh peeled shrimp (save the shells for stock pot)
1-2 lbs. of crawfish tail meat, if you have the heads/tails set aside for the same stock pot
1-pint oysters save and use liquid
1 can of whole tomatoes, or use 2-3 firm fresh tomatoes, diced
2-3 tbsp. of oil
1 large onion, chopped
2-3 quarts of prepared seafood stock
2-3 sprigs of celery, chopped
2-3 sprigs of green onion, chopped
2-3 sprigs of parsley, chopped
1-2 bell peppers, chopped
4-5 cloves of garlic, chopped (or 2-3 tsp. of minced)
1 cup of okra, chopped (fresh or frozen)
1 cube of seafood flavor bouillon cube
2-3 tsp. of Soumas Creole Soul Seasoning
A few drops of liquid crab boil
*Add seafood the last 10-15 minutes of cooking.

In a large aluminum Dutch oven pot, add oil and sauté all your fresh vegetables for about 6-10 minutes. Add your roux and seafood stock and your seasoning to taste. Cook on a medium heat for about 25-35 minutes. Add all other ingredients; continue to cook on a medium-low heat for approx. 30-40 minutes. Serve over a bowl of hot fluffy rice, place a dash of *file* powder over rice with a few chopped green onions…'wit' some hot buttered French bread. Feeds about 8-10…

*File — (fee'-lay) — Ground sassafras leaves brought to us by Native Indians.

~~GUMBO- from the word "kingombo"- the African word for okra, original spelling was "gombo". African slaves brought this vegetable dish to this country from their traditional tribal foods of vegetables and herbs. This well diverse recipe was considered to have both spiritual and health-giving purposes as well as its savory taste! To the ancestral roots of this dish… I give proper respected acknowledgment!

-Panderina Soumas

CHAPTER IV
~SPIRITUAL GUMBO~
BLESSINGS AND GIFTS

"How long will we continue to wait at the end of the rainbow before realizing that we, in fact, are the pot of gold?"

~Joylynn M. Jossel

Girl of Grace…Woman of Peace

I woke up this morning and looked in the mirror.
What I saw today was different than any other day.
Yesterday, I saw myself…a sinner, ugly, black, scarred, stained.
Before I went to bed, I said my prayers to the One who created it all.
I woke up this morning and looked in the mirror.
What I saw today was different than any other day.
Today, I saw myself…saved by grace, beautiful, black, washed cleaned, eyes filled with hope and peace.

What caused the change?

I finally decided that there was One who was greater than I was.
One who promised me that He would wash me white as snow….
My only responsibility was to proclaim HIM, call HIM by His name…
Believe like I have never believed…. trust like I have never trusted.
I had to forgive, as I now understood that I was forgiven.
I had to love like I now understood that I was loved.
I had to extend mercy and grace, as I now understood that grace and mercy was mine.

What I see today is a girl of grace, kissed on the forehead by a Father who
Not only created me, but constructed me divinely for His purpose.
I see what I will be tomorrow, I see what I was in the past, and I see what I can be on this day.

I am a girl of grace fashioned in the image of the Creator, who makes me new each day.

Dear Creator, I except my commission as a girl of grace.... a daughter of yours. Destined for greatness.

Yes, I am a girl of grace. I now walk with my head high filled with the grace and mercy that was extended to me due to a beneficent and merciful Creator.

-Tanya R. Bates

10th Anniversary Edition

For My Boys

I was young when you came to me from GOD.

Out of my mouth fell "Now what am I going to do?

Over the years the answers just came.

When I fell ill you became my strength and my courage

never shedding a tear or showing fear.

And when GOD healed me, there you were telling me "We told you so!"

Now it's off to work I go once again thanks to my GOD and his two

gifts from heaven.

To J'Von & Javonte'

    I was diagnosed at age 30 with Poliomyelitis. It affects EVERY muscle in your body. My mom always said your body changed when you hit your thirties but man! The disease left me barely walking, rising up from a chair was a challenge and even getting out of bed was a chore. Then, the falling for no reason occurred. I would just trip over the least little things and had to get help just to get up. For the tomboy who used to play basketball, run and climb with the best of them, this was a shock to my whole being. Learning to be dependent on other people when you are used to being "superwoman" was the hardest part. I was always the strong friend but now, I needed help. I thought I was going to "die" when it was time for me to take a year off from work.

God surrounded me with good friends who would give me rides home from work, call me with some natural healing recipes, scriptures, etc. Tracey, my best friend, kept me laughing and her mom (my second mother) who is a physical therapist gave me exercises to do and prayed for me. My dad had more knowledge of my disease than I did. He called me with suggestions every week. His phone bill must have been so high. (He lives in Mississippi and I live in Ohio).

My boys and my mom were the biggest surprises. I am my mom's only child and my sons' only caretaker, plus they were only 13 & 11 at the time. Being without work was hard for me because I have been working since I was 17. They didn't let me fall into the pity party phase or make excuses for myself. They didn't cry or fall weak. My mom took me to every appointment and my sons cooked and cleaned for me. My boys took on things that I felt should being doing and all of this during a time when they needed me the most. Those teenage years! My mom would just pick me up for lunch just to get me out of the house. No lying on my behind, I was going to be healed.

My feeling is that God also used this time to show me I need a better relationship with Him and that there is no need to walk alone or try to be superwoman. It also taught me many things about myself—things I was in denial about and afraid to face. I am not a bad person but everybody needs some fine-tuning. I am back to work and getting around a lot better. My doctor said I healed faster than he thought I ever would. My whole attitude has changed and I am a lot calmer. I take risks and walk on faith. The Lord is still working on me with forgiving people.

10th Anniversary Edition

The life lesson here is that you don't have to walk alone; you will need help every now and again and sometimes when you to slow down, God will sit you down and give you the words and the way to make it in this world.

-Shawneen C. Hicks

No Earthly Father

One of the most important responsibilities of a parent is to encourage and support their children in all positive endeavors. Being raised in a single parent home, some would say I only received fifty percent of support; however, my mother gave me one hundred percent. My biological father chose too be a stranger to me. This left me feeling like a bird with one wing and unable to fly, but my father in Heaven assured me that He would never leave me or forsake me (Hebrews: 13:5).

When I read these words of wisdom from God, suddenly I am motivated and determined to avoid breakdowns in times of sorrow. The bible says in the Ten Commandments, "Thou shall not lie" so why did my worldly father lie? He told me he loved me but no love was shown. He told me he would write to me but no letter we received. He told me he would call me but the phone never rang. Then, I felt rejected and broken hearted but I picked up the word of God and it explained that, "The Lord is close to the broken-hearted and He saves those whose spirits have been crushed." Psalms 34:18 and from reading that, I've been relieved.

Then I was afraid, afraid that someone else I would love would leave me like my father did and again I read the word of God and it told me, "God didn't give me the spirit of fear but a spirit of power and self-control." No longer am I afraid because God has my back. I was then bruised because reality hit me in the face and made me realize that my father may never again be in my life. Then God said He heals the broken hearted and bandages their wounds (Psalms: 147:3). And that healed me. Studies reveal that girls with involved dads fare better academically, especially in math and science, socially, and emotionally than those raised without fathers. Then I worried if I would fail in life so I prayed and believed that anything I asked for in prayer I would receive (Matthew: 21:22) and through prayer and hard work, I applied myself and I received academic advancement, emotional guidance and friends to help me socially. No longer do I fit in this study.

The first man abandoned me in my life but then I was introduced to God and He told me that He guards those who come to him for safety. (Proverbs: 30:5). Then I felt protected. Then I felt unaccepted but again God was there to tell me that I could come to Him and He would always accept me (John 6:37). Now I am accepted. The studies reveal the difficulties that girls have are less recognized because their issues are quieter. Well, my issues are just as loud as any male's issues and that study doesn't reveal any legitimate reason why a father shouldn't be in a daughter's life as much as in a son's. When those loud issues hit my life, the Lord told me. "Don't let your heart be troubled. Trust in God and trust in me" (John 14: 1). Then my issues seemed to vanish and the rough grounds that I once walked on were smooth. Moreover, in the end I realized I was excellent despite my worldly father not being there for me. I realized that when everything else becomes destroyed, the words that the Lord has said to me will never be destroyed. (Mark 13:31).

I always told myself that no substitute father is good enough to fill that vacant spot in my heart but then God came along and I realized that He's the best father anyone could ever have. He has filled my vacancy. And when all was said and done, I smiled and I assured myself that everything would be okay in the end. Now, no longer do my tears fall from my eyes and when they do decide to fall, God will wipe my tears.

-Crystal Jones

Twenty Year Stew

Twenty Year Stew Ingredients:
Prayer anytime. Four cups of Christianity.
Three to five cups of love.
A large amount of wisdom--about five pounds.
Knowledge, stirred in from time to time.
Understanding: a whole heap of it.
Kindness always.
One marriage; one won't hurt nobody.
God; you can't leave Him out.
Two teaspoons of salt, you don't want the stew too salty.
Charity; always good for the soul

Now, put all the ingredients into one pot, turn the flame down low because the stew will rise too fast, and it may stick or burn. It was December, nineteen hundred and eighty three, when I went to a Christmas party with a friend to serve food at her workplace. Everyone there was eating, talking and having a good time. I noticed the cake was getting a little low, so I saved a piece for a guy that I knew didn't get any. The other guys there started to tease him; saying that I thought he was special. About two weeks later, he asked me to marry him. I said yes. We got married on February fourteenth, nineteen hundred and eighty four; it was a short courtship, but I loved him. Soon after we were married he started to slack off on going to work, he even stopped going to church. The "stew" was beginning to simmer; okay, so I added just a little more prayer, love, God, and kindness.

Now God, I always kept real close, never know when you might need Him. I found out later my new husband abused alcohol and drugs, and would lose his job because of it. I stayed by his side, did the best that I could for him; he was my husband, for better or worse, in sickness and in health. He would say to me that he just could not find a job or the job did not pay enough. Now, I knew it was time to add a pinch of salt to the stew, a little wisdom, some knowledge, prayer and God. So I said to my husband, "Shade from a toothpick beats the hot boiling sun." I had a full-time job and a part-time job, and between the two, I would go home and cook before heading off to work again. I was tired, and I thought I would not make it out of the door when he said, "You know God will not put more on you than you can bear." I stopped dead in my tracks and could not say a word, I slowly turned around and just stared at him, the "stew" was really starting to boil over.

Now, it was time to split the "stew" up into separate pots, because it had become too much for one. With each pot, I added more love, charity, prayer, Christianity, salt, a lot of God, some wisdom, understanding and kindness. I took God and put Him back on my side, because I knew He had my back. Still, I continued in my faith by going to church, singing in the choir and teaching. On June, nineteen hundred and ninety six, my daughter asked us to move to Minneapolis, where she and her family lived. I told her that we would need time to think about it. Therefore, we took a visit to Minneapolis and said okay we will move. In July, we moved to Minneapolis; the culture was so different from that of Wisconsin. A few Sundays after we moved, I found a church and I noticed there were many changes in the way service was carried out. I wanted to talk to the minister, so I invited him and his family to our home for lunch. At lunch, I asked the minister and his wife why things were taught so differently here than at other congregations. His reply was that he was trying to appeal to the younger generation so they would stay in the church.

Now the "stew" was boiling a little too fast, so I turned the heat down on both pots. I dropped in more wisdom, added knowledge, love, prayer; I put God in for sure, and kindness. I told the minister, you know, you can only lie for so long, when our children find out that they're being lied to and they read for themselves the truth they may leave the church and never return. I told him teach the children the truth because even though they may stray, at least they will know the truth and return. Our children have been lied to for too long and it must stop. I suffered a stroke at work in nineteen hundred and ninety nine. It left my legs weak and me very depressed; I still have minute strokes (T.I.A.). I was off work for about two months but I had to return in order to keep up with the bills. The "stew" was simmering very well, but I thought I would add another cup of God, much more love; you just can't seem to add enough at once, put in a little more prayer, took God and put Him back on my side. By August, nineteen hundred and ninety nine I found a new job so I worked there for three years, then the job began to sell off its work, one area at a time. Work was going to Mexico, then Canada, and Wisconsin. I received severance pay, my 401k and insurance for three months and by November I had a job that lasted about two weeks. My health was not improving; I was starting to get weaker and weaker, and the doctors could not find what was wrong with my heart. The chest pains were getting worse and worse.

On January, two thousand and three, I moved back to Racine to be near my relatives and friends, as I was getting weaker to the point I had to walk slowly. My husband did not want to move back to Racine, but my sister offered her upstairs apartment until I was able to get back on my feet. My husband was the first to put his things on the moving van. In February, I became very ill while getting ready for church, I had to be admitted into the hospital, and it was determined that I needed to have a triple bypass. During the two weeks that I remained in the hospital, I suffered two additional strokes. Well the "stew" was still cooking just fine, by adding God and prayer to the pot kept it just right. Three days after I was out of the hospital, my husband told me that he could not find a job in Racine, and that he would be going back to Minneapolis to find a job and send money back to help me out. The plan was, he would use my car to go back to Minneapolis, and then he would return it in two weeks; well, none of that ever happened. In June, I went to Minneapolis to visit and my husband could not leave his home for fear someone would break in.

The "stew" was burning; I had to turn the flame off until I could put all the stew in one larger pot. I got in my car and drove to my granddaughter's house then signed the title over to her for fifty dollars. I put all of the "stew" into one large pot because I was finished with it, burnt, but finished. My husband got his divorce; we were together twenty years, that's when I remembered that I had left out one main ingredient: "forgiveness." I prayed to God for the mistakes I had made and to forgive me, I then went to church and repented. I realized that I had let my anger "stew" while never really doing anything about it. God will do so much, and then I must do something for myself. I must forgive others and myself as well. I allowed anger get between my cross and my salvation. When you find that you are so angry, don't let the sunset, get it resolved right, forgive and forget. After all, the kindness and love of God is still there. Be kind one to another with tender hearts and forgive one another, even as God for Christ sake has forgiven us, not by the works that we have done, but according to His mercy. Keep forgiveness in your pocket; use it and keep God by your side at all times.

-Elsie Roberson

What True Beauty Is!

(While sitting in the beauty salon one day I was divinely shown what true beauty is.)

Out of pits of poverty and graves of greed and jealousy emerges an army of African American sisters. Some are battle scared and some are limping but still moving, still marching, still running, still rising and still conquering!

For centuries on the backs of this precious army, nations were built and countries were sustained. Emerging through some of life's most pressing and grueling circumstances these sisters persevered by finding strength in the mighty arms of God and power in the portals of prayer.

We have come through broken homes, through ruined marriages; we have rippled through the waves of prejudice and the floods of segregation. We have withstood through the avenues of anger and ditches of depression. We have been looked at through the binoculars of bias and now, on the horizon of today and the sunrise of tomorrow, we see successful sisters standing strong and steadfast.

I, too, find myself standing there as a product of poverty, a one parent home, educational barriers, social degradation and physical abuse and yet I've risen, holding the hand of God! While kissing the face of obstacles, we continue to climb. While rubbing the shoulders of road blocks, we still rise. We still conquer. We still are victorious!

<u>Beauty Salon</u>

Sistas …Sistas everywhere
Short and tall, prancing dancing silhouettes
Voluptuously plump, round and skinny
Sistas are everywhere.

Almond, Chocolate, Banana yellow
And Midnight Black…sistas are everywhere!
Smiles of joy and frowns of anticipation
Freckles of fear and dimples of disappointment
Rejected by mothers, betrayed by brothers
Molested by fathers and born through uncles!
Sistas erupting from volcanoes of heart wrenching circumstances
Hiding insecurities in tight curls
And covering shame under synthetic nails
Sistas
Some braiding up their troubles
Others perming away their painful memories
Sistas hiding their dark gloom
Under hues of red and auburn and blonde!
Plucking away their angry brows
Pampering feet that have ran from fear
Sistas…soldiers of sadness
Princesses of pain!
Wrapping up guilt
And hiding tracks of regrets
Too painful to reveal…sistas
Rinsing away their worries
Conditioning their concerns
Massaging away the tension of midnight…
From this place majesty is born
Queens are conceived
Our pain is pampered
Sculptures of royalty emerges through pain
For in this place Eve is recreated

-Kim S. Lee

Walker Baptist Institute

Emma Addie Douse read every single thing she could get her hands on. There were no public schools for colored people. Her father Warren and a lot of other people felt it was a waste of time for girls, especially Negroes, to get an education. They were expected to find husbands to take care of them while they nursed babies, cleaned, cooked and took care of white folks. Rev. Dr. Charles Thomas Walker founded Walker Baptist Institute.

Dr. Walker was also the minister of Tabernacle Baptist Church in Augusta. He'd become a very popular speaker and felt strongly about providing education for colored students. The school taught basic classes like math, science and grammar. There was also Latin and music. There was a fully equipped kitchen in the Home Economics Department and students cooked all kinds of foods. They learned how to manage any kind of kitchen duty. They even made candy for friends and family.

Emma had a maid's job that she went to early in the mornings. She fixed breakfast and lunch and got the family off to work and school. Then she took a trolley to Walker Baptist Institute. The people in charge gave her a special rate on tuition since her father, Warren Douse, was a member of the Ministers' Alliance that helped support the school. She spent every spare minute in the Home Economics Room. During lunchtime, Emma oiled sewing machines, and learned every kind of stitch that could be made. She also learned how to manage a household. At the end of the school day, she walked back to her job to cook the family's supper.

Young ladies who graduated from Walker Baptist Institute had to make everything they wore except their shoes! Hattie scrimped and saved and bought Emma a brand new pair for the graduation ceremony. Warren was as proud as a peacock!

-Jayme Washington Smalley

Just Keep Praying and Pulling

We each have a wagon to pull through life's journey
Some may pull it slow; others may pull it in a hurry
Just keep praying and pulling, don't give up the fight,
Whatever the load, whether heavy or light
Sometimes it may seem those you ask for a helping hand
Jump in the wagon, instead of pulling, which you don't understand
Just keep praying and pulling, God will open up a way
He knows that your load is extra heavy and you need help today
Then you see folks being helped who have lighter loads
Just keep praying and pulling, as you make it down those bumpy roads
Now you look up, there is a hill, your back is breaking
and your heart is aching...
While others are looking, laughing and saying don't help
Watching as you pull that heavy wagon by yourself
Just keep praying and pulling, don't give up the fight
God sees it all, He knows you're not being treated right
He didn't bring you this far for you to fall from grace
Just keep praying and pulling with a smile on your face
Suddenly, you're filled with the Holy Spirit to the top of your head
And there is no heaviness in your wagon, just love and kindness instead
Now you're praising and pulling because the load has become very light
God has answered your prayers and everything will be alright!

-Pastor Orphialasertrella Adams-Taylor

Sewing

I watched as she carefully began to stitch my prom dress from scraps of cloth she bought from the neighborhood material store, which stood on the corner of Mount Vernon's busiest street. Her eyes twinkled as she tied off the end of a piece of thread, being careful not to leave too much at the end of the knot. She slowly picked up a spool of red thread from the corner of the bed. She almost didn't see it. Over the years, her eyes have clouded with age and it becomes increasingly difficult for her to see. The bedspread is a bright floral pattern, with fully bloomed red roses that camouflaged the spool making it initially difficult for her to locate it. She pulled out a piece of thread the length of the span of her arms and broke it off with her teeth. Granny then rolled the frayed and almost cottony end between her fingers, licked it between her lips to moisten it so the fuzzy pieces would stick together forming a straight enough end to go through the eye of the needle and pulled it straight with her fingers again. She picked up the needle, which was amongst a dozen other sewing needles and pins stuck in a red-orange pumpkin shaped pincushion with green stems and leaves. The cushion was about as big as my fist and had lemonade juice stains from Granny drinking and sewing in the blazing heat in a room with no air conditioning. Beads of sweat ran down her face and it would glisten after just a few short hours of needlework. Somehow she never allowed sweat to fall on what she considered her masterpiece. She then closed one eye, held the needle up to the sunlight and slowly threaded it through the needle. I suppose in her day she was very good at it, but today it took her three tries before she finally got the thread through; this is after licking it two more times to re-straighten the end, which bent every time she missed. Her frustration was short lived once she was able to continue her work. She stopped to look out the window as the wind blew through the trees. At that moment she realized that the window was closed and that's why it felt hotter than usual.

She began her ritual in the twilight hours, before the sun came up and just before the cock would crow. Although she is no longer home on the island in her country home on the hill, it's as if she can almost anticipate when they would begin their cackling and beat them to the early morning crow. I heard her shuffling around at about 4:00 a.m., her slippered feet dragging across the wooden floor. I quietly got up to see what was going on and peeked in from behind the door like a five-year-old looking for Santa Claus. She sat on the corner of the bed cutting out the delicate pieces of royal blue silk cloth, pausing from time to time to admire the lace that would be used for the v-cut collar, which hung on the headboard of her bed. It took me days to convince her that I really did want my dress to be above my knees. She simply couldn't understand why I would want my "meager" legs to show. But she finally gave over to the idea and said that it would be my problem if I couldn't find a decent young man to dance with because my bones were showing. So as she was cutting the skirt portion of the dress, she laughed under her breath and mumbled something that sounded like "crazy gal."

She never needed a pattern to make basic styles, but she used the pattern I chose because she knew I wanted it to be special. After cutting the main parts of the dress she tossed the pattern to the side and continued from memory. She is almost done with the major sewing and focused on finishing the hems, sleeves and collar. She skillfully uses the sewing machine as if she were a professional race car driver and this powerful machine was her car. She would slam on the pedal of her Singer and take the curves of sleeves and hems like a pro. Speeding up and slowing down only to gather the cloth that would next receive its white and blue dashes that looked like the lines in a two-lane highway. She smiled and sang about how Christ gave his life on the cross so that she could be saved; and my dress transformed from a bundle of cloth into a beautiful, well-tailored "frock."

She called me in to try on the dress. As I suspected and expected, Granny tried to give her final opinion by making the hem too long; well below my knees and far longer than I had requested. She argued all the way back to the sewing machine. She finally ended up cutting another three inches off the dress. And grumpily told me that it was "such a waste of good cloth." She would later use that "wasted cloth" to make a little sachet where she kept a few extra dollars for some yams and salt fish. She sewed a string to it and pinned it to the side of her bra so that no one could steal her "food" money. It never left her side. She slept with it.

After she lowered her voice and raised the hem of my dress, I tried it on, turned to examine the finished product in the mirror, and satisfied, took my dress to be professionally pressed and cleaned. She complained as I thanked her and kissed her on her cheek. She swiftly brushed me away claiming that she would never make another dress like that for me again. As I walked off I could hear her humming another tune about God's goodness and grace.

-Pittershawn Palmer

Morning Coffee with Grandpa

Sometimes I need to go back. I need to return to the frosty mornings in the red clay hills of Beatrice, Alabama. I need to capture just a smidgen of the early 1950s. Things were simple then.

I need to remember having morning coffee with Grandpa, George Davison. I would sit on the floor in Grandma's kitchen next to his chair. The kitchen was filled with love and the warmth generated by the black cast iron wood burning stove. He would pour my coffee in a green or white milk glass saucer trimmed in gold as my grandma yelled to him. "Don't give her coffee. She is too little. It will make her black." My Grandma was a warm, deep chestnut brown color and my Grandpa fairly light in complexion. Upon hearing her reasoning, he would simply respond by pouring some coffee in a saucer and saying, "here baby". Since I was already dark, who cared? Certainly, not grandpa and surely not me. I enjoyed the syrupy sweet, richly brown, and almost black coffee. In true southern style, it was heavily laced with chicory. The aroma of the freshly brewed coffee perfumed the entire house. It was always piping hot. Grandpa would blow the coffee in his cup to cool it and I would blow my saucer full of coffee, just like Grandpa. It took the bite off of the nippy winter mornings when the ground crunched with ice as you walked. Those were special times.

I still remember looking out of the train's window in September of 1955 as my sister, Sallie Joyce and I left Alabama and moved to the sunny Southern California with my mother, Sallie Davison Wesley. I waved goodbye to Grandma and Grandpa long after the little sleepy town, nested between the tall pines, faded away from the train's window. The train chugged down the track and whistled goodbye to the Crimson Clay hills and dusty red fog that hovered over the fields of a little town called Beatrice.

We moved to the big city, Los Angeles, but sometimes I really long for those bitter cold winter mornings in Grandma's toasty kitchen. I don't drink coffee anymore. Maybe it is because Grandpa has passed on. I am sure the flavor of the coffee was overshadowed by the love I shared with Grandpa. I keep a jar of chicory in my kitchen, instant of course. On the days when I need to remember, I have a cup and I am transcended back in time to the days I sat on the floor and waited for my coffee, like a baby bird with its beak perched upward with anticipation of the morning's rations.

It's not as cold in California but there are cold times in life. A cup of chicory seems to easy the chill when I feel alone, unappreciated, uneasy about decision that must be made, when I am gathering the pieces after my heart has been broken, or facing uncertain future events. I return to warmth of Grandma's kitchen and remember Grandpa. I make a cup of instant healing. As the chicory starts to permeate the air I reenter the needed portions of the time chambers of years past. Once again the smell of chicory takes center stage. It seems to take the edge off of the cold and chilling realities of the world outside.

Somehow I didn't envision the importance of those times then nor did I realize how special those memories would become. At the time it seemed to be one of many small things. The mornings spent on the kitchen floor have proven to be a pivotal part of my education. Through college and the work force, I have been exposed to many profound teachers and philosophies. The teachings of my grandparents still loom as my rock and core. The arsenal of wisdom imparted on me in the eight years I lived with them still helps me weather the storms of life. When calamity comes, I deploy one of the weapons inherited at the feet of my grandparents, although neither of them graduated from elementary school, their wisdom is infinite.

Yes, sometimes I need to go back. I need to remember if only for a moment. I need to return to the early 1950s and to take hold of one of the anchors that makes me who I am today.

This cup is for you Grandpa. Thanks for the memories.

-Bertha Wesley Sanders

10th Anniversary Edition

In The Ruff

I self-published my first book of poetry in April of 2004. The project was very special and held a lot of meaning for me, because it was said that it would and could never happen. That is the reason that I wanted to make sure that every inch of the book had my name on it, not so much to show anyone up or to prove anything to anyone else, but to allow me to look at myself and say, "You did it. I had come through all the talk, negative vibes, and the non-supporting cast that I had around me. I was told things like: men don't become writers and you can't put a book together with no money. And you know, if I heard those things, there were many other things that I heard as well. There was one person other than my mother that used to tell me that my writing would touch and minister to many. I used to deny it, but then I continued getting negative and comments about my gift, that's when it became a personal goal of mine to become exactly what my creation was intended to be. That's when my inside voice, My God, spoke to me and said, there is one or two speaking and many others talking. You are more likely to be what those few see in you, opposed to being what everyone else says. That is when I made up my mind to develop my own thought process and I realized that I had to do what was in my heart and mind and not be defeated by what others had to say or think. I realized, thankfully, at a very young age that if anything in my life was going to happen it was going to depend on me.

Many are called to talk, but only a few are chosen to be listened to. In writing this, I chose to listen to the few, and used all the others as the next steps on my ladder as I pursued scaling to new heights. This brought me closer to my spirituality and set the tone for how I would carry myself through my days. I found strength in myself by paying attention and being mindful of everything around me, and at 17 at the time, I didn't miss any fun as a child. That was just a small part of what was then, which has resulted into being a small part of what is now.

There was a Pastor here in Houston, TX that bought my book, and after reading through it, he was so impressed that he asked me to attend one of his youth Sunday services to read some poetry and say a few encouraging words to the kids.

Now mind you, this was after someone had told me weeks prior that they saw me being a good mentor for children, which meant to me, that I had something positive to tell or teach them. And that came about two days after someone else told me that I could never teach anyone anything, because I had not learned anything. But I live life everyday, don't we live to learn, which means that if done right, we should properly learn how to live. So, even now, I still deal with, and put up with, things that can detour me if I allow them.

Anyway, I accepted the offer to come and speak. I mean why wouldn't I? This was an honor for me and a much higher one for the God that resides in me. When it came time for me to speak, I read two poems from my book and then I spoke to them on the topics that their youth department were focusing on, which were player hating, life's detours, being and staying focused and determined. I wanted them to see and understand that we all deal with the same things, just on different levels. I felt it was important because children always feel alone in what they go through and maybe if they understood that we went through what they are going through, then we could possibly see a change in them because they will feel that they have something to relate to.

I talk to them about making decisions and following their hearts. I tried to explain to them the importance of paying attention to the things that takes place around them, which allows us to formulate a substance, or foundation for who we will become. I wanted them to begin to see that at some point in life, there will be a time for them to have to be responsible for their actions and their words. I wanted them to understand that we do not become sound adults because of the mishaps that took place in our lives, but based on how we let those mishaps affect us.

That concept lead me to have a word with the parents that were there, because, the parents are the foundation. I am not a parent, but I have taken time with my nephew, helped others with their children, as well as looked back to my childhood and tried to see the good, the bad, and most of all I tried to see all that I learned in order to be able to pass something positive on as opposed to reliving my life through the lives of children. I think a lot of us pass things on just because they were passed on to us. I rather think that in doing so, we do nothing but pass on the pains of generations before us.

We should be passing on what we learned from those pains, instead of inflicting the same pains on children that can't handle them, causing them to grow up with an unexplained complex. It's unexplained because children have always been told, "Do as I say and don't question adults." Even the bible says, "Seek" that means ask, and anything asked is a question. So, ultimately we live in contradiction and confusion, causing us to raise just that.

Now, if we say that the children are our futures and they keep seeing us as liars, hypocrites, contradicters, and so on, then that is what they will become. We are products of what we grow from. Children are told, "Be what you want to be in life", but when they become young adults that is when we really try to control them. As parents, we get upset and frustrated with them for not doing or even doing good at the things that we want them to when we are really upset with ourselves, trying to figure out where we went wrong, when the majority of it is because we tried giving them the person that we want to see instead of respecting who and what we see. We actually spend more time confusing them than anything.

But can we be faulted? That is what happens to us, now we are adults passing the same thing on. In order to raise them and teach them, we have to re-raise and re-teach ourselves according to what mama and daddy gave, as well as what people and the world gave. However, we don't allow ourselves to do that because we were taught, told, and raised to do and stick with just what we were taught, told, and raised to do.

So we have become afraid to step out and learned for ourselves. When you take your learning; good or bad, and apply it, you can come up with a sensible substance to pass on. We cannot be dishonest with ourselves, the children, nor the people around us. The kids see this and they will become it. We are what we saw and heard. In other cultures (outside the U.S.) children step into adulthood at about 14-16 years of age. Because of the formation of life at this age, we have to look at them as being just that, young adults and not just as a child anymore. As young adults we make them deal with spiritual warfare, which defeats them and discourages them from the start. Now that we have become adults with no courage, we end up with another generation that has adopted the negatives of life and that becomes what gets passed on to the next.

We need to start asking them about themselves, instead of telling them what to do, when we don't really know about them and their needs, desires, or their likes. No one can tell you about you or what is really going on with you unless they ask and you tell. It is the same for the children, just on a different level. Just because we are the parents, does not mean that we know them. They know what is inside of them and what they want to do. The warfare comes into play because we tell them what we want them to do, opposed to helping, guiding, and governing them through what they want to do.

We have to stop taking their fair chance from them. Neither should we raise nor have children in order to compensate for mishaps that were disappointments in our own lives. We say things like: I want to give my children the things, opportunities, and relationships that I did not have. We now have two different adults, raising a family based on pains from two different backgrounds, instead of taking from those backgrounds and finding one common ground to raise a new family.

10th Anniversary Edition

Although those things are all needs, we should be focused on and excited about passing on, we need to learn from the positives, instead of focusing on using someone else's life as a platform of satisfaction to curve our childhood disappointments.

Bill Cosby gave a speech not very long ago, about his thoughts of certain parts of Black America. Although he took some criticism, I agreed with him. If we can redirect the way we handle our children, then our children can redirect the way they handle themselves.

Of the children that I have had personal talks and involvements with, their grades have improved, their conduct has gotten better and they have begin to see how to make a decision without worry about what their peers may have to say. If we can get these things re-iterated to our youth, then we have a fair chance of seeing a difference in them.

-Johnnie Roberts

Contributors

Ja Adams, a poet and psychological suspense writer, resides in Austin, TX. Presently she is collaborating efforts with Grapevine Star Entertainment to launch Beautiful Africa, a series of books dedicated to awakening global pride in African heritage. Ja uses her gift of writing to enhance multicultural awareness, tolerance, and appreciation for the human existence. To order a copy of award winning novel, *Chameleon,* go to http://www.authorhouse.com/bookstore
To order her latest novel *Purple Haze,* view her website: http://www.jaadamsauthor.bravehost.com

Orphialasertrella (Orphia-La-S-trella) Adams-Taylor is an ordained Minister, dynamic motivational speaker, Gospel Poetess, Senior Pastor of Scriptures Evangelistic Ministries and Director of The Ten Commandments Campaign for Children. She has a Doctor of Divinity Degree, Bachelor Degree in Pastoral/Biblical Studies and a graduate of Temple University's School of Social Admin. She is blessed with more than 50 speaking engagements yearly.

H. Renay Anderson has a M.A. in Organizational Management and a B.S. in Management/Marketing. Her first book is <u>Why Women Wear Shoes They Know Will Eventually Hurt Their Feet</u>. In 2005, she won a National AD contest for ADCandy. Former book reviewer for "Bella Online," "EuroReviews," and "BBW Reviews". Website: http://clix.to/renay

Mary Bains-Fort was born on December 18 in San Francisco. She is the wife of Bishop Wesley D. Fort, Pastor of NewLife Family Worship Center. Her education includes a Ph.D received from the Union Institute & Kingsfield University in Organizational Behavior

Psychology, Master of Science in Educational Psychology, Counseling, and a B.A. in Liberal Studies-Music Option, both from California State University, Hayward. Mary Bains-Fort is a Life Strategist Coach, former Host & Executive Producer of Cable TV and the Talk Show "How to Get Your Groove Back!" as well as the founder and ED of NewLife CDC, Inc.

Keyanna Celina Bean, www.keyanna.com

Toni Beckham is the president and CEO of PR et Cetera, Inc. a full service public relations firm based in the San Francisco Bay Area and publicist for Gumbo for the Soul. www.pretcetera.com

Gwendolyn Brown-Massey resides in Rock Hill, SC, is a mother of four girls and a copyrighted writer of poetry and children stories. For more information iamsilkyslim@yahoo.com

Monique Miles Bruner is currently an academic advisor at Rose State College in Midwest City, OK. She has a Bachelor and Master degrees in Public Administration and a Master in Human Relations, and is in the process of completing her PhD in Adult Education. Monique is an avid reader who reviews books for www.looseleaves.org. To her credit, Monique co-wrote a textbook entitled, _Strategies That Empower People for Success in College and Life_; a co-editor of _Delta Girls: Stories of Sisterhood_; and contributor to _Violets_. She spends family time watching movies, putting together jigsaw puzzles, and watching football with her husband, BK Bruner and two daughters, Angelique and Domonique. The Bruners are co-owners of the Diaper Outlet and they also established a non-profit organization to support family education called, Families First Foundation. Known for her quick wit and contagious laughter, Monique has dedicated endless amount of time and hard work to support the programs of her beloved sorority, DELTA SIGMA

THETA Sorority, Inc. and currently serves the community as President of the Oklahoma City Urban League Young Professionals.

Christopher Chambers, www.chrischambersbooks.com, chrichambers@comcast.net.

Lorita Kelsey Childress is from Antioch, California. She is married, has three daughters, and one granddaughter. Lorita is working on her first novel, *The Turning Point of Lila Louise*.

Heather Covington is the host of the Black Family Channel's Literary Living show, Author of *Literary Divas: The Top 100+ Most Admired African American Women in Literature* (ACGI, www.Amberbooks.com), one of the leading independent journalists in the literary arena and editor of Disilgold Soul Magazine. Her website is www.Disilgold.com and anti-negativity defying poetry books can be found at www.perSOULnalities.com.

Lynette Daniels is the founder of Nfinite Productions, LLC; a company that delivers educational media for children. The mission is to help children develop basic math skills and improve self-esteem through an engaging program that integrates educational concepts with popular culture. In 2004, Lynette launched her first product entitled Rap-A-Matics with a follow-up line of illustrated books expected to hit the market early this year. Please visit: www.Rap-A-Matics.com.

Yvonne Singleton Davis was born in New York, New York. Yvonne is happily married, the Founder & CEO of Sister to Sister: One in the Spirit, Inc., the Author of *Teachers Under Siege*, and Board of Directors Member of the New York Coalition of 100 Black Women. Her passions are writing, knitting & crocheting, and swimming/water aerobics. Yvonne is a multiple-year Honoree listed in Who's Who Among America's Teachers and a member of Mother A.M.E. Zion Church.

10th Anniversary Edition

Frank E. Dobson, Jr. is a native of Buffalo, NY and author of the novel, *The Race Is Not Given.*

Kimberly Etherith-Spence resides in Leesburg, Virginia, has a passion for helping others, and does so by volunteering for the Hospices of the National Capitol Area among other organizations. For further information, feel free to contact her at ladysoulgirl@yahoo.com.

Pierre Etienne is a young poet and speaker who aims to change the world with his actions and words. He was born and raised in Southern California. He began his love of writing at a young age, and has continued to develop his skills using various writing forms. Some of his past works have been featured in various publications for poetry. He is currently working on his personal anthology.

Lorraine Elzia is a paralegal, editor and author. Her work has been published in *Chicken Soup for the Single Mother's Soul*, *Chicken Soup for the African American Woman's Soul* and she is a contributing author in the upcoming anthology, *Surfacing...Phenomenal Women on Passion, Politics and Purpose.* Lorraine is Co Moderator of Essentially Women Writing Group, www.essentiallywoman.com, and Co Owner of Eve's Literary Services with Sharon Gray. For more information, visit her website at www.evesliteraryservice.com.

Shelia M. Goss currently resides in Louisiana. She's the Essence Bestselling author of <u>My Invisible Husband</u> and is an entertainment writer for various publications. To find out more about her, visit her website at www.sheliagoss.com.

Sharon Stinson Gray, M.P.A, *Editor, Gumbo for the Soul Anthology.* Sharon "Shaye" Gray is the Co-Founder of Essentially Women Writing Group, www.essentiallywoman.com, co owns *Eve's Literary*

Services with Lorraine Elzia and served as Sr. Editor of Bahiyah Magazine, www.BWMmag.com. Ms. Gray works full time as a high school teacher and part time as an evening adjunct professor for adult education; she has her B.A in English and Master's degree in Public Administration. Currently, she is pursuing her Doctorate degree in Higher Educational Leadership with an emphasis in Adult Education. Presently, Sharon Gray resides in Maryland and is working on several literary projects. You may visit her site at www.evesliteraryservice.com.

Benjamin Hicks is the CEO and President of Ingleside Press www.geocities.com/inglesidepressmd. He graduated from Towson University with a degree in Mass Communication. He has been writing for 16 years and resides in B-more, where he works as an outreach assistant for BCCC. He wrote eight books: *Life Conflictions, Distinguished Young Black Poet: Vol I, Christmas Poems, Diary of Black Love, The Myths About Condom Safety, Arithmecation (Children's book), Sexcrazy,* and *365 Degrees of Blackness.*

Shawneen C. Hicks, a payroll administrator and writer from Cleveland, Ohio, is a single, blessed parent of two boys and loves to write about everyday life. Contact via email at gemini61572@yahoo.com.

Jennifer Jackson is a graduate of Mount Holyoke College. She is originally from Uniondale, NY. She currently works as an education development volunteer through the US Peace Corps in Namibia, Africa.

T. Marie Jackson has been writing since elementary school. She is also an avid poet and was a regular on the poetry circuit in the Bay Area and Las Vegas. She has written for several internet websites as an editorial columnist, and currently runs a web log, *Really Smart Talk,* where she participates in the monthly *Radical Women of Color*

Carnival. She currently resides in Grand Rapids, Michigan with her family.

Beverly Black Johnson, founder of Gumbo for The Soul www.gumboforthesoul.com.
Beverly finds her passion in writing gospel lyrics. Find out more about her at www.beverlyblackjohnson.com.

Kyeisha Johnson is a 6th grade student who has been writing ever since she could hold a pencil. In 2005, Kyeisha was the recipient of a Young Authors Writing Contest writing award from Barnes and Nobles for her story, "<u>Trick The Trickey Trickster</u>".

Vanessa A. Johnson hails from Louisiana. She and her husband of twenty-eight plus years have four children, and three grandchildren. Johnson is the author of, *When Death Comes a Knockin'*, a self-help, inspirational book about loss and grief. (Lulu Press, March 2005, ISBN 1-4116-2470-X). Learn more about her at www.vanessaajohnson.com; Email: vjohns1@bellsouth.net.

Joylynn M. Jossel, a Columbus, Ohio native, is the Essence Magazine Bestselling author of *If I Ruled the World* and *When Souls Mate*. Joylynn is the editor of the Urban Books imprint, Urban Christian. You can contact her via email at JoylynnJossel@aol.com.

LB Lacey, MA has a BA in English & Theatre & Master of Holistic Counseling. She is CEO of SOULutions for Dynamic Living; (www.SOULutionsForDynamicLiving.com), co-author of *100 Words of Wisdom for Women*, and co-producer/ spoken word artist on "f o o d" The PaKoLi Project. "*My passion is using my talents, gifts and skills to empower & celebrate others in manifesting and developing their own.*"

Halima Lee, a San Francisco Bay Area native, is an aspiring novelist and Freelance Copy Editor. She is also the Editorial Manager for CityFlight Newsmagazine, a Bay Area based publication that serves the African American community.

Kim S. Lee, Native of Columbus, Ohio and author of *Diamonds of Grace,* a collection of poetry/biographies featuring Biblical Icons of God's grace. Kim is a motivational speaker and spiritual leader. Contact Kim at KL4795@aol.com.

James W. Lewis is an up-and-coming author originally from Virginia and now lives in Southern California. He has several print credits, including *Chicken Soup for the Mothers and Sons Soul* and Zane's *Caramel Flava.* His website is www.jameswlewis.com.

Matthew Lynch is an Exceptional Education Teacher at Sykes Elementary School, CEO of Lynch Consulting Group, LLC, and a Doctoral Candidate at Jackson State Mississippi. He is also the author of *Closing the Racial Academic Achievement Gap,* and an upcoming children's book, entitled *Matthew and the Money Tree.* Mr. Lynch is a contributing columnist for *My Brotha Magazine, Renaissance Man Magazine,* and *Emerging Minds.* Born and raised in Mississippi, he currently resides in Jackson, Mississippi.

Sylvia McClain is a freelance writer who currently writes for the business periodicals published by Equal Opportunity Publications, Inc. on engineering and information technology. She recently wrote about hair care and styles for "Braids World" and life changes for "Strut." She conducts workshops about money management, self-publishing, and freelance writing. For more info, visit her website at www.scribalpress.com.

Tamara Ashley McCullough hails from Dallas, TX. She is a junior at Southern Methodist University where she is majoring in journalism and psychology.

S. Raye Mitchell, Esq., is an Attorney and Business Consultant for most of the time, and an expressive creative for the rest of the time. She loves collecting African American Art, interior decorating, writing, working out at the gym and finding her purpose. She believes in mentoring and giving back. Her story is best found at www.mitchelllawgroup.com.

E. Joyce Moore is a Renaissance woman with a passion for fine art, writing and thanking people who walk their talk. Read her work on www.blackboardjournal.braveblog.com.
  Want to know more? Visit www.goodwood.bravehost.com.

Alicia Morgan is an engineer by trade with a deeply rooted passion for writing. She is a poet, essayist, short story writer and aspiring novelist. Her personal website is www.inseparable1.com.

Michael T. Owens doubled-majored in Sociology and Communications for Business at Florida State University. He is the author of *A Dream Come True, Pick-Up Lines,* and editor of *Truth Be Told: Tales of Life, Love, and Drama.* His works are also featured in anthologies and national publications. Email him at michaeltowens@yahoo.com or visit his website: www.getmynovel.com.

M. LaVora Perry became the first African American staff card writer, in 1995, for American Greetings, which is headquartered in Cleveland and is the world's largest publicly-owned greeting card company. She has appeared on the *Tavis Smiley Show* on National Public Radio to discuss her work and is profiled in the original *Marquis Who's Who in America* and *Who's Who Among American Women.* Perry is the author of the children's books *Wu-lung & I-lung* and *Taneesha's Treasures of the Heart,* which is included in the curriculum of Zambian public schools. Perry's Pictures of *My Days:*

An Art & Writing Workbook for Creating the Life You Want is a creative envisioning and goal-setting tool for all ages. She conducts writing, book publishing and promotion workshops for youth and adults. Perry is the founder of Forest Hill Publishing, LLC and lives in Northern Ohio with her husband, Cedric Richardson, and her three children.

Ryan Christopher Pinkston was born and raised in the Bay Area of California. He is a student at Berklee College of Music in Boston, Massachusetts. He has been singing since childhood and plans to make a career out of it by using his influence to positively impact the community from which he came, and reaching out to the global community as a Humanitarian.

Joe Prince. From the late 60's streets of East Palo Alto, to attending Oakland's Black Panthers' Liberation School, Mr. Prince learned the value of education. Misunderstood as a child, Mr. Prince was eventually diagnosed with Asperger's Syndrome, the mildest form of autism. Mr. Prince attended college but was stricken with cancer which dashed his Olympic dreams. Liberation Saturday is Mr. Prince's inspirational saga of "going the distance" to attain his college degree and eventual position as an educator to Special Education and Track and Field students.

Rolanda T. Pyle is a currently a New Jerseyer but is a native New Yorker. She is single, and authors the book, *FINALLY* - a collection of inspirational poems. Rolanda's passions include writing and grandparents who are raising their grandchildren. Find out more about her at: www.rorosrainbowcommunications.com

Angela Ray is a multi-talented artist--working as a writer, actress, and motivational speaker. She is the author of the book of poetry, Blackberry Whispers and the CEO of Mahogany Dime, LLC. To learn more about this diva in development, visit www.mahoganydime.com.

Sidalia G. Reel, was born and bred in Berkeley, California. She is a widowed mother of three adult sons. Sidalia is a Human Resources Executive in the Silicon Valley with a passionate commitment to diversity in the workplace.

Pamela Rivers who currently lives in Riverdale, NY, is a journalist, poet, author, public speaker and event producer who works for VH1 Cable channel. In addition to writing for television and radio, she serves as publicist and writer for Black Outdoorsman Magazine, is a contributing author to *Delta Girls: Stories of Sisterhood Anthology* and is a freelance contributor to Today's Child Magazine.

Elsie Roberson was born in Enterprise, Mississippi on March 14, 1944; she is a mother of six children and has been a member of the Church of Christ for twenty-two years. Her mother moved to Wisconsin when Elsie was ten years old. Elsie says she is blessed with the knowledge, understanding and wisdom of God's word; the Lord has given her the ability to write Bible lessons, and that's what she does at home.

Bertha Wesley Sanders is a minister of the gospel and has one daughter. Her articles have been published in local publications. She has 34 years of experience in writing business communications. Retirement allows her to finally return to some of her foremost loves: full time ministry, reading, and writing the things that nourish the heart.

Carla Sarratt is a resident of Charlotte, North Carolina who enjoys traveling, watching movies, and reading. Find out more about Carla as well as read samples of her writing at http://www.carlasarratt.com.

Jayme Washington Smalley has a unique gift for painting vivid word pictures for her audiences. Groups of all ages are enthralled by her mix of theater, music and powerful storytelling. Her book *As The Butterbeans Boil* is a collection of stories, poems and recipes that entertains as well as informs readers about the challenges of growing up African American in the late 1950s.

Panderina D. Soumas is owner and author of *Soumas Heritage Creole Creations Soumas Heritage Creole Cookbook, The "Creole-Cocoa" Cook, Public Speaker-Cooking Demos Wholesale, Retail - Festivals, Fairs & Trade Shows.* Visit www.soumascreole.com ~A Taste of Creole History of Creoles of Color~

Glenda Staten is a married, retired military who hails from Statesville, North Carolina. She is the owner of Staten's Picture Gallery (www.statensgallery.com). Glenda's passion is photography (nature and scenic).

Kara Ingrid Stevens, writer and educator, is a firm believer in power of self-love to transform and rebuild. She holds a BA in Political Science from Oberlin College and a MSED in Bilingual Education from Hunter College. She resides in Queens, NYC where she works as a bilingual kindergarten teacher.

Davidae "Dee" Stewart is the managing editor for Suite 101.com's African American Women Writers Finding Voice, a book reviewer for Romance in Color, the R.E.A.L. Reviewers, and other publications and a contributing writer for Shades of Romance Magazine, Rejoice Atlanta, Rejoice Valdosta and Common Ground, Inc. Newspapers and Atlanta Christian Family Life Magazine. She owns a custom publications/commercial writing consulting business and is completing her first novel.

Kathie Strother-Scholl seeks to inspire children, notably children of color, to strive to do their best, persevere and to help others.

Through writing for children, Kathie has been able to accomplish her goal. Her poem titled, *Walking That Line,* for the GFTS anthology, will be her first published work. She has completed five children book manuscripts, two of which are currently being reviewed by two different publishers. Kathie is also working on a book of inspirational poems for children.

Delores Thomas is the recipient of numerous poetic awards including 2001 and 2003's Poet of the Year from the Shakespearean Famous Poets Society, the Editor's Choice Award for Outstanding Achievements in Poetry, the Best Poems and Poets for 2001, 2002, 2003, 2004 and 2005. Delores is also the recipient of 2002's International Merit of Poetry, 2003, 2004 and 2005's Outstanding Achievements in Poetry, 2005's Editor's Choice Published Poet Ribbon Award Pin, and inducted into the *International Who's Who in Poetry*. Her poetic endeavors can be found in more than twenty anthologies and four Sounds of Poetry compact discs.

Delores Thornton, voted "Queen of Promotion" by C&B Books, is an Indianapolis native and lifelong resident. Author, columnist, radio talk show host and book promoter, Thornton invites you to visit her site at www.deloresthornton.com.

Jamie Walker is a poet and journalist who writes for *The New York Amsterdam News, The Long Beach Times, The San Francisco Bayview*, and countless other Black newspapers and media outlets. Originally from Oakland, California, Walker's first book is *101 Ways Black Women Can Learn to Love Themselves* (J.D. Publishing Group 2002).

Vickie L. Williams-Morris is a performance, visual, and literary artist from northeast Ohio. With a Bachelor's degree in communications from Cleveland State University, her stage play *Expendable* was read in the 9th Annual Arenafest Festival of New Plays at Karamu House and her poem "Slide Back" was published in the PWLGC' *Cleveland in Prose and Poetry* anthology. Currently, she is working on several children's books and co-authoring her sister's memoir.

Visit www.wilmorcreations.com.

10th Anniversary Edition

An Additional Helping of Gumbo?

While many of the stories, poems and recipes you have read in this anthology were written by well-known black authors, other submissions were accepted from readers just like you. Gumbo for the Soul is a mixture of the experiences of ALL our people worldwide. We invite you to contribute to our next anthology.

Submissions should be non-fiction, up to 1500 words in length and must be an original piece. Each submission must include a bio (5 sentences or less) written in third person. Electronic submissions must be saved as a word document attachment, written in Times New Roman 12 point font only. A query letter or a 1-2 paragraph summary of the poem or essay is encouraged. Only those selected for inclusion in Gumbo for the Soul will be notified of acceptance. Pieces not selected for immediate inclusion are eligible for consideration for publication on our website and/or in future anthologies.

To obtain a copy of our submission guidelines, please visit our website at
Gumbo for the Soul, www.gumboforthesoul.com.

Helpful Resources Section

Creating Key "Pieces of the Puzzle" That Shape the Minds and Souls of Our Children: Mr. Fred Stickney and UPI Education

He has served as the President and Chief Executive Officer of the YMCA San Francisco for three years and for 11 years as the President and Chief Executive Officer of YMCA East Bay. He is the founder of the "Latch Key" Youth Development Program concept, which was established in the late 1960s in Portland, Oregon – a concept that has grown worldwide. He is the author of numerous articles which have been published in journals and periodicals and has co-authored "Where Do the Children Play" a manual for "Latch Key" Child Development. He also is the author of "Ghana Planning Assistance – Vocational Rehabilitation." He has conducted a research project in Ghana at the request of the Sister Cities International Program and lectured in Hong Kong, Taiwan, The Philippines, Japan, Korea, Australia and New Zealand. During his career, he has created key pieces of the puzzle, which have enhanced and continue to enhance our children's positive intellectual, psychological and physical development. He continues to utilize his talents to empower families and communities. He is MR. FRED STICKNEY. Mr. Stickney, who has been active in fundraising and business development for over 35 years and has raised over US$100,000,000 for new projects in the non-profit and for-profit communities, is a key member of a team of individuals, which is helping to shape the minds and souls of our children through his affiliation with Unified Progress International Education ("UPI Education") -- founded in 2004 by Mr. Frank Crump, a successful international businessman – which offers a Life Skills Solutions™ curriculum. Stickney and UPI Education are creating key "pieces of the puzzle" that are positively shaping the minds and souls of our children.

Mr. Stickney carved out time from his very developing schedule to talk about, among other things, UPI Education, its Life Skills Solutions™ curriculum, his affiliation with UPI Education, and what our children need from us.

So, how is Mr. Stickney, a man who has embarked upon a path which has caused him to
become *"all things to all people"* able to sustain a sense of balance in his life?

"I have chosen to find things that I like to do. My balance is my total involvement with my family and their activities. I have a wonderful wife. I have two daughters, a son, and four grandchildren and I talk or e-mail with all of them daily. I am very self-disciplined and choose to consult or write articles because I am interested in learning. My balance comes from years of working on it. The YMCA experience early in my life gave me the principles of a 'strong mind', 'a strong body', and 'a strong spirit', which I have tried to follow all my adult life," Mr. Stickney responded.

Stickney has demonstrated a strong concern for children through his stewardship of the YMCA in San Francisco and East Bay, the founding of the "Latch Key" Youth Development Program concept in Portland, Oregon, the authoring of numerous articles and a manual and his current affiliation with UPI Education and its Life Skills Solutions™ curriculum. Why?

"I believe the heritage of our world is through the positive nurturing and growth of our children. Through my YMCA experience, I learned how to administer and provide programs for youth of all backgrounds and in urban and rural areas. I feel strongly about children having opportunities to participate in activities that broaden their horizons. I directed camps for ten years and saw how much children learned from outdoor experiences. I founded and managed child day care programs, which provided safe and secure environments for children. I am currently the Volunteer Chair of the Board of Directors of the NorCal Volleyball Club, which is a non-profit organization that serves girls aged 12-18 years of age. There are ten teams, twenty-two coaches, a sizable budget and the bonus is to watch two of my granddaughters play for the club. I'm able to give my expertise and enjoy valuable time with my family. Non-profit agencies are able to offer a variety of programs for children of all ages. The collaboration of non-profit agencies and the educational system need to continue to work together to support the broad life experience that children need," Mr. Stickney explained.

The discussion moved to Mr. Stickney's affiliation with UPI Education. Mr. Stickney talked about his role at UPI Education, its Founder – Mr. Frank Crump – and its team of leaders which include Dr. James Comer from Yale University and Mr. Tom Fleming of New Haven, Connecticut.

"I met Frank Crump, the founder of UPI Education and I liked his vision, his energy and concepts for the program. I am a consultant to UPI Education and have enjoyed being involved with its team of leaders, such as Dr. James Comer from Yale University and Tom Fleming of New Haven, Connecticut who have demonstrated the successes of UPI Education within the education process. UPI Education is a program that will enrich the educational experience for students. It will provide a curriculum that prepares students for the future -- and the quicker traditional educational systems adopt the UPI programs, the better off our society will be," Stickney remarked.

UPI Education has a Life Skills Solutions™ curriculum. It is reported that UPI Life Skills Solutions™ curriculum has produced a 16.4% increase in the grade point average in schools, a 23.6% reduction in school absences and an astonishing reduction in school disciplinary actions. How is this possible? How is UPI Education through its Life Skills Solutions™ curriculum able to achieve what a number of parents, school administrators, and educators have not? Is there a magic formula?

"I think we would be stretching it to say there was a magic formula, despite the fact that many people, myself included, find the percentages to be magical to the ear," Stickney replied with a wry smile. "The possibilities of UPI's educational process are endless and in fact, the entire process of UPI's program is inclusive of and encompasses educators, administrators, and parents as they rally in support of UPI's instructional materials and method of training; given the obvious benefits to the student(s). UPI exemplifies what can be accomplished and these accomplishments will be magnified when the above mentioned are joined by corporations, foundations, concerned individuals and government leaders who are committed to solving the 'real problems' which demise our current educational process and future outlook for our youth."

What does the fact that there is a need for a program such as UPI Education's Life Skills Solutions™ curriculum say about the state of affairs of education in the United States? In your view, what are we doing wrong? What are we doing right?

Mr. Stickney offered the following:

"The state of affairs of education in the United States has been readily documented and the bottom line is that our current system does not have all the answers and we have much room for improvement. Further, we must make a concerted effort to correct it and if necessary change the way we view education and the process thereof. Otherwise, the entire fabric of our nation and life as we have known it will suffer. The forefathers of our great nation fully understood the value of education as it relates to the growth, development, and longevity of a nation. It's important that we maintain such an understanding and, in fact, truly 'Leave no child behind.' UPI Education represents just one piece of the puzzle. The key to the puzzle will require that those with the ability to implement change within the vast historic past of education in America – open up their minds to the pieces of the puzzle that lie before them and act accordingly. Many have begun to realize that we cannot address these new problems with old worn-out tools. To this end, we are on the right-track and doing the right thing," Mr. Stickney observed.

The focus of our discussion shifted to the life skills that are taught to students enrolled in UPI Education's Life Skills Solutions™ curriculum – life skills such as conflict resolution, balancing a checkbook and career goals. Are these skills not being taught in our homes or in our schools? Are our children who spend twelve years in our educational system graduating without knowing how to balance a checkbook, resolve conflicts and prepare for a career?

"Many of the parents of our children have themselves been victims of our current educational system. Thus, when we truly look into the homes we find a lack of ability to teach the necessary life skills such as balancing a checkbook or setting realistic career goals. Likewise, most schools do not have a life skills curriculum and focus on teaching reading, writing, and arithmetic as their core set of courses -- in an attempt to meet national standards. Again, I'll repeat: 'The poor results of the above have been readily documented'. So, yes, many children who spend twelve years in our educational system are graduating without life skills knowledge, and for the many that drop out of school, they are ill prepared to live in a normal society. The result of a poor educational process is inextricably tied to other societal problems such as drug use, crime, incarceration, pregnancy and a number of repeatable negative cycles," Stickney said with unflinching honesty.

In what ways will UPI Education's Life Skills Solutions™ curriculum provide our children with the tools that they will need to successfully compete in a global marketplace when they reach adulthood?

"I think I can best answer that question by quoting Mr. Frank Crump, the Founder of UPI Education. Mr. Crump has said, 'The UPI Education life skills curriculum is a training program designed to prepare students for the rigors of life. Exploring life's most challenging obstacles, the curriculum makes sense of it all and allows a student to open their mind to the social, economic, and political possibilities that exist for themselves and those around them. The curriculum is designed to teach students what society will expect and demand of them and what it will take for success. UPI concentrates on developing a good citizen, one capable of contributing to the school community and society at large," Stickney commented.

So, in Mr. Stickney's view, whose responsibility is it to equip our children with the tools that they will need to successfully compete in a global marketplace when they reach adulthood? Does this responsibility lie solely with parents? Alternatively, is it a responsibility that should be shared with parents, academic institutions and concerned citizens?

"The responsibility has to be shared. The parents begin the process, the schools extend the process, concerned citizens, businesses and corporations share the entire process. The priority of all countries must be the goal to integrate the education process within our society," says Stickney.

What are the necessary steps, which need to be taken to positively shape the minds and souls of our children? Whose responsibility is it to positively shape the minds and souls of our children? Does the responsibility lie solely with parents? Is this a responsibility that should be shared with parents, academic and religious institutions and concerned members of our communities?

"The responsibility to positively shape the minds and spirit of our children is shared by parents, academic institutions, faith-based organizations, and the entire community encompassing both business and social aspects. Much of the failure of our education systems has been because of lack of funding and priorities of our communities. Our communities must place children as the top priority in the funding of education and provide resources for new and innovative programs such as UPI."

If a parent wants to enroll their child in UPI Education's Life Skills Solutions™ curriculum or wants to have the curriculum instituted in their school district or community, what should they do? How can one learn more about what UPI Education's Life Skills Curriculum Solutions™ has to offer?

"To learn more about UPI Education one should visit the website www.upieducation.org. UPI Education is a non-profit, tax-deductible 501(c)(3). Parents interested in instituting UPI Education within their school district or community should contact Heather Taylor at 818-990-3378. Likewise, parents and educators should inform their mayor, school superintendent and elected officials about UPI Education and get them involved in the process of bringing UPI to their school and community," Mr. Stickney advised. D.A. Sears

10th Anniversary Edition

Recommended Resources for Parents and Students

1. http://school.discovery.com

My favorite site. It has so many links and useful information, including pages that current students have created. Not only does it have homework help, but information about current school supplies, extra activities to enhance your child's learning. My top pick.

2. http://encarta.msn.com/encnet/departments/homework

This site is so well put together. It is clean, crisp, and very easy to follow. I love this site. There are so many ways to learn here. You have to check it out.

3. http://www.kidsource.com/index.html

Although I have this site at the bottom of the list, it should be the first for a parent to read. Created by the Department of Education, this web page explains the role and importance of homework for parents.

4. http://www.homeworkspot.com

The homework spot uses layman terms with listed secondary school categories: middle, elementary, high. It also has information about the National Spelling Bee. Don't mean to toot my own horn, but I placed well back in the day. There is a Parent Source link which has the National PTA. Great Site.

5. http://www.infoplease.com/homework

This site is so clever. It has a "This date in History" calculator feature, which promotes Black History, Women and Latino Heritage months. I like very much. It also has a word for the day. Love it!

6. http://school.discovery.com/homeworkhelp/bjpinchbeck

This site is created by a seventeen-year-old high school student named BJ. His site contains more than 700 links to sites that for homework help. It's a cool site and is a part of the Discovery School website. Very kid friendly and very useful.

7. http://www.thepie.org/learn/homework.html

This site not only has links, but gives you a brief synopsis of the site. Hosted by the Public Internet Exchange.

8. http://www.educationcoffeehouse.com/students/homeworkhelpers.htm

Basic links. Nice Home schooling link.

-Davidae "Dee" Stewart

10th Anniversary Edition

How to Become Actively Involved in Your Child's Education

"It takes a whole village to raise a child." African Proverb

Parental involvement is the best predictor of a student's educational achievement. Parental involvement demonstrates to your child the importance of school, resulting in improved student attitudes, moral, and academic achievement. Parents' active interest also results in increased attendance, lower dropout rates, fewer discipline problems, and higher aspirations in life. Children who have been supported this way throughout their education are also more likely to consult with parents when making educational decisions.

Education is the key to our children's future, whether they attend college, take up a trade, or join the work force upon graduating from high school. There is no way to overestimate the importance of instilling the love of learning into your child because it can lead to the development of a genuine love of knowledge, and not just the obligation to make good grades. When this occurs, you won't have to tell your child to study because it's already his number one priority.

Instilling in Your Child a Love of Learning

Show interest! Ask questions! To help a child have academic success, parents must show an active interest in their child's education. This is, in fact, one of the easiest things for parents to do, and it doesn't depend on their level of education. All you have to do is set aside time every day to talk to your child about school. If you are a working parent who is not at home when your child returns from school, make sure you talk to them as soon as you get home, or at least the first chance you get. Making sure you periodically talk to your children demonstrates your genuine interest in their lives. The lines of communication are kept open and strengthened. Your questions should be a jump-off point for a two-way conversation. Ask open-ended questions, which require more than yes or no answers.

Be a positive role model. Show your child your love of learning by picking up a new hobby, keeping up with current events, or reading a book. These actions will show your child that not only is one never too old to learn, but that learning should continue throughout life. Show your child that what he is learning is an important part of being an adult. Use math to double a cookie recipe. Help your child understand how you use these skills at work.

Visit the public library often and have reading materials available. A child's success in reading comprehension is directly related to the availability of reading materials at home. Filling your home with culturally relevant books, whether your own or from the public or school library, will develop a child's comfort with books. In addition to loaning books, many libraries have children's programs for every age, from toddlers and teenagers. Usually, they also have a section devoted to African American Literature. Make visiting the library a family tradition.

Build on school learning. Express to your child that learning does not just occur at school. One way to do this is to plan family activities, which support what your child is currently learning. If your child is studying different animals or their classifications, visit the zoo, an aquarium, or even a farm. Take your children to local historical sites when that time period is being studied. Teach them the importance of voting and the hardships that many African Americans had to go through in order to secure this right.

Observe your children to find out what interests them. Some children will tell you what they find interesting by discussing it endlessly. Other children need their interests to be drawn out. This just takes a bit of investigation. What topics do they bring up? What books do they check out from the library? What is their favorite subject in school? Start with an area your child already finds interesting. If you are at a complete loss, ask a teacher or one of their friends.

Educational opportunities are everywhere. While grocery shopping, have your child practice math skills, whether it be counting bananas or calculating sales tax. Have your child map out the best route to the city. Learn about the birds that arrive in your backyard each spring. The following are some natural connections and examples:

<u>History/Social Studies and Current Events</u>. Discuss the past and recent history of African Americans. When your child is studying the writing of the Constitution, discuss a bill currently being argued before Congress. Teach your children that Christopher Columbus was not the first person to sail to the "New World" and that an African gentleman holds that distinction.

<u>Literature and Society</u>. Read Richard Wright's *Black Boy*.

The Right Foundation

Before focusing specifically on what a child is learning, parents must lay the foundation. This starts with a healthy lifestyle. For example, a healthy, nutritious breakfast will start the day off right and has been proven to positively affect academic achievement. Make sure your child gets enough rest and relaxation. This means going to bed at a reasonable hour. Tired students are poor learners.

Organization and ritual are important cornerstones of the foundation. Organization will allow for a calm and smooth morning before school, setting the appropriate tone for the day. To do this, children should wake up at a specific time, dress and prepare for school at a specific time, etc. It also helps to have the child's belongings waiting in a specific spot, preferably near the door. In fact, have her prepare her belongings the night before. This organization and ritual will make for a more pleasant morning, one in which you can express your pride in your child and allow him to calmly head out for a school day. To help keep the school week organized, you can keep a central calendar with upcoming school events, including sporting events, meetings, and report card mailings.

African American parents should set rules and consequences for their children, because they instill a sense of law and order. These rules and consequences should be in writing but not set in stone, because there will be exceptions.

Some examples of disobedience of home rules and their consequences include loss of outside activity privileges for one week for incomplete chores or loss of driving privileges for older students when academic expectations (failing grades, irregular attendance) are not met. For home rules that are not followed like disrespectful or aggressive behavior toward family members, loss of all privileges may be a consequence for your child. Remember these consequences should be fair and related to the severity of the violation.

Priorities

Education must be made the priority and therefore a true commitment. Be mindful of activities, whether educational or otherwise, which detract from that commitment. A child's school attendance also demonstrates the priority given to education. Your child should understand that he will attend school unless he is ill. This includes not taking him out of school for non-medical reasons.

Goals and Standards

Once education is made a priority, goals and standards must be set. A child should understand he should always do his best. Emphasize the importance of completing assignments. Other standards of education may be imposed depending on the child's age and circumstances.

Behavioral standards are also relevant to a child's educational success. These behavioral expectations, determined by each individual family, must be clearly understood. The consequences for failing to meet those standards should be clear. Children must learn that poor choices result in unpleasant consequences.

Goals differ from standards in their specificity and immediacy. While standards are more general and long-term, goals should be short-term, specific, and measurable. An appropriate goal for any age would be to earn an A on the next math test. Children should be expected to set their own goals, with your help. Putting goals and standards in writing and placing them in a conspicuous place may also help your child remember what his goals.

Encouragement and Praise

Praise is important to people of all ages, children especially. Encouragement from the most important people in their lives, their families, is priceless. Be your child's cheerleader. This does not mean that parents should ignore areas needing improvement. Encouragement includes constructive criticism when necessary. For example, instead of criticizing your child for a messy paper, suggest that his ideas will be clearer if the paper is neater.

Rewards

Almost everyone can be motivated by incentives. Incentives can range from simple stickers for younger children to special trips to the movies or the music store for older children. Rewards can also simply be praise or special time spent together. Be sure that the incentive does not overshadow the goal itself. Children should work for good grades or positive learning experiences in their own right.

Report Cards

While we know that reports cards are limited in their ability to measure intangibles such as work habits and intelligence, you should always take your child's report card seriously. Remember to praise and reward a good report card. In the event that your child does poorly or does not live up to his potential, make sure that, you talk about the situation and develop an improvement plan with the teacher.

The Bottom Line

Parental involvement plays a large role in a child's academic success. Parents must instill a love of learning in their children and form partnerships with their schools in order to ensure they will succeed academically. Unfortunately, in African American communities, parental involvement in schools is often low, and until African Americans as a whole take interest and become involved in every facet of our children's education, we will forever be behind.

-Matthew Lynch

10th Anniversary Edition

Scholarships for African Americans

Everything you want to know about college but afraid to ask in at www.theu.com
~~~~~~~~~~~~~~~~~

FORD HBCU Business Classic Scholarship: Submit a business plan for your dream venture to the Ford HBCU Business Classic and compete for a share of $100,000
in scholarships for your team and your school.

http://www.diversityinc.com/FordHBCUClassic2006/index.cfm

---

100 Black Men of America Scholarship

The 100 Black Men of America, Inc. is committed to the growth and development of America's youth. In addition to engaging in mentoring, education, health & wellness and economic development programs, we feel it is important to aid in developing talented young Americans in pursuit of higher education. Through gifts provided by our corporate sponsors, the 100 Black Men of America, Inc. is able to provide scholarships to hundreds of deserving college students on an equal opportunity basis regardless of race, sex, creed, or religious preference.

http://www.100blackmen.org/

Taylor your own scholarship search and have the results emailed to you via: http://www.fastweb.com

Student Inventors Scholarships http://www.invent.org/collegiate

Student Video Scholarships
http://www.christophers.org/vidcon2k.html

Coca-Cola Two Year College Scholarships
https://www.coca-colascholars.org

Holocaust Remembrance Scholarships
http://holocaust.hklaw.com

Ayn Rand Essay Scholarships
http://www.aynrand.org/contests

Brand Essay Competition
http://www.instituteforbrandleadership.org

Gates Millennlum Scholarships (major)
http://www.gmsp.org

Sports Scholarships and Internships
http://www.ncaa.org/about/scholarships.html

National Assoc. of Black Journalists Scholarships (NABJ)
http://www.nabj.org/front/index.html

Thurgood Marshall Scholarship Fund
http://www.thurgoodmarshallfund.org/sk_v6.cfm

FinAid: The Smart Students Guide to Financial Aid scholarships)
http://www.finaid.org

Presidential Freedom Scholarships

10th Anniversary Edition
http://www.nationalservice.org/scholarships

WiredScholar Free Scholarship Search
http://www.collegeanswer.com/index.jsp

Hope Scholarships &Lifetime Credits
http://www.ed.gov/inits/hope

William Randolph Hearst Endowed Scholarship for Minority Students
http://www.apsanet.org/PS/grants/aspen3.cfm

Guaranteed Scholarships
http://www.guaranteed-scholarships.com/

Easley National Scholarship Program
http://www.naas.org/senior.htm

Maryland Artists Scholarships
http://www.maef.org

Jacki Tuckfield Memorial Graduate Business Scholarship (for AA students in South Florida)
http://www.jackituckfield.org

Historically Black College & University Scholarships
http://www.iesabroad.org/info/hbcu.htm

Actuarial Scholarships for Minority Students
http://www.beanactuary.org

International Students Scholarships & Aid Help

http://www.iefa.org/

College Board Scholarship Search
http://cbweb10p.collegeboard.org/fundfinder/html/fundfind01.html

Siemens Westinghouse Competition
http://www.siemens-foundation.org

GE and LuLac Scholarship Funds
http://www.lulac.org/education.html

CollegeNet's Scholarship Database
http://www.collegenet.com/

Union Sponsored Scholarships and Aid
http://www.aflcio.org/scholarships/scholar.htm

Federal Scholarships &Aid Gateways 25 Scholarship Gateways from Black Excel
http://www.blackexcel.org/25scholarships.htm

Scholarship &Financial Aid Help
http://www.blackexcel.org/fin-sch.htm

FAFSA On The Web (Your Key Aid Form &Info)
http://www.fafsa.ed.gov/

Aid &Resources For Re-Entry Students
http://www.back2college.com/

HBCU Packard Sit Abroad Scholarships
http://www.sit.edu/studyabroad/packard_nomination.html

Scholarship and Fellowship Opportunities

10th Anniversary Edition
http://ccmi.uchicago.edu/schl1.html

INROADS internships
http://www.inroads.org/

Black Alliance for Educational Options Scholarships
http://www.baeo.org/options/privatelyfinanced.jsp

ScienceNet Scholarship Listing
http://www.sciencenet.emory.edu/undergrad/scholarships.html

Graduate Fellowships For Minorities Nationwide
http://cuinfo.cornell.edu/Student/GRFN/list.phtml?category=MINORITIES

RHODES SCHOLARSHIPS AT OXFORD
http://www.rhodesscholar.org/info.html

THE ROOTBERT SCHOLARSHIP FUND
http://www.roothbertfund.org/

Access information on demographics, school scores, etc. for any school in the nation. http://www.greatschools.com.

10th Anniversary Edition

FOREWORD

It gives me great pleasure to pen the foreword for *Here's Our Child; Where's the Village?"* and participate in the efforts of the Gumbo for the Soul project. The joy one gets from a child is indescribable, but something everyone can enjoy in one capacity or another; especially if we believe in the old African Proverb, *it takes a village to raise a child.* When Beverly first asked me to pen the foreword, I immediately thought "Who Me?" because I really don't see myself as a writer. Yes, I am an avid reader, a literary enthusiast, and I have firsthand knowledge of the subject matter, but I wasn't so sure about the actual writing part. So, I consulted with a few friends before agreeing and when I shared the book's theme: *to help convey that every child deserves the opportunity to flourish as a happy, thriving and free spirit regardless of the displacement factors governing their lives,* they immediately eased my doubts. I was adopted, so their mindset was "who better to share their experience?"

I only have one child, a five-year-old daughter, who I love more and more each day, but I'm still constantly amazed by her. She is a happy, loving child who delights in learning new things. She's adventurous and pretty independent for one so young; yet, she's so much like me, it's very eye-opening just watching or listening to her. Children tend to mimic what they see, and in our family she sees hard-working parents who love her. She knows the difference between right and wrong, what it means to be responsible, how to value herself, and express love to her family and friends. Most importantly, she knows from Whom her blessings flow.

Unfortunately, not all kids have this type of foundation. They haven't been shown the tools necessary to develop. Instead, they are missing out on the proper support, both externally and internally, and are unaware of how to measure the right balance of each. There are those who aren't loved and wanted, and others who may be wanted, but the parents don't have the resources to take care of them.

My brothers, sisters, and I fell in this category pretty early in life, ending up in an orphanage and later in foster care. While I don't remember everything from those times, I do recall some pretty harrowing experiences; especially for a child separated not only from my mother, but also my siblings. I remember not feeling wanted and missing my family. As time passed I was taken in by a really nice foster family, and my twin sister later moved around the corner with another family, so I was able to spend time with her. Several years later, at eight years of age, we were both adopted. Even more amazing...we were adopted together and relocated hundreds of miles away from our birth family. Not every child is this fortunate.

As someone who was in the foster care system as a child, I understand the need for surrogate families and adoption. I had both good and bad experiences, but as a result of being adopted, I had the opportunity to rise above my situation, to live a happy life with family members who loved me, and to know I could be and do whatever I dreamed. As a first-time mother, I see what wasn't so clear as a young child growing up in a "village" in a small, rural town in Arkansas. I see why the community of mothers was always there to discipline and to encourage. I see why my parents worked so hard to instill pride and a sense of self-worth. I see how a smile, kind word or a bit of praise can light up a child's world. Most importantly, I see the magnitude of how my adoptive parents and their teachings shaped my life, and how my husband and our families are shaping that of my child, and any other children who may find themselves in our presence. Again, not every child is this fortunate.

Some of our children are suffering because people don't care anymore. The "village" in which we live neglects our children, and sometimes their own. Our communities are suffering because of the ease of turning kids over to the television or video games, and getting caught up in the hustle and bustle of our everyday lives. But, it's not too late to make a difference. We can ensure our children are cared for in all areas of their lives. I'm an old-school parent and if my child is in your presence, not only does she understand that she is to behave a certain way, but she knows you will have my back. But, I also challenge you to actually have it. We need more of this in communities across America, and throughout the world. We don't necessarily have to go back to past times, but we can take that mindset, and utilize it in our families, schools, churches, and communities.

10th Anniversary Edition

Through the pages of this anthology, you will hear various accounts of what it means to the contributors to give back, to honor those who have come before us and to support our caregivers: parents, grandparents, teachers, clergy, doctors, etc., because it truly does take a village to raise a child. Do your part and give back. We are all responsible for raising our children, for their well being, their sense of self-worth, their education, and their understanding of what it means to be loved.

Let's get some of those old-school tendencies back!

Tee C. Royal

Tee C. Royal is a freelance reviewer, editor and literary agent, but known most as the founder of RAWSISTAZ Literary Group (www.rawsistaz.com) which supports and promotes African-American authors and their work. She lives in the suburbs of Atlanta with her husband and daughter.

Chapter I

~ Soulful Gumbo ~

Essays Reflecting on The Village

What Happened to the Village?

I was fortunate to be adopted in the 1950's. My parents told me I was special because I was chosen. I always felt loved, supported and encouraged. I had a safety net all my life until they died. We were such a loving family, I never thought about biological parents. These two people were, and will always be, my parents. My mother talked to me about her upbringing in New Orleans. She described family history events and incidents so clearly that I could see them in my mind's eye. She told me about how she was raised by "the village". Although it was strict and disciplined back then, it was safe and there was a definite sense of belonging.

As I remember my upbringing and the stories my parents told me about how they were raised, I see now how the "village" has dissipated, been dismantled and in some communities vanished completely. Many of our children are not exposed to healthy discipline or constructive criticism. They don't feel safe or that they belong to anything. This in large part has resulted in the harsh reality that many of our children have no visions, dreams, expectations, or hope. Many of our children lack any sense of ancestral history, tradition, sense of belonging, connectedness, motivation, or self-confidence.

"The village" once included parents, grandparents, extended family, school, church neighbors and friends. The nuclear family for many is no longer a reality. When both parents are together, some are working long hours or two jobs, and/or going to school. Others are trying to keep the family together because one or the other parent is out of work, abusing drugs and alcohol, in gangs or in prison.

Parents and grandparents are dying at an early age due to illnesses and diseases such as diabetes, high blood pressure, heart disease, obesity, HIV/AIDS, stroke, not to mention black-on-black crime and other preventable causes.

Some parents simply are not taking responsibility for raising their kids, and others have lost control due to societal trends in child rearing. "Time out" and "the naughty chair" are not always appropriate for children living in highly volatile homes, neighborhoods and school environments where children are more afraid of their peers than they are of the consequences they will face from parents when they make negative choices.

Parents are not involved in their schools. Even though many parents know what they want for their kids, they don't know how to get what they want and often feel they are somehow unequipped to successfully advocate for their children. When parents aren't available or involved, principals, teachers, counselors, and others, consciously or subconsciously hold, promote and perpetuate low expectations for our children. These attitudes along with everything mentioned so far, permeate, whittle at and eventually destroy our children's self-confidence and belief that they are capable of accomplishing most anything they set their minds to achieve or obtain. In addition, children are raised by grandparents, placed in seven to ten foster homes by the time they're in middle school, wind up in gangs, on the streets or in juvenile halls. As a result, high school drop-out rates increase and high school graduation rates decrease.

Nowadays, family, friends and neighbors are less likely to get involved in other families' lives for a host of reasons. One reason is that neighborhoods have changed. When I was growing up, a family lived in one house and the same neighborhood for years. This resulted in lasting friendships and relationships that lent themselves more readily to "the village" concept. However, in order to find better jobs, schools, housing, safer neighborhoods, or as a result of divorce, and so forth over the last few decades, families move from neighborhood to neighborhood, from city to city, and even further, several times during the course of a child's life. As a result, we don't know our neighbors or at least not as well as we once did. We barely greet one another. This makes it very difficult to build, rebuild, develop or establish "the village".

Furthermore, many of us use media and technology - TV, radio, music, movies, video and electronic games as babysitters, toys, and constant entertainment for our children and ourselves. When used in this manner, our time becomes unproductive. We don't have the time to spend building meaningful relationships with our children, families or neighbors because we are too busy mindlessly entertaining ourselves. We allow the media to continue to portray negative representations of African-Americans (in many cases perpetuated by African-Americans). The unproductive and destructive behaviors displayed in some electronic games, videos and DVDs, coupled with lack of appropriate parenting, squelch the imagination and creativity of our young people. They are not encouraged to think critically, analytically, or problem-solve to make well-informed choices and decisions. Instead the children learn to handle and solve problems in the same way music video and electronic game characters do - through sex, drugs and violence.

have not covered all issues that have negatively impacted the concept of "the village". However, those that I have mentioned cross socio-economic and educational status in African-American families. By the same token, there are African-American families who keep "the village" concept alive and well within their families and extended families in their communities and are raising happy, healthy, productive young people.

How might we rebuild "the village"? We must first begin with ourselves. What do we want for our collective children, our Black people? What legacy can we leave behind? The village encouraged the practice of the basic principles our parents and their parents instilled from generations past - those of respect for self, family, elders and others. The village reinforced constructive self-pride; meaning, no matter what we chose or aspired to be or do, we were encouraged to do our best and to be the best we could be, from custodian to CEO. The point was to chose something, aspire to something and never give up hope, dream or imagination. It promoted honing the ability to effectively navigate between the "hood", home and the boardroom. It taught Black youth to learn to consider challenges, changes, and sometimes disappointments as opportunities. And just because some things in life like chemistry, physics or a new job seemed hard, or the candidate voted for didn't win, didn't mean that you dropped the class, or through false pride rejected tutoring, didn't apply for the job, quit the job, or never voted again. Not going to college wasn't an option. Unfortunately, some of us didn't listen. But it wasn't because we didn't know any better.

What happened to the village? We adults stopped talking and listening to our youth and our people. We let go of our history, traditions, and upbringing. We assimilated so well we got addicted not only to alcohol, drugs and sex, but to a fast-paced stressful lifestyle to acquire more and more material things we don't have time to enjoy while we forget what is really important - our children – all of our children. We must stop, think, and reflect. We must develop the philosophy and belief that each one of our children deserves a quality of life that includes hope and the opportunity to have dreams that can in fact be realized. This belief must permeate every family, church, school, parenting course, juvenile hall, judge, social worker, probation office, police officer, adoption agency, community, neighborhood, early childhood education program, tutoring program, library, Boys & Girls' club, YMCA and so on. To do this we each must take responsibility for rebuilding "the village" in our communities and across this country. This means we must take risks, take the lead and talk to one another, listen to one another, learn to trust again, reach out to those who need help and encouragement, build friendships and strengthen relationships. We cannot continue to perpetuate the hopelessness that is choking the life out of our people and communities across this country. Regardless of our individual educational or socioeconomic backgrounds, we can, and must find proactive ways in which to actively participate in our children's daily activities. We must learn our African and African-American history and share it and other ideas and information with each other through web sites, newsletters, churches, sororities and fraternities, community and senior centers, parent meetings, workshops, conferences, everyday conversations and through books like this. We must work together with adoption agencies, foster care, community organizations, schools, parent groups, and others who want to rebuild "the village" and promote a "plan of action" to benefit our children such as the Covenant with Black America, for example, and other local, state and national efforts. We must not give up on rebuilding "the village" for the support of our children or there will be no more healthy, productive children.

-Dr. Marie-Elaine Burns

10th Anniversary Edition

Will

Will (n) – The mental ability that allows one to purposefully choose or decide on a course of action.

I'm not really sure why, but I began to watch him. I watched him roam the halls and hook classes for several weeks. Today would be different I thought. "Whose class do you belong in?"

"I ain't got no class." He smiled.

"You don't? Well, you'll be my hostage until you figure out where you belong." He just smiled as I grabbed his arm. He willingly followed. "Mrs. Jones, do you know where this child belongs?"

"No. What's his name?"

"What's your name boy?" I scowled, as I shook the arm I held captive. He smiled.

"I don't know." It had become a game to him. I lovingly popped him on the back of his head and yanked his arm. Now we were going to the principal. He continued to smile as he followed.

"Miss. Stone What Will do?"

"Nothing!" I looked at him. "Will?"

"Nothing? Well why you got him all Jacked up? You always botherin' somebody." Deniera huffed. Aaaahhhhaa! Will how you get caught hookin' Mr. C. class? You stupid!" I gave him *the look* and continued to pull. I walked him to his class and dropped him off.

"Come on Miss Stone!" I put down my pen and walked to the door. At this point he would only go to class if I walked him. Later, I would have to stay. "I ain't going unless you come with me" he would say.

"I'm not coming to your class. I will walk you, but I am *not* staying." Very shortly after, he would be right back in my room. "Mr. C. put me out."

"What did you do?"

"I ain't do □othing' he don't like me." It was a c-o-n-spiracy. He would purposely get put out of class, so that he could come back to my room. Every day I arrived at the door with Will, Mr. C. would look with

Gumbo For The Soul

disappointing eyes and sarcastically say, "Thank You Miss Stone." Will immediately picked up on his tone.

"Miss. Stone can I get my work and do it in your room?"

"You need to ask your teacher."

"He don't care. Man, give me my work so I can get out of this class!"

"Is that how you talk to adults?" I snapped.

"Naa man, he don't!"

"Watch your mouth! You are not coming to my room with that mouth!"

Will went to Mr. C and got his assignments daily and returned to my room. His class was eventually changed. He had become my child and now my student.

"I didn't call him no faggy. I said he need to stop actin' like one"

"Will, you can't just say whatever you want to your teachers or any adult for that matter." Ms. Williams growled. "You are going home!"

"He always sayin' something to somebody. He don't never say othing' to them girls."

"I don't want to hear it! What is your mother's phone number?"

He smacked his teeth, folded his arms and leaned back in the chair. "I don't know."

"What do you mean you don't know? You better stop playing with me boy!"

Will scrunched his face. "Man, I don't know where she at!" He was annoyed now. "You can call this number." Ms. Williams wrote as he recited the number.

"Whose number is this?"

That's my grandfather's number."

"Hello. This is Ms. Williams I have William here and we can't seem to get in contact with his parents. He seems to be having trouble with his mouth. His teacher is fed up and will not allow him back to class until he has a parent conference. Now, this is not the first time we have had a problem out of Will."

" I can't come!" He spat. "I live in Pasadena, MD and I'm not coming all the way up there for that."

"Mr. Foster." Ms. Williams pleaded. "We need someone up here or he will be sent home for three days. Even then, he will not be able to return without a parent conference."

"Well send him! Ain't nobody to come up there! Now yall do whatever yall 'gon do 'cause I ain't comin'." Ms. Williams listened as Mr. Foster hung up the phone. She leaned back in her chair. As she placed the phone on the hook she took a long silent look at Will's scrunched face. "Go over there and sit down! Don't you move from that spot!" She pointed at the couched in the Main Office. Will had plenty of company on the couch.

Mrs. Williams walked to the cafeteria for the first lunch period. When I entered the cafeteria, I had already heard the news. After all he was my child. Anything he did teachers and students alike would say, "Miss Stone your child is in trouble." I knew immediately who they were talking about. I went to her, because I knew his situation and I wanted to help.

"Miss Stone your child is in trouble—again."

"Don't talk about my child like he is bad!" I smiled, because he had given us all a fair share of trouble. She lowered her head and peered at me over her glasses and shook her head.

"He called Mr. Douglass a faggy. I need your help Stone. I know that you two are pretty close. I can't send him home because there is nobody to bring him back to school. We have to do something. The grandfather said he doesn't know where the mother is, Will doesn't know where the mother is either. He gave me another number but no one answered. My heart goes out to him. Where does he live?"

"He lives with me."

"What do you mean he lives with you?"

"He lives with me. He has since January."

"Oh! How many bedrooms do you have?" Ms. Williams knew that I was single and that I had no children. "One. I made him a little room in a breakfast nook I have off of the kitchen. He has a queen mattress on the floor, a little blue comforter and a blue chair. It's cute. He even has a couple of posters up." I spoke proudly. It was nice for a makeshift room.

Both lunch periods had ended and there was an announcement. "Miss Stone please report to Mrs. James' office." I shook my head as my stomach churned. As I walked into the principal's office, I saw Ms. Williams sitting next to an empty chair at the front of Mrs. James' desk. I slid into the chair.

"Miss Stone, Ms. Williams shared with me what you are doing for the boy. So he lives with you now?"

"Yes."

"What you're trying to do is commendable but what you're doing is also very dangerous."

"Does his family know he lives with you?"

"I've spoken to his mother and we've seen her once."

"Has she given you legal custody?"

"No."

"Stone this is dangerous. These kids don't have any loyalties to anyone. He or his family can say anything. I was just watching TV the other day and they talked about targeting women on that *To Catch a Predator* show. You just have to be careful." I just listened but my mind spoke out angrily as my chest began to heat. I took a deep breath then released and leaned back in my chair. *What the hell is she implying? Why would she say that? Damn! People can't just be kind?* I had shut down and was barely listening.

". . . you need to get that boy out of your house." She was still talking. ". . . what your doing is dangerous. You don't know what that boy is capable of. His mother could get him to say anything—thinking she is going to get some money out of it. Is he worth losing your job?"

Everyone has thrown him away. I thought. *I can't do that to him.*

"There are plenty of agencies that can help him. Foster care, they have group homes. We can call Social Services. They can find him a place. *He didn't ask them. He asked me.* He needs to get out of there!" She continued.

"You think *he's* worth it—worth losing your job?" She asked again in amazement.

I spoke softly to mask my anger. "Yes! I can get another job. He only has one life." I could no longer hold back the tears. I was sure that her daughters or sons were worth it. It has been 8 months and I have purchased a home. He now has his own room with his own door. We have had a number of challenges but, I am not going to give up on him.

-Anna K. Stone

10th Anniversary Edition

The State of Motherhood in America

A writer once wrote, "No nation is greater than its mothers, for they are the makers of men" But, when I turn on my television and see the numbers of mothers who are killing their children I must ask myself, "What drives a mother to the point of killing her own child?" "What is it in our society that makes a mother feel so desperate, so alone, that she believes her only recourse is the death of herself and her children?" Andrea Yates, who killed her five children; Dee Etta Perez, who shot her three children; Deanna Lany, who beat her two sons; Lisa Ann Diaz who drowned her daughters; Dena Schlosser, who fatally severed her daughters arms; and now Gilberta Estrada, who hung herself and her children. Not to mention the countless number of babies that are born and left in dumpsters even with the passing of a new law that says they can leave them in safe places and receive no repercussions.

Loneliness, poverty, depression; what demons lurk behind the erstwhile smiles of these women that lead them to believe that death is the only option?

Women have suffered hardships for years. Slavery, the Great Depression, living during the Civil Rights Era, all of these times were hard, but you never heard of mothers killing their children. Instead they reached deep down inside themselves and mustered whatever strength they could to make sure that their children had better lives than they did.

What has changed? Nothing could be more devastating than being raped by a slave master, forced to have his illegitimate child, and then being forced to raise that child. Yet, these things happened and many of those children and/or their grandchildren grew up to be productive, effective citizens in our society.

During the Great Depression and the Civil Rights movement, money was scarce, but somehow people managed to take the little they had and turn it into something great. Material things were not the norm. What was more important was love of the family, togetherness, and morality.

I sought the Lord and he answered me. He delivered me from all my fears. Psalm 34:4.

I was sixteen years old and pregnant. What was worse, I was a "PK" (preacher's kid) for those of you not familiar with the term. And as long as

I could remember it was always rumored that we, "PK's" that is, were the worse. It had however been my mission to prove them wrong. I had excelled in school to the point that I would graduate one year early. I was respectful to my parents and to my elders. Until now, I had really been of little trouble to my parents. Now this! The problem; I truly was in love and I felt compelled (now I know by the enemy), to prove this love and as a result I had to face the consequences. I mean really, just say no is great in theory, but in the midst of raging hormones it's really not meaningful. How on earth would I tell my parents? How would I raise a child? How would I continue my education? How would I withstand the ridicule that would come my way; the disappointment of my parents? After all, we have an image to uphold. The statistics were grim.

Fast forward 24 years. My oldest son is now a college graduate and teaching computer technology in the local school district. My youngest son is nearing completion of a college degree and will soon be among the work force. I am happily married to my second husband of fourteen years and I have become an author, mentor, and educator. I have never been on welfare and both of my children went to school with academic scholarships. Raising two sons was not an easy task. God placed many people in my life to help me make my transition.

How did I do it? I sought the Lord and He answered me. He told me in His word that I could do all things through Christ who strengthens me. He said that a good woman, a worthy woman was worth more than rubies and that is what I wanted to be. He said that He would do exceedingly and abundantly more than I could ever ask him for. He said in His word that if I made myself at home with Him, and made His words at home in me, that I could be sure that whatever I asked would be listened to and acted upon. God became my ultimate source. He did not give me a spirit of fear but of love and a sound mind. I became like Paul, it mattered very little to me what others thought of me or my situation because only God could judge and as a result I can now stand firmly and testify to the fact that God is faithful and that He will honor His word.

Could it be that as a society we have focused so much on gaining material wealth that we have forgotten about people? There was a time when neighbors knew neighbors, intimately; when everyone in the neighborhood had a stake in raising good, well-rounded children. If, a mother was suffering and needed support, she could go to the neighbor's house and be assured that whatever they had would be shared with her and her family. What happened to the village?

Motherhood is a gift from God and it should be cherished. However, in our day it has been massacred. It is mocked. Unfortunately, too many mothers exercise selfishness with small regard for their children whom they largely ignore.

Then their are those mothers who really try to do better, but because of bureaucratic red tape, and long waiting lines, they are left to their own devices to try to make it. Where is the love and support? Where are "Big Mama", "Mamaw", and Grandmother, who can help teach and nurture these young mothers? Or have they become a sign of the past as well?

None of the successes that I have achieved in life would ever have been possible without my God and my mama. The bible says that the older women should teach the younger women how to love and care for their children. My mama did just that. Her favorite words to me were:

"You must teach by precepts and examples."

In other words, "Do as I say; not as I do" was not in her vocabulary. She tried to exemplify the traits of a good mother each and every day. She has been giving, kind, trustworthy, a good worker, and above all else she trusts God. Now her children rise up and call her blessed.

My mothers support for me during this difficult time in my life was unparalleled. Her love was unconditional and she was determined that I would not falter. She supported me emotionally, physically, and financially. She was even in the corner of the delivery room helping me to push when my oldest son was born. She was a mama lion protecting her young at all costs, even fighting for me when necessary. Her love for me made me even more determined to be a good mother for my boys. If I could instill in them one half of the things she instilled in me they would be well on their way.

Even when my first marriage faltered, (no, I didn't listen to her on that one), she was right there to help me pick up the pieces.

She is even part of the reason that I never received public assistance. The Department of Human Services said that she and my stepfather made to much money. I believe that God orchestrated this matter so that I would not become dependent on the system as so many young women do.

The bottom line here is that everyone needs a champion, a mentor, a confidant, to help them through that time in life. In my case it was my mother.

But ladies, if you don't have someone like that in your corner, seek God first and then ask Him to place someone in your life that can provide guidance and a listening ear when you need it. It makes a world of difference.

Mothers are supposed to be the teachers of compassion, love, forgiveness, honesty, and integrity. It is more than a biological imperative. Yet, because society has all but given up on these qualities, they are forced to spend their time looking for their next paycheck. Many of them can't even be with their children when they are ill because their jobs won't allow them to be off. Instead, the children drag off to school feeling bad and lacking the security and comfort of a mother's love. What have we done?

If, we don't cure the disease that is eating away at motherhood and do it soon, our nation is headed for destruction

-Cheryl Donovan

10th Anniversary Edition

The Day I Entered a Group Home

It happened so fast; that the little bit of 16 years of my life had run by me in a minute. Today, I was entering a group home.

I remember sitting in the kitchen talking to Natasha. I had been staying at her house because I had no where to go. I knew that this was my last morning there. All the arrangements had been made the day before. BCW (Bureau of Child Welfare Services) was expecting me before 5:00.

Natasha and I were talking and listening to music. She was telling me about that time she had gone into a group home herself. She had given me some pointers about how to act. She explained that I should keep to myself and get to know people before I become too familiar and friendly.

She said she still knew some people in the "system" and that she would put the word out so that others would be aware and look out for me.

The social worker's name was Ms. Valerie. I had spoken to her many times before that day. That same morning I had gotten a phone call from my boyfriend's (at the time) aunt, who had the name Valerie as well.

Natasha handed me the phone; I began talking as if I was speaking with the social worker. When I realized that I had gotten my signals crossed, and I was really talking to his aunt she had given me the bad news. He had been shot!

I recall standing in the bathroom. It was cold. There were no pictures or pretty bath towels or fluffy bath mats. Just a tub, a toilet and a sink with a towel rod to my left. Above the cold sink was a dull mirror. I stood in front of the mirror and sink. I stared at myself crying. I had no other emotion. There was no shaking, shuttering or screaming. Just my face in the mirror accompanied by the top collar of the housecoat I had been sleeping in.

Natasha came in and asked what happened, but I stood there looking in that mirror, staring at the little girl inside of it. Natasha went back to the phone, said some words and hung up. I came out and picked up my bag and returned back to the bathroom. I dressed slowly. Combed my hair, straightened out my bag, and said my good-bye's and left.

Gumbo For The Soul

I walked right out of that two story red brick building. I watched my feet walking slowly. Seeing the front of my shoes bend with each step. While I walked I looked on the ground noticing every crack and all the small pieces of grass that had grown in between them. The sky was gray that day. I remember looking at the Brown Line buses pulling into the depot across the street and a woman with a child walking the other way.

There was no train going by as I walked under the tresel, but there were many cars on the street, either parked or passing.

As I reached the corner I wanted to scream, shout, and cry. I wanted the world to notice me. To notice my pain and recognize it. I wanted them to know the real story of how my family had treated me. I was 16 in age but much younger inside

No one heard the noise inside of me. Life went on. In my whole life I had never felt more alone than I did then.

I walked to the office. At first they were going to send me to "the mount". It was famous for its blanket parties. Instead I went to the Bronx. The social worker called my grandmother telling her to pack my things and she would come to get them.

When we got there the light on the porch wasn't on. She came to the door with a green suitcase. I took it and walked out. If they said anything I didn't hear it. I wouldn't have wanted to and didn't care.

I got into the white car. I sat in the back seat. I stared at that house through the window. The driver started to pull off, but right then my brother ran out the house waiving his hands for us to wait.

I rolled down the window and he passed me a sandwich wrapped in tissue. He told me not to let anyone know I had it. I smiled, rolled the window up, and we were gone.

I remember the highway and bridge lights being lit brightly. It was the longest ride of my life. I sat through it with my head tilted on my hand as I stared out the back window. I cried a little.

We got there fast. There were so many girls out in front of the house that night.

When we got inside, the social worker said a few words, gave me a number were she could be reached, and then left. The woman in charge was fat and black. She had big hair. She asked me to open my suitcase. She counted everything I had.

The lady called down the girl I would be rooming with. Her name was Lisa. She was 19 and on her way out. Lucky her.

I got my bag together and followed her upstairs. There were 3 beds and 3 closets in the room. I picked the one against the wall, but I chose the middle closet. The lady came upstairs and showed me around the floor. It had 4 bedrooms, and 3 bathrooms. She gave me a padlock to put on my closet and left.

I pushed my dresser into the closet, unpacked, grabbed a towel; some clean clothes and headed towards the shower. I felt as if I washed all the "dirt" off of me.

It was too late to call anyone when I finished. So I lay in the bed and thought about all that had happened to me that day. I turned the lights out, checked the lock on my closet door, and went to bed.

-Tonisha Johnson

Never Leaving Home

It was nightfall and the coolness of the evening was refreshing after another long, hot, and sticky day. I could see her silhouette reflected in the moonlight as we approached the place I had always called home. She seemed so much at peace. I was afraid to break the spell of the evening by calling out her name.

It had been too long since I had last seen her. The memory of my mother sitting on the porch on a cool summer's eve, always brought a smile to the corner of my lips. Only this time, I suddenly realized as we approached my childhood home, that my mother wouldn't be there. Instead, I would find the often-stern face of my younger sister, Renee, who would be waiting as my sons and I returned to the one place, I knew I could always call home.

Driving down the streets of my childhood brought back so many forgotten memories. As I looked at the neighborhood where I had spent so many years growing, learning, and longing to get away from, I became conscious of the fact that no matter how far we travel away from home, we never truly leave.

I left home at the ripe old age of eighteen. Not by choice, but because I knew more than my mother did at the time. She felt it best that I put my great wealth of knowledge to use by caring for myself. Since her home had simply become a place that I sometimes stopped by to change clothes and voice my disdain at being treated like a child.

That first time that I moved, I had nothing to carry with me other than my seemingly endless amount of clothes and make-up. Actually, the only thing that I took with me that first night was my wounded pride of being thrown out of my mother's house over some slight misunderstanding that I felt at the time had nothing to do with me.

I moved into my brother's one bedroom apartment with him and his new wife for the first week, as they tried to convince me of how wrong I was in the situation. Since I already knew the answers to life at the wise old age of eighteen, there was no way possible that my mother could be right in her decision. Suddenly full of newfound eighteen-year-old pride, I refused to apologize but opted instead to become even more independent and move in with my grandmother.

Living with my grandmother did give me more freedom, or so I had assured myself. Yet, there was something missing from life that I couldn't quite put my finger on. Could it be that I couldn't bring myself to argue with my grandmother about anything? She and my great-grandmother treated me like a ten-year-old.

I would cringe at the thought of "back-talking" my grandmother. So instead, I continued to work and save money so that one day, I could move once again. That day came just more than a year later.

I had found a furnished studio apartment that was half the size of my current bedroom at my grandmother's, but who cared? It would be mine; my very own place to live, out from under the watchful eyes of my nosy, albeit loving female family members.

Once again, with clothes and make-up in hand, and very little else, I moved. My little studio apartment became my first real stab at trying to be independent and on my own.

I was in for a rude awakening when I realized I was the one who had to pay my own bills. I didn't have the extra cash flow that had once been the source of my joy as I continued to build my closet instead of a bank account. Not only that, I now had to learn to cook for myself.

Ah, but the thrill of being an adult, making my own decisions, coming and going as I pleased, was heaven! Or so I thought. As the months progressed, I realized that I had no idea what it took to be a responsible adult.

There always seemed to be more bills than money coming in. Additionally, I was dating a musician who traveled a lot. For some strange reason, when he was in town, he actually must have thought we lived together. He spent constant nights at my place, eating my food, sleeping in my bed, driving my car; never contributing a dime to my existence. I did the only sensible thing a twenty-one year old could do in my situation. I moved home.

I had gained a new respect for my mother and her sense of responsibility. This time around, my mother and I seemed to get along much better. I tended to listen to her a little more and she treated me more like an adult.

I remained at home with my mother for a few more years. Life was good. Sure, I still had chores to do, but I didn't have to pay any household bills. However, once again, I was free to shop for the latest in fashion to add to my already overwhelmed wardrobe collection.

Then one day, I announced to my mother that I was getting married. The young man whom I've been dating had proposed and I accepted. I would prepare to move out of my mother's house one last time or so I thought.

My father had died the year prior to me getting married. My brother, another sister, and I had all moved out on our own. The baby of the family, my youngest sister graduated and moved away to college. My mother's house became a quiet and sometimes lonely place for the two remaining family members; my mother and my sister.

I would visit often and my mother and I would usually spend hours playing her favorite game. Backgammon. Then one day, my mother was gone. No longer would she be there to be my safe refuge in the storm. But her house would.

So once again, I find myself moving my clothes, make-up and a few extra things home. This time I bring my two sons home to find refuge in the place that always offered shelter, comfort and a place to rest before the next move.

-Jacqueline D. Moore

10th Anniversary Edition

What happened to our village?

When I was young, there were many things that I saw and heard that were probably too much for my young ears. These incidents included arguments between adults, children fighting each other, parents using drugs and children reaching out because they were left alone. I even heard stories from adults about children being sexually abused. Most of what I heard and saw was because I intentionally placed myself in the wrong place at the right time. I was again sticking my nose in grown folks business.

Although I loved hearing about what was happening to people, I found myself tossing and turning at night with worry. I always felt that if only the children had better parents or if only the child was good and not causing problems, they wouldn't be having so many problems. I was too young to understand that it was not the child's fault, but that fault was in the hands of the adults. Because of these experiences and exposures, which were too mature for me to comprehend, I made sure that as a teenager I stayed in my place to avoid getting myself in negative situations that I couldn't handle. So I was careful of my associations and the places that I visited. Yet I realize that these were the experiences that shaped who I am today. Many children today miss out on opportunities to learn from others because they do not have the family and community around to teach them lessons that can benefit them in the long run.

Back in the day, it wasn't uncommon for teens to experience negative peer pressure, or to find ourselves doing something our parents warned us against. Oftentimes, we messed up, but we survived because our parents taught us to obey rules and when we didn't, we suffered the consequences and were punished.

Looking back now, I realize that life for me and most of my friends was not as difficult as we may have believed because the world was a lot different back then. We had our parents, brothers, sisters, our extended family, the community and the church to give us a hand and help guide us when we needed it. Today, times have changed. No longer can a small child go safely to a neighbor's house to wait until his parents arrive home from work. No longer can a child reach out to a stranger if he is lost because people have changed. Not only have they stopped caring about children, many of them no longer care about themselves. No longer do children go home to hot meals waiting after a long day in school. This is because our communities are breaking down, parents are working two jobs to make ends meet and some parents are addicted to drugs, gambling or something else that takes their focus off of their children.

In addition, many parents have left their children to find their own way. Due to the problems in our communities with drugs, crime and neglect, many of our children are finding themselves without families. In fact, too many are put into foster care because there is no one to give them the care, love and support they need. Even still others find themselves on the streets getting into trouble.

In the days of the Clinton administration, Hilary often recited a simple African- American proverb that drew national attention, but had been uttered by people in our communities for years. The slogan, "It takes a village to raise a child" still holds true. But I wonder what happened to our village? What has happened to programs and activities in the neighborhoods to keep children and teens out of trouble?

Now, I see fathers and mothers pushing their children to excel in sports and extracurricular activities to the point that the child no longer enjoys participating. In one incident, at a little league football game, a father threatened a coach with a gun. Another time a coach in a different state, who was charged with teaching our children how to play sports ran onto the football field during a game and knocked a young player to the ground. Why? Because he was upset with a tackle that a child from the opposing team put on one of his players.

What is wrong with society when those we entrust with our children turn out to be worse than the neighborhood thugs who terrorize their residents? Why can't a young man or woman seek counseling from a priest or other church leader without being touched or forced to do something sexual? These actions break down our children's trust in authority figures. What's wrong with a teacher, who comes to class drunk, touches his female students inappropriately and then sends students to his car to fetch him another drink? Yet there are many other children who don't have parents to push them to excel so they look to outside forces to take the role of their missing parents. What can we do to help change the negative turn of events that are consistently happening to our children at school, on the sport's field, and in the church?

Are we talking about these issues? Are we meeting, strategizing and teaching our children how to protect themselves? If we are not, we should be. If we don't start trying to address these situations now, things are going to get worse. As parents, teachers, community leaders and business owners we need to participate in PTA meetings, attend community meetings and talk to our leaders about our expectations for them to protect our most vulnerable citizens; our children.

We should also encourage people to get involved with children through mentoring programs, volunteering at schools and to adopt children who do not have parents. We can do so many things to change the negative path that awaits children who have no parental guidance. As the mother of an adopted child and the sister of adopted siblings, I know the value of having a solid family support system. When children feel valued, loved and have the support of a family, they can accomplish anything. Without the strength of families, children lose the willpower and the desire to exceed in life. Adoption changes people lives. It enhances the lives of the children and the families who chose to adopt. It is one way that we can help to change the life of a child who is in need of love from a family.

As parents, social workers and others in the helping relations field, we must begin to collaborate, communicate and then implement our ideas. We can't sit at the table too long talking because the longer we stay there, the more children we lose. We must also include children and teens in our discussions because they are the ones living the pain and going through many negative experiences. They can tell us why, what we need to do and how. As adults we need to listen. Oftentimes, we are so busy doing what we want to do that we fail to hear what the youth are saying. Ignoring their needs silences their voices.

When kids think we don't care, or that we don't have time to listen to what they have to say, they begin to listen to their friends. That is where peer pressure begins to rear its ugly face. Kids feel compelled to have someone in their corner who cares and who will hear what they are trying to say. The problem is that many of those who are willing to listen to our children do not have good intentions. We have to give our children confidence that we believe in them, we love and trust them and that we, in fact, want to be there when they need us the most. We must support them by showing them that we care. If we don't act now, the village that should be helping us to raise our children will disappear as quickly as we can say abracadabra. Adopt, volunteer to mentor, or give back to our communities to help our children but we must do something now, or we will risk our children's futures and inadvertently ours as well.

-Rose Jackson-Beavers

10th Anniversary Edition

My Story

Because They Exist

I really believe that having God-fearing, Jesus-loving grandparents heavily influenced the development of my loving, unselfish character. They were my baby sitters until I was 14 years old. Having 13 children of their own resulted in many grandchildren; every time there was a need, a welcome and opening hand was there. Everything was stretched and divided so none ever went hungry and always a place to eat.

This was my environment; where nothing was mine, but "ours", where love for the materialistic never existed. An unselfish, loving, devoted not just talked the talk, but walked the walk, home built by Eston and Wilda Putman.

Because They Exist

It's several contributing factors that make good foster parents. For me it was the heart.

For others because it's the thing to do, dedication, a helping hand, because it's right. Growing up as an only child there was always a wanting for sisters and brothers, my heart hungered for their companionship. I couldn't bear to see anything suffer, human or animal. Some say I had gentle, extreme loving heart. Because of this I was often in distress. Many hurts because I couldn't understand how others could be deceitful, and not return my love and friendship. I was naive. I couldn't comprehend why they didn't feel the sorrow or be upset when children were sick, hurt, or homeless.

Headstart

While teaching headstart. I witnessed much neglect and some abuse. My heart made me push myself to the limit to help. Taking some of the children home for the weekend and during the summer months, these are the times when most of the neglect occurred. I love them as if they were my own. I didn't teach in my hometown but a city 25 miles away. So I was surprised when a distant family member enrolled her little boy in my class.

As time went on I noticed symptoms of neglect; dirty clothing lack of baths, uncombed hair, etc. I made a home visit. Lights, heat and water were all turned off. His nine-month old baby sister had a severe cold. I new immediate intervention was necessary; I asked the mother if I could take the children and just keep them until things improved. After a few months she asked for them back. The utilities were turned on. The five year old still showed signs of neglect. I worked closely with the Department of Children Services monitoring the household. One day I received a call that the children had been placed in foster care but I could have them if I agreed to take the children. After agreeing I immediately went to the home and picked them up. The mother had visitation rights but only showed up for about three weeks.

As time went on I was told that they would be put up for adoption. I had first choice. Two months later they were mine. I can't say it was easy but I can say it was a joy. They are on their own now living far away. I'm still mom and receive calls weekly. LaShawn and Nikki are mine forever, along with two other children Shaka and Ashanti we raised since childhood. They are now in high school and every basketball and football game is filled with over-the-top excitement.

They give my life meaning. Just looking at them warms the shackles of my heart. Thank you LaShawn, Nikki, Shaka, and Ashanti for bringing happiness in my life.

Honorable Mention

Thank you Ms. Arnold, Ms. Pruitt, Ms Leahey, Ms.Balbuze, and Ms.Kassouf, for being Ashanti's mentors, counselors, life skills teachers and friends. Because of you Ashanti was the only student selected from our county, to attend the youth

Leadership conference held at Emory University in Atlanta Ga. You go baby girl!

-Betty Nandi Cantrell

10th Anniversary Edition

The Village

"Pump your gas, ma'am?"

I barely looked at the young Black man as I shook my head *"no"* and went inside the station to pay. It had been a long day; beginning with a 6:00 a.m. morning drive radio show and duties as the station's program director, followed by an afternoon of teaching creative arts at an after school program for at-risk youth. And the day wasn't over; after getting gas I was heading to rehearsal for a theatrical production.

My foot tapped impatiently as the customers slowly progressed before me. Something was wrong with the man at the front of the line's credit card, and this snafu was holding up the line and eating up my time. I shook my head, exasperated, and in the process looked outside the gas station window. The young man I'd turned down to pump my gas was being systematically denied by each motorist he approached. Dejected, his shoulders slumped a bit as he walked to yet another car with his now weary offer to pump somebody's, anybody's, gas for whatever gratuity would hopefully be paid him. Payment was the desire, not a guarantee.

As I watched him, something tugged at my heartstrings, and at my conscience. Here was a young man, probably twelve, thirteen years old, out hustling to make a few dollars. He wasn't selling crack, stealing or begging; but asking if he could perform a simple task in return for a small remuneration. Standing in line, I wondered at the story behind the weary smile. Where did he live? Was his a single parent family? Was this money a much-needed addition to the family coffers? Was this money to buy his dinner, and would he eat if everyone, like me, shook their heads *"no"* as they went about their busy lives? I stopped thinking of him as some kid interrupting my day and asking for money, and saw him as somebody's son, brother, cousin; as a person with feelings, hopes, and dreams. I looked at him as one of my students, all too aware of how those bright, talented, energetic boys and girls were "at risk" because too little time and attention had been paid to their spirits, and because too many adults, beginning with their parents, had either literally or figuratively shook their heads *"no"* to pleas for help, attention, direction, love.

Gumbo For The Soul

I paid for my gas and returned to the pump. "You can pump my gas," I said to the youth, as he lounged against the pump and twiddled with the windshield cleaner sponge. "And you can do my windows, too," I added.

The young man bounced over to the car and grabbed the gas pump. "What do you use?" he asked.

I told him regular was fine, and watched as he expertly placed the nozzle inside the tank.

"What's your name?" I asked.

"Rashad."

"Hi, Rashad. How's business today?"

He seemed a bit surprised that an adult was engaging him in conversation and simply shrugged his shoulders.

"You do this every day?" I continued.

"Almost," he replied.

I asked a few more general questions; how old he was, where he went to school, simple things that defined a life behind the handsome, brown-skinned face. Then I asked him what he wanted to be when he grew up.

Rashad thought briefly before answering, "A mechanic."

"Oh," I replied, pondering his answer for a moment. "So you want to own your own business, open your *own* garage."

I watched his face as this almost imperceptibly offered idea took root in his mind. He'd obviously never considered it before, but immediately embraced the possibility; his chest almost visibly expanded with the power of the thought.

"Yeah," he nodded confidently. "I'm gonna own my own shop."

He finished my windows and I paid him a couple dollars. With a perfunctory "thank you," and "you're welcome," we went our separate ways.

As I rushed to rehearsal, I thought about the seemingly inconsequential act that had occurred; a random meeting between two strangers. But for me, coincidence is simply God being anonymous, so I knew much more had happened than a chance encounter. In those few, brief, moments, I'd helped raise a child. I'd planted a seed, nourished a dream, patronized a "business" and encouraged an enterprise. I'd helped a young man see that it was possible to earn an honest living, and to know there were people ready to support him. The bothersome boy asking for money had become the young man named Rashad, who perhaps one day would service my car at his establishment.

10th Anniversary Edition

And in return, Rashad had given me a few things. He'd given me a feeling of accomplishment, and the joy that comes from simply doing something to help somebody. He'd reminded me that seeing anyone as a "stranger" is an illusion; in truth we are all connected, all each other's mothers and fathers, sons and daughters, brothers and sisters. He'd helped me understand that instead of waiting until we can do a big thing, that Oprah kind of giving, we can do a lot of little things, and make a real difference in people's lives. One doesn't have to birth the child to help raise the child. One may not be able to adopt a child for a lifetime, but most of us can adopt one for a few moments.

For a mere two dollars, I'd taught a lesson, and been reminded of one as well. I remembered that this type of positive adult/child interaction is what had happened with me in the small town in which I grew up. Every adult had been my "parent": nurturing, encouraging, admonishing and teaching me with small, seemingly inconsequential acts, every day. I felt that the simple deed of helping him to not only dream, but to dream big, might keep Rashad from being "at risk," make him more aware of the greatness within him, and move him closer to his date with a successful destiny.

I never saw Rashad again; but now, all these years later, our encounter still makes me smile. And I still remember the valuable lesson of planting positive seeds and helping others grow; a lesson I've continued to implement everywhere: whether with a kid pumping gas, or selling candy in a parking lot, or cookies at the front door. Every adult is the village; and every child is our own. That's how we make the world a better place: by nodding our heads *yes* to our children—one positive word, helpful act, or well spent dollar at a time.

-Lutishia Lovely
Novel Ideas Unlimited © 2007, All Rights Reserved

Gumbo For The Soul
Through The Eyes of a Foster Child

As a former foster child and an advocate for foster children, this will be something that children will always remember. In my latest book "Through the Eyes of a Foster Child" I wrote an essay with the same title describing what children go through when being taking from their homes and placed in the system.

Free your mind and imagine that you are 2, 5, 10 or 13 years old and you're playing with your favorite toy, video game or something that you really enjoy. All of a sudden, there's a knock on the door (knock, knock, knock). Your parent reluctantly opens the door and in walks a nicely dressed lady. The lady briefly speaks to your parents, then walks over to you and says that you need to go with her. You don't know where you're going, but your parents think its ok. As you are leaving, you notice your parents walking behind carrying a packed suitcase. At this point, you don't understand what's happening; your heart starts to beat fast, you want to ask where you are going but you are afraid. You take a deep breath and say, "Where am I going?" The nicely dressed lady looks at you and replies, "You are going to a nice home to live with a wonderful family." Your mind starts to travel, "What did I do wrong? Will I see my friends again? Will I go to the same school?"

Now, imagine that:

You are living in a different environment

The culture of your family is different

You have to follow new rules

You share a bedroom with someone you don't know

You eat different foods than you normally eat

You go to a different school

You attend another place of worship

Your friends are many miles away

At this moment, all that you have ever known has been taken from you; everything, except your name.

This scenario is played over and over for the many children that are faced with entering foster care. Sometimes, we are given a second chance in life; the opportunity to come full circle. What we do with what is offered is totally up to us and no one else. Being a foster child is not what we choose to be; but something that has been chosen for us. I often see us as "a product of the system", viewing the world differently than others may view it. In our world, I've often seen pain, mistrust, abuse and even hatred. We are given a stigma that is hard to shake. Words are spoken to us that hurt to the core. We, in turn, create our own world where we find that little piece of love, happiness or stability that was taken or absent in our lives. We use this as our defense mechanism. Whether it benefits or harms us, this is the world we create; one, which I've created. My world was in the basement of my foster parent's home; where I chose to spend many hours in front of a small black and white television set.

As foster children we want to belong, to be loved and to have our existence acknowledged. We want to belong in a world where we are like your own children, your own relatives. We wish to belong to a family that says I am theirs no matter what. We don't want pity, we don't need pity; we just want to be loved and cared for without the presence of mistreatment, misrepresentation or dismissal.

Here's a little reality check for you. You say that your child "will not do this", "will not do that" because they are living in your house, under your roof and in a religious home. I've got news for you, you need to wake up and wake up fast. This is not the 60's or 70's where everything moved a lot slower. Many of these foster children have been abused, seen abuse and in their minds feel that –

1. They cannot trust you or anyone else
2. You really can't tell them what to do - you can only ask
3. Your home is just temporary like all the rest before yours

Allow me to break this down a little further . . .

You say that your foster son or daughter will not have sex until she is 18 or out of your house. And you say this, believing that you have control over what goes on with that child. I'm going to tell you straight, like it is in their world. They hear you, but are they listening to you. Some of these children have already been abused and feel that all they ever had has been taken from them. I'm sorry to say, but the one thing you cannot take from them . . . their right to decide how they use their body. You can scream about religion until hell freezes over. You cannot control what they have already made up their mind to do. Instead, it is your responsibility as parents, teachers, and counselors to educate your children as well as foster children about the pitfalls of being sexually active at an early age. However, if you keep closing the blinds, the light will never shine through. Don't be afraid to talk to them about birth control and sexually transmitted diseases. My sister, Theresa and I both learned from the streets. I had my first sexual experience between the ages of 14 and 15, my sister Theresa, even earlier. Yes, we lived in a Christian home.

As foster children, we experience special occasions such as holidays and find them especially difficult. We don't really look forward to them and can't stop them from coming. We see kids with their families, and wish that it were us. We lie in bed at night and ask "why me?" I often asked that question as a child. I didn't get my answer until age 39; to be able to tell the world that we exist; that we also belong. I now find myself in a position to assist other foster children in ways that I was not assisted. 1G-d does things in His own time. When I was young, I resented my bio-parents for what they had done and often my foster parents for what they didn't do. As I've matured, I've come to accept the hand that I was dealt and often view the negative events in my life as stepping-stones to my future. I was fortunate to have been raised with my sister, Theresa. She was only 18 months and I was 2 years old at the time that we entered foster care. This is not always the situation for foster children. There are many who do not know where their siblings are or if they have any siblings at all. When I was older, I learned that I had another sister, Tracy. She is the youngest of the three of us. Recently, at age 41, I discovered that I have several other brothers and sisters which I had the opportunity of meeting in late 2003.

For those of you that are fortunate enough to have your own children or foster children, this is the time to look at them, even if they are not "a product of the system," and tell them how much you care. Don't let them have to wonder if they will ever find parents to love them. Don't let them go into a world that will do more harm than good. You could be the parent that they are seeking, the parent that will put them on the right path. Be the parent that says, "I love you"; no matter what has happened or will happen throughout their life. Every time you look at your child and say how much you care it helps. When they don't have to wonder if they will ever find parents to love them, it lets them know that you will always be there for them. When they go out into the world and find people that are good to them, it helps. Every child will have a story to tell. Whatever story it is; it will depend partly on you. Will they tell the story of hate, sorrow, mistrust and pain? Or, will it be one of love, a story of someone that made a difference in his or her life.

-Dahveed

10ᵗʰ Anniversary Edition

Light Beyond the Shadows ...

The ages of twelve to sixteen, where divided between four foster homes and two group homes. The first home was foreign and a short stay. I was beat up in one home, for what could only amount to not being liked. The group homes were full of girls from every imaginable circumstance; and some not so much. Freedom was too accessible. Looking back, there was any number of things happening that shouldn't have been. The yellow house, as I'll call it, (I proudly helped paint it) would be no different.

The yellow house was home for two years. My foster mother worked part-time, could burn in the kitchen and had an old school, no non-sense Madea-like way about her. My foster father was a blue collar man; who loved to hunt. I remember tasting beef tongue and rabbit for the first time. My foster mother cooked Monday through Thursday. Fridays and Saturdays we had leftovers or as she was known to say *"go for what you know;"* which meant frozen pizza. Sundays were spent at her parents' church; followed by "Sunday dinner." If we wanted our allowance early (who didn't) and to hang out on the weekends, chores had to be done Friday night. The sounds of the adults trash talkin', washin' dominoes, Bobby Blue Bland, and B.B. King (and Lucille) albums were the regular. There were only girls in the house. Some of us were long term, while others came and went. Our stories were varied. There were fights and punishments. What began to feel like normal would end soon.

Journaling late at night while listening to music was a natural occurrence. This particular night it was Michael Jackson's BAD album. There was a knock on the door. It was my foster father, making the rounds to check the house. *"What are you doing up?"* he asked. *"Just listening to music,"* I said. Without any warning, he grabbed my breast. Just like that, standing there in the doorway of my bedroom while everyone else slept. Time stopped. *"Turn that light off,"* he said, *"I'll be back."* To this day, I do not know where I went in my mind or why I did what came next.

Instead of closing the door, I went to the front of the house where their room was. He was about to return to my room, when he saw me standing there. *"Dad,"* I said *"may I have some Tylenol?"* All medicines were kept locked in their room. Not that makes it makes any sense. He stood there for a second; then got the Tylenol. My adult self so wished the girl I was would have woken her foster mother. That didn't happen. He took my hand in his and placed two pills in my palm. *"I have a headache,"* I said; pulled my hand back and walked away with my heart drumming in my ears. The way he held my hand stayed with me for years. Something about it made my skin crawl.

Back in my room, I stood there for what seemed like forever; feeling like I was in some sort of parallel universe. It was real and unreal at the same time. I didn't know what to do. What if he came back? Block the door; I thought. The chest of drawers was too heavy to move. I spent the rest of the night hugging my knees, praying he didn't come back. I didn't say anything right away; except in my journal – where I could always speak freely. A few nights later, on a visit with my family I told my mother I didn't want to go back. The details of the next few days are unclear. After leaving the yellow house, I spent time in a short and long term group home before ultimately returning home to my family.

One of my foster sisters at the time was ten years old. The perfect embodiment of a pesky little sister: nosey, mouthy, and always wanting to be with the older girls. Snooping around, she unearthed my journal; read it and promptly ran away. It turned out that her mother's boyfriend had molested her. She was terrified it would happen again. I felt it was my fault and that I was to blame for her running away.

Sometime later, I learned their license had been revoked. Ugliness and shame settled on me like an old familiar coat. This was not my first experience with molestation. Between the fourth and then eighth grades, there were five occasions (not all in foster care) in which five individuals thought it alright to touch me (and other things I won't detail here). As an adult, my mother shared with me that when I returned home, I was different. I was; for many reasons. Among them being that another part of my spirit had retreated into the shadows. Journaling no longer comes easily.

I don't understand why these things happened to me and know not every foster care experience mirrors mine. It was never my fault. I am clear about that. I am clear that I am still standing, light shining.

10th Anniversary Edition

It is my hope to be even the tiniest flicker of light to someone still in the shadows.

Kenya Williams, is an Air Force veteran, mother of one and owner of Butterfly Belly Beads (www.butterflybellybeads.com); where she designs waist beads as hand crafted instruments of self-awareness for women, assisting and encouraging them to embrace their bodies and stand in their feminine power.

1. *The spelling of "G-d and L-rd" is used throughout to respect the Jewish prohibition against spelling the name or title of the deity in full.*

In Our Ghetto

"If we could capture wisdom... then this religion of indecision would not become our prison". And maybe we'd have something more to believe in".

There's a darkness still bleeding from this wound, because were I'm from has become a place with a drums for children just a slum in need of rebuilding.

The Ghetto

In Our Ghetto...we no streets of gold or angels standing at crystal podiums

waiting to greet you at the pearly gates. There are no harps, or rainbows, or grand

piano's... nothing beautiful...

And maybe this.. is why children... hoping for brighter tomorrows...keep slippin through the cracks.

To get to our ghetto, you just step through a hole in a barbed wire fence, leading to an empty playground where dead pygmies hang from monkey bars like little pot bellied bats whose wings have been clipped by an angry God too busy to answer prayers.

Near the entrance, there's a giant dumpster overflowing with the battered spirits of abandoned babies screaming for their teenage mothers... and I suppose **that's** where lost souls go.

Inside, a man wearing an "I love Bush" T shirt smiles like a pimp, as he checks his list for section 8 rape and motions to an rickety wooden ladder where drug dealers circle and grin.

In the courtyard, Billie Holliday sits beneath a hanging tree with noose-shaped leaves holding an empty syringe... dying....from spiritual laryngitis.

10th Anniversary Edition

To my left... Martin stands barefoot, handcuffed...surrounded by confederate soldiers yelling, "Ain't no dreams here NIGGAH", you took the wrong DAMN turn at the mountain.

To my right...The Klan rapes Abe Lincoln, Malcom is on his back in a straight jacket and James Byrd is still running behind that damned truck, in Jasper Texas... struggling to pick up the pieces of his soul.

In Our Ghetto...The police, play paint ball with the blood of lost children while Osama and Jeffery Dahmer place bets. And the ancestors, just sit on stumps like black leprechauns watching... as priest turned pedophiles drool as they wait for lil Hansels and Gretels to lose their way.... and history makes damn sure they do.. by leaving trails of broken promises scattered with the restless souls of a million slaves.

In Our Ghetto, the bombing of the 16th Street Baptist Church is a national celebration, where heroes like Hitler and Hoover propose a toast to the ghosts of dead daughters.

And ANYONE caught believing in themselves ...ANYONE... Would have their spirits lynched by the rope of their own hope. Cause in our ghetto it's a sin to DREAM!

Foster homes become concentration camps for children starving for attention, and there ain't no such thing as college because knowledge is NOT the key to success, and HERE they don't give a DAMN if you don't do your best. IT DON'T MATTER....THIS DON'T MATTER ... WE DON'T MATTER...

You see...THIS is what we see in our ghetto and if things don't change....

This is ALL WE'LL BE in our ghetto....

This is what we believe our ghetto to be. Cause in our ghetto.....

There IS NO TOMORROW ...just the hell of living ...TODAY!!

- Michael Guinn

Every Child's Voice Should Be Heard

A question one might ask is; what exactly do you mean by "Every Child's Voice Should Be Heard." Back in the day, for those of us that remember that far back; we were told that "children should be seen and not heard." We all have something that we want to say, need to say; something that we wish to share, but don't really know how to express it. As children and young adults; you may assume that no one wants to hear what you have to say. Here's a tip for you; when you express yourself in a positive way; people will not only hear you, but they will talk to you. When I write, I write with passion and from the heart. When I speak I give it to you raw; my truth, my voice. There's no sugar coating, no cream or strawberries mixed in. But I do it in a way in which others can relate, and also feel what I am expressing to them.

Forty-two years ago, which may seem like forever, I was a child that was placed in the foster care system. Forty-two years ago, I would have never dreamed of what I am doing today; advocating for foster children.

My story is not unique in any way. But it is one that has been told over and over again by other children; the children that wanted their voices to be heard. By writing "Through the Eyes of a Foster Child"; it helped me to tell a story that I may not have ever told; because I was afraid to let my voice be heard. Today, I say to you; I emphatically believe that every child's voice should be heard.

A few years ago, I wrote an article and put it on the internet. Someone from a foster care agency in Rhode Island read it and contacted me. They asked if they could put the article in their newsletter. I didn't think anything of it; so I said sure, go ahead.

After they sent me a copy of the newsletter, I read it and thought; why not put it in our newsletter; the agency that I was working for at the time. I did; and a few days later, as I was walking down the hallway and was stopped as I passed the Executive Administrator's office. She had recently read the article that I had written titled; "Through the Eyes of a Foster Child." Our conversation went as follows:

"David, may I speak with you for a moment?" She asks. "Sure, Carol, what is it?" "I read the article that you wrote for the newsletter. I am very

impressed and touched by it. I had no idea that you were a foster child."
I looked at her and replied, "Too many people don't know that about me Carol. I just don't share that information with everyone." She looked at me with bewilderment and concern and says "David, you have a gift. You have a way with words." Now I'm looking puzzled and have no idea as to where this conversation is headed. "Excuse me Carol, I don't understand;" I replied, with a puzzled look on my face. "David, you have a lot to say and everyone needs to hear this, people need to hear your story. Have you ever thought about writing a book, writing your story? You need to write." I looked at her and I laughed. "Carol, I don't know the first thing about writing a book, and who would be interested in reading it." She stares at me as though she sees through my eyes; "David, you have a special gift and you should really think about it." "Ok Carol, I'll think about it." As I walked away, I thought to myself; "yeah right, write a book."

I'm sure that some of us, if not all of us have been told something positive about ourselves and didn't want to believe it. We have even convinced ourselves that we are not even worthy of the acknowledgement. I realize now how true it is when they say "people come into your life for a reason or just for a season." Carol passed away a few months later from (ALS) Amyotrophic Lateral Sclerosis, known as the Lou Gehrig's disease. Upon her passing, I began to think about our conversation and what she was trying to tell me.

> *I remember you*
> *As you*
> *Looked at me,*
> *Stared at me,*
> *As though . . . you really knew me.*
>
> *I looked in your eyes*
> *And saw that you cared,*
> *We shared,*
> *As you looked past*
> *My pain, my shame,*
> *"You're not to blame" you said.*
>
> *We conversed,*
> *Smiled,*

Chatted . . . just a little while
And got to know,
Feel and learn
Each other's style . . . as we smiled.

You taught,
I listened and learned;
In return . . . I yearned . . .
Your knowledge, insight,
As you suggested
That I should write and unite;
Red, yellow, black, brown and white.

And so, I sit here, stand here;
Pen, pad, and sometimes mic in hand;
Allowing my words to flow . . .
So others may understand.

It was on a daily basis that I use to sit at my desk and watch so many foster children come into the office and I think; does anyone hear them? Are people really listening to what they have to say? Do people feel their heart crying out for love, crying out to belong? Are their little voices being heard? What stories do they have? I sat and I pray . . . God, if it's your will, guide me on this journey so others can see – through the eyes of a foster child.

Every child will have a story to tell. Whatever story it is; Our Children will look to their teachers, social workers, clergy, and parents, as their guide through life. Will they tell the story of hate, sorrow, mistrust and pain? Or, will it be one of love, a story of someone that made a difference in his or her life.

Over the past few years; I've had the opportunity to speak and listen to so many foster youth, foster parents, and those that wanted to become foster parents. And with each occasion, I've learned so much more about myself and about what my purpose is in this life. It took me many years to find my place in the world; to find the one thing that made me who I am; the person that I've come to be. Sometimes, we try to run from those things that are set in place to guide us. I chose to ignore and not accept what was meant to be until that one person entered my life and said

10th Anniversary Edition

"David, your voice need to be heard." I can now say without shame that I was a foster child; I am a former foster child. I AM who I AM and ACCEPT who I WAS and have become. Not only will I let my voice be heard, I will shout out to the masses that every child's voice should be heard because I'm still . . .

Trying to look Beyond the Horizon
Where the sun goes to set
One day ends . . .
Another begins
As
seagulls
 descend

On our California shores
Discussing the philosophy of life and more,
As my brother Pablo and I explore
The reality of an unpredictable war

Where hatred turns to love
Looking to heavens above,
For The Answer to the Question
Forgiving
all
our
 transgressions

Where religions are amassed
Gangs become outcast
To a society that's meant to last
Never forgetting . . .
Never forgetting ones past

Where death's no longer mourned
Babies safely born
Abuse unheard of -
Children
treated

with
love

Where AIDS has no face
No black, brown, or white race
In a society that lives as one
Still waiting . . .
for
HIM to come

As we look beyond the horizon
Where the sun goes to set

-Dahveed

10th Anniversary Edition

Do The Math!

Our babies are being condemned to failure as they go un-adopted.
Not enough is being done to remedy this problem or halt it.
There is a simple equation that is being over looked.
No the answer to this problem can't be found at the back of the book.
The solution to this problem starts and ends with the race.
We hold the key to creating prosperity in the face of disgrace.
The only way to truly have a sense of pride
Is to be able to take your last breath knowing you've tried.
I know that my life's work is not yet done
Until I have changed the possibilities for someone.
It starts with a symbol and ends with a choice.
But the two together give each silent victim a great voice.
In separation we see the bigger picture.
For adoption "Ad(ds) + Options" to their future.
An option can be defined as variety or abundance.
But the next definition is the one that fits them best.
The dictionary says option is the equivalent to opportunity.
Something that every human being deserves to receive.
Once we *add* a child to a caring home,
This simple addition problem takes on a positive life's journey of its own.
The next step moves a little more swiftly.
Simply because we have created much more equity.
We no longer are dealing with the negative connotations.
There are now only positive integers in the life of their equations.
Although we usually find a finite answer, this case has become a rarity;
For our solution has an outcome that will *multiply infinitely*!
The children are being given an extraordinary life-line due to their new found variety.
Now the race holds another key player as we move toward true equality.
Ad(ding) options yields a vast many opportunities.
Now they get the choice of disparity or victory.

Gumbo For The Soul

In our country too many take the high road of charity and travel it far from home.

When here in our own backyard we have a problem weed that is far too overgrown!

If just one fortunate family took in a less fortunate child,

Our race's ability to rise would continue for miles.

These tender souls who had no choice in setting the path of their life,

Would have end results with opportunity rather than strife!

So it's our choice in how to view the glass.

But if we want to opportunely fill our children's half,

By affixing our names to their papers, we must triumphantly DO THE MATH!!!

-Shawnda Tate

10th Anniversary Edition

Too Old

As a child it is difficult to imagine that you may not be able to have as many children as you would like…even if that number is 100!

In kindergarten I was able to count to 100; so why not have 100 children?

Oh, to be 5 years old again…

Growing up in the early 1960's, I remember our first television: black and white- not color.

My favorite show was Perry Mason, a criminal attorney who won virtually every case. He was a white and I was black but without "color" I failed to see the distinction between us and my dream of becoming a lawyer became a reality years later. I was a "late bloomer" in when it came to starting a family. My first child, a beautiful daughter, was born a couple of weeks shy of my 35th birthday. I was blessed to have two stepdaughters who graced our home on their weekend visits but I still longed for more children to love.

After literally years and years of failed fertility treatments, my husband and I decided to adopt. I was 42.

We initially considered adopting an African American child from the United States-preferably a boy as we had three girls. With all the literature about African American children needing families, particularly boys, we assumed that we would have a bundle of joy in our arms in no time.

Did we? No.

The adoption world we entered was not "parent-friendly."

The first hurdle we stumbled over was that as prospective adoptive parents, we would experience placement delays because we wanted to adopt a boy. The fact that we were specifying the sex of the child would result in not being readily matched with a child as many expectant birth mothers who had made the decision to place their child for adoption early in their pregnancy, did not know the sex of their child and wanted to identify a family that would adopt their child prior to delivery.

In addition, we were told that "open adoption" was becoming a popular choice of many birth mothers.* The facilitator of the first adoption seminar we attended discussed open adoptions, this was the first time we had heard that term. To familiarize the audience with the concept several examples of open adoptions were shared. We were told that the birth mother would set forth the terms of the adoption and those terms could range from something as simple as keeping the name the birth mother chose for the child to having the child spend several holidays a year with the birth mother. The agency sponsoring the seminar informed us that the majority of birth mothers using their services already had at least one other child in the home. In addition, it was highly recommended that we have professional photographs taken as this was in actuality an "interviewing" process where the birth mother was the interviewer; we were the interviewees.

My age could also be a deterrent to many birth mothers, some as young as 13, as they would view me as "too old" to raise their child as they may have grandparents-or even great-grandparents my age.

We opted out of that process and turned to African adoptions. I have had the good fortune of traveling and living in West and East Africa throughout my adult life and felt a definite connection to the Motherland.

I searched the Internet for adoption agencies and my husband and I settled on one that had all the requisites of what we perceived a good agency to be. We indicated to the agency director that we wanted to bring an infant into our home, a boy.

Unbeknownst to the agency director, the batteries finally ran out on my biological clock, but the face of the clock still shined. Well, that was until she told me that at age 43, I was "too old" to adopt an infant and would only be eligible to adopt a child the age of two or above. The fact that my age "disqualified" us from adopting an infant was another conventional "wisdom" that was coaxing me to steer far away from an infant and "settle" for an older child. I had older children; I wanted an infant! But, my fear of not being "suitable" for any child, I begrudgingly accepted the restriction and was ecstatic when we were "matched" with a toddler who we love and adored. We never met in person but holding and caressing is not a prerequisite to loving-at least not in my book.

The months of waiting crept into a year and though all our documents were in order, we still had no clear indication of when our son would be coming home. Between the lack of plausible explanations for the delays and soured communications with the adoption agency, tensions peaked, and I made one of the hardest decisions of my life-we terminated our relationship with the agency and decided to go it alone-sans agency.

10th Anniversary Edition

One of my favorite motivational speakers is Jim Rohn. In his book, Seven Strategies for Wealth and Happiness, he discusses "The Four Emotions that Can Lead to Life Change:" Disgust, Decision, Desire and Resolve. ** I was disgusted that arbitrary age restrictions stood in my way of expanding my family through adoption.

I made a decision to travel to Ethiopia to adopt an infant, on a hope, prayer and support from those who told me my age would not be a bar.

I had a desire to return to Africa, the continent of my ancestors.

I resolved that I would stay in Ethiopia until I could return home with my son; no matter what.

My mother and I flew to Ethiopia September 2004. I kissed my husband goodbye and told him that I may not be home for Christmas. I only had four weeks of vacation available at work. I spent three and a half weeks in Ethiopia. My two-moth old son and I were home in plenty of time for Christmas.

-Karen Felecia Nance Ransom

*The American Association of Open Adoption Agencies (AAOAA) defines open adoption as "a form of adoption in which the birth family and the adopted child enjoy an ongoing, in-person relationship." (www.openadoption.org)
 **Seven Strategies for Wealth and Happiness by Jim Rohn

Through the Eyes of a Child

Aunt Louise's Red Pumps

Introduction by Jackie Moore, Author:

The story of the <u>Aunt Louise's Red Pumps</u> is a love story. It is a story about the love and admiration that a small child has for her Aunt Louise. It is a lesson in love, tolerance and acceptance. Mama Boo admires her aunt more than anyone else in the world. She sees her aunt as the epitome of all that she believes a woman should be. Mama Boo admires her strength, her passion and her courage to be true to herself. Nevertheless, her world is turned upside down when she discovers Aunt Louise's secret.

It is a reminder that children see us and learn things from our actions as well as what we say. There is a lesson that every adult needs to know, be very careful on what we teach, because we never know when little eyes are are watching.

10th Anniversary Edition

Aunt Louise's Red Pumps

By Sharon Stinson Gray

Aunt Louise's crimson dipped pumps intrigued me. Actually, everything about her intrigued me. The 3-inch heels sat studiously and obediently in the right hand corner of her lavish closet. Many sequin gowns and elaborate silk scarves reign superior; hovering over the 3-inch pumps. The heels weren't alone, though because she had an array of fabulous and exquisite shoes. Mama said that Aunt Louise spent her entire paycheck on frivolous material items. I didn't quite grasp the meaning of frivolous then, but if it meant 'cool' then yes, Aunt Louise was frivolous in my book. These particular pumps resided in the right hand corner of the closet. The right hand corner. Today, they were in the left corner. Foreign territory. That wasn't right, I thought to myself. Aunt Louise always replaced her items appropriately. She was particular like that.

Mama called my name four times yet her voice seemed transparent and lost in my magnitude of thought. I was worried. I was steadfast and hungry for the 'know'—why had Aunt Louise's pumps been moved? I was on a mission—of the highest priority, I pondered to myself. Amused at my creativity in this matter. I felt compelled to investigate further.

"Go out and play," the faint rumble of vocals blended in the background. The voices seemed humdrum compared to the significance of thought that penetrated within. My feet were transplanted. I was transfixed in the midst of my own chaos.

"Come on Mama Boo, let's play hopscotch" my older sister whined. I could never resist her wishes when she used my nickname, Mama Boo. I dared not move. I'll hide instead I contemplated. It was 2 p.m.

4:30 p.m. my eyelids were molested by the shadow of lights illuminating the room. My dream state was no longer. I dare not breathe in fear that I would be discovered. This hiding space was my haven; my escape from reality and propelled me into my Hollywood fantasy. Mama never allowed us to play in Aunt Louise's bedroom. She said it was *'no place for a growing girl to be'*—didn't mama know when she said I can't do it that made me want to do it even more? Because of the secrecy and forbiddance, I was drawn to the room. I was fascinated—the thought of voyeurism plagued me and hunted me until I could no longer resist. What was so special about Aunt Louise's room? I convinced myself that I must venture to this world—the adult world of roguish pleasures such as grown music (Marvin Gay's words were too mannish for a girl my age, Mama would say), hot red lipstick (Mama said only streetwalkers use bright red lipstick & bleached their hair blonde). But, what mama didn't know wouldn't hurt her, I thought. I liked the sexual healings and the Bright Red Passion #43 lipsticks of the world. I yearned to be like my Aunt Louise. I wanted this so much; my heart ached in anticipation when she walked around in the room. Her actions were bronzed with perfection in my eyes. She could never do any wrong.

My heart engrossed in the moment, seemed to skip a beat due to my utter excitement. What would she wear tonight, what would she sing? I secretly voted for her gold sequined mini dress and her newest song, "Little Girl Blue."

10th Anniversary Edition

"Okay, Pearl. I'll be out in a minute! Let me change, PLEASE!" Louise roared in frustration.

Aunt Louise's voice lingered in the air. Her charming perfume trailed the room and hid in the corners. The intoxicating aura seemed to set the mood. She began to hum a tune. The same and noticeable tone that caressed the airways as I listened to her song, "Bitter Sweet Heartbreak" perused the record when I privately played it. Mama said that a real woman didn't fancy herself as a nightclub singer if she wanted respect. She also said that Aunt Louise was too old to be hanging out and singing in those places. Those places, I winced when remembered the malicious tone Mama used when pronouncing the word but those places captivated me. Well, I wanted to be transported to those places. I desired to bellow out earthy tones and sing about love and a man leaving me. I didn't quite grasp why a man leaving you would be a bad thing, but then again, I didn't like boys so it wouldn't bother me.

I would be just like Aunt Louise one day. She was my idol. She embodied truth and always stood her ground. I've never seen her back down from ANY fight, confrontation or argument. Just like the time when Mama told Aunt Louise that she could no longer stay out all times of night and still come home to the house. Mama said she was setting a bad example for the kids. Aunt Louise stood emotionless as if she was absorbing each word.

Then, ever so slowly and softly she whispered, *"I am who I am and I will NOT be ashamed of my comings and goings. If you have a problem with me and what I do or what I don't do, then I shall move out by the end of the month"* Then, she grabbed her handbag and walked fearlessly out of the room. Not once did her voice shake. Not once did she wince or look back. She actually stood up to mama. I was in awe.

When Aunt Louise said that, my eyes started to swell with tears. I couldn't bear her departure. I wanted to run after her and tell her, *'Mama was just kidding. You can stay!'* but I knew I couldn't get involved in grown folks' business. I just knew I had to absorb as much of Aunt Louise's essence as possible before she left permanently.

My secret place was safe. It was just compact enough for a lanky nine year old. It encompassed the wooden portion under Aunt Louise's king side bed. The soft silk sheets overlapped the crook of the mattress and gathered elegantly on the corner of the bed.

Gumbo For The Soul

Cling, Cling. I heard the soft murmur of her jewelry embracing one another. My leg has gone numb or as my Mama would say, *"fell asleep"* so careful not to make any noise, I readjusted my leg so I could maintain my view of her powerful legs. I unconsciously rubbed my own legs as I mentally compared them to my idol. She hummed and it was mellow and sensual. I remembered listening to this tune when she went out of town and mama thought I was outside playing "red-light, green light, and 1-2-3". It was simply divine.

The room suddenly became silent—what happened to her voice, I thought. My heart began to skip a beat in eagerness of the unknown. I adjusted my legs to propel my head higher so I could grasp my surroundings. Where was Aunt Louise? Her legs have disappeared but I can still smell her perfume so she still must be present, I thought logically. She must've moved, but where was she?

Because of the cramped space, I had little desire to move again in fear that my covert operation would be discovered. Then I saw it.

It rested. Motionless. The rich caramel color from my innocent face was drained and replenished with dread and apprehension. It was curly, blonde and lifeless.

I saw it. Her hair or rather her wig.

My image of perfection started to flake. Unbeknownst to this facade, I craved those same natural curls. I would religiously curl my hair with my slender index finger in hopes of acquiring the exact movement and grace of Aunt Louise's hair. I was astonished. It wasn't real. Paralyzed, at first, but then, I begin to push myself up. I didn't desire to complete my mission any longer. I just wanted to go outside and play hopscotch with my big sister.

The rumble of the hollow wood erupted in a loud noise. As I emerged from my secret place, my peripheral vision caught a glimpse of a body shuffling away in fear and surprise.

Sweat gathered at the temple of my forehead as I clumsily unfolded my 9-year-old slender body out of the compartment. My heart was pounding mercifully but I knew I needed to get out!

"What the hell are YOU doing in here?" yelled Aunt Louise in complete astonishment.

Still avoiding eye contact, I looked down and shrugged my shoulders hopelessly. Sweat continued to bead on my forehead. My hands became clammy and slippery. My nerves were no longer balanced. I was caught so I stood peacefully in all of my innocence.

I wanted to speak, I truly did but I couldn't. I couldn't understand my feelings at the moment and I certainly couldn't muster up enough confidence to speak back to my idol. So, I stood there, looking pathetic and sneaky. I stood there with my head held down in embarrassment. I didn't want to look up.

A few uneasy and silent moments passed. Then I felt her tender fingers brush my face. Then she nudged my chin upwards. Still, unable to give eye contact, I clenched my eyes shut. I couldn't bear to see Aunt Louise incomplete and without her glorious golden locks. I didn't want to distort my image of perfection. So I halted in silence.

"Child, open your eyes. It's okay sweetie."

"No, I don't wanna" I mumbled out of confusion. I shook my head nervously and silently prayed that this moment was not happening. I wanted to run out and go play.

"Please, Mama Boo, open your eyes. It's time that you know the truth." She said in a nurturing maternal voice.

What truth? I pondered. I didn't comprehend her words. I just yearned to leave but her endearing tone made it hard to resist her request for me to open my eyes.

"It's okay, sweetie... Come on Mama Boo, open your eyes," She continued to sway my stubbornness with her bold persistence. It started to work.

Deliberately and gradually, I embraced her hand with my small hand. I opened my eyes while tears were simultaneously cascading down the side of my face. I wasn't prepared for what I was about to see.

Aunt Louise stood tall and proud. She had a short crop haircut and she lacked all signs of womanhood. There was no makeup, no jewelry, no nothing. I searched deeply in her eyes for some recognition of my sensational Aunt Louise. I was unsuccessful. Instead, I gazed in the eyes of a slim man who resembled my Aunt Louise. A man, I thought. Wow. She was a he.

"This is me, sweetie. In the flesh. No more secrets. I'm still your Aunt Louise and I love you more than anything. You're my special Mama Boo.'

I shook my head no; indicating my resistance to the truth unmasked before me and began to cry. My tears were long, vigorous, and full of sadness. I tried to break her embrace as Aunt Louise held me closer. She rocked me as I wailed and started to hum. That sensual hum that usually brought calmness to my spirit. The mellow sound of her voice soothed me. This was my Aunt Louise. I felt less constricted once I heard her voice and inhaled her sweet perfume. She rocked me slowly. I felt safe. I abandoned the thoughts of running away and relished this moment for what it was worth.

Aunt Louise was still my idol and I loved her very much.

-Sharon Stinson Gray

10th Anniversary Edition

A Tribute to Grandparents Raising Their Grandchildren

Thank You

We celebrate you for all you've done
For caring for your granddaughter and your grandson
You took on this awesome task that no one else could do,
Because no one loves and cares for your grandchild quite like you.

You had the courage to start all over again
Raising your grandchildren at an age when
You thought you might retire, travel and rest
But the children needed caregivers, and they needed the best.

Some came to you in pampers and most in tears
Needing nurturing and someone who cares.
Others came as toddlers, exploring the world on the run
You couldn't believe this happened – after you thought that you were done.

Still others came at school age, when they needed guidance and direction
Science may have you baffled but you are great at giving affection.
And some of you have teenagers, oh my, what can I say.
Just keep reminding yourself that they won't stay this way.

We know it has not been easy – often quite a heavy load
And there have been many bumps along the road
You've been misunderstood, labeled and denied the services you need
Often criticized and not recognized for your labor or your good deed.

But we are here to honor you who have done so much
To change the lives of children with your special touch
We thank you grandparents: we thank you once; we thank you twice
And know you are appreciated for the rest of your life.

Thank you, grandparents.

Rolanda Pyle
– Copyright

This poem is one in the collection of poems in the newly released book,
FINALLY,

by Rolanda Pyle.

10th Anniversary Edition

A Diamond in the Rough

It was the fall of 1989 and I remember being so excited about my new community service assignment at Terrence Cardinal Cooke Hospital. My high school in Manhattan made it mandatory that all students volunteered during the school day to give back to the community. I could not wait to work with the babies in a special ward of the hospital. These children were either at this facility because they did not have a home or they were receiving extensive medical care. As the weeks went by there was a rumor around the hospital about a special little baby that was being admitted into our ward. Her Mother abandoned her in another hospital without any trace as to how to find her. I could not believe that someone would do this to their child. The nurses told us that her Mother was a crack addict and that Baby Hanley was special because she lived after being born blue. Baby Hanley is what everyone called her because all they had was her Mother's last name. She was not breathing and the doctors after many attempts freed up her lungs so she could breathe. She was also shaking and could not stop moving. After many tests the doctors found traces of crack in her system. She was the first generation of "crack" babies. In New York City everyday someone was giving birth to a baby that was addicted to crack or cocaine. Some of the children turned out to be fine and some ended up medically challenged where they could not walk or talk. The doctors never knew how the children would turn out and had to closely monitor them.

The next day a few of us arrived at the facility and discovered all of the nurses fussing over a tiny baby girl. I looked at her and just rubbed the sides of her head. She was beautiful. Her eyes almost looked black and she had a bad rash on her face from the oxygen tubes being taped to her. The nurse turned to me and asked if I wanted to hold her. I smiled as I extended my arms. I knew I had to hold her tight because even though she was only a couple of months old she could not stop moving. She would reach out and try to grab things because her body did not know how to relax. She still had crack in her system and the doctors told us that the damage was permanent. After a lot of tests they placed her in the nursery during the day with the rest of the babies. She would look up and smile at you with her wide grin. Her legs were always kicking and she seemed okay from the surface. As time went on I told my Mother about Baby Hanley and how she had to see her. My Mother was hesitant at first since she was already taking care of me and my adopted sister Ayana but she met me after school the next week and we went to visit Baby Hanley.

My Mother laid eyes on her and instantly fell in love. Baby Hanley loved my Mother too and after a while I started to see my Mom at the facility a little more often because she wanted to spend time with her. As time passed the nurses decided it was time to give her a name. We all put names in a hat and had a drawing at lunch one day. The first name picked was Christina and then her middle name was drawn from the hat which was Simone. She finally had a name like the rest of the babies. Christina was now old enough to start crawling around the nursery and she would crawl over other children as she caused a slight disruption. She was the only child in the nursery that was mobile. The other baby that started crawling went home to his Mother after a while. The facility said that she would have to be moved into the foster care system because no one from her family was responding to their request. They asked them to please claim her and start the process of foster care by having a caseworker visit the house of the Grandmother. The family did not want to have anything to do with her since she was medically challenged. Christina was hyper, she often had temper tantrums, her speech became slurred as she got older and she would need someone to take care of her for the rest of her life.

My Mother Marguerite Wills did not want to see Christina in the foster care system. Because of her challenges it may take a while for a family to take her. After a while she would end up in an institution. My Mother called Children's Aid Society and asked if she would be eligible to become Christina's foster Mother even though she had two children already, one with severe medical problems. After a few phone calls, a home visit and a lot of paperwork Christina was coming home with us in February of 1991. My Mother had to deal with the negative feelings that some people had towards her about bringing another child into her house since she already had both Ayana and me. By this time my Mother developed tougher skin and saw the darts coming as soon as people threw them in her direction. She was polite and told them to mind their business.

I was now in the 10th grade and I was able to support my Mother since I was a little older. There would be evenings where I would watch

Christina while my Mother would tend to Ayana or vice versa. Christina was more able then my sister Ayana, she could walk and had a little speech. However the crack that caused permanent damage was becoming more evident as time went on. Christina would have temper tantrums and did not know how to calm herself down. Her body would get worked up and did not know how to come down just like a crack addict that gets a high and does not know how to relax without some assistance. My Mother had to start going to more doctors appointments to find out what was wrong and after a lot of tests they came to the conclusion that the drugs were still in her system. The doctors were new to this as well since she was considered part of the first generation of crack babies. As time went on Christina had less temper tantrums.

We received a lot of support from the caseworkers and in September of 1993 my Mother was in front of a judge in the Queens Family Court adopting my sister Christina. She is my diamond in the rough. She was a little treasure that I found in Harlem, NY. Who would have known that God was blessing me with another sister? Christina is now 17 years old and she walks around the house singing. We all get a kick out of her deep voice. Even though she will never be able to take care of herself we are not as worried as we once were since she loves to do little things for herself. She can watch a cooking show and with some assistance can make a simple meal. Her mother or family never bothered to find out about her and after many years we have forgiven them.

My Mother Marguerite Wills is a very selfless person and people can learn a thing or two from her. Her courage to go up against the odds is what I admire the most about her. She always puts her children and family first. My Mother and two sisters still reside in Queens, NY. My Mother wants to open up a group home for children like Ayana and Christina where they could get physical therapy, medical attention or a place to be loved until they find a loving family.

-Serena Theresa Wills

Eva Cara

When I look at Courtney's baby Eva Cara

I remember

I remember understanding, the first time I saw Gabriel Antony lying there on my chest, that scene in "Roots" …

…the *"Behold, the only thing greater than yourself,"* scene where big Papa holds his tiny newborn son up to the sky …

I remember seeing, in Gabriel's being – his sweet eyes and pink lips, his long thin fingers and long already muscular legs, in all that dark curly hair – I saw traces of every single ancestor – all my ancestors, each of his father's ancestors – all the way back to the first two human beings that ever existed.

I say again – the first time I saw my baby I could see in him every single person it took to create him dating all the way back to the very first human beings who ever walked.

As I held him to my breast for the first time, I held his tiny hand in mine and told him, "You are limitless simply by virtue of the fact that you exist. You are living, breathing, and completely amazing proof that the possibilities for human beings are endless, limitless and infinite. You are everything. I am here to honor you, to love and protect you, to grow, learn and change with you, to guide and be guided by you, all of my days."

I was 17.

When I look at Courtney's baby Eva Cara

I remember

I remember that, less than 3 years later, I was looking at a second brand new baby boy – more infinite possibilities created through me.

I remember telling him, my little Brandon Jorell, during our first moments alone, "Someone once said that the Universe – the stars and sky, the sun and moon and everything beyond, are the only things greater than you. Today, I re-vamp that. Behold, dear child, behold the stuff you are made of. Behold, you are as limitless, as infinite and as perfect as the Universe. Know that I am here to honor you, to love and protect you, to guide and be guided by you, to learn, grow and change with you, all of my days."

10th Anniversary Edition

I was 19 ... a few weeks shy of 20.
I knew then, owned fully then, something I saw clearly in my babies that I couldn't yet see –and wouldn't see for many years – is also true for, and about, me.
When I look at Courtney's baby Eva Cara
I remember
I remember that there are no limits
that we are all, every single one of us, formed from the first two humans
and therefore, we are the stuff of Gods
We are formed from the stuff of Gods

When I look at Courtney's baby Eva Cara
I remember
that there is only choice
only change
that finite equals illusory
that existence equals infinite-limitless-ness

In her tiny face I see all that is beautiful, powerful, capable, miraculous and delicious in this world
in every world
in her tiny grasp I feel that there is no separation
no her, no me
no them, no us
no colors, every color
through her tiny touch I am able to know Oneness

When I look at Courtney's baby Eva Cara
I am able to know perfection
I am finally able to release all my illusions
all the "symptoms" and "syndromes" I've allowed to hold me back
I've created to hold myself back
I'm able to burn every memo I've ever read, or written, that said "no," "don't," or "can't"
from the ashes of those limiting memos I am able to rise
I am able to be
 and live my own infinite-limitless-ness

Gumbo For The Soul
I am the perfection I see clearly, feel deeply and know *sem dúvida*

When I look at Courtney's baby Eva Cara
"sem dúvida" = without doubt in Portuguese

-Erica Y. Woods

10th Anniversary Edition

Against the Odds

The doctors already considered her dead. They were bold enough to tell my Mother that her niece at that time would not make it passed the age of two. Ayana was born April 30, 1983 to my Aunt Doretha who had full blown AIDS. Ayana is considered the first generation of "AIDS" babies and the doctors did not know how to handle the situation. They looked my Mother straight in the eye and said, "Ms. Wills there is no way a child that has this many medical complications can survive. She may even still contract this disease from her Mother." The doctors could not wrap their minds around the fact that my Aunt Doretha was dying of AIDS and she just gave birth to a baby girl who had no string of the virus in her system. I was eight years old at the time and was not allowed to go to the hospital with my family. I wanted to tell those doctors that there is nothing to understand, it's just God's work. He wanted Ayana to live and her spirit was so determined that it didn't care what shape or form her body was in.

Ayana is severely brain damaged due to the drugs that were in my Aunt's system and also having a stroke while inside of the womb. She has the complexion of mahogany but was born white because she was barley breathing and from all of the stress and trauma that her poor body endured during the nine months of her being subjected to AIDS and drugs. All in all, she was born just under four pounds and after a few weeks she gained her color. Ayana should not have made it; she should have died before my Aunt gave birth. But she wanted to live and she did!

My Aunt Doretha died in September of 1983 at the age of 24 just a few months after giving birth to her beautiful daughter. The doctors didn't allow Doretha to hold Ayana during those months. Imagine a Mother not being able to hold her child and then die shortly afterwards. My Mother Marguerite Wills made a promise to her sister that she would raise her daughter and never see her enter the foster care system or worst case scenario an institution. My Mother didn't know how she was going to do it. She thought back and forth about the odds that were against her. After Aunt Doretha died my Mother wondered about Ayana, she was left at the hospital to fend for herself. Between the doctors telling her that Ayana was going to die, family members turning their backs on her telling her she could not physically and financially do it and the straight ignorance that people had about the disease. AIDS was so new in 1983 that nurses would not touch Ayana because they feared that they would contract the disease by washing her or changing her diaper.

My Mother received a call in October from someone that told her about Ayana and that she had to take her home. The funny thing is that this gentleman was in the facility with my Aunt and after that call my Mother never heard from him again. She barely had to pick up a phone and do anything. Mom came home one afternoon and sat me down and asked if I wanted a little sister. I knew about Ayana and wanted her to come home and be with us. At such a young age my Mother had already taught me to not turn my back on my family or friends and to always be there whether the sun was shining or a storm was brewing in their life. I knew she would not be like my other friends sisters where she could come outside and play with me and that it would be different. I still wanted her to come home and not have to be in the hospital any longer.

The ball was rolling fast and my Mother didn't have to go through the same procedures that most had to go through in regards to the foster care system. Several months after that phone call Ayana went through numerous doctor's appointments, a case worker from The Children's Aid Society called to really get things started, house visits were made and everyone in my house had to take an HIV/AIDS test Ayana was finally ready to come home. She suffered from severe seizures and could not be outside a lot because her immune system had not fully developed. Ayana would scream when she had seizures but my Mother would run to comfort her. We were blessed to have such a positive group such as the Children's Aid Society support us. They helped with doctor's appointments, financial assistance, counseling and physical therapists for Ayana. They also helped with a very important piece of this puzzle, which was the adoption. My Mother treated Ayana as if she gave birth to her. We loved to dress her up and once her immune system was starting to build up she would travel from Queens to Manhattan with my Mother so she could take me to school. My teachers would always commend my Mother on what she decided to do and how God will always bless her. On the other end of the spectrum when word got out that my Mother wanted to adopt Ayana we had people turn their backs on us. Those who we thought would understand the most told us it was a mistake, we should not do it and to just put her into an institution. The statements at first angered me but as the years went on and I matured I came to the realization that it was simple ignorance. They could not understand that God blessed Ayana with the gift of life and that she was here to stay whether people liked it or not.

I remember going with my Mother after school to the Children's Aid Society and listen to them talk about Ayana's health, the last home visit by her caseworker and they would sometimes just listen to my Mother as she had to vent about the negative feelings that some people had towards us because of her decision.

After four years I remember sitting in the Queens Family Court on June 30th, 1987 where my sister Ayana Doretha Washington-Wills was adopted. The smile on my Mother's face was priceless. I was happy to officially call Ayana my sister. The doctors at the hospital where she was born were still deeming her as dead in 1987. As the years went on Ayana's medical conditions became more complicated. She lived on a vent that helped her to breathe, had a trek, a feeding tube, a collapsed lung, colitis, severe scoliosis and numerous other complications. Ayana passed away on September 22nd, 2007. We are naturally saddened because we will miss her smile, rubbing her forehead, kissing her and telling her we love her. Her spirit was and still is tremendous. The one thing a child like Ayana will do is show us unconditional love. Now a days, it is rare to receive and even give it. Her spirit was not tainted by anything and lived life the best was she knew how. My Mother and I believe that she is doing all things that she could not do on earth. She is free and happy and beat the odds!

My Mother Marguerite Wills is not just your average woman. She is woman of compassion, emotion, strength, courage and confidence. Words can't tell a person about a Mother's true love. It is indescribable and unconditional. We miss you Ayana and may you rest in peace.

-Serena Theresa Wills

Call Me Ma'am

I require that I be addressed as "ma'am," because I make it my business to address the young men and women who have been assigned to my care as "mister" and "miss." In my opinion, this requirement builds a foundation for respectful exchange and mutual growth. And since the overwhelming majority of people assigned to my care haven't really known respect in its purest form, I take it upon myself to plant the seeds for something that is inarguably imperative to their success once they have surpassed the limits of our association. My charges and I are not bonded by love and affection, but rather criminology and, more often than not, recidivism. They do not come to me because they want to come, but rather because they have been given an ultimatum. It is either the chair across from my desk once, twice or even three times a month, or a cell in one of many overcrowded penal institutions, for who knows how many years. Yet, for many of these young men and women I am not only a probation and parole officer, I am something of a foster parent.

The line is often blurred when, as an educated African-American woman, I am confronted with the reality of the broken village on a daily basis. Approximately 95% of the people under my supervision are African-American; roughly 85% are males and at least 75% haven't realized their twenty-fifth birthdays. Similarly, approximately 80% of my clients did not complete high school and an equal number of them now have a criminal record that will follow them for the rest of their lives. This tells me that somewhere along the way a disconnect has occurred, to the detriment of our children. This reaffirms for me that I must step up and do my part to foster reconnection. When they meet me they have lost faith in the villages, have been ousted from their villages, have blindly helped destroy their villages and have never learned to define *village*. They expect me to pick up where their worlds leave off, chastising, belittling and setting them up for certain failure, but I refuse to be anything other than part of the solution.

Is there anything more disparaging than meeting a client who is a "junior" and remembering a time in the not so distant past when you supervised his father, two or three of his brothers or at least one of his uncles? I've known entire families who have come to be known as the "so-

and-so family," the ones not to be trifled with, the ones who pass the legacy of negative notoriety down through the generations. Many times the client sitting on the other side of my desk is third generation and the look in his eyes speaks volumes. His village has led him astray and he believes his future is behind bars, where, unfortunately, he says a great number of his relatives already are.

Then I come at him like this and like that, spinning his world on its axis and speaking to him in a foreign tongue. Before he knows what's hit him I have him sitting up straight in his chair, wearing a belt in my presence to hold up his sagging pants, turning his cell phone off and taking his hat off as soon as he hears my voice. I have him bringing his mother into my office with him to see me and verifying thrice weekly attendance to the local GED class. I'm throwing job leads at him left and right and telling him that there's nothing wrong with an honest day's work. I make him understand that life is for living, for contributing and giving back to the village, and that the sins of his father do not have to be visited upon him. I insist on receiving drug-free urine and I ring his doorbell in the middle of the day to verify that he is working; good and ready to say, "Why aren't you at work?" and to start fussing like a foster mother if he answers the door. He cringes when he walks into my office and I say, "Close the door," because he knows I am about to call him to the carpet, and he counters with, "I can explain..." because he knows accountability is what we are about to talk about. Accountability to self and to the village.

Sound familiar? It does to me. Sounds like my parents, my granny, my aunts & uncles, neighbors, teachers who've dragged me out into the hallway to straighten me out and the old folks in church who pressed a dollar into my hand and dared me to fall asleep during sermon. One look from any of them and I knew...

The fact that I have been charged to uphold the law and many perceive my office to be the last stop before prison does not alter the duty I have inherited. Like a stoplight, I stand before the clients assigned to my care with my arms extended, one labeled "stop" (the criminally destructive lifestyle) and the other "go" (to prison if you don't). I explain the pros and cons and allow them to believe the choice is theirs alone. Sometimes it takes them a minute to understand that the reason the stoplight very seldom changes to "go" is because I work hard to avoid flipping the switch. It's not about ushering our young people to prison; it's about stepping into their paths and turning them in the opposite direction, the same way someone stepped into my path. So I require respect from the onset because not only do I appreciate receiving it, but also by giving it I hope to instill an identical appreciation in my clients. Respect for self raises the bar for what we will and will not partake in. It can be a powerful deterrent when even the idea of going to prison doesn't seem to be powerful enough.

I don't mean to insinuate that my clients are children, because they aren't. What I propose is that, when many of my clients were children, the village was in a chaotic state of disrepair and so then was their sense of support and security. The lack of these things brings them to my office with tales of drug-addicted caregivers, horrific abuse and pervasive disrespect. They have their own children and they struggle with either creating or seeking out a nurturing village in which to surround themselves and their children. Thus, I have placed myself in their paths as a member of this illusive village.

As a foster parent of sorts, I lend support in the ways I know best. I counsel my clients, I provide resources to assist them in bettering their life circumstances and I advocate for substance abuse & domestic violence treatment and education. I encourage my clients to be the best they can be, not only for themselves but also for their children. The babies they bring with them to my office, the little and not so little ones they have dreams and hopes for, the ones whose eyes shine with the light of possibility, these are the children I have endless opportunities to touch in vast ways. By touching their parents and caregivers, I in turn touch them. I in turn become a part of their village.

So you ask, "Where is the village?" And I answer, "Parts of it are often found in unlikely places. For each of us is led into a vocation for a reason. Everyday I work for the good of the village, not because I have to but because, how can I not?"

-Terra B. Little

10th Anniversary Edition

Chapel in Turquoise for the Children of the Land

O stone of sea color
O stone of color/O people, people of color
if sand made a sea
and
the heart was a sailing ship—a wing
and
that vessel that carried the heart was
a wing, a ship on a shifting sea
and you and I were the children of
a land without beginning or end...
Children gathered around
a sea-colored stone, a sky-colored stone
a hand-size, palm-warmed stone.
Children bound by silver, by blood
by legend and
by a thousand
thousand
broken promises.
Would it matter?
About the darkness?
About the promises made in the name of the land?
About the fate, the fate of the little red children...
About the dark-haired child and
the child of dark eyes and
the child waiting in darkness
And what about
the absence or the presence
of the animal brothers
—my brother is an eagle—my brother is a fox—
What about my sister—my sister is a tree—
What about our mother the earth or
our father the sky?
What about the enormous silence
Is this our answer?

Gumbo For The Soul

Broken promises, broken dreams
memories of a language only the grandfathers understand
or do we have another?
Can a space be found?
Can we draw a sacred circle?
Can a chapel be founded?
a chapel full of promise—arched in desert color
a chapel made in turquoise
for the children of the land

-Cheryl Hanna

10th Anniversary Edition

Keeping It in the Family

I guess reasons run the gamut when it comes to why some mothers choose to relinquish their parental rights to someone else. My niece's reason was mainly financial. Barely able to take care of herself, she acted on the advice of her grandmother and agreed to place one of her two children in the care of an auntie—me.

There have been areas throughout my niece's life that have warranted stern criticism. How she came to be in her predicament could easily be considered one of them. She was given opportunities and taught to make good choices. Unfortunately, those choices were compromised by situations that didn't necessarily hold her best interests in the highest regard, and costly consequences soon followed. At least one of her decisions, however, won't get any criticism from me. That was her choice to make my husband and me the legal guardians of one of her children.

It couldn't have been easy to own the decisions responsible for her and her children's depravity. People like to throw stones at mothers who don't live up to what they think should be nature ability. That's why putting their best interest in front of whatever pride or fears might have stood in the way of her doing what she needed to do gets nothing but the highest praises from me.

I must admit that in the beginning I, too, was afraid. My second marriage (which was still in the newlywed stage) had made me a mother and grandmother instantaneously. The transition from being alone to mass activity carried challenges of its own. We were also working our way through some debt issues. The thought of adding a one year old to the mix was a little overwhelming at first. But assistance from family and friends helped to level the anxiety.

I believe that God really does work things together for our good because many prayers were answered by way of that decision. The obvious answer was to my niece's prayer. She was struggling with too many bills and not enough income. It was a sink or swim situation and she was going down fast. Placing her children with relatives gave her room to exhale. It also kept the children in the family. (The other child went to live with other relatives.)

A less obvious answer was to the prayers uttered by my husband and me. We had entertained the idea of a pregnancy, but had not been able to see our plans fulfilled. Having a little one in the house has been a wonderful blessing that we would not have known as a couple had this opportunity not presented itself.

If babies pray, I suppose my great niece received an answer, as well. Moving in with us gave her a two parent home that offered her a love and stability that over the years she has come to expect and, at times, even take for granted.

And there was a bonus. A bridge was built. See, my niece is related to me by one of my brothers who spent most of his life incarcerated. Due to this disconnect and the miles between us (different states), we had corresponded all of her life, but had never met. This circumstance led us to a full circle moment. After many years of separation we were finally able to look into each others eyes and talk person to person. I sometimes wonder if that ever would have happened had my niece's need not existed.

The day I met my great niece God spoke a word into my spirit. He told me that she was going to be someone special; and, like the Virgin Mary after being visited by an angel, I pondered those words in my heart. Today, as I look back on what's already happened, I'm beginning to see some of what makes her special realized. As she continues to blossom and mature, I am sure that the person she is becoming will reveal even more in the years to come.

-Karen Elaine O'Bannon

Chapter II
~ Poetic Gumbo~

Here's Our Child, Where's The Village?

The Village is the mother who God chose through which to birth to me
The Village is the father that planted the seed
The Village is you, the Village is me
The Village is the extended family.

Through times when I was too weak to go on
The Village was the ones that kept me strong
My Mama that fought to keep my kids from being adopted
When she asked friends and family to keep them and they opted

Going to court on their behalf when I couldn't appear
Being there for birthday's and calming their fears

My Mama was the Village when I was sick in my disease
When God delivered me she helped provide for my needs.

The Village was the man who cared enough to help me
When I got my kids back and tried to be a family.

The Village is the people who became a part of their lives
They too loved and cared for them and won't be denied

The Village is the play cousins, play aunties and friends
The one's no matter what were there to no end.

The Village holds the key to the whole community
Mentoring, providing after school care and being a second family.

The question is not, "Here's Our Child, Where's the Village?"
The question is-"Who's Village will you be?"

Beverly Black Johnson

10th Anniversary Edition

A Myriad of Hands

We come together on common ground--

Palms open, fanlike, reaching toward the Nubian sky.

Recalling always the Niger River and our great legacy--

Linking, clasping and meshing hands as one.

Hands of a wide array of earthly hues, a spectrum--

Offering up centuries of fervent gifts and talents.

The original race of man—we nurture and give,

Relishing our ebon triumph; celebrating our collective imprint.

-Bonita Sanabria

You Talking to Me?

You talking to me?

You trying to buy me with lollipops?
I can buy and sell you and still pay the cops.
You're asking me how old am I?
Ask your mama, unless you want to die.

You talking to me?

I'm "old enough,"
so don't ask my age.
What I make in a week
beats your whole year's wage.
When I go out, it's not to play.
Go ahead mess with me
and make my day.

You talking to me?

Don't even think about my size.
I carry something that will equalize.
I'm not worried about being tall.
My game ain't about no basketball.

You talking to me?

10th Anniversary Edition

I don't talk loud.
I don't have to shout.
If I don't like how you look,
I just take you out.
Nah,
you're not talking to me!!!

-Lindamichellebaron

Yes, I'm Talking to You

Yes, I'm talking to you.

I hear your brags,
and I see your name-brand rags.
You're obviously money obsessed,
but I'm not impressed.

Yes, I'm talking to you.
It's clear to me, you're a serious dude.
I can hear your attitude.
I have absolutely no doubt
that you can take me out.
But—yes, I'm talking to you.
I know you never raise your voice.
                            Weapons are your words of choice . . .
a gun, machete, your fist, a knife,
or one of your "dawgs" could take my life.
But—yes, I'm talking to you.

I'm taking the risk because it's possible
that I am partially responsible.
I might have missed the beat
that could have kept you off the street.
Maybe you needed a different interaction,
and I was present but missing in action.
I don't know what has occurred.
I know I spoke, but who knows what you heard?

So, yes, I'm talking to you.

10ᵗʰ Anniversary Edition

Yes, I'm talking to you.
But—I don't know what to say.
Can we talk?

Lindamichellebaron
Copyright © 1998, 2002, 2007
All rights reserved.

When Momma and Daddy Couldn't Be There

When momma and daddy couldn't be there,
You taught me the meaning of love and care.
You wiped my tears when I cried.
You gave me the strength that I needed inside,
When momma and daddy couldn't be there.
You were my source of hope
When it seemed that I had no one else,
You taught me to believe in myself.
I now know that there is so much I can be,
Simply because you had the courage to believe in me,
When momma and daddy couldn't be there.........

-William C. Bell

10th Anniversary Edition

RESCUE ME

    Rescue me from my only-ness.
I won't survive this loneliness.
I yearn a family—a home—
    An existence that is my own.

Don't desert me out in the cold,
Waiting for fortune to unfold.
Shelter me with your sincere love.
Prove to me that God is above.

Find room in your heart to claim me.
From worthlessness, set my mind free.
Beam light into my soul's darkness.
Release hope into this starkness.

Commit to this rewarding task.
Share yourself with me is what I ask.
I, too, shall return the favor.
Life—let us together savor.

    Neglect not my plea—take action.
It will grant you satisfaction.
Know the feeling of saving one
From damage hard to be undone.

Adopt me—a motherless child.
Prevent our race's wrong revile.
Show the world that we care for us.
Give them new topics to discuss.

Destroy the old stereotypes
And silence the ignorant hype.
Demonstrate the impact we make,

Gumbo For The Soul

When duty, we willfully take.

Redeem a foster kid today.
Offer me life—a better way.
You decide where my feet will land.
My future remains in your hands.

-Sylvia Larane Green-Chatman

10th Anniversary Edition

Tribute to Foster/Adoptive Parents

Thankful you care enough
To lend a helping hand
Through cries of despair
You proudly take a stand
Providing love and courage
To embark on a new day
United we all flourish
And provide that change
The path has its obstacles
Don't lose sight of hope
Remaining on your guard
Creating new ways to cope
Challenges creates success
The shift begins with you
Utmost gratitude and respect
For all the things you do
Spread kindness around
Touching other's hearts
Generosity profound
Giving lost faces new starts
Trying to make a better way
By answering desperate calls
More than any words can say
We appreciate you all

-Kenya Acy

My Grandma Would

My Grandma would give us treats.
My Grandma would bake us sweets.

My Grandma would have long talks.
My Grandma would take us for walks.

My Grandma would give good speech.
My Grandma would preach, preach, preach.

My Grandma would pinch our ears.
My Grandma would bring us to tears.

My Grandma would sew us clothes.
My Grandma would paint our toes.

My Grandma would take us on trips.
My Grandma would let us steal a sip.

My Grandma would wash and braid our hair.
My Grandma would swing us around in the air.

My Grandma would dance and sometimes sing.
My Grandma would dress us up in her wigs and her rings.

My Grandma would turn our frowns upside down.
My Grandma would drag us with her all around town.

My Grandma would cook our favorite meals for us.
My Grandma would take us for rides on the bus.

My Grandma would always speak her mind.
My Grandma would drink hot tea to unwind.

10th Anniversary Edition

My Grandma would take us to the park and swing.
My Grandma would do all of these things.

My Grandma would give us advice and all that.
My Grandma would often wear many hats.

My Grandma would make the best tomato pudding in the west.
My Grandma would win The Best Grandma contest.

My Grandma would be the best of the east, south and north.
My Grandma would be the best of all the world then…of course.

An illness has taken my grandma away.
Locked in our hearts, my grandma would stay.

-Nikki Nicole

Mother Me

Mother me
Please do not sever our bond
I stemmed from your internal womb
Grew out of the bosom of your blood, sweat and cells
I need you
Nurture the offspring of your fondest recollection
Gather again your love of creation
Be the giver of my joy and peace
Fill my spirit with sweet memory
Be the light I have yet learned to give
Teach me how to live
Guide me that I may walk with sure-footing
Hold my hand that I may not loose sight of my path
Teach me in song of truth and innocence
Let me not wander this world alone
Allow me to experience the grace of your presence
The warmth of your home
Mother me
Do not abandon the gift we can be
Please do not give up on me.

-Michelle Alexandria Payne

10th Anniversary Edition

Mama Cries

Mama cries because she claims that her village died,
No, she says that eventually the village died out.
The adults were like the air and water to the crops,
I mean to the children, and now where left with drought.
Mama told me she remembers how,
When there was a problem at home
There was always another house,
Warm with open arms always willing to help out.

Whether if it was for a butt whooping
Or to feed an extra mouth.
And that's pretty much how things worked out.

Then, mama started to cry harder, and I asked why?
Then she lifted her head and asked God
 "Why did he let her village die?"
I took her hand and then, I looked her in the eyes.
She gave me a stare that took me by surprise.

Then I realized the real reason mama cried.
Because she too had died….a long with the village.

-Demetrius Phillips

Children Raising Each Other

"Sisters for Life"

I believe in you and you in me
We will always be there for each other
Not depending on one another
But lifting each other up
By loving, caring, and saying what's up
We are strong and beautiful
We can conquer any obstacle
As long as we stand by each other's side
And reach for goals, which will change another's life
By coming together as sisters
And to unite as one family!

Dedicated to my girls, who have been there for me, through the good and bad.

-Marie-Alicia Burns

Where is the Village?

"Umoja" (Unity)

Umoja we need you,
Where did you go?
Our brothers and sisters need you
Why have you gone?
Our villages have fallen apart.
We are strong, but without you we are weak
Brothers and sisters walk through the streets
Shouting Umoja! Umoja!
Fight the fight we've been fighting for centuries
Yes, the fight continues
Hopefully one day it will end
Until that day we need Umoja
Alone the battle will kill us.
UNITY is the key idea.
When we stay together, we out more fear into mainstream society
Yes, the more fear they have the tougher life will be
Until they give up.
Together we can conquer it
Stay strong, stay together
Unity!
Umoja!

-Marie-Alicia Burns

Am I Tomorrow's Keeper?

There used to be a time when Big Ma and Big Papa was the norm. When we knew if we acted out of line, well, that's what switches in the back yard were for.

There used to be a time when kids knew their actions weren't just watched by Mom and Dad; a time when thought of the consequences of our actions, and responsibility for choices was had.

A time when neighbors parented all children, not just worried about teaching their own. A time when molding tomorrow's leaders was the standard and the norm.

But that time has since perished and what remains is insane. Mastery of thievery, trickery and scamming is the height of today's youth's game.

Can we fault them when we fail to teach them wrong from right?
When we turn our backs to correcting the course of their immoral plights?

We're afraid to talk to our own children, let alone chastise those that are not our own. But in doing so, can we question the direction of the path our world?

Can we point fingers at our leaders, when we fail to lead our youth?
Can we scrutinize tomorrow's economy, when we say by our actions its okay for kids to sell drugs as they do?

Let today be the day you play Big Ma and Big Papa,
the day you get involved,
a day you implement elements that are worthwhile.
Let today be the day YOU open your mouth
and outline our future by leading a child.

Let today be the day wisdom and knowledge you share

10th Anniversary Edition

Instead of turning your back, waiting for someone else to correct the problem,
be Tomorrow's Keeper and say to your village today……..
I CARE!!

-Lorraine Elzia

2,4,6,8

2 sets of family
2 sets of kin
1 more black child told
that she can't win
4 different foster homes
killing all my dreams
2 eyes witnessed abuse
1 mouth yelled out screams
4 cruel foster parents
didn't want to stay
6 foster children denied of
childish play
2 sets of family
2 sets of kin
1 more black child
told that he can't win
4 needy children waiting
to receive
1 sets of parents in which
they can believe.
2 sets of family
2 sets of kin
1 positive family breaks
the cycle to prove
that they can win.

-Donna Felton

Color-Free

The color of my skin shouldn't define me
Because when I go out of this country,
American is all they see.
My Brown-sugar, Caramel, Ebony, Hershey-chocolate,
Mahogany, Mocha, Vanilla complexion
Is only an outer shell.
You have to dig Deeper,
If you want to know
What's embedded in my mind.
My skin color might hint to my Races
Past struggles and pain,
But don't lose the fact that we're
Individuals and not all the same.
One day I hope we can all
Be one big happy family
In the meantime; I'll leave a legacy
To the younger generation.
Show by example on how to get through
Life's complications.
I will teach them how to love
Through my own interactions.
I will show them how to give
And not wait for someone's reaction.
I will encourage them to dream and not
Let society dictate who they can be.
I will show them the benefit of believing in
Oneself, but most of all in a Higher Being.
I hope to see the manifestation of my vision
A society that's COLOR-FREE.

-Shelia M. Goss

I Am a Child of God

I am not unwanted, unloved, discarded, forgotten.
I am not the image of failure or someone's mistake.
I am not a burden or just another mouth to feed or monthly check.
Please don't speak about me as if I'm a nameless shadow in a room to be seen and not heard, nor put your face against the glass and stare at me as if I'm a pet in a store to be ogled at and then left behind.

I am a loving spirit created by God's hand.
I am wanted, loved, thought of, kept.
I am an image of survival, strength and promise. I am a voice to remind you that others like me no longer wish for turned backs, but wish for open arms.
Look at me, speak to me, I am life, I am joy, I am jumping out of shadows into the fullness of possibilities, into the hope of family.

For I am a child of God, I am deserving of love and belonging.
I am a face with a name, I am you.

-Pamela S. Rivers

I am a Mother

Not quite sure on what they all means
But I know having been blessed with you
Together on this journey God will see us through

Some may say, your eyes are not like mine
Your smile's not like your fathers'
But never let that bother you
It's my love that breathed life into you

Some are given by God
Others – chosen
How blessed my steps, some many, some few
That ultimately led me to you

Just like any new mother
Where do I begin?
I haven't been doing this too long
and already I don't want to get motherhood wrong

I give you my history,
my family, my name,
But if you decide later
I will help you find from whom you came

But know now, in this time in this moment to the next
you are all mine, the child I love, cherish and choose
who I now clearly see,
ended up choosing me.

Pamela S. Rivers

IN PLAIN SIGHT

When I take a look around at each and every one of you
Do you know what I see?
I see that all of you have the potential to be anything you want to be.
Your roots come from greatness
And your spirits from times beyond
Each one of you posses your own powers
But together, in UNION, you are forever strong.
Many thousands of years ago, your were Kings and Queen – pure royalty
Now you must rebuild your paths with knowledge – courage and loyalty.
Reading is fundamental
But understanding is essential.
That is the only way that you will be able to build your potential and temple.
Mathematics - we created
Astrology – we plotted
Architecture – we began it
Medicine – we thought it
Writing – we invented
Irrigation – First to grow
Communication – First to speak
Civilization – First to know
Spirituality – Always have been
Originality – Always will be
Musicianship – We made the drum
Travel – We made the first ships to sail the seas
We came to the Americas long before Columbus as the FIRST Native Americans
Now some called us Olmecs, Mixtecs, Mexicans and Indians
We've lived in kingdoms made of gold
And also lived in ghettos full of despair
They wrote about us in the bible
With our skin of bronze and wool-like hair

10th Anniversary Edition

We were here before Christianity, Islam, Catholicism and Jehovah

And now I've come back here today just to teach and show ya.

That when I look and each and every one of you

Do you know what I see?

I see that all of you have the ability to be ANYTHING that you want to be.

I see a doctor

A lawyer

An entrepreneur

A banker

I see you owning you own country with your own oil tankers

I see you with your own television station

And YOU with you own NBA team

I see you with our own school

Helping others to fulfill all of their dreams

But nothing in life comes easy

You have to study hard, listen, stay healthy and keep trying

You'll never get ahead by robbing, stealing, deception and lying

Be truthful

Learn to speak clearly and directly

Then other will see the GOD in you and treat you with respect, see?

If you need help – ask for it

If you fall down- get right back up

If you get lost – stop and think to yourself and about your surroundings before you start to erupt

Remember

You can do MORE than you probably think that you can

But you have to stay focused, understand and always have a plan!

-Douglas Stewart

Love Stew-Cooked in a Slow Cooker

1 tablespoon of pride for who you are, and
1 cup for who you'll become
2 pinches of discipline for your mishaps,
3 cups of tolerance, plus one

2 lbs of answers for the questions you'll ask,
6 ounces of "I don't know"
10 lbs of support as you begin to stand
5 cups of trust as you grow

At 18 years old, turn love up to a boil and stir in the ingredients above.
Once the communication starts bubbling; turn down the heat until the relationship simmers into love.

-H. Renay Anderson

10th Anniversary Edition
WE WON'T LEAVE OUR CHILDREN BEHIND!!

From the depths of my soul, the call emerges
With my every breath, my being searches and
I Soon find, the enlightened message that our
Future is a reality…only if we don't leave
The children behind
My heart throbs and aches,
Its' pain is of a wrenching and un-healing kind
We can't go forward, for there's
No place to go, if we dare live the Children behind
Our ancestors cry out from the ocean floor
Their pleas reach the underlying realm of my mind
They only want us to follow their lead
And not leave the children behind
They tell us we are the product of their past deeds
So, our future will surely spring forth from our own seeds
Looking back, I see we must continue to forge ahead
For by the hands of the innocent, we all shall be led
Thou we've walked down the paths cleared
By Tubman, DuBois, King and others
Our journey is not yet over and the future
Looks bleak unless we arise, hand and
Hand as brothers
We stand on the shoulders of our forefathers
Peering into the future, we strain to get a better look
Thou we gaze, we don't get a clear unobstructed view
But, that's another chapter of an unwritten book
How will we measure our success?
If we don't carry the children
If we don't lift them up
If we don't elevate them
If we don't educate them
If we don't stimulate them
How will we succeed and make it there
If we don't…

Gumbo For The Soul

Organize them
Mobilize them
Energize them
If we don't
Direct them
Protect them
If we don't beseech them
Reach them
Teach them
If we don't
Guide them
Walk beside them
To our breast – hold them
Into our best – mold them
We're stalled in our tracks
If we don't also carry on our backs:
 What once was—the past
 The here and now—our present
 What will be—our future…?
Our children

                                                -Dee Freeman

10th Anniversary Edition

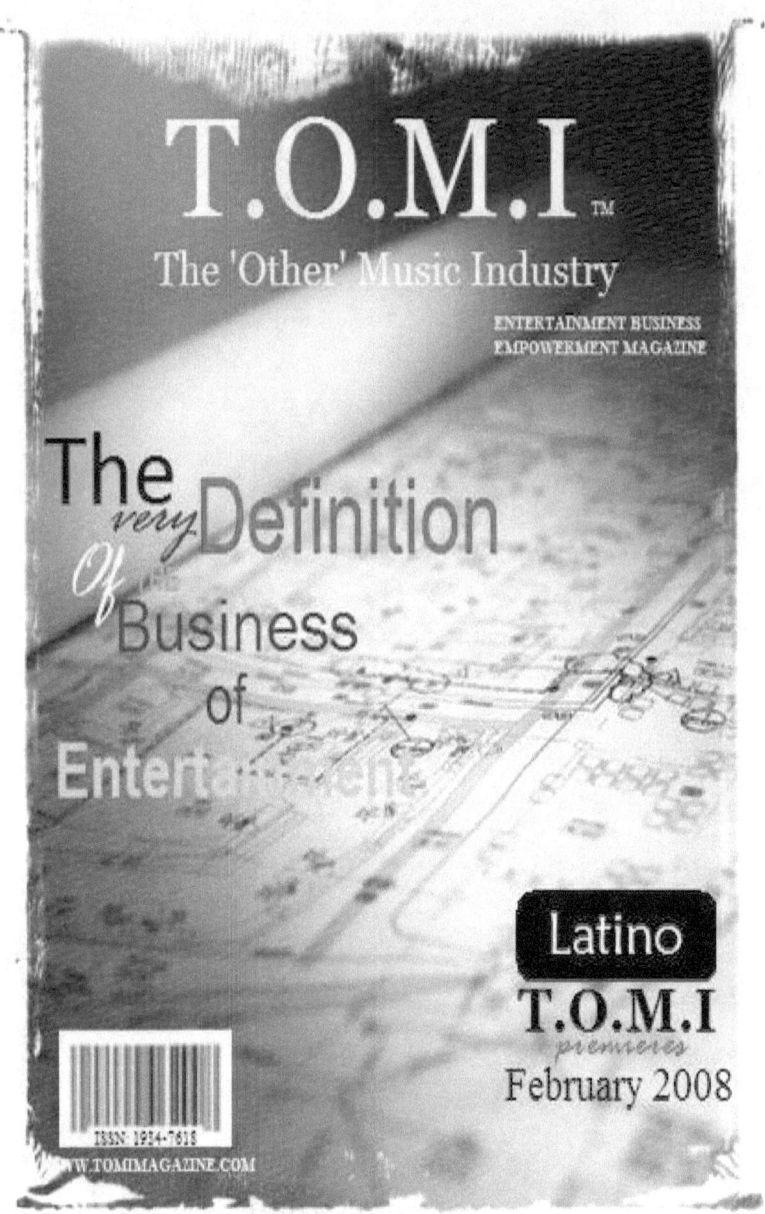

TOMIFILMFESTIVAL.ORG

African Cradle
Inc.

Dedicated to building and nurturing adoptive families for African and African American children

www.africancradle.org   info@africancradle.org

ETHNIC GIFTS & ACCESSORIES
www.karibugifts.com
e-mail: karibugifts@yahoo.com

Fannie A. Mohamed
Karen Nance Ransom
Arianna Ray Ransom

427 Water St.   *Jack London Square*
Oakland, CA 94607   *510-444-6906*

10th Anniversary Edition

Resources

Review of Qualification Requirements for Prospective Adoptive Parents

Although the laws and policies that regulate who can adopt will vary from state to state and from agency to agency, there are general requirements that most adoption agencies will look at when they talk to people about adopting. It is important to realize that, with the exception of the actual provisions of state law which cannot be waived or modified; there are usually very few requirements or rules that are inflexible. If you run up against a guideline or rule that gives you a problem, you should always ask if it could be waived in your particular case. You might be surprised by what exceptions can be made under the right circumstances and for the right people.

Frustrated adoptive parents have been heard to claim that they feel they should have a "right" to adopt, and they demand the cooperation of others in protecting those rights. Although it is true that everyone has a "right" to desire and to attempt an adoption, from a practical standpoint, no one has an absolute "right" to adopt.

As you do your research and examine the rules and guidelines that are imposed by different adoption agencies on adoptive parents, you will begin to recognize the interaction that exists between the following four levels of qualification criteria that must be satisfied in order for any adoption to take place:

1. **Mandatory Legal Criteria:**

These are the legal and procedural requirements that are imposed by the laws of the state and county where the adoption will actually take place, which is generally the county and state where the adoptive parents reside, although there are some states that will permit adoptions to be processed in their courts by non-residents of that state. In most cases, these requirements are not very flexible and cannot be waived or modified.

2. **Preferred Agency Criteria:**

These are practical requirements that are imposed by individual adoption agencies, which are above and beyond the legal requirements imposed by state law. These requirements will vary from agency to agency, based on the focus of the agency, the type of adoptions the agency handles, the human and economic resources that are available to the agency, the social philosophy of the agency and/or the commercial, non-profit or public entities that provide support to the agency. Each agency is free to establish its own criteria, but within the framework of its charter, may also be able to waive or modify the criteria under the right circumstances. A good example of this might be the maximum age restrictions that are imposed on adoptive couples. Because of the type of adoptions they handle, some agencies will not work with couples over 40 years of age, while other agencies will work with individuals who are older. In almost every case, there are very valid reasons for these restrictions. Adoptive parents will need to shop around until they find an agency that has criteria they are comfortable with.

3. **Criteria Sought by Birthparents:**

Especially in cases that involve independent open adoptions, birthparents are playing an ever-increasing role in the selection of the families who adopt their children. This means that birthparents can impose whatever individualized criteria they feel are important in their situation. Adopters are free to walk away from an adoption opportunity if it is felt that the qualifying criteria are unacceptable. They cannot "force" a parent to place a child for adoption on terms find unacceptable. This is not necessarily a bad thing, in fact, most often it can be a wonderful thing, but it does throw criteria into the matching process that will be totally subjective and individualized to the particular circumstances of each adoption. To a great extent, this level of criteria will be absent when the adoption involves a non-infant adopted through a public agency, because in most of these cases, by the time the adoptive parents get involved, the parental rights of the biological parents will already have been legally terminated by the court.

4. **Adopting Parent Limitations or Criteria:**

All adopting parents have practical limits beyond which they will not go in an adoption. These self-imposed limitations may involve financial considerations, age considerations, health considerations, or a wide variety of other considerations, which are specific to their personal comfort level. If they cannot feel good about the totality of factors involved in a particular adoption opportunity, they will not move forward with that adoption.

Examples of Areas Under Scrutiny

In general terms, some of the factors that will be considered as part of the evaluation process (homestudy) that adopters will undergo when they seek to adopt will be the following, which focus on determining if a child placed with these parents will be in a safe and stable environment, with loving and supportive parents who will be available to parent and nurture the child:

Marital Status: Generally, it will be easier for you to adopt if you are married than if you are single. This is more of a practical consideration than it is a legal one, because one of the predominant reasons that many parents give for wanting to place their children for adoption is that they feel as single parents, they will not be able to give their children the attention, care and opportunities that it could have if it were raised in a two-parent family. So even though single parents are some of the hardest working people in the world, if birthparents feel it is important for their children to be placed in two-parent families, that is what will happen.

Length of Marriage: If an adopting parent is married, a minimum of a three-year marriage is a common requirement.

Previous Marriages: Generally, divorced persons are legally permitted to adopt. From a practical point of view, this will generally not be a problem as long as the current marriage is stable and the current spouse is supportive and also eager to adopt.

Age of Adoptive Parents: The minimum legal age for adoptive parents is generally 18 years of age. The upper age limit that is used by most agencies is 40 years old, although some agencies will now consider adoptive parents who are older. In most situations, there will be a requirement that the adopting parents must be at least 20 years older than the child they are seeking to adopt, although there will always be exceptions to these rules under certain circumstances.

There is also a general rule of thumb that there should be an age differential of no more than 40 years between the child and the adoptive parents, although exceptions may be made if the adopters are very active and healthy. The rationale behind this is that one of the most trying times in the life of an adopted child can often be the teen years, when identity struggles tend to emerge. It is thought by many agencies that at this time in a child's life, the child will especially need the help of healthy, involved, and active parents, who will still have enough energy left to accommodate the physical and emotional needs of the child. It is also the feeling of some birthparents that they don't want their child adopted by someone who looks and acts like their own parents, because it feels like they are jumping a generation for the child. On the other hand, some mothers actually value wisdom and experience in adoptive parents, and may actually prefer a more mature couple to adopt their child, especially if the birthmother has already been involved in the parenting process herself and appreciates what it takes to be a good parent

Maximum Age Exceptions for International Adoptions: In many foreign countries where children are available for adoption, age and maturity are often considered sought-after virtues in adopting parents, rather than an impediment to an adoption. I these situations, more mature adoptive parents may actually have an advantage over younger and less experienced adopters.

Health Issues: The health of the adopting parents must be good. Some agencies will have rules that prevent adoption by those who are obese or underweight, although there are also exceptions to this rule. The primary reason for this is that agencies consider that adopted children need an opportunity to be able to grow to maturity with both of their parents around, since the premature loss of a parent will be traumatic for any child.

Disabilities of Adoptive Parents: Having some form of a disability does not necessarily disqualify an adoptive parent from being able to adopt a child. Although some adoption agencies will work with prospective adoptive parents who have disabilities, not all agencies will have the expertise or resources available to properly handle this kind of an adoption. Naturally, there are some disabilities that may make it difficult, or even impossible, for a hopeful adoptive parent to physically or emotionally provide the kind of constant care, supervision, and nurturing that a child will require. There are other disabilities, however, where adjustments can be made for in a variety of ways so that the individual with the disability to become a parent. In making these difficult determinations, an agency will focus on the ability of the prospective parent to properly care for a child and to meet its needs through its entire childhood, since it would not be in the best interests of the child to allow bonding with an adoptive parent, only to find out later that the child must be separated from that parent as the result of an inability to provide adequately for the child's care. Although each situation will be considered on a case-by-case basis, it needs to be realized that no one has an absolute "right" to adopt a child, especially if the input of a birth parent is necessary in order for that to happen. Naturally, one factor that can weigh heavily in favor of allowing an adoption to go forward, both for an agency and for a birthparent, would be if the disabled parent was already successfully parenting children, or even was providing a significant amount of care for the children of someone else.

Use of Drugs, Alcohol and Tobacco: Because of the growing awareness of the significant health problems that follow the use of tobacco, including the problems that can be caused by the exposure to second-hand smoke, some adoption agencies are now prohibiting placements with adoptive parents who smoke. Some of the agencies that are sponsored by religious organizations that oppose the consumption of alcohol by their members are also prohibiting placements with adoptive parents who consume alcohol. Even some non-sectarian agencies see the current use of alcohol as a problem if there is an indication that the level is excessive, or that it is getting in the way of responsible living, which is the foundation of responsible parenting. Without exception, all agencies will screen out drug-abusers, and will look very carefully at individuals with any prior history of drug or other substance abuse. Many agencies feel that this can be an indicator of potential current or future substance abuse. Even if hopeful adopters who are users of any of these substances are able to get past the screening of their adoption agency, they may still have to deal with the negative stigma when attempting to be matched with a birthmother who may not want this lifestyle for her child.

Fertility Status of Adoptive Parents: As a general rule, many adoption agencies will give some degree of preference to infertile couples in the placement of healthy infants, although this preference can be easily waived under the right circumstances, or when required by the preferences of a birthmother. In the adoption of children with special needs, or in international adoptions, fertile couples may also qualify to adopt on an equal footing with infertile couples.

Religious Considerations: As a result of requirements contained in their enabling charters, many sectarian adoption agencies will give priority to members of their religious group. Some of these sectarian agencies may even totally limit their adoption placements to members of their own group. Although some adopting couples express concerns that these kinds of practices appear to be unfair or even discriminatory, in reality, if a religious group provides all of the funding and supervision for its own captive adoption agency, it is certainly free to set its own preferences. In most cases, adopters are free to join, support, and be supported or given preferential treatment by any religious or other groups that they choose. Adopters with no particular religious preference or membership can anticipate this and may want to direct their efforts to non-sectarian agencies, where they will do just fine.

Other Children in the Family: Some agencies will not place more than two healthy infants with any adoptive family. If a family already has one child by either birth or adoption, they may be allowed to apply for and receive another child. For many years, the process of selecting adoptive parents was focused on fulfilling the dreams of "childless parents." Although this was certainly a worthwhile goal, more recently, the tide seems to have shifted to give some consideration to the advantages of placing a child with "experienced" parents who already have one or more children who will be siblings, role models, and protectors for the new child. How this plays out in each situation will depend a lot on the preferences of the birthparents. Placements with families who already have children in the home seem to be significantly more common in independent adoptions, where placing parents seem to have more input into who adopts their children. If adopters already have two children in their family, they may still be able to adopt through a private adoption, where they may receive a child from a birthmother who already has several children in her own family, and wants this same kind of an environment for the child she is placing. There are no laws that limit the size of a family in a private adoption setting.

Stay-At-Home Parent: Generally, it is recognized that both parents may be required to work outside the home; however, some agencies ask one parent, usually the mother, to remain at home for the first six months that a baby is in the home. In private adoptions there also seems to be a growing recognition of the short and long-term benefits of placing children into families that will have a stay-at-home parent. In international adoptions, some countries ask for assurances that one parent will stay at home with the new child for a period of time.

Financial Status: The ability to pay the costs and fees that will be associated with an adoption placement is a pretty important element in any adoption. Some privately funded adoption agencies are not subsidized by outside financial sources and may not be able to offer much flexibility in payment options. Others (usually those that receive outside or public funding) will have a sliding scale for fees based on total family income, or reduced flat fees, based on need. Beyond that, it is important that an adopting family will be able to manage its available family income and other resources to properly support all of its children, including the child the family hopes to adopt. The federal <u>Adoption Expense Income Tax Credit</u> can also be a source of useful financial assistance for those families who qualify.

Employment Stability: Since the stability of employment by the breadwinner(s) in a family can significantly impact not only the financial well-being of a family, but also its social and emotional well-being, a history of employment stability, and the prospect of future employment stability, are always considered to be big plusses in the eyes of birthparents, who in many cases may know from their own painful first-hand experience what periods of unemployment can do to the morale and stability of a family. The adopters' type of work may also be significant to birthparents, if it involves a lot of time away from home or dangerous activities.

Housing: The adopters' family home can be in the country or in the city; can be an apartment, a townhouse, a mobile home or a house; can be owned or rented, and can have a big yard, or no yard at all. The family home should, however, be safe, clean and able to adequately accommodate the child, along with existing family members. Some factors that will be addressed by the adoption caseworker in the adoption homestudy will be: the fencing of a swimming pool or other water feature, the fencing of a back yard, the status of other individuals who are living in the family home, the presence of firearms in the home, or the presence of large dogs or other potentially dangerous animals in the area.

Medical Records: A complete medical history will be required for all adopting parents, regardless of whether they are infertile or fertile. In some instances, a psychological evaluation may also be required.

Criminal Background Check: Those who seek to adopt will have their backgrounds checked thoroughly in an attempt to uncover evidence of any prior legal or criminal problems, or any problems with child abuse, financial instability, or substance abuse. It is not uncommon for this to be the first time that a prospective adoptive parent learns of a problem in his or her spouse's past that can prevent them from obtaining approval for an adoption. All adoption agencies should be very willing to discuss their specific eligibility requirements and placement options with you, and you should be forthcoming and honest about problems in your past before the background check is done.

Source: http://adopting.adoption.com/child/review-of-qualification-requirements-for-prospective-adoptive-parents.html

10th Anniversary Edition

Resource: What is adoption?

Adoption is a legal process that creates a new, permanent parent-child relationship where one didn't exist before. The adoption proceedings take place in court before a Judge.

Adoption bestows on the adoptive parent(s) all the rights and responsibilities of a legal parent, and gives the child being adopted all the social, emotional, and legal rights and responsibilities of a family member. Sometimes, court language will include the words "as if born to" to describe the new parent-child relationship.

For the purpose of this article, reference is made to the adoption of a minor child, although many jurisdictions also have statutes covering the adoption of an adult.

Before parental rights are assumed by adoptive parents, the court determines that biological parents have, legally and with full understanding, either voluntarily relinquished their parental rights, or that those rights have been terminated by the court. Depending on the circumstances and state laws, these two actions - the severing of biological parents' rights and the bestowing of parental rights on the adoptive parents - may be done at the same time, at finalization.

During the court finalization hearing, the judge reviews information about the child, the biological parent(s), and the adopting parent(s). This information can include:

- The homestudy and/or other evaluation of the adopting parent(s) and their suitability for the child,
- Reports of pre-adoption counseling and education for both placing and adopting parents,
- Case workers' notes and recommendations, and
- Other reports.

Those who appear at the finalization hearing (either separately or together), in addition to the Judge, may include, but are not limited to:

- Adopting parent(s)

- Their attorney
- Placing parent(s)
- Their attorney
- The child/ren
- The child's legal advocate and/or case worker
- Adoptive parents' case worker
- Placing parents' case worker

The Judge reviews all supporting information about the adopting and placing families, and may ask questions of all parties, including the child/ren if they are able to communicate their feelings and wishes. The Judge will then approve or disapprove the petition to adopt.

If approved, the adoption is finalized and an Adoption Decree is issued.

In most U.S. jurisdictions, at the time the adoption is finalized, the child's name is legally changed, and the court orders the issuance of a new, amended birth certificate for the adopted child. This amended birth certificate:

- replaces the name(s) of the biological parent(s) with the names of the adoptive parent(s), and
- replaces the child's birth name with his/her new name.

The original birth certificate and other documents relating to the adoption are sealed, and are generally not available to parties to the adoption, as detailed in state law in the U.S.

For international adoptions, U.S. federal and state laws must be observed, as well as the laws and regulations of each country. Depending on the country and the immigrant visa issued for the child, a finalization process may need to be completed in the adoptive parents' home state.

Source: http://adopting.adoption.com/child/what-is-adoption.html

Adoption Term Glossary: http://glossary.adoption.com/

10th Anniversary Edition

Resource

By Rolanda Pyle

Across the United States, more than 6 million children- approximately 1 in 12- are living in households headed by grandparents (4.5 million children). As the children's parents struggle with substance abuse, mental illness, incarceration, economic hardship, divorce, domestic violence, illness, military deployment and other challenges these caregivers care for the children inside and outside the foster care system.

There are another 1.5 million children in the United States who are living in households headed by other relatives.

U.S. Census 2000 data tell us that nationally, 2.4 million grandparents report they are responsible for their grandchildren living with them: 29% of these grandparents are African American.

Contributors

Kenya Acy (28) has been writing since age 3, where I wrote my first short story. I have been writing poetry for the past 14 years, with 5 books written (over 700 poems). I am an avid speaker of spoken word, and I love to rap. I have an Associates Degree and I currently attend Bryant & Stratton College (4.0 G.P.A.) for the past 2 years to obtain my Bachelors Degree.

H. Renay Anderson has lived in the Austin, Texas area for over 20 years. She is originally from the Bay area of Northern California. She has Bachelor's in Management/Marketing and a Master's degree in Organizational Management. She wrote her first book in 2003: *The After Party Why Women Wear Shoes They Know Will Eventually Hurt Their Feet'*. In 2006 and 2007 she contributed to three anthologies; Chicken Soup for the African American Woman's Soul', 'How I Met my Sweetheart' and 'Gumbo for The Soul: The Recipe for Literacy in the Black Community'. She has written reviews for Bella Online and for BBW Reviewers. Writing has always been an outlet for her. She often refers to the quote "The ultimate of being successful is the luxury of giving yourself the time to do what you want to do" Leontyne Price, 1976.

Marie- Alicia Burns is seventeen years old. She recently graduated from high school and has completed one year of college through the Middle College program, which allows high school students to attend college and finish high school at the same time. She plans to attend Clark Atlanta University in the fall of 2008. Some of her hobbies are swimming, rollerblading, and writing poetry.

William C. Bell is the President and CEO of Casey Family Programs in Seattle, Washington. Prior to joining the foundation, Mr. Bell was the Commissioner of the New York City Administration for Children's Services. Mr. Bell has written articles for numerous child welfare journals and publications. He is a minister and the proud father of two beautiful daughters.

Dr. Marie-Elaine Burns, Higher Education Administrator, President and CEO, Mammoth Concepts, Consulting for a *Changing* World

Betty Nandi Cantrell, Cleveland, Ga., attended Fort Valley State University; she is a novelist and freelance writer.

Dahveed was raised in foster care from the age of 2 to 17 years of age. He began writing poetry at age 16 and did not fully embrace his gift until he was forty two years of age, at which time he published his first book, "Through the Eyes of a Foster Child: A Poetic Journey." In 2005, he created Dahveed's Voice and Vision, a California licensed Online Resource and Information Network; with the emphasis on bringing awareness to foster children and all children that will become *Our Future*. As an advocate for foster children, Dahveed's Voice and Vision serve as a resource, support system and a voice - in an effort to bring about a change, awareness and a new vision.

Cheryl Donovan is an author, educator, entrepreneur, mentor, and internet radio personality. Her book *Women What the Hell are You Thinking* was number 10 on the Amazon.com Hot New Releases List. She has been happily married for 14 years with two adult sons, a step-daughter and grandson.

Lorraine Elzia is a paralegal, literary artist, editor and author. She has published pieces in two of the Chicken Soup for the Soul Anthologies; The Katrina Anthology, Surfacing...Phenomenal Women on Passion, Politics and Purpose; and Gumbo for the Soul. She is Co-Moderator of Essentially Women Writing Group, and Co-Owner of Eve's Literary Services. Lorraine has always had an admiration for both the spoken and written word. That love affair coupled with an addictive need to express herself, gave birth to a compulsion to write, which is a gift she is constantly nurturing.

Donna Felton is a single mother of a ten year old son Akinda. She was adopted at age seven, and one day plans to adopt a child as well. Donna has a bachelor degree in English and is currently working on her Master's degree at Queens College.

Dee Freeman: www.deepoette.com; deekfreeman@yahoo.com

Gumbo For The Soul

Sylvia Larane Green-Chatman is the chief graphic designer/owner of the design and publishing company, Distinguished Design, and the poet/author of *Gift of Life*, a collection of inspirational poems. Writing poetry over 15 years, Sylvia has read her poems at various church, school, community, and literary events and published them in journals, newspapers, and the previous *Gumbo for the Soul* anthology. To view and purchase her poetry, go to www.cafepress.com/distinguisheddp and www.distinguished-poetry.com.

Sharon (Shaye) Stinson Gray is co founder of Essentially Woman Online group and Eve's Literary Services (www.evesliteraryservice.com). She has a Bachelor's of Art Degree in English from Palm Beach Atlantic University in West Palm Beach, Florida and a Master's Degree (M.P.A.) from Nova Southeastern University. With her passion for words and love of children, she entered the teaching profession in 1998. She currently teaches High School English Literature and Adult Education courses. Sharon is also a corresponding Editor of Gumbo For The Soul, as well as served as Senior Editor of Bahiyah Woman Magazine.

Shelia M Goss is the author of the Essence Magazine and Black Expressions Book Club Best seller My Invisible Husband, Roses are thorns, Violets are true, Paige's Web and Double Platinum. Shelia has received numerous accolades over the years, including 2006 Infini's Outstanding Author, Literary Divas: The Top 100+ Most Admired African-American Women in Literature, Honorable mention in a New York Times article and Three Shades of Romance Magazine Reader's Choice Awards. Besides writing fiction, Shelia is an entertainment writer. To learn more, visit her website: www.sheliagoss.com.

Michael Guinn is a former child abuse investigator for the state of Texas who began writing poetry as a way of dealing with the horrors of child abuse and neglect. His unique style of poetic expression captures and then nurtures moments in a therapeutic outlet he coins "Tear-prints". Michael is also the founder of the Fort Worth Poetry Slam Team has published many chap books of poetry, written numerous editorials and has been the subject of local and national media for his social philanthropy.

Cheryl Hanna is an artist, book designer and illustrator. She has illustrated several children's books including the award winning books *An Enchanted Hair Tale* and *Hard to Be Six*. Hanna's collages and paintings have been widely exhibited in a number of venues including The Brooklyn Museum of Art. Illustrations from her books, *An Enchanted Hair Tale* and *Stagecoach Mary Fields* have been exhibited at the National Museum of Women for the Arts and also form part of the collection of the Mazza Museum, a museum dedicated to the art of children's book illustration, in Findley, Ohio. Hanna is currently at work on a novel, *Tunisian Moon*, which is set in North Africa and combines her love of fairy tales, fascination with magic and the imagined lives of animals. She is a longtime member of the writer's group, Pen & Rose and lives in Brooklyn, New York.

Beverly Black Johnson is the founder of Gumbo for the Soul. www.beverlyblackjohnson.com

Lindamichellebaron has been publisher and president of Harlin Jacque Publications for over 20 years. Her poems are collected in *The Sun Is On, Rhythm & Dues,* and *For the Love of Life*. She has won numerous awards including the designation as Hempstead, New York's "Village Griot." Lindamichellebaron holds a doctorate in Cross Categorical Studies and is presently an assistant professor at York College, of the City University of New York (CUNY) in the Department of Teacher Education. You can find out more about Dr. Baron on her website www.lindamichellebaron.com.

Terra Little holds Bachelor of Science degrees in Criminology and Sociology, respectively, and a Master of Arts degree in Professional Counseling. Currently, she is a native of St. Louis, Missouri, where she is a Community Corrections professional and a Crisis Intervention Counselor. She is also the mother of a teenage daughter and a published author.

Lutishia Lovely is a published author, actor, motivational speaker and publishing consultant. Among her many past pursuits were several years spent teaching in a variety of alternative instructional settings. In addition to working as the creative arts instructor at Images, the after school, at-risk program mentioned in the story, Ms. Lovely performed culturally educational one-woman shows for grade and junior high school students, produced original children's theatre, and had a children's book published that focused on the benefits of a diverse culture. Visit Ms. Lovely at her website: www.LutishiaLovely.com.

Jackie Moore is currently pursuing her undergraduate degree in religion and offers spiritual words of encouragement daily on her website www.virtuousliving.com. She and her two sons, James and Joseph reside in Detroit, Michigan. They are members of New St. Mark Baptist Church under the leadership of Sr. Pastor, Larry Smith.

Nikki Nicole is a freelance journalist/writer who currently resides in San Diego, CA with her family. She has been published online on various sites as well as in print in such magazines as American Cheerleader, Jr., Teenage Buzz and Fire Magazine. Her first novel, A Little Bit of Sin, is scheduled to be released Fall of 2007.

Karen Elaine O'Bannon is the author of *A Song for You—Women's Stories in Rhyme*, *A Song for You—Parables and Pearls*, and is a contributing author of the anthology *Tal'i-tha cumi: Daughters Arise* chief edited and complied by Andrea L. Dudley. She also writes monthly blogs for the internet newsletter *The Soul of Louisville (www.thesouloflouisville.com)*. Karen resides in Louisville, Kentucky with her husband and great niece.

Michelle Alexandria Payne is a Writer, Performing Artist, Mentor, Teacher and Activist.
A lifelong student, she believes that the arts are an integral part of healing the human soul and that the importance of the artist is to utilize their innate abilities to incite social change, growth and unity.

Rolanda T. Pyle is a certified social worker and is the Associate Director of the Relatives as Parents Program at the Brookdale Foundation. . Rolanda is the coauthor of the chapter "Support Groups in the Lives of Grandmothers Raising Grandchildren" in the book "To Grandmother's House We Go and Stay. She is also a contributor to the anthology "Gumbo for the Soul- 1". Rolanda recently released her first book, "FINALLY" – a collection of inspirational poems. For additional information on her book go to www.rorosrainbowcommunications.com

10th Anniversary Edition

Karen Felecia Nance Ransom, Esquire, co-owns Karibu Ethnic Gifts and Accessories in Jack London Square in Oakland, CA with her mother, Fannie Mohamed, and daughter, Arianna Ransom. In addition to practicing law, she is an adoption advocate working vigorously to find homes for children in the US, Africa and the Diaspora. She lives with her husband, Fabian, daughter, Arianna, son, Fabian Menelik, Jr., and stepdaughter, Mariah. Stepdaughter, Jaquela is away at college.

Pamela Rivers, a writer, author, on-air talent and entrepreneur of her own event planning company; not only extends her scope as a writer/producer into radio and television but is a contributing author to the anthologies, *Gumbo For The Soul: The Recipe for Literacy in the Black Community, Delta Girls, Stories of Sisterhood* and the upcoming *African American National Biography (Oxford Press/Harvard University)*. She has served as an editor for *Innercity Magazine* and for the *Bolognese Club of America* newsletter and in addition to her print and voice work with VH1, she currently serves as publicist and contributing writer to *The Blackoutdoorsman* magazine and contributing writer to *Today's Child* magazine. Pamela is also a proud and active member of Delta Sigma Theta Sorority Inc.

Tee C. Royal is a freelance reviewer, editor and literary agent, but known most as the founder of RAWSISTAZ Literary Group (www.rawsistaz.com) which supports and promotes African-American authors and their work. She lives in the suburbs of Atlanta with her husband and daughter.

Bonita Sanabria wrote this poem to celebrate and thank the many "Hands" of our Village that partake in nurturing our children. Bonita's "Betrayal and The Bully" was featured in Anthology #1. As well as being a writer, she volunteers for the National Black Arts Festival, a glorious summer happening held annually in her home city of Atlanta. This former English teacher also enjoys her visual art projects, especially collage. In addition, every fall she conducts workshops for guidance counselors at the Power Over Prejudice Summit held at Georgia Tech. This event draws students and counselors of diverse ethnicities from all over Metro Atlanta for a day of breaking down the barriers of prejudice.

Anna K. Stone resides in Maryland where she teaches high school English and works as a freelance graphic designer.

Shawnda Tate is a Freelance writer; entrepreneur, poet, educator, wife, and mother don't exactly sum up the many hats author Shawnda Tate wears. You can sense her passion in every aspect of those cherished areas. With the unwavering conviction that words are power, she has made it her life's work to help unlock the voices of those who have been silenced. Driven by cynics and determined that her gift would not be squandered; she placed her power in words. As a product of early life lessons, Shawnda Tate has always been an emotional writer. Using poetry as an outlet from the age of 10, she never was a stranger to written expression. Life and opportunity allowed her the avenues to add elements and tools to her raw talent and to produce works with refined edges. Yet, her true essence is always present in her work. Her fervor for poetry can often find itself intertwined in her novels. When not consumed in her own aspirations, she is often a vehicle for other's written expression. Her writing service offers others an avenue for written communication. You can explore her services at www.giftdink.com.

Serena Ther□sa Wills was born and raised in Queens, New York after receiving her Bachelors Degree in Public Policy from Syracuse University she relocated to Alexandria, VA where she completed her Masters in Public Administration from Virginia Tech. Serena now resides in Dallas, Texas. She realized she had a passion for writing when she was a young girl. Her teachers would steadily encourage her to write. It is therapeutic and is an escape from the everyday hustle and bustle. She has worked in the nonprofit field for ten years and in her spare time when she is not writing she is traveling home to spend time with her family, enjoys running and loves to serve her community through sisterhood of Delta Sigma Theta Sorority, Inc.

Erica Y. Woods has been writing all her life. She's honored to have a piece in the first Gumbo anthology. She also has two novels she's shopping to the world of publishing. She currently resides in Bahia, Brazil, where she has created a non-profit that creates housing, healthcare and educational facilities and employment opportunities for homeless people. Her greatest work, however, is her sons. They are 21 and 19 and are her greatest joy.

10th Anniversary Edition

GUMBO FOR THE SOUL:
The Recipe for Literacy in the Black Community
Available via barnesandnoble.com

"Gumbo for the Soul" dares to call it like it is. This serving of Gumbo is a must-read for every parent, teacher, mentor and all who believe it is important that our children can read and comprehend the English language."
-- Tavis Smiley, Author, Television and Radio Host

Foreword by
Heather Covington, author of Literary Divas: The Top 100+ Most Admired African American Women in Literature and NAACP Image Award Nominee.

"*GUMBO FOR THE SOUL* tells African-Americans exactly what the recipe for a good life is. . . it is inspirational, uplifting, and recommended for people of all ages, colors and aspirations."

- Alice Holman, RAWSISTAZ.com
Rawsistaz Reviewer rates Gumbo 5 out of 5
Bookcover ©1990 "With Honors" by Synthia SAINT JAMES

Beverly Black Johnson

Here's Our Child, Where's The Village?" conveys that every child deserves the opportunity to flourish as happy, thriving and free spirited people regardless of race and the displacement factors governing their lives.

"We must bear each others burdens. Though the village has been replaced by concrete and Roe v. Wade, there remains innocent children deserving of love and a safe haven. They may be parentless, but they are not Godless..." –Bruce George, Co-Founder of Def Poetry Jam

"Connecting kids to permanency is paramount."
Stacia C. Hammond- Executive Director/Founder
Adoption Support & Consultation Services of Florida, Inc. (ASCS)

"It gives me great pleasure to pen the foreword for *Here's Our Child; Where's the Village?"* and participate in the efforts of the Gumbo for the Soul project. The joy one gets from a child is indescribable, but something everyone can enjoy in one capacity or another; especially if we believe in the old African Proverb, *it takes a village to raise a child"*. –Tee C Royal, founder of RAWSISTAZ Literary Group

Book cover- Grandmother Spirit© by Synthia SAINT JAMES
Edited by Eve's Literary Services

Gumbo for The Soul Publications and logo are registered trademarks of Beverly Black Johnson. All Right Reserved
www.gumboforthesoul.com

Dedication

This book is inspired by Bruce George Media. Mr. George's vision for a platform that honors women led to the birth of Gumbo for the Soul: Celebrity Moms (under development) and Gumbo for the Soul: Women of Honor ~ Special Pink Edition.

Gumbo for the Soul: Women of Honor ~ Special Pink Edition seeks to heighten awareness in the fight against breast cancer while giving special honor to those women that are fighting or have fought the good fight!

In honor of women everywhere, the Gumbo for the Soul family would like to especially thank the women that have made a difference in our lives and the lives of those we love. Not all have been necessarily affected by breast cancer but have managed to rise above adversity in this journey we call life. We salute you, Women of Honor.

Along with our many generous contributors that make this book possible, the Gumbo for the Soul family gifts Women of Honor to Sister's Network Inc. San Francisco Chapter in honor of the chapter's president, Gail D. Bishop. Our hats are off to you. You are a strong woman, a portrait of perseverance and a woman worthy of honor. We salute you and all you do towards the fight against breast cancer. 100% of the proceeds from this book will benefit Sisters Network Inc. San Francisco Chapter.

We appreciate your support and hope you enjoy this serving of Gumbo.

Gumbo For The Soul
Women of Honor

Celina "Bigmama" Cargile, Hilda "Mama" Noel, Cassie "Bigmama" Black, Clara "Nana" Dixon, Betty Dixon, Wanda Lee Dixon, Lillian "Peanut" Jackson, Linda Henry, Yolanda Black, Auntie Reba, Auntie Geneva Cooper, Auntie Mary Joe Black, Deborah Renee Black, Aunt Ruth Black, Aunt Magalene Goins, Aunt Vera Johnson, Aunt Re, Aunt Tina Bit, Marsha, Teresa and Eleanor Johnson Mama Ruby Smith, Willie "Momo" Bean, Brenda "Punch" Hayes, Helen "Fassy" Castine, Mary Bradford, Earldine "Dean" Powell, Mary Lee Swayzer and Evelyn "Mom" Hartley the honor is overdue to the women that made a difference in my life being there for me as I journeyed through.

Teachers like Mrs. Harris, Mrs. Haysbert, Kerry Townsend Boucher impacted my life while friends like Valetta Robinson Sturns, Dianne "Blueboy" Shorte' Debbie Castine, Jeanette Combs, Cynthia Bean, Pam Bean and Rhonda Lamb White Stood by me through life's most difficult times.

Grown and sexy now, here I stand but not on my own
These sistahs stand with me helping to carry the baton
Toni Beckham, Sharon "Shaye" Gray, Lorraine Elzia, Shawnda Tate, Shelia Goss, Rachel Berry and Synthia SAINT JAMES too while just as beautiful- my daughter's Keyanna and Kyeisha are my glue.

Women of Honor are the ladies that saw me through many seasons
Some still standing, some passed on and some unmentioned for other reasons
So my hats off to you, I salute you the only way I can
And thank God for including you in my life's master plan.

By Beverly Black Johnson

Beverly Black Johnson is the creator of Gumbo for the Soul, she hails from San Francisco, CA. Look for her autobiography, *'A Wretch Like Me'* an awesome testament of God's power to bring you out of anything, including HELL!!

www.beverlyblackjohnson.com

Chapter 1
~Soulful Gumbo~
Reflections on Women of Honor

I will use my words to empower myself and others.
~Synthia SAINT JAMES

Foreword

By Synthia SAINT JAMES

Beverly Black Johnson truly honored me when she invited me to write the foreword for Gumbo for the Soul: Women of Honor. Thank YOU Beverly for the blessing!

This incredible anthology provides emotional and spiritual cleansing, healing, and encouragement for the reader, as well as for the many women who so candidly shared their life stories.

Henrietta, Cousin Rose, Hattie, Goldie, Willie, and Lena are at the top of my ever growing list of women who I love, honor and adore. They individually created or enhanced all the components that make up the complete person that I am today.

Henrietta, my biological mother, not only contributed her love, support and her DNA, but her spirited, yet humble, personality. I also inherited her love of Latin and Caribbean music and dance, and her ready smile. She taught me to be respectful of all people and how to find joy and happiness in the simplest of things; she gave me her gift of grace.

Cousin Rose, my paternal grandfather's first cousin, lived in Harlem, was like a grandmother to me. She lived to be 102 and had a great sense of pride which was completely void of vanity. She taught me how to carry myself, how to laugh out loud, and how to enjoy whatever life gives you. I dedicated the book that I illustrated 'No Mirrors in My Nana's House' to Cousin Rose since it was based on my relationship with her.

Now, Hattie is my spirit mother. Although we met when I was only six years old, we quickly grew to love and respect each other. She is the nurturer of my creativity, the one who believed in me as an artist on all levels. She sent me care packages when I was a so called "starving artist",

Gumbo For The Soul

I took the train to go visit Aunt Beatrice. That was the first time I ever witnessed prejudice; it was on the train from Northern California to Pennsylvania. My grandmother and I were asked to move from our assigned seats to the back of the train. I rode in my Grandmother's lap from California to Pennsylvania. She was angry, but never said a word. Her pride and dignity shined through it all. She made so many friends on the train. I remember folks would stand up awhile to give her a break and so that I could sleep. I learned about pride, friendship and love on that train ride.

My Mom has always been a free spirit. All my family loves her. She is the baby of her nine siblings. She is a great cook and she definitely puts love into her dishes. There were often requests for her potato salad and turnip greens; she was often the life of the party. I must admit, she taught me spontaneity and having fun with what you have no matter how little it may be.

Nanny was my sounding board, my friend, and my first true love. I can remember singing love songs along with the radio and replacing the names in the song with the name 'Nanny'. Once when she was going on a trip and I was about seven years old, I sang *"Nanny, please, please come back, don't take the train going down the track. Oh no, no don't leave me, don't leave me in misery..."* I think about her almost every day since her passing in 1988. The three greatest things she taught me was the golden rule, "do unto others as you would have them do unto you", repeat the 23rd Psalm feeling unsure or uneasy about something, and when I am at my lowest say to myself: *Renay you can either lay down and die now or stand up and be a woman"*. Now, I have been standing up for several decades.

I learned from My Women, My Family that Nanny was due respect and love as the Matriarch of this family. She had taught all my aunts and uncles about the importance of family and togetherness. Although many of the family have gone on to Heaven, those of us remaining here will never forget those family picnics when Nanny was here sitting in the middle of the park with her hands folded on her knees while looking at all the love she had created.

-H. Renay Anderson

10th Anniversary Edition

My Aunties!

It is a great opportunity to honor three special women who have touched my life. Let me begin at the beginning. My paternal grandmother stepped in to assist my father raise my siblings and me and my three aunts were instrumental in our child rearing.

As life would so have it, after being born, I was brought out of the hospital to live in my great Aunt Margaret's home where my parents resided. Now Aunt Margaret, a very personable person, was married and a beautician--hairdressers they were called in those days, and she conducted her business out of her home. Aunt Margaret and her husband had been married more than twenty years by the time I came on the scene, but they had no children, and she immediately bonded with me.

So my first official home was at Aunt Margaret's and I stayed there for a little over a year then I moved to Brooklyn. After moving, my siblings and I spent many weekends with Aunt Margaret. She was the one who gave us our first experiences of going down south to Columbia, South Carolina to see our grandparents and other family. It was Aunt Margaret and Uncle Stone who were also the ones who would take us to Radio City every year to see the Christmas and Easter shows, to our first and following Mets baseball games, to the movies and to shows at the world famous Apollo Theater. Wherever we went, Aunt Margaret brought along snacks – hard boiled eggs, sandwiches, cookies and soda. Aunt Margaret loved to take pictures and we would go over her house and go through tons of photo albums as she patiently told us about each one. She kept in contact with all the family members, so she basically knew what was going on with everyone.

Aunt Margaret was a talker and she loved to socialize, so being a hairdresser was the perfect line of work for her. Her customers would confide in her and being the nosy child that I was, while the others were playing, I would sneak and listen to their stories. Aunt Margaret also loved to go out and often went to plays and shows. I really believe it is because of her that I developed a love for both the theatre and traveling. It was after graduating from college that I took my first trip with Aunt Margaret and Uncle Stone to Bermuda. One thing about her is that when she arrived to new territory, she would want to explore the island and we did. I am the same way now; whenever I travel somewhere new, I want to learn and see as much of the place as I can. Other trips included Bermuda and within the U.S. - Saragota Springs, Texas, Boston and Vermont, where we enjoyed our time together.

Aunt Margaret had an older sister named Aunt Bernice. Although just two years apart, Aunt Margaret and Aunt Bernice were like night and day; Aunt Bernice never had a lot to say but was direct with whatever she said. Aunt Bernice was not only a sports buff, but she was athletic. She was on a bowling league and used to horseback ride. Annually, these two close sisters, who lived next door to each other, traveled together South to see their older sister, Aunt Baby. They were always my connection to my Southern roots. Being born and raised in South Carolina, they were the ones with the photos and the stories of our family down south. With them, I learned about my heritage and had a sense of belonging. The many Southern meals I ate as a child were at their homes. I learned to love candied yams that Aunt Margaret made. I admired the way she would scurry to make black eyed peas, rice and collard greens on New Year's Eve, and how she just had to have bread at every meal. My first connection to my Southern roots was through my aunts via their talks, traditions and travels. Aunt Margaret and Aunt Bernice both lived in Harlem for many years. Going to visit and stay with them on holidays and school vacations was instrumental in building my love for Harlem. I already knew a lot about Harlem because my father grew up there and he shared his many experiences with us. Just as they shared some of the memories and history of Harlem and the Black Renaissance with us, my aunts shared some of the Southern Jim Crow era and the Civil Rights Movement also. Some of their stories were not so pleasant; but it was all part of a history we needed to know--a history that they had lived.

About a year after my birth, my parents moved to Brooklyn to live in the brownstone that my grandparents owned. My grandfather had just died and my grandmother and her only daughter lived there. So I went from the home of living with one aunt to living in the home of another. This aunt was my paternal Aunt Daphne, who we affectionately called Auntie. Now Auntie was single, attending college and she latched on to the three of us like we were her own. Auntie assisted my grandmother in caring for us. Auntie married when I was five and she relocated to Boston to live with her husband and start her own family.

We would visit Auntie often during the summer breaks from school and sometimes during Christmas vacation. She would always welcome us and take good care of us while we were in Boston. Now Auntie was a feisty woman who would speak her mind. She had very few friends and spent most of her time with her family. Auntie, like her mother, was short and as we grew older, we would hover over her. She was my connection to my father's side of the family. Auntie would tell me stories of her early years hanging out with her two favorite cousins in Harlem. She would also tell stories of my grandmother and friends who were all Barbadian. Whenever Auntie came to New York, I could be sure that she would visit her mother's friends and take me with her. The other thing she always did was to attend church with me. I always felt so proud to take my aunt to church. Up to that point in life, very few of my other family members had expressed any interest in church, so having Auntie with me was special. When I was about in the third grade, my grandmother fell and broke her arm. She appointed me to write letters to my aunt in Boston. This continued until my aunt's death. We would communicate by mail and later by phone. Even as an adult, I would take at least one week of my vacation time to spend in Boston with my aunt. By this time, her children were married and she lived alone. I enjoyed our private times together. One of the things we enjoyed was to go shopping at Filene's Basement or to Cambridge Square. My aunt and I would sit up late laughing and telling jokes. She loved to laugh. Like me, my aunt would laugh so hard until tears would roll down her cheeks. One of the things I remember about her is that every night, like clockwork, she would read her Bible, before going to bed.

When I was in my early twenties, I was diagnosed with a tumor on one of my ovaries. I had to have both the tumor and the ovary removed. When my gynecologist first told me, I came home and called my Aunt Margaret whom I talked to every night. She quickly recommended that I get a second opinion. My aunt went with me to every appointment. After I was hospitalized and had the operation, she was at that hospital every day. My Aunt Bernice often came with her. My Auntie Daphne came down from Boston that weekend and came to the hospital during the entire weekend. My three aunts never missed one of my birthdays, or a graduation. I cannot think of an important event in my life where I didn't get some type of communication from my three aunts. So when I think of honorable women, I think of my aunts who were connected, loving and there for me. Aunts have played a huge part in my life. I only hope that I can be half as good as an aunt to my nieces and nephews as my aunts were to me. My life has been enriched because of three women and for that I thank God for my aunties--my great aunts.

-Rolanda Pyle

I will see miracles in each morning's light.
~Synthia SAINT JAMES

Surviving My Breast Challenge

It was in 2000, when I walked into the medical screening room at New York's renowned Columbia Presbyterian Hospital, one of the most prestigious health care facilities in the country. I was there to get my annual mammogram, and expected to walk out as happy as I did when I walked in. But that was not about to happen. After the mammogram was performed, I waited patiently for the results, only to be told that I could not leave. Needless to say, being held captive was not my idea of anything pleasant. I was devastated, because when I was momentarily stripped of my freedom to leave, I immediately felt in my spirit that something was wrong. I was called into a private office; it was there when I was gently informed that I had a fibrocystic breast, the precursor to that of breast cancer; a condition that warranted close monitoring.

When I returned for another mammogram in 2001, approximately six months later, I learned that the fibrocystic breast had now turned into one of my greatest fears and challenges: breast cancer. I couldn't believe it! My mind was racing; my thoughts were bouncing from every bit of available wall space surrounding my brain while finally landing in its wondering mode. I began to question how I would handle this challenge; this uninvited, unwelcomed guest, who had suddenly taken a seat at my table of life? And, what was my plan to move forward? I did, however, have the presence of mind to call my husband, who reacted to the unexpected news as if he had just received notice of someone's death. He was in total shock!

As I sat and listened carefully to the health care professional, I felt as if I wasn't in the room. It was almost as if I were somewhere else; almost like I was having an out-of-body experience. However, somewhere in that space of time, I was referred to the highly skilled surgeon, Dr. Mahmoud B. El Tamer, who would be responsible for performing the lumpectomy. As he compassionately explained this disease, he informed me that it would take about two weeks before the surgery would be performed. What? Two weeks? Are you crazy? I wanted this stuff out of me! I had some living to do, so my immediate question to him was, "Why are you waiting so long?" His response was interesting, yet, very reassuring. "My dear," he said, "If anybody wanted to get breast cancer, yours would be the one they would want to get." I didn't understand that rationale, but I did know that I had sighed a breath of relief. You see, I had carcinoma insitu. It was not going anywhere. As a matter of fact, it had not even penetrated the duct or lymph nodes where it was found. So, I was truly blessed that my breast challenge was discovered in its very early stage. Yes, it was caught at an early stage, but it was breast cancer nonetheless; and in my particular case, the lump was much too small to be discovered through self examination, but discovered by the mammogram that I will never fail to get.

Prior to the surgery, I was given three options. One was a mastectomy, the second was chemotherapy, and the third, was radiation. I opted for the latter, which turned out to be thirty-three treatments of radiation. I received these treatments on a daily basis, from February 14 to April 6, with the exception of the weekends. Every day I walked to Columbia Presbyterian from my strenuous teaching position in a New York City middle school, took the elevator down to the basement, where my treatments in radiation took place. Each time, with great care and precision, the technicians were able to target and radiate the same spot. I was impressed by that precision and their compassion. My decision to receive radiation, introduced me to one of the best female oncologists in the healthcare profession, a Dr. Shermian Woodhouse; and I was very impressed with her, and the healthcare that was provided.

I knew I had a fight on my hands. But remembering the strength of my now deceased mother was how I struggled and fought to survive. She left me with a legacy of her strength and courage, and she taught me how to fight with faith. And that's exactly what I did. I fought with faith.

At some point during this unexpected challenge, a third physician was assigned to my case. He immediately put me on Tamoxifen, and sorely downplayed its side effects and risks. Although I continued to work and proceeded with my daily routine, between the activity of it all, I was able to research this disease, and this medication. I discovered there were foods I could eat that would help prevent the onset of breast cancer, and I found that exercise would be a great benefit to me. Armed with this knowledge, I immediately changed my eating habits, which weren't that bad to begin with, and began an exercise regimen which included walking, swimming, as well as aerobics in water and on land. More importantly, I discovered that Tamoxifen had more deadly side effects than I was willing to risk.

The doctor who prescribed the medication was not thrilled that I took myself off of it, but I felt he was using me as a guinea pig, and I had sense enough to know that I had to be my own medical police. So, that's when I shifted gears and went into the investigative mode. When I became knowledgeable of the risks involved with taking Tamoxifen, I could not continue or justify taking something that would possibly cause me to get cancer in another part of my body, just to keep me from getting cancer in my breast; so I walked boldly on faith, and immediately stopped taking the medication. So, after taking approximately eleven Tamoxifen tablets, which I was told I would have to take for five years, I refused to take any more. That's right! I absolutely refused, and threw the remaining pills in the garbage. It was my faith that allowed me not to take any more of the drug; and it was my faith that allowed me to choose to control my breast challenge with the proper diet, exercise and the power of prayer. And, guess what? I've been cancer free for eight years. Thank God for Jesus!

I have since started an organization called *Sister to Sister: One in the Spirit, Inc.*, an empowerment and health conference service for women of color in New York's Harlem community. Through this outreach ministry, we provide health screening for those African American women who have no insurance, or those who are under-insured. As I do with our sisters in Harlem, I encourage every woman to be smart about her health care. However, as the years fade, so does my scar; but I'm reminded that early detection was to me, worth a pound of cure. So my sisters, be your own medical police. Get annual mammograms, and perform self breast examinations. In the final analysis, it can only save your life.

-Yvonne Singleton Davis

10th Anniversary Edition

The Buck Stops Here

CANCER: First my mother. Then my brother. Followed by my sister. All in 18 months. Whew! Finally, a breather. But only for two years before my beloved husband was stricken. Prior to my late husband's departure, we had been community activists in Detroit for more than 30 years. He loved Detroit and everyone knew it. So often we heard him say, *"I was born here. Raised here, and I will die here."*

Strangely enough, following his retirement in 2002, he said, *"I believe I can leave Detroit now."* We were all amazed. Rev. Eddie K. Edwards had been a Michiganian of the Year, received a Presidential Award for his community service work, and was highly regarded by the city, state, and county governments for his commitment to Michigan. More importantly, most of our family lives here. This sudden change of heart was hard for us to understand. Nevertheless, in December 2003, we began to make plans to relocate to Texas.

During the Christmas season, we looked for a home in Texas. It didn't take long for us to find a lovely one. Negotiations began on the purchase; pending the sale of our Detroit home. We rushed back and put our home on the market. The real estate agent we worked with felt sure our home would sell quickly. We were all surprised when thirty people looked at the home and, even though many expressed their love for it, not one put a bid on it. Thank God they didn't.

In March 2004, Eddie began to complain about having a pain in his side. At first, the doctor diagnosed it as an infection and gave him a prescription for antibiotics, which he took for about a month. When his condition didn't improve, he had a biopsy. That's when we discovered that he was in stage four of cancer and only had four to six months of life left! He was a health-conscious person and it was difficult for us to understand how his condition could develop to stage four without us knowing something was terribly wrong. He left this life in July 2004, just five months after his diagnosis.

My husband's passing left me in a stage of utter shock and the need to make important decisions alone. But the transition from wife to widow wasn't the only major crisis I had to deal with. Before I could catch my breath, I WAS DIAGNOSED WITH CANCER MYSELF. I've always been faithful to have my mammograms on a consistent basis. Upon having my annual mammogram, the test showed something "abnormal" was on the film. I needed to have a biopsy, which I did. The biopsy came back as stage one of breast cancer. Naturally, I was panic-stricken. Images of death began to dance in my head. I thought about my mother, my brother, my sister, and my husband – all dying from this awful disease.

Once I got over my initial fears, I rose up and prepared myself for battle. I have always been a fighter and it's a good thing. Now, I was fighting for my OWN life and the life of my grandchildren and great grandchildren. ENOUGH IS ENOUGH! I refused to sit idly by and watch this deadly disease take the lives of my offspring.

Being a writer, I have a very creative imagination. Immediately, I began to see myself healed – instead of dead. Instead of writing out my obituary, I wrote out my goals for the next five years. And I wrote my autobiography. I also designed and posted signs all over my home for my eyes to see. One of the signs said: "THE BUCK STOPS HERE!"

When it came time for my scheduled surgery, I can truthfully say that all fear was gone. Although I had to go back twice for the disease to be removed, (it was so small that it was hard to pinpoint) it was removed on an outpatient basis! Today, I'm cancer-free and the buck stops here.

-Minister Mary Edwards

I will steadily plant GOOD seeds that
will grow into beautiful plants of success.
~Synthia SAINT JAMES

A Whisper of Hope

If someone had asked me where my life would be in 2009, I would have painted a future full of joy, hope, and expectation of spending the rest of my life with my husband Kevin, the love of my life, and the father of our two beautiful daughters Meghan (16) and Kaylah (12). But life took a dramatic detour on November 16, 2007. That day was the beginning of many unfolding events in my life. I was diagnosed with a metastatic carcinoma of the left breast, which is called breast cancer. I was shocked and surprised by the diagnosis. I could not believe that it was me since I took the initiative to have annual mammograms, exercised, and maintained a healthy life style. I did not linger on the negative, instead I became hopeful because I have three girlfriends who were breast cancer survivors, and I believed that I too would survive breast cancer.

I was fortunate to have been able to schedule an appointment with the Breast Center at Anne Arundel Medical Center the following Monday. There I received the positive confirmation that it was cancer and that biopsies of the breast and lymph nodes needed to be performed. Days later it was confirmed that cancer had been found in the lymph nodes and immediately an MRI of the breast was ordered. The result of the MRI was a diagnosis of breast cancer with a questionable abnormality in the liver. A team of doctors consulted and ordered a CT scan of the abdomen. The CT scan found extensive biliary ductal dilatation present which caused concern. There was suspicion that there could be possible cancer of the pancreas.

Although negative medical diagnosis continued to be thrown my way, I believed and stayed positive that God was in control of my life and body. I also believed that I had a greater purpose to live, and cancer could not destroy my life. I was determined that cancer would not wipe away my hopes and dreams. God blessed me with a husband and two wonderful daughters who love and needed me. I knew that God would not take me away from them. I was prepared emotionally and mentally to wage war on this cancer. I would not allow the cancer to control me and my future, so I was prepared to do everything possible to regain my health. I began to live my life with expectancy that God would restore my health and I prayed the Psalms of Hope. My favorites Psalms were 23 and 27. I also prayed I Philippians 4:13 "I can do all things through Christ …who strengthens me".

Prior to the breast surgery I consulted with a gastroenterologist regarding the abnormality in the pancreas. He felt that it was safe to move ahead with the breast surgery.

As my faith grew stronger, my husband Kevin became distant and withdrawn; I saw his spirit and faith begin to diminish. I felt hopeful, while my husband felt hopeless and helpless. He cried constantly and wanted to take my cancer away. On the morning of December 6, 2007, as I prepared for surgery, many of my friends and family called to offer prayers and words of encouragement to us. I was aware that the focus was on me, but I asked them to also take care of Kevin and the girls. As I was being prepared for surgery, I was relaxed and safe in the arms of God as Kevin led a prayer for the team of doctors who would perform the surgery.

The surgery was a success. I had a left breast partial mastectomy, margin reexcision lymph node procedure. During surgery a Penrose drain was placed in my breast to remove the excess fluid from the tissue, which minimized the swelling and diminished pain. Kevin made it his duty and cared for me as if he was a trained professional. He became our daughters' primary care giver, he prepared meals, checked homework, and shuttled them off to school and other activities. He made sure that their schedules were uninterrupted. By Christmas, Kevin was still unusually quiet. I did everything to exhibit that I was going to be whole again and I returned to my normal activities.

Kevin continued to play a major role in my care; he scheduled all of my upcoming doctor's appointments, and consulted with the numerous doctors. On January 7, 2008 we met with the medical oncologist at John Hopkins Institute who laid out the protocol for treatment through the use of chemotherapy and radiation. The protocol was four cycles of Adriamycin and four cycles of Taxol and thirty-six treatments of radiation. We had planned to begin chemotherapy on January 18, 2008.

I was about to celebrate my birthday on January 14 and my daughter Meghan's fifteenth birthday on January 16. What usually was a double celebration became the birthdays from hell. Instead of a celebration, I was now planning the funeral of my husband who had committed suicide by hanging the day before my birthday.

To this day it is still difficult for me to come to terms with the fact that the man whom I spent twenty-seven years with, thought I knew like no other human being, whom I loved deeply could make this drastic decision to end his life which would have long term effects on so many other lives. While I was choosing to live, he chose to die. I instinctively reassured my daughters that mommy would be healthy again, and that although daddy is gone he still loved us.

The morning of February 1, I began chemotherapy. It was surreal. I stood in the bathroom hunched over the sink crying, and wondering why Kevin chose to leave the girls and me. We were supposed to fight this cancer together, but instead I must fight for my life without him and raise our children. Thank God for the Grace that He has shown me. He promised that he would never leave me nor forsake me. I began to live and believe in his promises. I completed chemotherapy and radiation without complications. Additional test proved that the abnormality in the pancreas was of scar tissue from an earlier surgery.

I had been healthy during chemotherapy. I continued to stay active through modest exercise, and maintained a healthy diet. I received specialized skincare treatments for chemotherapy patients, and did post chemotherapy detoxifying, I continued a customized antioxidant therapy, and as a result of detoxifying I did not experience edema or mouth sores. As an added bonus, I went from a size 14/16 to a size 8. Through antioxidant therapy, I continued to maintain rejuvenated cell health.

The support of family, friends, and the community during that time was critical. I am blessed with strong and loyal sister friends who continued to love and support me. They shared the responsibly of taking me to chemotherapy and doctors appointments. My dad and stepmother stayed with me during the first few weeks after the death to support the girls and me, and continued to visit frequently. My daughter Kaylah's fifth-grade class families were very, very supportive and provide weekly meals. Many people from the community contributed towards an educational fund for the girls, while the tennis foundation provided tennis scholarships.

Coping with the loss of a husband and father has been a sad and lonely road to travel. We will never understand the reason for the decision that Kevin made, and it was important that the girls and I receive psychological therapy to help cope. Cancer in itself is difficult to deal with on its own, but to have it compounded by their dads' suicide was too much for the children to deal with. Therapy offered us an outlet to express our hurt and disappointment. I wanted to make sure that my girls were mentally healthy, and would be able to cope and maintain stability in their lives. I did not want them to be ashamed nor embarrassed by the death of their father. Cancer and suicide as a result of depression has not been openly discussed in the African-American community. I wanted to let them know that it was healthy to talk about it.

Today I am healthy, vital, and feel more alive due to the success of my medical treatments, my supportive group of friends and family, the holistic services of my esthetician Caprese, the encouragement of my life coach Raphael, our therapist Dana and Meredith, my friends Grant and Synthia for believing in my story and encouraging me to share it with the world.

Currently I am drafting my first book titled *Solid in My Faith: Surviving Breast Cancer and Suicide* to encourage other women who have experienced breast cancer and other life tragedies to let them know that "Joy Cometh in the Morning".

-Marcia C. Hodge

Marcia Hodge is currently cancer-free and lives in Bowie, Maryland with her two daughters.

I will turn on the joy when times get rough.
~Synthia SAINT JAMES

Neecee's Shine

Six impressionable young teenage girls adored her; spending time at her house was Disneyland to us all. She was more than a role model; she was our Auntie Neecee and a mortal Goddess in our eyes. Dripping with the allure of sensuality and sassiness, she was the Diana Ross of our family and the world, as we knew it. She had no kids, lived in a big house in the suburbs and her husband was a light-skinned Billie D. Williams that fit the bill of what a man should be as far as we were concerned. Neecee could do no wrong in our eyes and her style captivated us as the epitome of womanly form. Not only did we want to emulate her every action and move, we wanted to be her when we grew up. She was all that to us, plus a bag of chips, pickle and medium drink on the side. — Simple and pure satisfaction, with no additives needed.

Every other weekend, Neecee would give her two sisters and one brother a gift- a break from their lives as parents. She agreed to take all six of her nieces for the weekend. In hindsight, I often think it was her way of experiencing the children she never had of her own. Much like the way she lived the rest of her life, Neecee would go for the gusto; instead of taking any indulgence in small dosages, it was all or nothing for her. In doing so, her life would go from childless, to six girls at one time in sixty seconds flat. Neecee seemed to thrive on the energy rush of pubescent estrogen as we walked through her door and she never failed to deliver entertainment, as well as, education to her nieces. We loved our weekend excursions with her. Her house was our haven and her personality was our goal of attainment. Unlike our parents, Neecee just seemed to "get" us. She was the ultimate girly girl and as we stood firm on the assertion that adults just didn't seem to understand; she was different – she understood. We wrapped ourselves in her essence. She personified for us, the definition of a woman.

As we each settled in her family room on Friday nights, she would tell us the itinerary for the weekend. "Tomorrow is 'Showtime at the Apollo Thomas style', you each have twenty-four hours to get your outfits ready and practice your performances. I am the judge and at the end of the show I want to see a group number with all of you in it. Done in a manner that could only be pulled off by girls as talented as you. You are each wonderfully and uniquely made and I want to see your shine." Neecee was all about making us see the beauty within us and teaching us to embrace ourselves.

So we practiced our individual performances and worked on a group act as well. It was all about performance with Auntie Neecee, and she promoted self-love and embracing our womanliness and beauty. She insisted upon it, and we grew from her encouragement. She pushed uniqueness on us like it was essential to us as much as the air we breathed and we suckled each and every word from her lips.

Neecee opened her closet to us and as we looked at her belongings, we saw the things that made a woman a woman. She had it all. She was the total woman and gazing at her clothes put us in a stage of astonishment. She had wigs, Go-go boots, dresses, even boa feathers and then there was the jewelry. Her collection could put any name-brand department store or boutique to shame. Our eyes buckled each time she allowed us to look at, much less, try on and model her treasures. As an adult, I remembered my time with her as an old black and white memory of a simpler time, a moment when family connected and encouraged the beauty of each family member. Aunt Neecee did that for us.

With her six nieces, she forced us to put on a show in the confines of her sunken family room. She encouraged impressionable teenage girls to see the beauty that resided in them just based on their gender--she encouraged us to shine. She provided the costumes, the accessories, the music, the AURA and the confident and encouraging words that enabled six little girls to feel like Diana Ross, if only for a moment once or twice a month.

I loved her for that feeling.

I loved her for that small gesture that will forever touch my soul.

Then one visit was different. Neecee's eyes were a little less bright and seemed clouded over with something too heavy for her to verbalize as we prepared for our monthly show. Neecee made the experience as special as always, but something was different. Something was off. She went through her normal motions and the normal routine. She tried to be inspirational to the six of us like before; she tried to put on her "Diana Ross" aura, but it just was not the same. Maybe I smelled it in the air before my cousin counterparts did because I was the oldest, or maybe the air was filled with a different smog to all of us, yet we didn't voice it. But "it" was there. Neecee wasn't Neecee, and her Diana Ross flair was an impersonation, at best, of what it normally had been. We had no idea, at the time that the culprit that had stolen her womanly air was Cancer. We had no clue that the Big C had captured our Auntie Neecee and put its scent on her as a victim for life.

That weekend, we had our normal *"Showtime at the Apollo Thomas Style"* show. Our group song was "Car Wash", with exceptional gyrating moves delivered as best as six teenage girls could do. At the end, she kissed our foreheads, told us how well we did and then took us to her bedroom to further educate us on the tolls of life and the threats to our outward appearances as women.

I'm forty-three now, and I still don't know the exact timing of when my aunt received notification that she had breast cancer. I only know that at some point she was notified and someone told her of her fate and the actions that had to be taken to fight the demon known as Breast Cancer. I can only surmise that someone, most likely God, told her to share what she was going through with the six girls that worshipped her.

Did she find out a day, a month, two months or more before she shared it with us? We'll never know. In the scheme of things, that's irrelevant. All we know is that true to her phenomenal nature of teaching her nieces the upside and the pitfalls of being a woman, breast cancer was included in the curriculum of her coming of age lesson plan.

As we entered her bedroom, plopping ourselves at the foot of her bed, she made some small talk about what being a woman meant and how it was much more than outward appearances and accessories. Then she removed her top and her bra. Underneath she revealed that she had one real breast and a flat counterpart on the opposite side. Built in to her bra was a falsie, a term I was clueless to as a child, but one, as an adult, I have come to understand. She showed us her battle scar and in doing so, she held her head high as if to say, "All wars have casualties, my breast just happens to be it in my personal battle with cancer." As a spectator to her war, her revelation made her come out in my eyes more beautiful than before.

Each 'Showtime' moment after that one became better than the last as Neecee seemed to be on a mission to instill "Beauty in spite of" in all of us. She let us know that true beauty did not reside in packaging, but in what lay beneath the skin, in the internal qualities that allowed us to shine. She showed us that being a woman was not determined by accents and physical body parts. Breasts were just accessories to an already fabulously made creation of God. The essence of a "real woman" was not determined by cup size and what fleshly supplements filled a bra. Cancer could win the battle but a real woman could win the war.

There was a sense of sorrow in her voice that night when she stood topless before us and taught us the evils of the world and the effects it can often take on a woman. We sensed the melancholy loss of her breast; one of the things that make a woman feel like a woman, yet the moment was victorious as well. In sharing her loss, she taught us to let our beauty shine in a way that is not enveloped and defined by outward appearances and packaging. As she talked to us, she was vulnerable, yet her words and her presence were glorified in being a woman and all that it entailed. She maintained the iconic persona that she always had and in some ways, lifted herself higher, if that were possible, by the way she handled the hand that Cancer had dealt her. She was still, if not more so, an ultimate diva because of what she had endured.

Years have passed now and I've thought about that event repeatedly in my mind; remembering when Cancer added my family to its roster of victims on its ultimate roll call. And when I do, I think of Auntie Neecee and smile at the fact that even as a victim of breast cancer, her spirit, her persona and the essence of what a woman truly is emerged. And to me, one less breast or not, she was even more beautiful than before.

-Lorraine Elzia

10th Anniversary Edition

Memorial of Janice Carol Tillman
May 30, 1960 – December 13, 2008

When do you know you have touched someone's life? When over 1,000 mourners filled Faith Assembly Church on December 20, 2008 in Pasco, WA to attend the Homegoing of my sister Janice Carol Tillman, I knew that day that she was no ordinary woman. That December day was bitter cold, the city was at a standstill; snow packed several feet high everywhere, and the roads were questionable for traveling. What would make all those people – family, friends, coworkers, neighbors, and acquaintances want to give honor to this 48-year-old African-American woman? You might have called it an international funeral because there were people from many nationalities present – Asians, Mexicans, Whites, and Blacks. Her husband of twenty-five years, Andrew Tillman, has assisted me in memorializing her service to her family, her friends, and the community.

I know my sister as the giving sister – each birthday of mine she never failed to honor my birthday and she did the same for her other eight sisters as well. I remember one birthday receiving a card from her with $5.00 in it with a note that said lunch is on me. It was not the amount she sent, because she was by no means needy, but it was the love behind the gesture. She became the matriarch of our family after our mother passed, taking the lead to keep the family connected. When two of my nieces lost their mother (my sisters), it was Janice that stood in the gap, extending motherhood to them and at the same time being a mother to four of her own. She was loyal to her family and would do whatever she could for them. She was a giver beyond measure of her time and treasures. She was a devoted servant to St. James CME Church of Pasco, WA acting as President of the Stewardess Board for over ten years.

Janice was honored with numerous in-house awards at Energy Northwest where she worked for twenty-four years before her passing with the last fourteen years managing a workforce. She was also one of eight women from the Columbia Basin Region to be chosen for the Women of Achievement Award which recognizes women for being leaders at their prospective companies which was followed by a recognition letter from United States Senator Patty Murray. In addition, she received The National Management Association Woman of the Year Award for the region.

Friends and coworkers would say Janice simply cared about people and she loved connecting people to life. That was evident by the many camping trips and vacations that she planned with her friends and her involvement in the Ivy Glades Homeowners Association where she served as Secretary. In December during the Christmas holiday, she organized a luncheon where women gathered for some girl talk and gift exchange. That is where the Janice Tillman Scholarship Fund was established in her honor by some of the ladies; Sadie Henderson and Andrea Ramsey, who knew that education meant a lot to Janice. The Scholarship worth $1,500 was given to a graduating senior (who met certain criteria), at the annual AAAS Awards Banquet honoring African-American students for maintaining a 3.0 average throughout the school year. The significance of the scholarship is the fact that not only did Janice work her way through college, graduating from Eastern Washington University with a degree in Business Administration, but she only had a school loan for $1,500 when she finished.

It was well known that Janice was committed to community service where she lived. She has volunteered countless hours on numerous school district ad hoc committees with the last one being the Pasco Facilities Task Force. She was also on the General Board of the African-American Community Cultural Educational Society (AACESS), which spearheads community event fundraisers for youth education and community activities. AACESS also sponsors the Miss Juneteenth Pageant where funds go toward educational scholarships for girls.

What sets Janice apart from others? She was a model of a woman using every gift God had given her to the fullest. Janice is deeply missed but her spirit remains to those she has touched. It is my hope through this short biography of Janice that women will be inspired in their gifts and talents, that women will encourage other women to stay strong during their life journey, and that women will desire to leave a legacy of service to others.

-Elaine Bean

10th Anniversary Edition

I've Got a Hookup 'cuz God is a Friend of Mine!

I've known some strong and courageous women in my lifetime; my mother, grandmother, and oldest girlfriend among them. The latter having suffered a debilitating stroke in 2004. They, along with many other of my female friends and acquaintances have endured physical pain, emotional trials, horrendous tribulations, and a lot more of the cruel stuff that visits us during our respective lifetimes. Each of the women deserves recognition for having fought their respective battles with strength and dignity—some won and some lost.

Now, don't you just love a woman who is consistent in thinking positively, setting goals with clear objectives, motivating others, smiling frequently, not complaining, being a loyal friend, and praying regularly? I know of one who is all of that and more. She is my hero!

My friend, Gail D. Bishop, is a God-fearing, church-going, highly favored middle-aged woman who was diagnosed with breast cancer in 2000 at age forty-two, and suffered subsequent associated complications as cancer cells metastasized to one of her lungs in 2004 and to her liver in 2008. Gail's cancer treatments have included one lumpectomy, four lymph node dissections, and an untold number of radiation and chemotherapy treatments. She continues chemo treatments today, ten years after her first diagnosis.

Currently under a clinical trial, Gail's weekly chemotherapy medications include Avastin®, which works to inhibit the formation of new blood vessels that supply cancerous tumors with the oxygen and nutrients needed to grow, and Taxol®, a medication that slows the growth and spreading of cancer cells in the body.

The chemotherapy procedure is wholly uncomfortable and its side effects are certainly more agonizing than the average person can endure. I've called it a misfortune that she has had to suffer so much. She's called it a blessing [to be alive]. I can rarely conjure the "right" words to comfort her or to let Gail know that I feel for her. The best that I know to do is pray to God to relieve my friend of her suffering, and ask that He help me learn to be a soldier like her.

Gail has encountered hair loss, memory loss and weight loss, yet carries a broad smile every time I see her. In spite of having experienced changes in nail appearance, taste and smell distortions, and extreme fatigue, she gives thanks to her Lord every single day.

In 2000, one year after her initial breast cancer diagnosis, Gail Bishop established and became President of the San Francisco chapter of Sisters Network, Inc. It was Gail's giving heart that motivated her to head the organization's San Francisco chapter that provides breast cancer sufferers, survivors and their families with group support, agency and medical referrals, joyful activities, encouragement, education, advocacy, friendship and prayers. In addition to its ongoing work, annually Gail's San Francisco chapter hosts a free health fair, a young women's breast health summit, and a benefit luncheon and fashion show at which prime, pretty and proper breast cancer survivors proudly take to the runway to model the latest of fashions.

Gail has known many women who succumbed to breast cancer or related complications. Among them, three were members of her Sisters Network support group, and one was her 85-year-old aunt whose cancer returned after thirty years in remission.

Gail reminds me over and over again that I have much for which to be grateful. She is joyful and thankful all of the time.

If asked, "How can you be so pleasant, and have such faith with all that is happening to you," I imagine Gail Bishop's naturally optimistic outlook would bring her to reply, "I'm going to be alright. I've got a hookup 'cuz God is a friend of mine!"

To learn more about Sisters Network, Inc. or contribute to Gail's San Francisco chapter, please visit www.sistersnetworksf.org.

-Toni Beckham

I will know that I am essential and
that I have a definite universal
purpose and responsibility.
~Synthia SAINT JAMES

I had Cancer on my Wedding Day

Have you ever thought you were "all that?" Untouchable? Invincible? On top of the world? That's how I felt on my wedding day. I was a successful single mother and Houston entrepreneur with several major awards under my belt, an Ebony magazine top bachelorette and had reconnected with my college sweetheart after a sixteen-year hiatus. Yes, I was finally getting married after a string of painful relationships at the age of thirty-five and ready to live happily ever after.

As I flip through my wedding album, all of the details are a blur. I don't notice the flowers or the detailed cake. What I cherish is the genuine smile on my face, which reflects the love in my heart for so many things: life, my husband, my daughter, my family and friends. Dazzling in my strapless wedding gown, little did I know I had breast cancer. Ironic isn't it? I look so happy while cancer was dwelling inside me.

I never would have imagined that I would grow up to have breast cancer. When I first noticed the marble sized lump under my armpit eight months prior to my wedding day, I dismissed it as a swollen lymph gland as a result of a sinus infection. Life went on while the tumor grew. I found every excuse not to go to the doctor. My grandmother had breast cancer so I knew that there might be a slight likelihood that I would have it but I convinced myself that *Superwoman* doesn't get cancer.

Shortly after my honeymoon, my husband urged me to go to the doctor to determine the cause of the lump, which was beginning to get bigger. Within four days of seeing the doctor, I was diagnosed with Stage III A breast cancer. I had a lumpectomy and axillary lymph node dissection with sixteen positive lymph nodes. Due to the positive nodes, chemotherapy would be a treatment option. The thought of chemotherapy was terrifying to me. I had always had a head full of beautiful long hair, which was highly prized in the Black community. I couldn't imagine being bald and taking my new husband through the negative cosmetic changes.

After much research and consideration, I opted for four cycles of chemotherapy. My hair began to fall out about twenty days after my first treatment. One day while driving, I got a wave of courage and drove to the nearest salon. I decided it was time to empower myself and just shave my head. It was falling out daily and was matted and dry. To my surprise, I didn't shed one tear in the chair. The big picture was extending my life; hair couldn't rob me of that.

Since the thought of losing my hair was so frightening to me, I went on a Houston, Texas community affairs program bald to show viewers that being bald wasn't so bad and what the result of chemotherapy looked like. I even shared home video of my hair falling out to help other women facing this medical challenge. For a former Texas beauty queen, this took a lot of courage.

As my one-year "cancerversary" approaches, I realize that God was holding my hand the entire journey. He gave me strength and courage when I needed it and he broke me down so I could grow strong with Him again. I also realize the meaning of true beauty and it isn't based on external features.

I never heard my thirteen-year old daughter say to me that she was proud of me, despite my numerous accomplishments, until I showed her my baldhead. She gave me the biggest hug and I knew that it would be ok. I am forever humbled by this experience and hope to share my testimony with other young patients someday. Cancer doesn't care if you are all that and a bag of chips. Cancer doesn't care at all.

-Crystal Brown-Tatum

My name is Crystal and I am a breast cancer survivor.

Her-Story. Mattie Sanders Carter

My mother was born 80 years, 8 months and 6 days before the day she died.

My mother was born to a Southern Preacher who was also a farmer. She lost her mother early in life, and her father followed a few years later. She gave her life to the LORD as a child, and followed the way of the LORD thereafter the many days of her life. She instilled a Christian lifestyle in us, her many children, through instruction, games, family activities and the example of her own daily lifestyle. My mother taught me, at a young age to read the Bible. We would read the Bible together nightly. Through these teachings, I routinely earned the award of "Sunday School Scholar."

As a family, we played board games that dealt with the word of God, our favorite was a game called "The Bible," as well; we had an encyclopedia of biblical books, which we read often. Not only was a loving Christian atmosphere created within our home, we were also taught family value, respect and unity. We were taught to love our neighbor as we loved ourselves. We were taught to be kind, honest, loving and respectful of others. The lesson of obedience was big in our house. The girls were taught to crochet, knit, sew and needlepoint. We were also taught to love and to honor our Mother and our Father, which we did, individually and as a collective unit. Our parents knew beyond measure that they were loved, respected, cherished and adored by all of us.

October 31, 2007 is a day I will always remember, that is the day my Mother was diagnosed with stage 4 colon cancer. Whoa!! My world begun to spin, seemingly out of control. We met with the doctor and he advised us of the diagnosis and the short prognosis of life expectancy. Three months to live without chemotherapy and six months to live with chemotherapy.

I looked at the face of my Mother, and it was unchanged; unmoved; unyielding to the words this man, the doctor, spoke. I was filled with terror, confusion and a lack of understanding. Yet, she, my Mother, sat there as if she had not heard a word that man, the doctor, spoke. I fought back the tears that were trying to well up in my eyes, and to keep the sure signs of fear/terror from my face. I tried to behave as a strong soldier, like the one I sat across from in that room.

When I got the chance to have a private conversation with my Mother, I spoke to her wondering if she actually heard and understood what the doctor said about the cancer that had invaded her body. She advised me that she had both heard and understood, and then she said "I Trust God, and if He wants to heal me, I will be healed." At that moment, I realized, I had no choice but to join my Mother in her journey of Faith. That day I walked away with a broader, more defined Faith in the God of my Mother, whom she shared with all of us.

My Mother has many children, but gave birth to only nine. We, the nine, came together and sought all and any information relating to fighting cancer. We sought a second opinion, which gave us empowerment and time that the first, initial diagnosis, took from us. After the second opinion, we were stronger and armed with more information.

My Mother had surgery to remove the cancerous portion of her colon. Chemotherapy was used to control the metastasized cancer on her liver, lung and lower abdomen. Immediately we changed her diet, consisting of organic foods and specialty water. We also used a non-traditional medicine (Zeolite) in between chemotherapy treatments. We, the nine, came together as a family unit, as we were taught to do, and we discussed treatment options, family expectations, requirements and job duties of each family member. None of this was equated as a sacrifice, but was considered an honor and a privilege. My Mother never asked for any of this, and was exemplary and outstanding. We never imagined cancer would affect our immediate family, certainly not our Mother, our matriarch, but we had been prepared for this in the early years of our lives, through the lessons our Mother taught us. We, her many, worked well together in servicing the needs of a virtuous woman of God.

My Mother's chemotherapy treatments were intense, yet through her labor of love to God and His given mercy and grace, she endured it with ease—without problems. The six-month prognosis turned into seven months, then eight months, then nine months, and then ten months. It kept growing. Increasing in time. Not one of us, her many, even noticed we had passed the six-month mark, because not one of us, her many, expected that diagnosis to be true. Our expectation lay in the hand of God.

Gumbo For The Soul

My mother's faith in God, the Father, never wavered. She continued to read a chapter in the Bible every day, to say her prayers, to create beautiful quilts, to bake "birthday" pound cakes, to tend to her roses and her vegetable garden and fruit trees, to play *Tetris*, to do word search puzzles, to keep her appearance up, to attend Sunday church services, to enjoy watching her favorite television shows *Jeopardy* and *Wheel of Fortune*, and to be a JOY to her many children.

We, the many children of Mattie Sanders Carter, are grateful to God for first blessing us to have this dynamic woman of God as our own momma, and second, for the Agape love of God she gave to the world around her. My Mother was a remarkable woman with many talents that sustained us as a family. She was a fantastic friend, sister, church member, co-worker or whatever role she filled in the lives of those who had the opportunity to know her. She was a great wife to her husband. If I can have only half of what she had...

November 25, 2009, is another day I will always remember. 2 years and 25 days after diagnosis, and 1 year, 6 months and 25 days beyond prognosis... that is the day my Mother died.

The memories. The lessons. The gifts. Her God. Her Faith. Her Trust. Her spirit of service. Her spirit of excellence. Her warmth. Her unyielding compassion. Her lifestyle. Her wisdom. Her teachings. Her recipes. Her valor. Her touch. Her smell. Her smile. Her way. Her voice. Her style. Her grace. Her charm.

These things will live forever in us, individually and collectively. The seeds she planted in us, her many, will grow forever. We are the fruit of her labor...

-Jacqui Roberts

I will send out love with my silent touch.
~Synthia SAINT JAMES

Commanding Respect

"She's faced the hardest times, you could imagine, the many times her eyes fought back the tears...."

In this day and age, we often hear of women who are verbally "demanding" their respect. However, there are few who are capable of *"commanding"* respect; Mrs. Alpha Mae Sanders was one of those women. And if God ever blesses you with someone in your life who's willing to share a pearl or two of hard-won wisdom on how to command respect, it is strongly suggested that you pull out a pen and paper and take notes.

Growing up in the South, Alpha was the child of former slaves, and at an early age she experienced the unfairness of being Black in America. Her parents worked hard picking cotton, enabling them to buy property and make a better life for their children. Determined that their children wouldn't grow up experiencing the injustices of the South, they moved to California during Alpha's teen years.

Married at a very young age and bearing seven children, even motherhood didn't begin well for Alpha, as her first-born son was stillborn. However, God blessed her with six more healthy children and she juggled the responsibilities of raising her children and keeping house, while caring for her ailing mother. Being the fortified, strong woman that she was sometimes came as a curse for Alpha. Because so many people leaned on her, she was often the one who was depended on to step up to the plate. As a result, she assisted in the upbringing of many of her nieces and nephews.

Alpha was determined to be the "hand that rocked the cradle," so it wasn't until all of her children were of school age that she began to venture outside of the home. As a result of her "on the job training," in taking care of so many family members, she was able to obtain a job in the nursing field, despite a lack of professional training, and continued working full-time while efficiently balancing taking care of her own family, her household and extended family members. Even with all of this, Alpha still managed to instill the love of God in her family and attend church on a regular basis. She didn't just "teach" that God is love, she showed it!

Being one who was raised in the "old school" way of doing things, Alpha exuded confidence and gave the impression that her life was not challenging. Being the only girl of six children, she was accustomed to hard work and had been taught at a young age that working hard did not mean you had the luxury of not taking care of your children, or your home, or any other family member that required help to focus primarily on yourself; it simply meant you added one more ball to the juggling act!

Befriending one of the Sanders children, I met Mrs. Sanders when I was in Jr. High school and I was afraid of her. She made it clear that she wasn't accepting mess from anybody! What I didn't understand at that time was that she was bearing the weight of the world on her shoulders. Despite being married, her husband was seldom home, often working two jobs to provide for his family. That left Alpha to be a single mother. Additionally, because she was the only girl, her extended family leaned heavily on her, so it wasn't unusual for her to also be caring for one or more of her nieces or nephews while taking care of her own children.

Mrs. Sanders became a widow at a fairly young age, and I believe that was the turning point in how I viewed this woman, because in spite of truly being left alone to finish raising six children, she didn't miss a beat! You would never know, by her demeanor, that she bore the weight of raising six children alone while mourning the loss of her husband. She never muttered, complained or uttered a harsh word regarding the challenging hand life had dealt her. She simply held up her head, stuck out her chest and smiled as she continued moving forward and doing what needed to be done. Her children no longer had a father, but she maintained the household.

Soft-spoken, she rarely had much to say, but when she spoke, Mrs. Sanders commanded a respect that rivaled the likes of E.F. Hutton. She stood a little over five feet, but had the ability to reach heights of giants, not because of her physical stature, but because of the way she lived her life and carried herself. The epitome of a tea bag in a hot cup of water, it seemed the hotter the situations in life got, the stronger she became.

Wearing as many emotional and relational hats for the people she loved, as the physical hats she wore to church each Sunday, Mrs. Sanders was a wife, mother, grandmother, great-grandmother, sister, aunt, cousin, and friend. It's difficult to understand how she was capable of being so much for so many and still make each person feel special, but she did. It simply amazed me that this little woman was capable of meeting so many challenges and always encouraged; always had a moment to talk and to remain non-judgmental, regardless of your lifestyle. She had a gift of making people feel welcomed at her home while at the same time conveying that she was a force to be reckoned with if you were disrespectful!

Life dealt Mrs. Sanders emotional blow after blow, but she remained strong, not allowing anything to get her down and not allowing the people around her to let anything get them down. When she was diagnosed with cancer, she didn't give the impression that life was over, she took whatever treatments she needed to take and continued to live life the way she wanted to. Nothing stopped her. Not the deaths of loved ones; a stroke or being diagnosed with cancer seemed to be able to shake this remarkable woman.

The plain and simple truth is that in spite of the many things that Mrs. Sanders had to endure during her life, she did so with style, class and grace. She was a phenomenal woman and it only took meeting her once to know that she deserved every ounce of the respect she commanded.

-Linda Brown

10th Anniversary Edition

The Power of a Mother's Love

"I have breast cancer and the surgeon has scheduled for me to have my left breast removed on Friday, March 5, 2010." My mother spoke these words to me on Wednesday, February 24, 2010 while I was driving home from work. There were other words spoken during that conversation, but truthfully I have no recollection of them because I immediately became numb and emotionally paralyzed within seconds as tears began falling down my cocoa brown cheeks from hearing the words *breast cancer* and *surgery*. After hearing the devastating news, I immediately got off the phone to try and gain my composure because otherwise I was going to end up in a terrible car accident. I thank God that when receiving the troubling news I wasn't far from home—actually I was around the corner.

After arriving home albeit dazed, I grabbed a Kleenex to wipe the tears from my blood shot eyes, said a quick prayer for strength and called mom back to get more details about what I had just been told and to comfort her. It was one of the hardest conversations that I've had in my entire life. During the conversation, truthfully mom ended up comforting me more than I did her because of my emotional state. I know deep down that I should have been more consoling, but I was just a basket case. Mom was doing her best to keep it all together even though I can only imagine how frightened she was about the battle that was before her.

Writing in my journal became one of my coping mechanisms, and proved to be of great help. Although I've been journaling for over two decades, I hadn't consistently done so in a long time until this situation occurred. Each time that I wrote down my thoughts about how I felt about mom's breast cancer, the emotional pain lessened and rather than wallow in the pain, I turned my focus to conducting as much research as possible to learn all that I could about this horrible disease in which women from all ethnic backgrounds have been diagnosed and unfortunately succumbed. In fact, according to the Centers for Disease Control and Prevention (http://www.cdc.gov), breast cancer is the common form of cancer in women aside from non-melanoma skin cancer. As for Hispanic women, breast cancer is the number one cause of cancer death. It's the second most common cause of cancer death in white, black, Asian/Pacific Islander, and American Indian/Alaska Native women. I found these statistics disturbing. Although it is not very common, men can also get breast cancer.

Armed with more information about breast cancer, I was more comfortable accompanying mom to see the oncologist on Friday, March 19, 2010. While at the appointment, the oncologist thoroughly explained mom's treatment options, and I asked various questions and was satisfied with the answers that were given. During the doctor's visit, I felt at ease that mom was in good hands, which was reassuring since I live approximately 180 miles from her and my father. Ironically, while leaving the doctor's office, one thing that came to the forefront of my mind was how I really discovered since mom's diagnosis and others finding out about it, just who my *real* friends were and what family members *genuinely* cared. It's interesting how God will reveal things to me *when* and *where* I least expect. And, this was one of those moments.

In general, throughout the whole ordeal, the research that has been conducted, the learning that occurred, as well as the above revelation, don't compare to the selflessness and power of a mother's love that has been reinforced for me. I now truly understand what it means to be a *true* hero. In my eyes, mom's heroism upon getting the diagnosis of breast cancer, preparing for the mastectomy, actually having and recovering from the surgery and considering the feeling of others while enduring everything was remarkable. As a result, I want to publicly acknowledge the hero in my life, Carline Newell Curtis! I love you mom!!

Carla J. Curtis

10th Anniversary Edition

QUIET SOLDIERS

Quiet **S**oldiers stop the silence
The lack of communication is creating division
Leaving us without fighting for answers and
Keeping us from spreading the message when
We need to unite, fight and use our sisterhood
To create bonds and safe havens in the hood
For if and when the enemy strikes again
We're prepared to help another sister-friend.

In the early 1980's, my sisters and I were called together at Stanford Hospital to be at my mother's bedside before her procedure. As memory serves, no explanation preceded the hospitalization. After my mother was released to come home she became sick. She couldn't eat, threw up what little she could muster down and started losing weight and hair. Helplessly, I watched and was unable to offer much assistance, under the circumstances, aside from a water glass refill, a small meal or some bedside adjustments. There was an eerie taboo about what she was going through.

No one seemed to talk about what was wrong with Mama. Mama didn't talk about what was wrong with Mama-not to me anyway. I didn't know what questions to ask. I'm what—22 years old and don't have a clue.

Weeks would pass as time assumed its sporadic chain of events. I watched Mama go from this weak state of helplessness to a butterfly unfolding in her later stages of life. She started regaining her strength and mobility. Her hair grew back and she rocked a cute little salt 'n pepper afro until it was long enough to press and ponytail.

Mama had a mastectomy on her right breast. They removed her entire breast, nipple and all. All that was left was a horizontal scar. Mama began fitting her bras with a pad and being a small size 'A' cup, she was able to match her other breast in form and size. She had to retire from her job but most of her activities that she enjoyed were resumed over time. Mama wasn't much on words about her seemingly near-death bout from my perspective. An avid reader, she would quite often clip articles out of newspapers and magazines to pass along to loved ones. Everyone was accustomed to checking the kitchen table for an article with their name hand written above the header. If you were going in another person's direction, you delivered his or her article and vice versa. I shared a laugh with my elder sister about Mama's form of teaching with these articles. I wish she'd just tell me certain things. My sister informed me that I was lucky because while growing up Mama had given her and our other sister a whole medical reference book to read. I saw it with my own eyes. That thing was about six inches thick! I sure learned to appreciate my articles, often taken for granted, after hearing that!

Passing along these articles was Mama's way of handing down some knowledge. Not having much to say about her story was her choice. I remember asking her years ago if she would tell her story. She declined at the idea. Mama, though she never talked about it, was nonetheless a warrior and an over comer at a time when there were no support groups, aftercare services, programs or even discussions amongst the sisterhood. I'm not even sure if there was an alternative to the medical choices that were made back then. Mama's return visits to the doctor over the following months reported cancer free results. Hallelujah! She led an active lifestyle for the next thirty plus years and lived to be eighty-two years old. The Taboo Factor would loom long past Mama's experience with breast cancer.

In today's information age and technology, we are still battling this horrible disease. Much has changed by way of advancements in the fight from medical treatment, after care services and prosthetics. Full clothing lines and specialty items can be found online. Groups form events and raise funds around the world. And still we fight. We, the sistahs, have yet another fight within the fight. The silence. The quiet soldier that fights the good fight of faith would benefit from lending to and garnering support from advocacy in the community. We have to engage ourselves in the information and have the discussions with our sistahs and daughters. We must take extra measures in the fight and make commitments to get our annual mammograms and encourage our sistah friends to do the same. Bring pamphlets back from your doctor's visits and share with each other. I can now look back and piece together Mama's events as close as possible but I have two daughters and if I don't share what I know and what measures I'm taking in detail, they will be left to piece it together too! The first question doctors want to know about females is most often about their mother's health. Due to my mother's experience, I was concerned early on about my breast care so I've been getting my mammograms annually since around age 40. Praise God I have never had any incidents.

My friend and contributor to this anthology, Elizabeth Udell, recommended I have a BRCA* Test. (BRCA1 and BRCA2 are human genes. Mutation of these genes are linked to breast and ovarian cancer) When she explained what it would reveal, I became extremely interested and contacted my doctor to request a BRCA Test for myself. Of course, now I need to have a consultation first and grit nearly even tooth in my head to influence the decision. I was reminded of the cost, nearly $3000.00, but I was stern. As much as the monthly premium cost to have insurance, it's time some were spent on me. I was not playing as the doctor hammered some other questions my way. Soon, he concluded that since 'I'm not sure' about how old my mother was when she had breast cancer; he would submit the referral to my insurance company.

I was grateful and pissed all at the same time. How dare they; I ruffled under my breath. I deserve this test and more. My daughters need to know! As I awaited the approval, I marveled at the idea that there was a simple blood test that could tell me if I genetically inherited a gene linked to breast and ovarian cancer. I also feared the answer in a way. Prayerfully, I did not carry the gene and thankfully this type of information would prove invaluable to my two daughters. The approval came in about a week and another two weeks or so after the blood draw, the results were in. Negative. HALLELUJAH!

The conclusions of my test results rule out my daughters when it comes to inheriting the gene, as well, but not my sisters. They would have to have their own test performed.

It's a good thing I had the test done then. I have since become unemployed and with losing the health care coverage I have sought free services through community programs specifically for women. An organization called, A Woman's Place in Santa Clara County gave me a referral to Mills Hospital in San Mateo, CA with a wing that services the needs of women and breast cancer. Completely free to me, I was very grateful that such a place existed and I was able to adhere very closely to my regularly scheduled annual mammogram.

Now, I have some articles of my own to pass along with much more information reflecting the signs of the time. I would like to encourage the sistahs to engage ourselves in living a better quality of life. Let's Stop the Silence when it comes to our health. Please.

-Beverly Black Johnson

Written in honor of Hilda Rose Noel ~September 19, 1924 ~ July 12, 2007. I love you, Mama.

* BRCA1 and BRCA2: Cancer Risk and Genetic Testing Source:
http://www.cancer.gov/cancertopics/factsheet/Risk/BRCA

I will take the time to renew and restore.
~Synthia SAINT JAMES

Forever In My Heart: Her Quiet Strength

"Honey, I need to talk to you right away," Mama's voice crackled through the phone. Missing was the lively "Hi, Trisha Ann," punctuated like the crescendo of a sweet harmony. This off key, monotone voice was not my Mama's. Her crisp chit-chat ranging from the spices in a pot of beef stew to Mrs. Jones' cat knocking over her pottery on the balcony was cut from the conversation.

Within an hour, I was sitting at Mama's kitchen table sipping coffee and nibbling on a piece of homemade pound cake. I studied Mama's smooth, ebony brown face, her high cheekbones and the scant creases in her forehead. Her medium length, black and gray streaked hair curled in small ringlets around her face. Age was merely a number for my seventy year-old mother, who relished life to the fullest in her latter years. Without a notion of what to expect, I was unprepared for the news that would drastically change our lives. I noticed her uneasiness as she stumbled through her words.

Erratic pulsations pummeled my chest wall and beads of sweat popped through my skin. Several deep breaths throttled my adrenaline rush and shock transitioned to pain, fear, and then anger. "Breast cancer! Why my Mama?" I asked God in my mind, knowing better than to question Him. "Don't worry baby, I'll be okay," Mama said, reading me like the fine print in a newspaper. Anger rapidly changed to humble pleas to the Lord to heal my closest friend and confidant. Grandmama lived until she was ninety-eight, so surely this must be a mistake, I thought. Then I remembered Mama telling me about a quarter-sized lump she had found in her right breast nearly two months earlier. She shrugged it off as nothing more than just a cyst and said the doctor would schedule a biopsy. The biopsy was done. She never told a sole about the biopsy or diagnosis until that day.

The oldest of seven children, Mama stood out as bold, outspoken, and cast iron tough. Often mistaken to have the temperament of a lioness, though caring and softhearted, she just refused to put up with anyone's foolishness. She quit school in the ninth grade, set off before daylight for the swelter in the cotton fields, cleaned houses, and worked other odd jobs to make extra money. A divorced mother of two children, she raised me and my brother alone. "Lord, please spare her," I silently prayed. My reverie ended when Mama poured another steaming cup of coffee. Sensing my hurt, she pulled her chair close; her crinkled hands covered mine before she asked about my 10 year-old son, Damon's next baseball game. Her quiet strength.

Mama kept her routine schedule. Her active life included monthly visits to her physicians, weekly trips to the Grand Central Market, a "turn around" trip to Las Vegas every other month, and our once a month shopping sprees. Mama's closet was fit for a queen and she cherished the wardrobe she had meticulously put together over the years. Suits, dresses, hi-heels, and other clothing, all in pristine shape, lined the racks and floors of her closet. Some items still wore price tags. Treasures that she could only wish for while growing up, now replaced the worn work clothes and one "good" dress for church on Sundays. Her golden mottos – "when you work hard there's nothin' wrong with rewarding yourself, but always place God first in your life." Those words of wisdom trickled down through the family like a waterfall from my grandmother to my mother, and then to all the children and grandchildren. Faith in God, strong work ethics, and reaching out to help others were the essence of their beliefs and values. I inherited the traits in the matriarchal chain and passed these valuable family gems to my own children.

Time sailed faster than a fading flame. The year seemed to end prematurely and changes had transpired during the course of several months. Mama started radiation therapy. Shortly thereafter, the daily intimate aroma of her southern cuisine dwindled to two days per week, once a week, and then to none. After spending the day in bed, she would often insist on helping me prepare dinner. Her low energy crises would bring moisture to my eyes, but I shed not a tear. Not in front of Mama. "Lord, please spare her," I silently prayed.

She always managed to rejuvenate within a couple of days and once again, take on the world. Damon's little league baseball games meant everything to her and she rarely missed that special event. She sat in the crowded stands munching on popcorn, proudly cheering for her grandson, who seemed to "energize" and play even better when she was present. Her quiet strength.

"Six months or maybe less. There's nothing more that I can do." I defiantly protested this prognosis. "How could this happen? Mama followed all of your recommendations," I said to her physician. His blank stare never wavered as he placed his hand on Mama's shoulder. "I'm so sorry, Mrs. Gentry." His only consolation was a referral to hospice, which Mama politely refused.

The physician's words replayed in my mind for days, evenings, and nights. Grief mounted deeper within my soul, burning the pit of my stomach. I called off sick for three days in a row while my brother stayed at Mama's house. I mustered just enough energy to rouse my son in the mornings, fix his breakfast, and send him off to school. After he left the house I spent hours in prayer as tears showered my pillowcase. As the days passed, the Lord gradually granted me solace and a change of heart. My vows included no more dousing in a dungeon of self-pity; no more bargaining, pleading, or blaming other people—just acceptance of God's will. Suddenly, I opened up and spewed out my hurt and pain to my spouse, friends, and family, anybody who would listen. At that point I received overflowing love and emotional support from all the people I had literally shut out of my life. "Lord, thank you for your grace and for my renewed strength."

When my brief hiatus from work was over, I returned to a desk piled with new projects that kept me busy for weeks. I stopped by Mama's place one afternoon and found her still in bed. While I rustled with pots and pans, she eased into the kitchen, sat at the table and began cutting vegetables for a salad. We gorged on smothered chicken, rice and gravy, green beans, and salad. Our chatter and laughter roared through the apartment for hours as we reminisced about our memories. Memories of my first day at a new elementary school and my embarrassment with wearing a pink ruffled dress with hair bows to match. Memories that made us laugh and cry. I knew it was coming, but I did not know when. She never asked what happened or why, but silently watched me for several minutes before she spoke. "You needed a little break, and you look better now that you're rested," she said, smiling. Her quiet strength.

Three months later, my phone rang. It was early morning, about an hour before dawn. My brother announced that Mama had peacefully passed away in her sleep. I closed my eyes, inhaled and exhaled before saying a silent prayer. "Lord, thank you for the time we had together, the ability to be of good courage, and for her quiet strength. Amen."

10th Anniversary Edition

The remembrance of my mother's strength, perseverance, faith in God, and her love for life and loved ones, keeps her spirit alive forever in my heart.

-Patricia A. Bridewell

Starr Power Pilates: Taking Back Your Physical Power...One Muscle At A Time

I have had the privilege to interact with hundreds of breast cancer survivors from all walks of life -women of all ages 30, 40, 50, and 60 years and beyond. I have worked with strong lean athletes, mothers who have infants too young to walk, beauty queens, non smokers, women too busy to take time for mammograms, women who have had regular examinations, smokers. No one is exempt from getting cancer.

I have taught and I have learned. I have laughed and I have cried tears of joy for the triumphs of determined women, with the will to live, diagnosed with breast cancer. I have drawn and gained much of my own capability and strength...from women who have managed to inspire others by giving hope while battling cancer themselves.

I have been commissioned by a higher power, to tap deep into my spiritual and physical "potential" to empower others to get in touch with their own body awareness...even with their respective limitations. After cancer surgery, radiation and chemotherapy treatments, exercise can play an important role in helping a person regain strength and fitness levels prior to surgery. In many cases, patients are able to progressively reach new heights in strength, flexibility and cardiovascular conditioning program.

I have been given the gift to create adaptive restorative strength and core training programs, for cancer survivors for flexibility, endurance, stamina. The cancer survivor program begin as a result of requests from healthcare providers and cancer survivors expressing concerns about rehabilitating the body through an adaptive progressive fitness program suitable for cancer survivors- six weeks operative- through full recovery.

You never know what is in store for you in life. The creator had a plan for me all along. You see...I am not only gifted in being able to work with cancer survivors through strength and flexibility programs. I have also been royally blessed to guide breast cancer survivors through a progressive restorative healing journey to the road of recovery. You never know what a cancer survivor has to endure unless you have experienced the disease. If you have never walked in a cancer survivor's shoes, you can only imagine the pain and the suffering when someone is given the news; no one wants to hear the devastating news that "you have the big C cancer word." You see...I have shared some of the experiences that my class participants have endured. I am a Cancer Exercise Specialist...but I am also a Cancer survivor.

To date, I am pleased to announce - hundreds of women have completed my Starr Power Pilates Program for Cancer survivors. These courageous women have excelled in proving the possibility of re-gaining strength, full range of motion through flexibility exercises and renewed energy through diaphragm breathing, standing and mat exercises.

The Concept of Starr Power Pilates for Cancer Survivors

The concept of Starr Power Pilates for Cancer Survivors is designed to introduce the participants to mind and body integration techniques. The strength-training program concentrates on the following principles: Centering, Breathing, Precision, Control, Concentration and Flow.

Starr Power Pilates for Cancer Survivors begins with a system of building blocks conveying the fundamentals and principles for each Pilates move from a basic to intermediate level. At the basic level, each participant masters reviewing and reinforcing alignment, breathing, adaptive and modification techniques before transitioning to the next level. Participants are encouraged to move at their own physical capability- all of the Pilates exercises are implemented in non- competitive slow systemic moves to ensure proper form and technique.

The powerful mind and body integration moves provides a gentle restorative exercise regiment, to get cancer survivors to progressively recover and rebuild their bodies. After completion of each session, participates often describe the movement session as a reawakening and energizing the body from head to toe.

Cancer survivors are often amazed how well and quickly their bodies began to respond to the slow, controlled movements. The upper body Pilates stretches are extremely beneficial in the recovery from mastectomy and breast reconstruction surgery. After a few sessions, participants experience increased muscle tone, lung capacity, enhanced flexibility and range of motion, while progressively gaining stamina and confidence to become functionally fit to enjoy a better quality of life.

Frequently Asked Questions about Cancer and Exercise

Q. What are the most suitable exercises for cancer survivors when starting a program?

A. Gentle Restorative Yoga, Adaptive Pilates Tai Chi, and water based programs are recommended for starting a fitness programs for post-operative cancer survivors. These mind and body integration exercises are ideal, because the movement places less stress on the muscular skeletal system while improving flexibility, muscle strength, balance, systolic blood pressure, cardio-respiratory fitness. As the participant becomes stronger, the movements from these exercises can be adapted to increased challenged levels.

Q. What is the best way to start to improve strength, motion, and reduced pain after breast surgery?"

A. Follow your physicians' recommendations immediately after surgery. Your physician may permit to start off slowly with gentle movements. Wall crawls with your hands will decrease stiffness of the arms and shoulders for postoperative -surgery.

Here's a time line factor and suggested exercises to help you get started:

Six weeks post surgery- This is the time to start to rebuild your strength and prevent more weakness in the upper body region. Try slow controlled palates movements to help improve muscular strength, and flexibility. Using the Pilates deep diaphramphic breathing technique- (inhale through the nose and exhale through the mouth) will help you to relax and helps for pain control. If you are feeling well enough, take a few steps daily to start the weight bearing to help keep good muscle tone.

Seven Weeks-Eleven Weeks- Try to take short walks without swinging the arms; swimming- using the breast stroke, and side stroke only (No back stroke at this point)

Twelve-Weeks —Add low impact activities, walking at faster than slower intervals- add exercises that will increase your flexibility and strength. Examples: Yoga, Pilates, Treadmill (low speed) Aquatics program (adding the back stroke). You may want to try a modified exercise program that will include flexibility, cardio respiratory (low impact) and strength training.

Note- Always check with your physician for medical clearance before engaging in any physical activity.

Q. Am I too old to start an exercise program after my surgery?

A. No. Exercise is the important vehicle to improve both physical and emotional health. There is always a physical activity that can be modified to suit your physical status. If you are breathing and able to move- there is an adaptive physical activity move for you. Anyone can benefit from moderate levels of exercise- young, mature, weak or strong individuals, and those rehabilitating from an injury.

A. When should people with cancer avoid exercise?

You should not exercise if you are not feeling well, feeling the effects from chemotherapy, pain, nausea, fever, dizziness, shortness of breath, low blood counts, heart problems.

Starting the Healing Journey

Find a quiet place in your own private space- where you can go to reflect, mediate, exercise and relax. Cry if you must and laugh if you can. It is cathartic for the soul and the body. Focus on centering yourself by concentrating on the calming effect of uniting your mind and body to create a serene balance throughout your day. Don't push yourself into doing too much too soon. Your body is a work in progress on the road to recovery. Rest as often as possible and move as much as you can to help strengthen and fortify the immune system. The body is a miraculous work of art so be good to yourself and have faith that *You Can Do It!*

Remember it takes one step to begin the journey. Take back your physical power one muscle at a time.

In Great Health,

-Starr Carson Cleary

Annie Pearl's Ballad

Dedicated to the entire Stinson/Haczynski Clan:

It raped my family. Ravaged our soul like no other. A tornado of destruction sullied the essence of our perfect dynasty. The beast kidnapped her body and was holding her captive.

The words seeped from him as he enunciated each and every dreadful word. It was crisp and normal that afternoon. Everything was at ease in the world until he said the unforgettable: *"Ma has cancer."* Those words were deep bellowing sounds that unearthed the worst in me. So much so, that I couldn't finish talking to my daddy, my hero. I dropped the phone as tears plummeted down my face. At that very moment, the phone was a metaphor of my spirit when it crashed to the floor and scattered to pieces.

MA HAD CANCER.

Annie Pearl, the eldest of her family, was born and raised in Valdosta, Georgia; she moved to Florida, where she met her soul mate, my father, Edward Stinson and they raised their own family of five beautiful and resilient children. Even though my mother is in her mid sixties, you would never decipher her age from her flawless skin and ageless smile. She was the ultimate nurturer for all of us. I remember how she would give her last of anything she had for one of us if we needed something—anything, just to ensure a smile on our faces. My mother's sacrifices did not go unnoticed because she bestowed those same selfless qualities to us, which are reflected in our own lives and professions.

The Cancer was a menace and it finally captured the matriarch of our family. We knew there was a possibility that Ma had the dreaded disease because she had noticed a lump in her left breast a few weeks earlier. It was hardened and the doctor did a biopsy on it. The possibility of that reality lingered in the back of our minds even though we did not allow it to take up permanent residency there.

We dreaded the day of announcement; it poisoned our thoughts which in turn, ignited a torch in form of the devil.

The devil sat at my desk and smiled at my brother and me while we mourned our present with the awful, awful news.

Ma had cancer.

We were clueless how to absorb it.

She lived two hours away and our business hours were in effect. My youngest brother, Brian and I owned and operated a Learning Center in Central Florida. We had teachers under our supervision, and many students scheduled for tutoring that day. Life continued even though we had just heard the worst news thought possible.

Time did not stand still—not even for us.

Classes were to begin in ten minutes so teachers started arriving to the learning center and preparing for that evening's tutoring sessions. Yet we sat paralyzed in my office—in a staring match with the devil. He wanted us to fall apart and shake us to the core. As the raptor, that was his duty to take our souls and dangle it for his amusement. The devil was in the business of making us feel and act sourly. But, he wouldn't win. Not that day or any other day.

As the older sister, I crumbled as my tears took over my body. I sobbed for my mother and the pain she was experiencing at the doctor's office alone without her entire family. We were so far away. Her children, whom she needed there with her, weren't there. My father, as papa bear, was deteriorating with each moment that passed. He was strong but when he heard the cracking of her voice; his wife of forty plus years, a small part of him was lost. He was not as strong on the inside as he portrayed on the outside, and indeed, he needed the combined strength of his children to help shoulder the burden that threatened the mortality of the matriarch of the family. He summoned us silently with his inward tears while he stood, magnificently, next to his wife and listened to the doctor's words spewed upon them. He listened attentively and squeezed Annie Pearl's hand to reassure her safety during his watch. Unrepentantly, my youngest brother, Brian, took the presence of the devil as a joke and superseded his existence with his own power. He stood up and spoke to me with great confidence.

"This is what we're going to do, Sharon. We will be there for Ma tonight but we have to make sure the teachers, parents and students do not know we're in turmoil. I am going to keep it together while you handle the Stinson business."

I dared not look at him due to the fear that I couldn't hold his glare without crying even harder. His words were so brave when I knew he shared our family's pain just as I did. I knew he wanted to curl up in a ball and cry but he didn't. I stared in silent admiration at his resiliency. Our mother's strength summoned him to make a decision and he did.

Assertively, he continued with his instructions and as our roles reversed, I obeyed my baby brother.

"You will leave now to go be with our family and I will run the business. Then tomorrow, we will switch off so someone will always be there with our parents. On your way to visit them, contact the rest of the family and make further arrangements."

I reached for my phone and realized it was destroyed earlier when I heard the dreadful news of Ma's cancer. With effortlessness, Brian unclipped his own phone and passed it to me with ease. My tears slowed down as my heart followed suit. In the background, I could hear the sounds of good-humored youths playing *Connect Four* games intertwined with the voices of our energetic teachers joking along with them. So much love was in the other rooms—oblivious to the mayhem that seemed to transmit throughout our souls in my office. The devil was a liar because from that moment, I felt my mother's arms wrap around me. She had instilled so many wonderful gifts within us, unbeknownst of the extent of them to me at that moment. The gift of faith was reopened in that instance because of her words said to me years earlier.

The memory flooded my mind like a gush of fallen rain on a hot summer day. Crisp and defined, the recollection conjured a smile on my face to contradict my swollen red eyes. I even remembered the smell of *Pine Sol* in the living room while we cleaned together. Our conversation replayed in my mind, which made me giddy. I remembered my mother's big, beautiful brown eyes and glowing light brown skin. Her persona simmered contentment in the midst of the mess we were cleaning. How was that possible--I remembered while reflecting upon her positive demeanor. How could someone be so blissful when the house was in disarray from a party we concluded earlier that evening; but my mother was just that—content.

"Look at this clutter in the house. There's junk everywhere. It's a hot mess just like society at times. But, at least we can clean this mess up! God will take care of the other messes. There is much chaos out there but, you know Sharon, chaos can be controlled when you walk on faith and believe in God's glory." My Mom said with ultimate authority.

I rolled my eyes and in my usual rebellious nature, I rebutted, *"Ma, Chaos can't be controlled—that's why it's called Chaos. There is no order so we have to MAKE order and take control. That's the problem with society and life in general."*

"So, you're calling me a liar, Sharon?"

10th Anniversary Edition

"No, Ma... I'm just saying...why would someone walk on faith in the middle of a chaotic time. That's when you have to act and do something to control it."

I stood my ground with certainty. I knew I had a point. Finally.

"But, Mama Boo, you are doing something. You're walking on faith. God answers prayers and believe me there is a reason for that chaos in the first place. It will be revealed to you when you have faith. You have to give your burdens to God."

"Whatever, Ma. I gotta get ready for school"

And to my surprise, I realized her point was much stronger than my own. She was right and I liked that. I admired my mother for being who she was with no regrets. She raised me to be the same way. I walked out of the cleaned living room and smiled because I felt the weight of her words. With faith, you can find calm in the midst of madness so I made a mental note and locked it away.

As I refocused on the present hour, God revealed that day would be the day I would unlock the same calmness to conquer the situation at hand. At that point, Brian had finished his game plan and started packing some items in my office. My heart still ached but I knew in a few hours, I would be in my parents' arms—comforting them the way they had always nurtured and comforted us.

For the next few months, my siblings and I did just that—comforted our family. Every few days, a designated sibling would visit our parents for moral support and everything else they needed. Life was more optimistic for us and every day, I made an effort to tell my mother how much I loved her. I needed her to hear me say those words to her even though, I knew she understood the depth of my emotions for her.

I also told her to 'walk on faith' and she beamed. She knew I wasn't as spiritual as she was but for that moment, when she saw the sincerity in my eyes—she knew that I was full of my own spirituality. A spirituality that was defined by my own faith and set of beliefs.

The first Chemo therapy session was the absolute worst. If I could, I would have exchanged my young, strong body with my own mother's feeble body. She couldn't handle those poisons. The chemotherapy left sores in her mouth, sores in her hair and long and horrible bouts of nausea. Ma couldn't taste anything because her taste buds were fried from the chemotherapy; she couldn't eat anything but baby food; and slowly, but surely, her hair had begun to shed. Who would want to see their mother deflated, weak and sickly? It broke my heart. But after every chemo session, one of the children and my father would join her and provide her some comic relief. Our family came together for a common cause; despite our internal differences, we were as one in our mother's presence. The company was therapeutic for Annie Pearl Stinson, my mother.

During the entire ordeal, I never saw her shed a tear or even whisper any type of negativity. Instead, she held fast to her faith, recited Biblical verses and blessed us with stories from the Bible. It was divine and serene to see my mom's faith shining through all of the madness---the chaos.

Since the chemotherapy made the lump small enough for surgery, Ma had to have her left breast removed. That scared us to no end. The breathlessness feeling returned and I believed the devil decided to reappear to arrest my thoughts. The devil wanted to hold me in his arms and embrace all that was unholy of the situation. When I felt the devil's presence, my knees buckled in fear. I did not want to give in to the powerful nature of the devil; he seemed to attack me and the tears started to flow as I felt my body retreating.

My mom sensed it and told the nurses to leave the room after they recorded her vitals. She instructed me, in the gentlest and calmest way that I'd ever witnessed from her, to sit next to her and close my eyes. My mother, my flower of love who birthed me, had spoken and I was to obey. Secretly, I wanted to crawl into her arms and sway like I was a baby but I knew that wasn't going to happen.

She told me in her soft caring breath,

"The devil is a liar. Continue to embrace your faith and leave the things you can't change alone. Give your burdens to God. Do that for your mama, please."

And with that, the devil was a puff of smoke from our lives. Sickly and frail, my mom still managed to handle her baby's problems. She has been a truly amazing woman who will forever be my inspiration. Without a doubt, I believed my mom's unbreakable will to survive and her venerable force to overcome breast cancer were the driving forces to her recovery. Her faith, bold and reassuring, was the catalyst to her embodiment of everything beautiful. God's unconditional love wrapped around my mother and she extended it to her own family. Her love never crumbled. Never shaken. Never doubted. My Mama was, and still is, the epitome of love.

That fall, the entire family gathered as we prepared for a celebratory dinner. My mom was going to showcase her falsie breast in a new outfit. The entire family was present. She was glorious in her smile with a sweet

10th Anniversary Edition

feminine swag that sent chills down my father's spine as he recalled why he still loved his wife of more than 40 years. She sported a black sequined hat—in the absence of hair—so her look was complete.

With her face glowing and her long flowing dress accentuating her entire body, I knew at that moment, my mother was going to be just fine. Breast Cancer is a beast that was demolished. The Cancer is in remission and Annie Pearl Stinson still continues to walk on faith. Don't we all? I know I do.

-Sharon Stinson Gray, M.P.A

Chapter II
~Poetic Gumbo~
Rhythmic Honor

I will take a restful moment
And make it my perfect moment.
~Synthia SAINT JAMES

"I Am" Said So

It called me—no time to acknowledge a monster— black, unhappy, alone, and always preying

Sunshine, cool breezes, cotton candy, Fruits of the Spirit—the greatest is love

Honeysuckle-scented supplications—mirror you and me—our raison d'être. "I Am" said so

My closet filled with consecrated remembrances

Exorcised purifications—I rejoice in preparation for battle with three

Flesh subdued, aligned, and suited-up—"I Am" and I merge as One

Undefiled, undefeated—TKO—certain

No bumps, lumps, or bruises—free—whole—and in perfect harmony

Yes—free—whole—and in perfect harmony!

-Audrey Forrest-Carter, Ph.D.

Your Strength

Your strength is not measured by how much hair is still on your head or by the breast that is no longer there. Your strength is measured by your inner beauty. It's the beat of your heart and the spirit of your soul that rises from within.

Your strength is not measured by the chemo that makes you sick and frail. Your strength is measured by your grace and dignity that always prevails.

Your strength is not measured by your doctor's diagnosis. Your strength is measured by your character. It's the way you nurture your family and friends, your warm embrace, or your gentle kiss reassuring us you will always be there.

Your strength is not measured by a moment in time. Your strength is measured by a lifetime of trials and tribulations, joys and triumphs that make you the woman you are today.

Your strength is not measured by the tears you shed. Your strength is measured by your faith for He shall wipe every tear from your eye.

And when your strength can no longer be measured or defined and the battle has been fought: come to me, all you that are weary and are carrying heavy burdens and I will give you rest. (Matthew 11:28).

-Lorita Kelsey Childress

The Battle

Sometimes the battle is just the beginning.
Sometimes the reason is unclear.
Sometimes the light becomes dark.
Sometimes the pain is severe.

Oftentimes, the question is "why me?"
Oftentimes, the answer is not clear.
Oftentimes, the reason is eluding.
Oftentimes, the journey seems unfair.

Just know…

You can find purpose in the fight.
You can find strength despite the weakness.
You can find faith in the unseen.
You can find courage in the dark.

A warrior lies within.
A prizefighter's soul emerges.
A lion's heart beats loudly.
A Queen's will to live will persevere.

-Kimberly Albritton

Women of Honor Full of Spirit and Light

You have been the blessing and the beast
The joy and the pain
The life taker and life giver
Different experiences felt the same

You've never defined the person,
Never blocked their spirit or their soul
You've only been the part
But never their whole

A small dot on a breast
Barely for the eyes to see
That grew changing the lives of many
To great uncertainty

One breast or two taken
Yet never her heart
Trying to chase away her dreams
Of hope and for a new start

But she stands in battle,
Pink ribbons worn
Her body may be tired
But her will carries her on

And if only for God's purpose
She should lose the fight
Cancer you only took her physical
You never dimmed her light

For those shining brightly
Survivors of the storm
We're here to remind

And carry on everyone's song

See my story's been my Aunts
Jackie, Marion and Gwen
One – won the battle
Two fought till their untimely end

Breast cancer has touched my family
In more than just one way
It has left its hurt, pain and sting
But we trust God for the new and brighter day

Breast Cancer
May I be so bold
To say I stand strong with others
Until all the her-stories are told
Stories of Women of Honor
Full of spirit and fight
Women of Honor
Full of spirit and light

-Pamela S. Rivers

I will believe in my limitless abilities.
~Synthia SAINT JAMES

Gumbo For The Soul

The Wisdom Keepers

We see Them everywhere--The Wisdom keepers

The Matriarchs of our lives

Guardians of Truth

Sisters to Love

Enforcers of Discipline.

The Ones Who raised us and kept us safe.

The Ones who said GOD is Always

And Love is GOD.

Our Idea of Strength when we were weak.

The Protectors of our self-respect, Who said,

"Let no one put You down, You are much more than that."

Gumbo For The Soul

We see Them everywhere

The Discoverers of the Lost

Teachers of Faith

Friends to Insight

Keepers of Wisdom.

The Wisdom Keepers--Who are They?

Your Mother and Mine.

-Vernon J. Davis, Jr.

10th Anniversary Edition

Abundant Love

Her touch and embrace
As she wiped the tears from my face
Holding me tightly and whispering, "It's going to be okay"
Cleaning the dirt away from my scars
I remember those days
When Mama would make everything feel like brand new
Between cuts, scrapes, bruises on my skin from falling on my knees yet again
Mom has a tender touch as she told me to hold on tight
The sudden burn disappeared as Bactine was sprayed on my wound
In between sobs saying, thank you Mommy
Always wiping away the pain; whether it was a scrape on my elbow
Or another love that didn't go
In the direction that I thought it would be
Times when I couldn't understand what was happening to me
Laughing now cause I was going through mere puberty
Causing her drama
But all mama could say was
Everything is going to be okay
Mothers have a way with words like no other
To this day I'm amazed of your strength and often wonder
How did we make it through
I love you
For being my warrior, knight in shining armor, pillars in my temple
Tending to my every sniffle, sneeze, fever, body ache and shiver
Raising all three on faith, hope, love
Reminding me that we were no one's charity case
I still hold tight to the memories
How you struggled to raise us
Yet no matter what jokes were made by cruel kids my age
You would stroke my cheek and say
Better days are coming our way
Somehow you managed to pull another smile out of me
Mama, my Iya, Sauti my love

Gumbo For The Soul

I can say on and on how much I love and adore you
Worship the ground you walk on and I feel
It still wouldn't be enough
Relationship like no other
Blessed to call and have you as my mother
God had a master plan and although times were tough
You made it work for us
And today
I salute and honor you and every other mother
By simply stating, I love you

"Dedicated to my mother, Marguerite "Sauti" Wills, and every woman of honor who has raised children, been an inspiration to someone or a role model. Thank you for your love. God bless."

-Serena Theresa Wills

Who Am I?

(Dedicated to my mom, Exie Goss and the rest of the Mothers)

I am a woman of class,
With a show of elegance a sense of pride
One that cannot and will not be compromised.

I am a woman with many degrees
Not speaking of formal education, but life experiences
That help developed me into what you now see.

I am part of the evolution, some might say revolution
With my innovation, yet sometimes filled with frustration
But still stand tall as one of God's finest creations.

See I am a woman of hope
Full of life's possibilities, trying to live up to my abilities
Not accepting what life is trying to offer me.

I am a woman in spite of the complications
Still moving with strong determination
To reach the highest regardless of the situation.

I am a woman filled with sensitivity
Not letting just anyone get close to me
Because positivity is what surrounds me.

That's Who I am.

— Shelia M. Goss

Mama

(Dedicated to my mother, Cora L. Franklin, and mother-in-law, Stella M. O'Bannon)

Of all the things we can recall
From birth to date, both big and small
What we remember most of all
Are memories of our mother.

She wiped our tears,
Calmed our fears,
Rendered patient, listening ears,
And for our sake
Forgave mistakes,
Made sacrifices mamas make
For children she must raise.

Our mom considered it a must
To go the extra mile for us—
A Christmas wish,
A goodnight kiss,
A bedtime tuck,
Our favorite dish,
A useful tip,
A weekend trip.
Our mother did so much.

And Mama knows the power of God.
She trusted Him to guide our fate,
Taught us prayers that built our faith,
Lives the life we imitate.
For that we sing her praise.

Today we celebrate you, Mother.
For each of us your life's been lived.
It's only right that we should give
Our love back in return.

-Karen Elaine O'Bannon

The BIG "C"

This deadly killer is on the rise
Cancer is its name
Fear takes over a family
As this illness terrifies the home and the land

It doesn't care who it claims
Instead it wants to leave its name
Cancer a surprise like no other
Claiming victims even your mother

A suffering illness it is
One we wish would go away
But unfortunately it's here to stay
Steadily lurking like a predator

Slowly victimizing people
Until they are no more
Cancer is its name
And there is none like it quite the same

-Donielle A. Smith

Woman of Faith

Someone great whom I recall
Was a lady, Mother Walls.
She wore white clothes every day.
Much about God, she would say.

A woman of faith she was.
She believed God just because.
She claimed a testimony:
Jesus could heal her only.

To God's goodness, she'd attest,
Sharing miracles with zest.
Though she often testified,
Her time arrived to be tried.

Her body put her to test;
Cancer invaded her breast.
It was the malignant kind.
Her health began to decline.

To her belief, she held fast,
Trusting this would soon be past.
It seemed Satan had control;
Her condition took its toll.

Her nipple had rotted so,
That it existed no more.
The disease grew so severe,
The end of life loomed near.

Still, God held the final say.
Here, He wanted her to stay.
God sent Bishop Woods along.

10th Anniversary Edition
He prayed God would make her strong.

By His power, God would move.
Her plight started to improve.
The destroyer had been beat.
Wellness returned to her teat.

She nursed two more babes with it.
Giving thanks, she never quit.
She spoke boldly without pause
'Til she died of other cause.

-Sylvia Larane Green

I will make a place in my life for love, peace and prosperity.
~Synthia SAINT JAMES

Black Women, Tired

Black Women, Tired
Black Women, Tired
Years of Tiredness
      Fighting, pushing, hoping
Tired!

Slavery, freedom, wifehood, motherhood
Tired!

Losing our identities and our children,
Tired!

Possessing years of tired!
      Our grandmother's tired,
          Our ancestor's tired,
              Sojourner Truth's tired,
            Rosa Park's tired,
                  Winnie Mandela's tired!
All rolled up into one Tired!

Working the fields,
Cleaning their houses,
Caring for their children,
Cooking their meals,

Rearing our children,
Supporting our men,
Holding together our families,
Helping our people,
Tired!

Can't you see it in our faces?
Don't you hear it in our voices?

Gumbo For The Soul

We can feel it in our shoulders.
Tired! Tired! Tired!

But we rise up
We stand tall
We march on
We work on
We carry on!

We overcome our tired!
We don't let tired keep us down!
We can't let tired keep us down!

Can't you see it in our dancing?
Don't you hear it in our singing?
We can feel it in our living!
Victory! Victory! Victory!

We replace our tired with Victory!
Years of Victory!
      Our grandmother's victory
        Our ancestor's victory,
          Harriet Tubman's victory,
            Marva Collin's victory,
              Maya Angelou's victory!
All rolled up into one ...Victory!

Black Women, Victorious!
Black Women, Victorious!
Years of Victory
    Fighting, pushing, hoping
Victory!

                                      Rolanda Pyle

10th Anniversary Edition

Threshold

Sixty! Oh, it can't be!
It seems that only yesterday
I was watching Howdy Doody.
No gala surprise soiree for me—
Choose to spend the day at Spa Chateau Elan
Pampered like Nefertiti.
Do not want the "how-old-are-you-now",
The usual chant at a party—
Sixty is a shock—I don't deny it.
So I jog; go to the gym; eat right
And give up tobacco--
 People say I don't look my age.
Upon this occasion thoughts turn to my Mom
Who never got to own the full bloom I now possess—
Forty-five when she died.
I could be *her* mother—consider:
Fifteen years beyond Mom's sojourn—
Missing not sharing in her seventy-fifth cycle.
Cheated out of all that time--
Abruptly stolen--leaving
Progeny she never got to know.
I cross this threshold for us both—
Mom would approve of where I am
And how I embrace this journey.
I will walk the path
Into my ripeness---feeling
Her presence gently brushing against me.

(At age 60, I wrote this poem to celebrate the life of my mother. Even though she passed away at a relatively young age, her positive, optimistic teachings have had an immeasurable effect on my life.)

-Bonita Sanabria

Mirror of Friendship

Let me be your mirror. Look here at what I see.
Step outside, let your mind take a ride, and see yourself through me.

I'll first reflect your beauty; show you the angel I see inside,
That gorgeous giving spirit who puts others before her pride.

See your figure in all its glory. Study every curve and feature.
Realize what's looking back at you; one of God's most brilliant creatures.

As you stand there face-to-face with the lady in the looking glass,
I want you to see her spark; a combination of grace and sass.

Lean in and look a little further. You'll see a woman staring too.
A woman of strength and courage who can do anything you choose!

I'll turn the mirror over and over then back again
Until your frown is flipped around and replaced with a grin above your chin.

Now look away from my mirror and into one of your own.
Look there and tell me if you can see the person that I've just shown.
Girlfriend, you are beautiful. Let no one (not even you) cause doubt.
I'll always keep this mirror. And when you need it, I'll whip it out.

Sabrina LaBord-Smalls

With Pride and Grace
In honor of Celina Davis Cargile
Thank you for teaching me about God's love and Word.

With pride and grace
None other can take your place

10th Anniversary Edition

More than a grandmother to me
I'll love you throughout eternity.
You showed your love
In your special, gifted way
In showing my love, somewhat the same
I have the honor of my first-born daughter
To carry on your name.

-Beverly Black Johnson

Gumbo For The Soul

Wisdom on my Sleeve

As we stroll arm in arm, I'm on a mental walk through
the fields of my dreams and the meadows of my memories.
I recall the stories, the lessons, the blessings, and all that you've taught me.
The seams of my moral foundation were handcrafted by you.
I remember the tales you told of those who were sold…of winters so cold
and how I came to be in the fold.
I am but a leaf on a limb of a branch that is rooted in you.
I was carved from the bark of your tree.
That's how I came to be.
I am proud to be fruit of your fruit and seed of your seed.
So today I walk with wisdom on my sleeve.
Every silver strand of your hair makes you lovelier and dearer.
Your testament, growing pains, heart aches, back aches, sweat,
blood, and tears bring me nearer.
Nearer to your struggles and the lessons you learned from your mother…
Your younger years working the cotton fields, and how you made it through…
Nearer to that five mile walk to school one-way each day
with a hole in the sole of your shoe.
You taught me that life's a journey and not a race.
And so today I am conscious to keep a slow and steady pace,
Pull my shoulders back and I smile as a smile graces your face.
And when that day comes for you to leave,
My heart will surely grieve,
But I'll be thankful for time well spent. The time you invested in me
and the person that I have come to be.
Thankful for all the knowledge that school and college couldn't teach me…
It was your words of wisdom and encouragement that reached me.
As we stroll arm in arm, I walk with wisdom on my sleeve.

I will believe in my limitless abilities.
~Synthia SAINT JAMES

Contributing Authors

Dr. Audrey Forrest-Carter's teaching career began in 1979 after earning a MA degree in English, with a concentration in Afro-American Literature from North Carolina A&T State University in Greensboro, North Carolina. In 1990, she garnered a PhD in English, with a concentration in Rhetoric and Composition from Miami University of Ohio, in Oxford, Ohio. In addition to publishing two juried novels, _The Wages of Sin_ in 2004 and _Judge Not!_ In 2005, Audrey is listed in Who's Who Among Teachers, Who's Who Among African Americans, Who's Who Among Americans, and Who's Who Among Executive and Professional Women. Currently, Audrey is the Interim Chair of the Department of English and Foreign Languages at Winston-Salem State University, where she teaches composition and literature courses.

Shelia M Goss is the author of the Essence Magazine and Dallas Morning News Best seller _My Invisible Husband, Roses are Thorns, Violets are True, Paige's Web_ and _Double Platinum._ Shelia has received numerous accolades over the years, including 2006 Infini's Outstanding Author, Literary Divas: The Top 100+ Most Admired African-American Women in Literature, Honorable Mention in a New York Times article and Writer's Digest article and the recipient of three Shades of Romance Magazine Reader's Choice Awards. Besides writing fiction, Shelia is an entertainment writer. To learn more, visit her website: www.sheliagoss.com.

Minister Mary Edwards is an ordained minister in Detroit and has been a community activist for more than 30 years; she is an author, book coach and editor. She is featured in "Who's Who is Black Detroit" for her publishing efforts. Minister Edwards is the founder of The Called and Ready Writers and Widows with Wisdom; she was Voted "One of the Most Influential Women in Metropolitan Detroit". Friends call her "The Holy Hookup Lady."

10th Anniversary Edition

Crystal Brown-Tatum is the CEO and President of Crystal Clear Communications; a Houston based advertising agency and public relations firm. Crystal is a San Antonio, Texas native and Honors College graduate of The University of Houston with a B.A. in Radio-Television. She is the author of a breast cancer memoir entitled <u>Saltwater Taffy and Red High Heels</u>. She is a three-year stage III breast cancer survivor.

Lorita Kelsey Childress lives with her husband in Northern CA. She has three daughters and a granddaughter. Lorita's first published work titled <u>The Path</u> is in the anthology, <u>Gumbo for the Soul: The Recipe for Literacy in the Black Community</u>. She has published first novel, <u>The Turning Point of Lila Louise</u>. You can visit her on the web at www.loritawrites4u.com or email her at www.loritawrites4u@yahoo.com.

Vernon J. Davis, Jr. has been writing poetry since the early seventies. He was first inspired by Langston Hughes's poem "Impasse", which started his journey and adventure into the world of poetry and the spoken word. Vernon's very first published poem, "Beautiful Black Woman" (the basis for his poetry book) was published in 1978 for a magazine called Black Forum. More poetry followed in other magazines like SoulWord and Dawn, a magazine supplement to the Los Angeles Sentinel, an African-American newspaper. Mr. Davis has also taught Creative Writing and recited his poetry in talent shows, church gatherings and open-mic forums. He is still inspired by and in awe of his idols: Langston Hughes, Nikki Giovanni and Maya Angelou. His creative collection of Love poems, <u>Love is the Beautiful Black Woman</u> is his first book.

Karen Elaine O'Bannon is the author of <u>A Song for You—Women's Stories in Rhyme, A Song for You—Parables and Pearls</u>, and is a contributing author of the anthologies: <u>Tal'i-tha cumi: Daughters Arise</u>, chief edited and compiled by Andrea L. Dudley and <u>Gumbo for The Soul: Here's our Child, Where's The Village</u>. She also writes monthly blogs for the internet newsletter The Soul of Louisville (www.thesouloflouisville.com). Karen resides in Louisville, Kentucky with her husband and great niece.

Rolanda Pyle is the Associate Director of the Relatives as Parents Program (RAPP) with the Brookdale Foundation. In 2004, she published her first book entitled *FINALLY*, a collection of her poems. She is a certified social worker. She attends Love Fellowship Church, NY in Brooklyn where she is involved in several ministries. Rolanda is a contributor to the first two, *Gumbo for the Soul* publications.

Donielle Smith is a freelance writer/poet of numerous poems, magazine articles, quotes, greeting card verses, and eight stories that have been converted into books. She presently resides in the state of Louisiana. In her journey as a writer, she has written about a variety of topics such as: life, relationships, money, spirituality, infidelity, economy, war and much more. She has featured work on her blog at http://www.donarie.xanga.com/weblogs including publications featured on www.justsaynotomarriedmen.com,

www.articleshow.com/Relationships/Domestic-Violence/love-that-is-deadly and many other publications throughout the web.

Bonita Sanabria was a contributor for both of Gumbo's earlier anthologies. She composed her currently featured poem to celebrate the life of her mother. Even though her mother passed away at a relatively young age, her influence on Bonita's role as a successful woman was immeasurable. In addition to her writing, Bonita continues to enjoy her work as an amateur artist. She also remains an active volunteer in the fields of the arts and diversity training in Atlanta.

Sabrina LaBord-Smalls was born in Augusta, Georgia; the third of four sisters. She was left in the care of her maternal grandmother from the time she was just three months old. After losing her grandmother to cancer in 2000, Sabrina found herself writing poetry as a means to cope with the flood of emotions she experienced. Today, she is a wife, mother, and a soldier in the United States Army. She continues to write and aspires to become a schoolteacher after retiring from military service.

Patricia A. Bridewell is a native of Los Angeles, California. She earned an Associate of Science in Nursing from Los Angeles Southwest College, a Bachelor of Science in Nursing from Holy Names University, and a Master of Science in Nursing Education from Mount Saint Mary's College. She is a registered nurse and adjunct nursing professor for California State University – Dominguez Hills and West Coast University.

Her first Christian Fiction novel, *Reflections of a Quiet Storm*, was published by Xpress Yourself Publishing on March 10, 2009. She is currently working on her next novel. Contact information: www.patriciabridewell.com

Starr Carson Cleary is a Corporate Lifestyle Wellness Consultant, Cancer Exercise Specialist, Master Fitness Motivational Trainer, "Empowerment through Movement Seminars" Advanced Power Pilates Instructor, and Cancer Fitness Specialist. She is also an author - *A Woman's Guide 30 Days to A Better Body*, and DVD Producer-Starr Power Pilates and Wellness Event Promoter.

Serena Theresa Wills was born and raised in Queens, New York. After receiving her Bachelor of Arts Degree in Public Policy from Syracuse University she relocated to Alexandria, VA where she completed her Master's degree in Public Administration from Virginia Tech. Serena currently resides in Dallas, Texas. Her publication credentials include being a contributing author for *Gumbo for the Soul, Here's Our Child Where's the Village* edited by Beverly Black-Johnson, *Have a Little Faith*, edited by Vanessa Miller and *How I Freed My Soul Volume 1*, edited by Khadijah Ali-Coleman of Liberated Muse. Serena is also featured in an upcoming artistic compilation titled *Angels of Nightmares* by ArtLoveMagic, which is a book that intertwines poetry/prose with artistry such as paintings, photography and more. Serena is also a poet/spoken word artist and plans to publish her poetry book entitled, *Pieces of Life*. Check out her poetry, stories and event updates on
   http://divinewryte.blogspot.com.

H. Renay Anderson has lived in the Austin, Texas area for more than 20 years. She is originally from the Bay area of Northern California. She has Bachelor's in Management/Marketing and a Master's degree in Organizational Management. She wrote her first book in 2003; *The After Party: Why Women Wear Shoes They Know Will Eventually Hurt Their Feet?*; In 2006 and 2007, she contributed to three Anthologies; *Chicken Soup for the African American Woman's Soul*; *How I Met my Sweetheart*; and *Gumbo for the Soul: The Recipe for Literacy in the Black Community*. In 2008, she contributed to *Gumbo for the Soul:*

Here's Our Child~Where's The Village? She has written reviews for Bella Online and for BBW Reviewers. Writing has always been an outlet for her. She often refers to the quote "The ultimate of being successful is the luxury of giving yourself the time to do what you want to do." Leontyne Price, 1976.

Carla J. Curtis is the author of *A Single Woman's Parenting Journey: Survival Tidbits*, *Grip the Rope: Prayers for Single Mothers* and *A Date with Jesus: A Woman's Guide to a Closer Relationship with the Lord*. Women from all walks of life can be blessed by reading Carla's inspirational books that have become wonderful bedside keepers for some of her loyal readership. Carla holds a B.S. in management and a M.S. in managerial leadership. She is the mother of one daughter, and grandmother of two granddaughters and one grandson. Carla enjoys spending time with her family and friends, reading, writing, playing the piano and traveling. She currently lives in a suburb of Chicago, Illinois. To find out more information about Carla, please visit her web site at www.carlajcurtis.com.

Yvonne Singleton Davis is an educator, masterfully working with at-risk children in the New York City public school system. Her excellent style of teaching has been studied by novice and experienced teachers alike. She has a gifted ability to connect with children of all ages, which is unprecedented, and highly revered. She uses her extensive research of the African Diaspora to help students develop an appreciation of their heritage while bringing the cognizance of self, full circle. She was a featured educator in a past documentary of WABC's "Like It Is." She is the author of the powerful, eye-opening book, Teachers Under Siege, and is the Founder & CEO of *Sister to Sister: One in the Spirit, Inc.,* a 501(c) (3) not-for-profit empowerment organization for girls and women of color. She currently resides in New York City with her husband, Wesley Davis.

Elizabeth Udell is an aspiring writer and breast cancer survivor. She shares her message of strength and faith in the hopes that others will so that others will find comfort in the midst of pain.

Sylvia Larane Green, the poet/author of the inspirational collection of poems, Gift of Life, has been composing inspiring verse for family, friends, and others for about 20 years. She began writing poetry in her late

10th Anniversary Edition

teens when she accepted Christ into her life and made a conversion from creating secular rap lyrics. Her book, *Gift of Life*, is available at www.amazon.com and her official website is www.sylvialaranegreen.com.

Sharon "Shaye" Stinson Gray has a Bachelor's of Art Degree in English from Palm Beach Atlantic University in West Palm Beach, Florida and a Master's Degree (M.P.A.) from Nova Southeastern University. She is co-founder and co-moderator of an online writing group called *Essentially Woman* and served on the Editorial Staff for all of the Gumbo For The Soul Anthologies as well as served as Editor-in-Chief of Style-ology Magazine and Bahiyah Woman Magazine. With her passion for words and love of children, she entered the teaching profession in 1998. She currently owns and operates Sylvan Learning Center of Fort Pierce, Florida (www.fortpiercesylvan.com).

Toni Beckham is president and CEO of PR, et Cetera, Inc., a full-service public relations and marketing communications firm. The company serves the communications needs of small public, privately held and non-profit companies and organizations throughout the San Francisco Bay Area and beyond. Toni's professional communications experience also includes 12 years as Investor Relations Manager for a Fortune 1000 Silicon Valley company, and eight years as writer and Corporate Communications Director for CityFlight Media Network. Toni is a proud literary contributor to the first award-winning Gumbo for the Soul anthology series, "Gumbo for the Soul: the Recipe for Literacy in the Black Community." www.pretcetera.com

Linda Brown was born in San Francisco, raised in Menlo Park and East Palo Alto, CA. She's a recovering alcoholic and heroin addict with 16 years of sobriety. As a result of her addiction, Linda served 10 years in and out of various county jails, state prisons and drug rehabilitation programs. Because of her desire to give back to the community, Linda has been a community organizer since 2003. She is a member of "All Of Us Or None," one of the fastest growing and effective grass-root organizations, committed in the struggle of working for the rights of those who are currently incarcerated and restoring the rights of those formerly incarcerated. Besides being a wife, mother, full-time employee and part-time community activist, Linda is also in the process of establishing a foundation called, "I Am My Siztahs Keeper", which will address the needs of HIV positive women with children.

Lorraine Elzia is an Editor, Award Winning Author and Ghostwriter. With stories in seven anthologies, two novels, several co-authored/ghost written books, co-owner in *Eve's Literary Services* and co-moderator of *Essentially Women*; a writing group for African American Women, all to her credit on her writer's resume of five years; Lorraine is proving herself to be a breath of fresh air in the literary field. Her debut novel, *Mistress Memoirs* released in 2009 by Peace in The Storm Publishing, received stellar reviews and allowed Lorraine to be the recipient of the AALAS *Break Out Author* of the year award. *Ask Nicely and I Might* is Lorraine's sophomore novel and is a continuance of her desire to present stories to the world that not only entertain, but have a message to tell as well. Visit Lorraine at www.lorraineelzia.com.

Kimberly Albritton is an aspiring writer who resides in Raleigh, NC. She is hoping to release her first children's book and collection of poetry in 2011. She is the creator and organizer of a writing group called, The Mahogany Experience. Feel free to visit the group page at www.meetup.com/the-mahogany-experience-writing-group.

Beverly Black Johnson is the creator of Gumbo for the Soul and she hails from San Francisco, CA. Look for her autobiography, *A Wretch Like Me* coming soon. www.beverlyblackjohnson.com.

10th Anniversary Edition
Helpful Resources Section

Association of Cancer Online Resources: cancer information system currently offers access to 99 electronic mailing lists and a variety of unique websites. www.acor.org

Breast Cancer Action (BCA): Breast Cancer Action carries the voices of people affected by breast cancer to inspire and compel the changes necessary to end the breast cancer epidemic. Their site is full of information you will be hard-pressed to find anywhere else. www.bcaction.org

Breast Cancer Classroom Screen: www.lbl.gov/Education/ELSI/screening-class-activity.html

Breast Cancer Fund: In response to the public health crisis of breast cancer, the Breast Cancer Fund identifies – and advocates for the elimination of – the environmental and other preventable causes of the disease. www.breastcancerfund.org

"Breast Cancer Lighthouse" Listing of personal interviews of women who have had breast cancer. www.commtechlab.msu.edu/products/bcl/index.html

Community Breast Health Project with a Web site devoted to breast cancer, this local organization provides information and support to anyone touched by breast cancer. All services are provided free of charge. www.cbhp.org

Breast Health Access for Women with Disabilities: www.bhawd.org

Lymphedema Web Page: www.lymphnet.org

Make a Splash for the Women's Cancer Resource Center! Help celebrate the 20th Anniversary of the Women's Cancer Resource Center by swimming in honor or memory of friends, family and loved one with cancer – so WCRC can continue to provide all women with cancer -- including women of color and women from low-income communities --

with free cancer resources, services, and support and advocacy. The Swim will be held at the Trefethan Aquatic Center at Mills College in Oakland on October 7-8, from 10:00 a.m. to 4:00 p.m. For complete registration information, please call 510-601-4040 Ext. 180, or register online at: http://www.wcrc.org/swim/index.htm

Sisters Network Inc.
A National African American Breast Cancer **Survivorship** Organization.
http://www.sistersnetworkinc.org/index.html

Susan G. Komen Foundation, www.komen.org

Susun Weed: Breast Health! The Wise Woman Way: By Susun Weed is for women who want to maintain breast health and for women diagnosed with breast cancer. This site empowers women in their health care choices. www.breasthealthcancerprevention.com

10th Anniversary Edition

Co-compiled by Bruce George and Beverly Black Johnson
Foreword by George C. Fraser

Co-compiled by Bruce George and Beverly Black Johnson
Foreword by George C. Fraser
Edited by Gift'd Ink and Eve's Literary Services
Front cover artwork, Fatherhood© Synthia SAINT JAMES
Golf photo taken by and of Homer Joe Black, Sr. ©Beverly Black Johnson
Represented by PR et Cetera, Inc.,
a Bruce George Media vision

www.brucegeorgemedia.com
~ Shedding Light On Life ~
www.gumboforthesoul.com

© 2011 Gumbo for the Soul Publications

Proverbs 10:14 -Wise people treasure knowledge but the babbling of a fool invites disaster.

10th Anniversary Edition

Gumbo for the Soul
Men of Honor – Special Cancer Awareness Edition
Copyright ©2011 by Gumbo for the Soul Publications

All rights reserved. No part of this book may be used or reproduced by any means, graphic, electronic, or mechanical, including photocopying, recording, taping, or by any information storage retrieval system without the written permission of the publisher except in the case of brief quotations embodied in critical articles and reviews.

Gumbo for the Soul Publications may be ordered through booksellers or by contacting:
Gumbo for the Soul Publications
www.gumboforthesoul.com
Because of the dynamic nature of the Internet, Web addresses or links contained in this book may have changed since publication and may no longer be valid. The views expressed in this work are solely of the author and do not necessarily reflect the views of the publisher, and the publisher hereby disclaims any responsibility for them.
ISBN: 978-0-9790-4793-0

Printed in the United States of America
Gumbo for the Soul Rev. Date 09-22-2011

Back cover photo © Beverly Black Johnson.
Photo credits: Michael Jackson per media pool rights granted Pearl Jr. Desmond Tutu, Lowell W. Perry, Sr.: Wikipedia.
Photo Editor: Zaji @ www.creative-ankh.com

10th Anniversary Edition

Dedication

In loving memory of Homer Joe Black, Sr.
An anthology of literary offerings honoring men
and supporting the fight against ALL cancers that affect men.
Gifted to Project Fatherhood | Los Angeles, California
in honor of the late Dr. Hershel K. Swinger.

"Project Fatherhood and Children's Institute, Inc. is excited about the possibilities of this new resource to heighten awareness. This consciousness raising will make a huge difference for generations to come and we're excited about being a part of it." Dr. Hershel Swinger, 2009 - founder of Project Fatherhood.

This book is inspired by Bruce George Media. Mr. George's vision for a platform that honors women led to the birth of Gumbo for the Soul: Celebrity Moms (under development) and Gumbo for the Soul: Women of Honor ~ Special Pink Edition, bringing forth this counter-part, Gumbo for the Soul: Men of Honor – Special Cancer Awareness Edition.

Gumbo for the Soul: Men of Honor – Special Cancer Awareness Edition – seeks to heighten awareness in the fight against ALL cancers affecting men; with great emphasis on prostate cancer awareness. Testicular exams are extremely vital and should be included in a male's annual physical examinations while monthly self-examinations are recommended by age fifteen. This is the kind of information we are carrying while honoring our fellow *Men of Honor* who may not have been necessarily affected by cancer, but have made a difference in the world as a whole.

This toast is for you, the *Men of Honor* who have touched the world, leaving your embedded footprint of valor and courage, stamped forever-- unchanged by time, upon the face of this planet. You've faced unkind conditions, assaults on your life, liberty, and pursuit of happiness; and yet you've stood boldly in the face of extreme adversity and unkindness to pave the way for all brothers of every nation. Your spirit is etched in the hearts and lives of many, including the contributors, both men and women, who have converged to pay this special tribute in recognition of you.

A percentage of the proceeds from this book will benefit Project Fatherhood.

We appreciate your support and hope you enjoy this serving of Gumbo.

My job as a social activist is to co-create movements to tell our story.

-Bruce George

10th Anniversary Edition
Foreword

By George C. Fraser

When I was asked to write the foreword to *Men of Honor*, I had to ask myself what single man would I say attributes most to my success? To whom would I pay tribute to being there for me? Being separated from my biological father at an early age and growing up in many foster homes, one might think I am at somewhat of a disconnection, but save for the Man above; I am most familiar and very much in tune with the man within.

I grew up with a deep sense of self-worth despite the uncertainties of my future. Against the better judgment of the school advisors who said quit and concede to failure, and regardless of the barriers I faced because of the color of my skin, I still believed in me. I refused to allow my lack of access or finance, kill the spirit—the man—that deep inner person that unequivocally believed I had the strength to persevere and beat the odds. I took the chance to invest in me. I knew that if I put God first, all things were possible. I pressed hard to overcome the obstacles in my way. I decided I was worth the struggle to meet the high demands to excel physically, psychological and spiritually. I developed a rule of value and purpose for every move I made. I knew hard work multiplied by time would make room for my gifts. Rather than dwell on the things I lacked, I chose to tap into my full potential. *What say the naysayers now?*

Today, black men, it is time to step up to the plate and take your rightful positions regardless of the cards that are dealt you, stacked against, or taken from you.

Against all odds, we have survived as a people of men and women, worthy to be honored, that have given their lives freely, so that we may have a better one. Men and women of greatness, too numerous to name, that we are collectively, connected to. The seeds planted inside each and every one of you, has already been equipped with the power needed to give birth to success. You have the potential to do life-changing, wondrous things. The debt has been paid, the time was yesterday and the final hour is at hand. It's time for black men to be real men as head of your households, providers for your children, educators in your schools, and leaders in your communities. The work of Project Fatherhood is to be commended for addressing these important issues and connecting men to what matters most. They have reached many but there are masses that remain in need. Supporting the efforts of Project Fatherhood and this book is one place to start if you want to help. Brothers, be encouraged to seek out that *Man of Honor* in you. Push beyond the stereo-typical media images that paint a picture of mediocrity over your life. Take charge of your health, family and finances. Consider going back to school to further your education and pursue your endeavors. Seek out advice and resources in the areas you are lacking in. Invest and believe in yourself. Had I listened to the "haters," I would likely have lived a street life, on a joy ride, down a road leading straight to hell. Instead, I have many accomplishments of which I am extremely grateful for. Mopping floors at night to put myself through school is one of them.

While we still have so very far to go, we can be encouraged by how far we've come. Had those before us not carved out a path to follow, we would not be where we are today, charged with the task of laying a foundation for our future generations. For that, I am honored.

What say you?

~George C. Fraser
Author of *Success Runs In Our Race, Click* and *Race for Success*

10th Anniversary Edition

"A daughter is a reflection of her father in the relationships that she seeks."

~Bruce George

Legacy of Honor

Homer Joe Black Sr.

Legacy of Honor - Homer Joe Black, Sr.

Life hasn't been the same
Since the day HE called your name
But I've managed to maintain
HE gives me strength and keeps me sane.
I miss you so much Daddy, words can't even explain
When I heard the unexpected news, I all but went insane.
The events that followed, keeping God in the midst
Pulled us together and got us through all this.
We celebrated you with style, praise dancing in the aisle
Cried, laughed, shared and hugged
Concluded outside releasing white doves.
I'm now standing in a world on my own
Life has taught me to be courageous and strong

10th Anniversary Edition

I guess it's all preparation for my destiny
For I have been handed the torch of your legacy.

In loving memory of my Daddy, Homer Joe Black Sr.

Thank you for being my rock. You taught me how to be strong and strive for what I want out of life. You saw my dreams the way I see them, and was always inquisitive about what was going on with me. Not a day goes by that I don't talk to you and look at your pictures. The proud gleam in your eyes at our first *Gumbo for the Soul* event will be forever etched in our hearts and minds. I love and miss you dearly. Thank you for giving me the money, marketing, emotional, and promotional support to launch *Gumbo for the Soul*. I'm honored to say it all began with you and your legacy continues.

~Beverly Black Johnson

Dear Pa-Pa,

First and foremost I want you to know, I love you, and I respect you for who you are to me.

A part of you lives in me and I will continue to represent every day I have left on this earth. You are one of the main people that helped to mold me into the man I am today.

You were the one who introduced me to the game of Chess, and photography, as well as late model cars.

I consider myself a man of many thoughts and few words; which I feel may be from your direct contributions and the many talks we've had.

The thought process that goes into playing a decent game of Chess can be infinite and a picture is worth a thousand words.

A lot of people are not fortunate enough to have somebody introduce them to positive pastimes that stick with them as they grow older. I have these two because of you.

I want to thank you for being a solid role model in my life, for being a man who voices his ideas, and takes action to see them come to reality.

I want to thank you for being my Grandpa, for being a true *Man of Honor*, and showing me the way. I'm representing till the day we meet again. I love you, Khaliid.

~Khaliid Bean

10th Anniversary Edition

Reflections

I met Homer in 1980...in Oakland, California. He offered to be my tour guide after recently moving from Illinois.

He was into physical fitness and I had the pleasure of visiting some of the most beautiful parks with him as we jogged and got to know each other. Homer, whole heartedly believed in entrepreneurship...he had been a general contractor once, building homes and his aspiration for productivity never waned through the years.

He was a no-nonsense kind of guy who believed that each day was precious and should not be wasted. He believed that integrity, honesty and enthusiasm were important in selling a product. He displayed those unique qualities in selling, Aloe Vera juice. He would use his 'fit' physique and good health to attest to the potent qualities of the juice.

Homer never told his age...his energy and zest for life kept him young, by far. On our numerous walks, he would talk about his children, a boy, Homer, Jr. and his daughter, Beverly. He preferred for you to just listen and not question when he spoke of them. I would listen, for I had children and could always learn from his wisdom. His family was the wind beneath his wings!

When he mentioned his son's death, I can still see the sorrow that watered his eyes!

I remember times when we would cut our exercise routine short so he could go tend to the needs of his mother who was in a nursing home. I was very impressed and never minded the interruption.

Homer, in the end, accomplished what he set out to do, and that was to be a role model, a motivator, a father and a grandfather with a winning attitude toward his daughter, Beverly, and his grandchildren. The apple doesn't fall far from the tree...Beverly is definitely her father's daughter!

~Donna Dortch

Gumbo For The Soul

10th Anniversary Edition

"MR. WILLIE SMITH"
Papa Sodie
My Grandfather…The Matriarch

M -   *Man of Honor*

My grandfather, Papa Sodie, raised his three daughters (one being my mom), along with his wife (my grandmother), Mama Ruby, with dignity and respect right smack in the middle of depression ridden 1930's. Suffering a horrific accident at a sawmill in segregated Louisiana, his head was split open by a saw and yet, he was refused medical treatment at a white hospital. He survived the night by people wrapping sheets around his head until morning. For the rest of his life, a gash on his forehead for the rest of his life was evidence of his ordeal. From then on, he vowed to make his own way, erecting a store right next to his house affectionately called the "Shack" which was his way of providing and protecting his family.

A -   Adventurous

Willing to leave the familiar confines of the South and venture out to California to start all over as an adult, he was armed only with what was the equivalent of a third-grade education.

T -   Trustworthy

Papa Sodie was a man of integrity who said what he meant and meant what he said, always clear, no confusion.

R -   Respectful

He did not have to raise his voice to make a point or use profanity to emphasis it.

I -   Innovative

One of the first in his community to own a business, home, car, and television; almost unheard of in the rural South where racial challenges were at its zenith.

10th Anniversary Edition

A - Available

If Papa Sodie said he would be there, if anything he would be early, you could count on that. I grew up with that comfort and privilege.

R - Regal

Tall and elegant, comfortable in working pants and shirt, but could switch to three-piece suit, hat and matching shoes with ease-a stylish man.

C - Courageous

Willing to put his life on the line for his family, he never allowed any man to be disrespectful to him or his family, even in the ethnically challenged South.

H - Holy Man

Through all that he went through, he refused to be bitter. He spent countless dollars on the work of the Kingdom. I remember him coming to get me to show me the land Faith Missionary Baptist Church would be built on. He was so proud; it stands on Runnymede Avenue in East Palo Alto, California today, with a plaque dedicated to him and my grandmother.

This is the example I have been honored and privileged to witness--Papa Sodie, a *Man of Honor*. I hope this encourages men and women facing challenges to be inspired and know you can overcome and be victorious too.

To God Be The Glory,

~Marvin Bean

Honored Vows

A mutual decision you and I made;
that we would share our lives
together, come what may.
Before God, family, and friends;
with love, and commitment, in a covenant agreement
we took one another's hand.
On that day and the years that went by,
we remained one together and with God;
you and I.
Loving, respectful,
faithful and true; our fate was
sealed the moment we said, *I do.*
Through ups and downs, the downs
being few; we honored and kept our
vows as God intended us to do.
I held your hand, heard you sigh,
as you took your last breath
and I said goodbye;
gently touching and closing your eyes.
As your spirit soared, I remained strong;
knowing the children
and I must journey on.
God answered my prayer,
you're healed and without pain.
He gave me beauty for ashes as we scattered your remains.
So enjoy the fishing!
We'll be ok.

In loving memory, My King ...Your Queen.

~Kelli Garden
This poem is in memory of my husband, Levon Garden, who died of colon cancer on October 28, 2006.

10th Anniversary Edition

Love Heals

Monica's left hand rested on a mound of green seedless grapes nestled in her lap next to a book she was reading while munching. I stared at cars vanishing into radiant heat waves on the horizon. She avoided looking at empty scenery populated with disappearing highway markers and swallowed.

"Do we have anything cool to drink?" I asked.

"What was that?"

"Do we have any cool drinks?"

"Wouldja like water, juice, or a soda?"

"Give me a *Coke*."

Monica reached into the small cooler next to the door. She opened the can while she protected her manicured fingernails, and wrapped a napkin around its base. I reached toward her fingers which were red-tipped with pink stripes. Our hands met above the stick shift, where she gave me the sweating can. I took a long sip, and then wedged it between my legs, never breaking my concentration from the highway.

"What're you reading?" I asked.

"An anthology of poetry from *American Negro Poetry*," she said. Cool air danced around her face.

"Would you like to hear one?" she asked.

"Sure."

She flipped through a few pages before stopping and clearing her throat.

Because I had loved so deeply,

Because I had loved so long,

God in His great compassion

Gave me the gift of song.

Monica looked at me, and then continued:

Because I have loved so vainly,

And sung with such faltering breath,

The Master, in infinite mercy,

Offers the boon of death.

(Poem by Paul Laurence Dunbar, from *Lyrics of Sunshine and Shadow*, published 1905.)

Gumbo For The Soul

The vintage 164E Volvo's smooth vibration lulled her to sleep, and I reached for the grapes near her thighs, engulfed in the tan leather seat. She awoke, staring at me—the man who took her grocery shopping and gave her Saturday rides from Oakland to the *San Francisco African American Cultural Society*, where she was the Executive Director. I became more than a volunteer worker; and in 1991, eight years later, we were married. We were in our early forties and it was the first time for both of us.

Four years later, shortly after turning 45, my tongue was sewed to the floor of my mouth for my first tongue cancer treatment. A month later I endured weeks of radiation therapy, which made swallowing difficult. Food had no taste and fifty pounds melted away from my body effortlessly. I was incarcerated in a starving body, tormented by food's aroma, too weak to play with our one-year-old son, Charles.

Eighteen months later I underwent surgery for neck cancer. Monica's love lifted my spirits and gave me strength to kiss Charles' chipmunk cheeks. His preschool teacher thought we were his grandparents and when he was five, the red glow from the fireplace reflected off Monica's face while she read aloud a children's book about adoption to him. His big brown eyes wandered before his attention focused on the flames. He didn't seem to care about the animal characters in the story. Monica gave me a perplexed look and then told him that, "Just like Fuzzy Bear, you are adopted."

Thirteen years later I had surgery for prostate cancer; however, the summer before the diagnoses we attended a family reunion. Afterward, we visited my mother's grave and our rental car hydroplaned en route as sheets of rain flushed away views of the trees' green canopies, and darkening clouds hid the daylight. Lightning lit up the sky, but that didn't faze Charles. Now a teenager, he stayed glued to his electronic game's flashing screen. Monica's voice crackled, and I pulled off the road. Unlike our first trip, we had no grapes to share as rain pelted the car. Our breath fogged the windows, and a crescendo of thunderclaps finally scared Charles. He dropped his electronic device.

Eventually, the sun came out revealing bake-dried trees that once were in the path of runaway slaves escaping through the thicket. Unfortunately, some of those slaves were trapped, returned, and hung from the branches. My great-grandfather survived that American tragedy and pooled his resources with several families to purchase land; after the Civil War, on which they built the Chapel on the Hill Baptist Church in Norlina, North

Carolina. He and his descendants, and members of those other families, are buried adjacent to the building. My mother rests a few rows down a gentle slope from them, a stone's throw from creeks that once nourished crops. Charles, Monica, and I held hands, bowed our heads, and said a prayer at her grave—fond childhood memories visited me.

Every summer, Mother would bring me to a big white house, surrounded by corn and tobacco, where her father grew up with his ten brothers and sisters, about a mile down a dusty road from the church. The elders would get up before dawn, eat a big breakfast, and go to work, many in the fields. I shared breakfast with them, but instead of working, I chased chickens and ran through the fields' red soil. Mother's thin lips would smile at me while we swung in the porch swing on those cool evenings drinking fresh lemonade.

None of the circuitous, mazelike, dirt roads had names then, but Mother navigated them with ease. Now they are paved, and many carry her relatives' last names. During a recent visit, one of Mother's cousins saw the resemblance in my face. "That's Rotelia's boy," she said. Those words made me feel loved. I want that kind of love for Charles too—the kind that heals—like the love I share with Monica.

Gerald's
Cancer Discovered
Emotions Explored
Life Constricted
Love Tested

Gerald's
Pain Gathered
Softness Found
Life Constricted
Love Rediscovered

Gerald's
Radiation Delivered
Tumors Killed
Life Constricted
Love Flowed

Gerald's

Gumbo For The Soul

Skin Burned
Sores Healed
Life Constricted
Love Exhales
Monica

~Gerald Green

10th Anniversary Edition

Man of Honor

A man of honor is very difficult to find,
For he is a rare specimen--he is one of a kind.
He is honest, strong, brave--just to name a few things.
He has pride in himself--carries himself like a king.

When he opens his mouth, true knowledge he imparts;
As a leader of mankind, he performs his part.
In the worth of his potential, he strongly believes;
He knows that nothing exists that he cannot achieve.

He is unafraid to be gentle and give his love,
For these are the qualities that a real man is made of.
He knows how to treat a woman with complete respect;
He would never hurt her--only cherish and protect.

His wife has no concern about his fidelity,
For he's a man of his word--he has integrity.
His rightful place as head, he knows how to claim;
To be what God wants him to be is his aim.

From responsibility, he fails ever to run,
For providing for his family is number one.
His children look up to him as example and guide;
His wife is glad that she decided to be his bride.

Who can find an honorable man? His price is high,
But waiting for him to come along is worth the try.

~Sylvia Larane Green

"I'm starting with the man in the mirror
I'm asking him to change his ways
And no message could have been any clearer
If you wanna make the world a better place
Take a look at yourself, and then make a change"

~Michael Jackson

10th Anniversary Edition

Man of the Millennium

Michael Joe Jackson

"Man of the Millennium"

Being the most famous entertainer in the world does not happen just because one sings and dances better than anyone else; it happens when the world sees beyond the glitz and glamour of superstardom.

Michael Jackson is undeniably the most famous man in the world and since the announcement that he died on June 25, 2009 at the age of 50, the man many have grown to know as the King of Pop was re-introduced to a young demographic barely old enough to talk. Suddenly, all ages can again sing and sway to the songs of Michael Jackson that made music history in the 1980's and beyond.

As the lead singer of the Jackson 5 appearing for the first time nationally in 1969 on the *Ed Sullivan Show*, youngest brother of the sibling musical group Michael, stood out from the very beginning and won the hearts and souls of millions.

The world watched Michael Joe Jackson grow while we enjoyed hit song after hit song for a span of 40 years. The 1982 "Thriller" album became the best-selling album in world history and it maintains that illustrious title to this day with no competitor even a close second. Throughout Michael's career, it is estimated that he sold more than a billion records and millions have purchased videotapes of his concerts and short films.

But hidden in the legacy of Michael Jackson is the fact that the *Guinness Book of World Records* granted Michael Jackson the award for the "Most Charities Supported by A Pop Star" in their Millennium Edition in 2000. This award meant the most to Michael because giving back was how he showed his appreciation to his fans from all over the world for their dedication and support.

Gumbo for the Soul is proud to honor Michael Joe Jackson as the recipient of the "Man of the Millennium" award for his tireless dedication as a humanitarian caring for the world's people.

Michael Joe's charitable donations are reportedly nearing $500,000,000, which is a staggering sum considering that in 2009, Michael Jackson was in debt nearly $400,000,000. Despite that, Michael knew his charities needed his annual donations. He would include his charitable contributions like a due bill that was in need of being paid, just like any of his other lifestyle budgetary demands.

The following is a small list of Michael Jackson charities and there are many others:

- AIDS Project L.A.
- American Cancer Society
- AmeriCares
- Angel Food
- Bambini – Gesu Children's Hospital
- Big Brothers of Greater Los Angeles
- BMI Foundation, Inc.
- Brotherhood Crusade
- Brothman Burn Center
- Camp Ronald McDonald
- Childhelp U.S.A.
- Children in Need
- Children's Institute International

10th Anniversary Edition

- Cities and Schools Scholarship Fund
- Community Youth Sports & Arts Foundation
- Congressional Black Caucus (CBC)
- Dakar Foundation
- Dreamstreet Kids
- Dreams Come True Charity
- Elizabeth Taylor Aids Foundation
- Give For Life
- Great Ormond Street Children's Hospital
- Heal the World
- Juvenile Diabetes Foundation
- Love Match
- Make-A-Wish Foundation
- Minority Aids Project
- Motown Museum
- NAACP
- National Rainbow Coalition
- National Action Network
- Prince's Trust (United Kingdom Royal Family)
- Rotary Club of Australia
- Society of Singers
- Starlight Foundation
- The Carter Center's Atlanta Project
- The Sickle Cell Research Foundation
- TransAfrica
- United Negro College Fund (UNCF)
- United Negro College Fund Ladder's of Hope
- Volunteers of America
- Watts Summer Festival
- Wish Granting
- YMCA - 28th Street/Crenshaw

Michael's charitable heart to give began back in Gary, Indiana, when becoming a world-class singing group was just a dream for the family. This dream became a reality due to hard work ethics enforced by both parents. Growing up in a large family of nine children, the Jacksons' childhood was one of struggling finances and limited space with eleven people living in a two-bedroom house. Parents Joseph and Katherine had one bedroom, the six brothers shared the other bedroom lined with two triple-decker bunk beds, and the three sisters slept in the living room. Despite their own limited resources, whenever they had just a little extra and knew a neighborhood family was struggling just to eat, patriarch Joseph, would have Katherine cook up some extra food and secretly deliver it using the game ding-dong-ditch. Michael and a few of his siblings would ring the doorbell, dropped off the food, and run. Joseph felt that a man had pride and wouldn't want to be confronted with accepting a handout, therefore, the Jacksons wanted to remain anonymous, and ran so their giving wouldn't cause anyone any embarrassment.

This heartfelt action to care for others was cemented in the soul of the King of Pop from a very early age and continued throughout his life.

Even though Michael is probably one of the most traveled people on the planet due to performing all over the world, he always scheduled time to visit sick children in hospitals. He wanted to bring smiles to their faces and offer some relief from their physical pains. As he learned from childhood, Michael never wanted media attention for his charitable efforts; he just felt people would follow by example. Michael wanted to be the type of role model that urged more people to involve themselves in giving and he thought that his celebrity status could bring attention to the world's ills. In this matter, the media let him down. Michael gave of his time and his money, and often said that's what entertainment is all about—sharing one's good fortune with others.

Michael's mother Katherine was struck with polio as a child and walks with a permanent limp due to the effects of that disease; therefore directly bonding the Jackson family to have empathy for anyone suffering from a debilitating illness. As fate would have it, a tragedy did strike that put Mr. Jackson in the hospital deepening his compassion for those in pain.

Michael suffered second-degree burns on his scalp when a faulty pyrotechnic set his hair on fire while taping a commercial for *Pepsi-Cola* in January of 1984. Although Michael was often brought to tears when he and his mother, Katherine, would see suffering people, Michael then learned precise understanding for the intense pain suffered by burn victims and opened up the *Michael Jackson Burn Center in Los Angeles* with the $1.5 million settlement paid to Michael for his injuries.

10th Anniversary Edition

Also in 1984, the Jacksons including all the sons of Joe and Katherine: Jackie, Tito, Jermaine, Marlon, Michael and Randy toured the world for their *Victory Tour*, which was the number one grossing concert tour at that time. Michael donated his $5 million share of profits to charity. In 1985, Michael teamed up with Lionel Richie and again with his producer on the *Thriller* album, Quincy Jones, who recruited other superstars for the charity single, "We are the World." At that time, this song became the number one fastest-selling recording in U.S. history and all the proceeds were donated to help feed starving children in Africa. The meaning of the song title was especially important because it reminds the world that we are all responsible for each other, no matter the race, the region, or religion.

As an African-American, Michael Joe Jackson loved all people of the world, but felt he had an added responsibility to help those within his own cultural group. The charities and Foundations that especially targeted the African-American population are:

~*Big Brothers of Greater Los Angeles* and the *Brotherhood Crusade*, due to the disproportionate number of missing Black fathers in the Black community, aims to reduce the effects of social ills, like incarcerations, repetitive cycle of deadbeat dads, poverty, over-abundance of children in the foster care system, high school drop-outs, gangs, drugs, and disrespect for authority; by offering mentoring programs and counseling to those in need.

~*Congressional Black Caucus* is made up of elected officials that work to ensure the needs and plights of African-Americans are not overlooked in national and local politics.

~*Minority AIDS Project* targets Blacks and Hispanics offering lifesaving education and testing in those minority communities.

~*Motown Museum* is targets Michael's appreciation to *Motown Records* for signing the Jackson 5 to their first major recording label that polished the already God-given talents of the Jackson family; ensuring this once Black-owned recording company and their achievements are never forgotten. Former owner of *Motown*, Berry Gordy, called Michael the greatest entertainer that ever lived. A compliment not to be taken lightly because *Motown* had some of the most talented superstars the world has ever seen.

~Mr. Jackson was also a reoccurring donor to social activism organizations like the *NAACP* (National Association for the

Advancement of Colored People), Jesse Jackson's *National Rainbow Coalition* and Al Sharpton's *National Action Network* who work on exposing issues especially important to the Black community by organizing protest and bringing media attention to problems in inner cities and beyond.

~Many people don't understand why Sickle Cell is a disease that strikes African descendants the most. The malaria epidemic is a part of natural selection (anthropological evolution) that attempts to aid the body with a mechanism that fights for building an added biological immunity for fighting off malaria. Malaria is widely suffered by people who have long lines of generations from tropical climates. Sickle Cell is an incomplete biological manifestation leading the body to fight off malaria naturally, but because this body correction is not finished, the disease of sickling of the blood is an illness that strikes African descendants more than other races of people.

~Other charities targeting Africans are the *Dakar (Senegal) Foundation*, which stems from a tour the young Jackson boys (including unofficial J5 member sibling Randy) and their father Joseph took in 1974, which chronicles the Jacksons visit to this "door of no return" exportation port of Africans being shipped and kidnapped into slavery for nearly 400 years. Michael also wanted to help all those on the continent of Africa by adding *TransAfrica* to his list of charitable contributions. Giving back to the motherland allows African Americans to remember their roots.

~*The United Negro College Fund* coined the phrase, "a mind is a terrible thing to waste" to encourage Blacks to attend and complete college because in America, education is the key to earning a better living wage and adapting to the world as a whole. Michael understood the importance of a college education even though he is not a college graduate—Michael's skill to earn a living was polished from the time he started singing at the age of five rendering him highly-trained in other ways, such as being the world's most loved entertainer. Racism is a terribly enabling principle that was once law which has stopped and/or handicapped many human beings in their pursuit of happiness and a decent lifestyle. During slavery of the African descendant, it was law that no slave could learn to read and write, which was an offense that was punishable by death. This trickling down and forced debilitating mindset seems to still have an effect on low high school and college graduation rates.

~Other charities that targets troubled teens are also foremost in Michael's charitable pursuit. Michael donated to *Cities and Schools*

10th Anniversary Edition

Scholarship Fund, Community Youth Sports & Arts Foundation, DreamStreet kids, Watts Summer Festival, YMCA - 28th Street/Crenshaw. Kids need productive things to do or gangs and drugs will waltz into their young lives, usually leading to criminal activity, so these charities helped slow degradation in many inner city communities.

Children were of great interest to Michael because he knew that if kids were loved and guided properly when they are young, they, more than likely, would grow up to be more loving and productive adults. This love of children eventually broke Michael's heart. Michael would often have sick children to his home known as *Neverland* where they could have a fun-filled time enjoying his amusement park, zoo, arcade, and train. Michael was falsely accused of child molestation which he was fully acquitted of all charges in 2005. Further clearing Michael Jackson of any wrongdoing were the covert actions of the *FBI* who had investigated Michael Jackson for 13 years to which they never discovered any misconduct on behalf of Michael Jackson. Michael's charities for children included *Camp Ronald McDonald, ChildHelp U.S.A., Children's Institute International, Juvenile Diabetes Foundation, Make-A-Wish Foundation,* and *Wish Granted.*

In order for most to understand the giving heart of the world's biggest superstar, one has to know the heart of those who raised him. Joseph Jackson, the man most blamed for the childhood ills of Michael, has been misjudged. This misjudgment was created by a media that was determined to demonize Joseph as a brutal father who beat his children. But to the contrary, and despite Joseph's intimidating demeanor, Joseph did raise the most successful family in music history who ALL have giving hearts.

Joseph is the one that made all his sons feel as valuable as Michael, by never allowing *Motown* to call the group, Michael and the Jackson 5. Joseph is the one who toured with his sons ensuring they were manner able at all times, and it was Joseph who gave Michael his love for animals. Joseph fell in love with Katherine Scruse and when it was discovered that unmarried Katie (her nickname) was pregnant, Joe married her with no consideration to the fact that she walked with a noticeable limp. All Joseph saw was Katherine's loving heart, religious upbringing, and unrelenting care for others—the traits of a good person.

The demonizing of Joseph Jackson could be a part of what many describe as systemic racism. Considering the Jacksons' image was well-crafted by *Motown Records* as a perfect family, the powers-that-be would be apt to tear this family down for the purpose of ensuring the Jacksons were not good role models for the African-American family. Replicating more Black families to follow step creates an atmosphere of widespread growth and prosperity within the Black population, which is in contrast to White Supremacy. Joseph's successful family structure and image that especially targeted Black fathers to be present and active role models does NOT ensure White supremacy, but racial equality; therefore demonizing this man's methods must take center stage rather than his achievements. Being a high-profile positive or negative role-model has far-reaching effects on those that witness such behaviors, so everyone must choose it's better for community to be positive than negative—each behavior breeds another.

Michael Joe Jackson also became a part of the same type of systemic racism. Michael grew to break records set by the Beatles and Elvis Presley and surpassed them in worldwide popularity, record sales, concert ticket sales, and out-charted them off of most number one lists. When Michael talked, people listened. Michael urged for world peace, racial harmony, and fair treatment. Michael was so fantastic at his job, he broke the racial barrier on *MTV* of not allowing Black artists to appear on this newly developed cable network—Michael Jackson's videos were the first of any Black artists to be played on Music Television (*MTV*).

Michael has always said he just wanted to make people happy by singing meaningful songs and entertaining the masses like no one before him, but Michael's ability to make the earth move caused panic to those in high places. Most conspiracy theorists believe dethroning the King of Pop was a must to maintain the world structure of White Supremacy.

It's always painful when anyone suffers from any disease or ailment, and even superstars like Michael Jackson would not be immune. Just before Michael Jackson ended his teenage years, Michael noticed white spots appearing on his body. His skin was turning colors, actually depigmenting, in effect losing melanin. Michael kept this a secret for many years, until he was diagnosed with vitiligo which afflicts about a million people in the United States. Vitiligo doesn't physically hurt, but it's quite emotionally devastating. Changing skin color for a private citizen is hard enough, but adding in the sex-appeal worldwide image of the world's biggest superstar had taken quite a toll on Michael who was turning white in front of a world stage.

The media reported that Michael Jackson bleached his skin to change his race because he hated the perceived inferiority complex of Blacks and/or he didn't want to look like his father who Michael had a temporary estranged relationship from due to childhood spanking. This lie would, naturally, enrage many African descendants worldwide, disconnecting Michael to his core audience, culture and longtime supporters. Even though Michael talked about vitiligo, little was reported about his disease and popular opinion was he bleached his skin so he would no longer be Black. All in line with the powerful purpose to promotes White Supremacy.

Coupling that with Michael's love for children another big blow was forced upon Michael Jackson—the child molestation accusations. The media spin about his *Neverland Ranch* was changed from its original purpose of providing a safe, fun and happy haven for sick children to a place created to lure children, so Michael could sexually molest them, became the proper feeding ground to generate more hatred for the once-beloved King of Pop. Michael also wanted to relive his childhood because he had worked through his own and once he could afford it, he vowed to get some of his childhood back and have playmate to boot. Michael felt adults always wanted something financial from him, but children just wanted love, happiness, and fun.

Michael was fully vindicated, despite the media manipulating lies, with a full 14 count verdict of not guilty in the biggest trial in world history in 2005; but was Michael worn down, a has-been, or was his image one that could be revived?

The world was going to get that answer. On March 3, 2009, Michael appeared at London's *O2 Arena* to announce his comeback called, "This Is It," which was going to set another world record by having fifty performances in London's *O2 Arena*, but that never happened because it was announced that Michael Jackson died on June 25, 2009 in his home due to acute propofol intoxication. The rehearsal footage for "This Is It" was made into a documentary, but many fans believe "This Is It" was always supposed to be a movie and the death of Michael Jackson is just a hoax.

Well, just like with other superstars, such as Elvis Presley, bigger than life figures can never die, but with Michael Joe Jackson is it really all over?

~Pearl Jr.

Gumbo For The Soul

10th Anniversary Edition

Thumbs Up!

When my mother met George Jones again, I was already nine years old, my younger brother was seven and my sister was about 18 months old. My mother had left California with the three of us in search of a new beginning in Michigan. That new beginning came in the person of George Jones.

My mother had dated George years earlier when she was a teen, but lost touch with him once she moved, first back with her family in Louisiana and then on to California. By and by, life took over and both moved on their separate ways. Imagine my mother's delighted surprise when she came back to Michigan almost twenty years later and found George still unmarried and interested in seeing her again.

To the delight of my brother, my sister and I, George quickly became "Daddy." Through Daddy, I was re-educated about everything that I thought was true about a man up until we became a family. I learned that a man *could* be loving and kind to his family. I learned that waking in fear and going to bed in fear was not normal, even though I had lived that way for years as my sister's biological father became increasingly more and more violent.

Daddy never stayed mad for long and he could make a joke out of just about any circumstance. Even though I know that it was no laughing matter growing up in poverty and as an African American male in the deep South during the 1930's, 40's and 50s, Daddy kept us rolling with stories about his youth, people he knew in the South, and animals that seemed to possess uniquely human or other unusual characteristics not usually seen in dogs, chickens, cats and mules.

I learned that I could go visit my cousins overnight and leave my mother at home and she would still be smiling when I returned home the next day. Mama wouldn't be hurt or hiding in their room embarrassed to come out and greet us. There wouldn't be plates broken in the sink, lamps and other items would still be intact and best of all; music to my childish ears, Mama and Daddy could be heard laughing together or talking lovingly as I stepped up and opened our front door.

I am most grateful to have had Daddy in my life for almost forty years because, through his example I learned the concept of God, the Father's unconditional love for us. Out of all those years, Daddy never had a harsh word for me. As I grew older and made my share of mistakes, he continued to encourage me and tell me that I would get things together one day. After years of fighting alcohol and drug addiction, homelessness and my own bouts of domestic violence, how happy and proud I was to have my mother and Daddy proudly being a part of not only my attainment of an Associate's Degree, but also a Bachelor and finally a Master Degree in 2005.

In 2006, Daddy finally retired from work at the age of 74. Aside from time off due to a work injury, Daddy had gone to work rain or shine, sleet or snow ever since I was nine years old. Most of his days began at 5 o' clock in the morning, and throughout the years Daddy raised four children, then my two children, his grandchildren, and had opened the family home to a number of our relatives as well as my grandmother who lived with my parents for ten years before passing away due to Alzheimer's disease.

Three years after retiring and vowing to take some much needed rest and relaxation, Daddy was diagnosed with cancer. After chemo and other medical treatments, we thought the cancer had been beaten but it came back even more aggressively. Never one to complain, Daddy, we later learned, knew that the cancer had advanced to such a state that there was little chance that he would beat it again. None of us knew in 2010 that we were spending our last months with him but we are sure now that he knew.

After my father passed away, my mother stated that she found various papers needed for his funeral, and for policies and the like, neatly placed where my mother could easily put her hands on them. He probably gathered those things together the last time that he came home from the hospital while my mother was still at work during the day.

The cancer rapidly spread throughout his body, yet Daddy bravely hid it from us to the end even though his hospital stays became longer and longer while his home stays became fewer and fewer. Daddy always had it conveniently set where my mother had just missed the doctor's round when she came to the hospital or if she caught the doctors their answers would be vague as they looked at Daddy propped up in bed. My uncles, my mother's brothers, also knew the extent of Daddy's illness but promised him that they would not share that knowledge with my mother.

10th Anniversary Edition

To this day, they've admitted that they made him a promise but they have not broken that promise.

On the afternoon of April 12, 2010, my father went into cardiac arrest and was placed on life support. He had seemed fine that morning at the hospital as he joked with my mother while she fed him *Jell-O* and he had even told her to go on to work and he'd see her later that evening. After my mother left the hospital, my father told my youngest brother that he could go to the family room and watch television but to stay close where the family could reach him if needed. Soon after, Daddy went into cardiac arrest. He never regained consciousness and passed away on the night of April 16, 2010.

It is now one year later since that night and I still can't believe Daddy is gone. I still find myself thinking that Daddy must be in the backyard, in another room or running an errand when I go to my parents' home and notice him missing. Then there are times that I'm there at their home and I remember and smile to myself as I think of Daddy smiling, laughing or joking around the house and playing with my mother or my youngest brother. Whenever the grief of my loss threatens to overtake me, I rely on my faith and my memories to see me through.

I have many fond memories. I even have two fond memories of those last days with Daddy. First I remember how one of the RN's came to my mother and me as we were sitting with Daddy in ICU before he passed away. She expressed her sympathy while telling us how Daddy continuously bragged on his wife, her good cooking and his sons while he was on her assigned ward. My father was such a blessing to our lives and I'm always comforted to know that even though he did not share the extent of his illness with us, Daddy was not feeling hopeless in those last days, he knew without a doubt that we loved him and were so proud to have him in our lives and I'm comforted knowing that he felt the exact same way about us.

Second, I remember the last time that Daddy was rolled into the hospital by EMS. He had come home for only three short days when he began complaining of chest pains and had to be taken back to the Emergency room. My father had never mentioned having chest pains before so we looked at this as something new to complicate his recovery. As we headed into the ER, my mother and I were walking sadly and silently behind the stretcher when Daddy, forever determined to see us happy, looked at my mother and I, winked and gave us the thumbs up sign. I still smile when I picture that moment. Daddy captured our lives best without saying a word. For all of our lives, for better or worse, our lives together have been one big thumbs up!

~Linda A. Haywood

10th Anniversary Edition

Little Big Man

Back in the 70's, Dustin Hoffman starred in a western called, "Little Big Man." I don't really know what the movie was about, but as soon as I started to write this essay, the title came to mind because my father, Thomas Franklin Brown, stood only five feet two inches tall, yet he commanded more respect than any man I've ever known personally. He was an entrepreneur and a church leader, but it's not the public man I want to tell you about. I want to tell you about Tommy Brown, my daddy.

One of my earliest memories is sitting with my cousins by the side of a dusty dirt road in Millville, New Jersey in front of my grandparent's house, watching him play softball with my aunts and uncles. Family was his top priority. We worshipped together as a family; we vacationed as a family and often worked together in the business he started when I was five years old.

Contrary to the well-meaning advice of friends and relatives; he started his own part-time printing business in our basement while he worked days as a pressman at a large printing company. Two years later he left the job and never looked back. When his business outgrew our house, he moved it to the first of a series of progressively larger rented buildings. Though he never had more than three full-time employees at any given time, he supported a wife, four children and, from time to time, assorted relatives on the income his business produced. I need to give my mother credit right here because part of the reason he was able to do this was because she made a lot of our clothes and knew how to shop to save money. He never worked another outside job again, which was an amazing accomplishment for a black man in the 1950's.

Gumbo For The Soul

By today's standards he would probably be considered strict in the sense that he expected us to be obedient. And we obeyed, not because we were afraid of him, but because the last thing we ever wanted to do was disappoint him. I'll never forget the time when I was in seventh grade and I got into a fight with the neighborhood bully. Embarrassed and humiliated by having his daughter involved in a street brawl, he made arrangements with the Chief of Police in our small town and the other girl's mother for us to be given a lecture and personal guided tour of the township jail by a uniformed officer in an effort to scare us straight. I don't know about her, but the experience sure did the trick for me. As a result of his "style," not one of his four children (now all over the age of forty) has ever been arrested.

We weren't rich by any stretch of the imagination, but Tommy Brown was a giver from his heart. He never failed to go overboard at Christmas and on birthdays, but when we wanted something in between those special occasions, his mantra was, "You save half and I'll give you the other half." Of course, we usually earned the money by working in his shop folding, stapling, and collating and sweeping. He definitely got his money's worth out of us.

A jazz fanatic who had an impressive collection of 78's and 33's, he always worked with his music on. I believe his children all grew up to be avid music lovers because, prior to moving the business out of the house, he built speakers into the walls of the basement in order to hear the music over the hum of the presses. When he cranked it up, we could feel the floors upstairs vibrate beneath our feet. Count Basie, Duke Ellington, Dinah Washington, Earl Grant, Jimmy Smith and Ray Charles provided the soundtrack for our childhood.

Even though he worked ridiculously long hours, he knew how to have fun. In his younger days, he loved to host big backyard barbecues for which; of course, my mother did all of the work. And those summertime gatherings usually ended with the kids toasting marshmallows over the fire on the grill while the grown-ups played rowdy games of badminton and horseshoes. I'm hard pressed to recall a time when our back yard wasn't much more than two huge bare spots on either side of the net at the end of the summer.

Never one to put vacations on the back burner in favor of the business, he and my mother always came up with fun outings for us. When money was low, we did local excursions to the early amusement parks, *Olympic Park* and *Palisades Park*, which have long since disappeared. With air fares being out of their financial reach back then, we traveled everywhere we went by car -- Atlantic City, Freedomland, Bear Mountain, Sebego Lake in New York and Hershey Park, Pennsylvania. Once we grew up, he and my mother we finally able to fly to Bermuda, Puerto Rico and Canada, and took my daughter, Crystal along with them when she was little.

Sadly, in telling this story to people over the years, I've often received looks of disbelief. That's when I realized just how uncommon my story is and how blessed we were. Tommy Brown's name will never be written in any hall of fame, but he was a man of incredible pride, faith and integrity. He didn't go out to bars or hang out with his buddies. He went to work, to church, to Chamber of Commerce meetings and spent his free time with his family, which included his nine brothers and sisters and their children.

During times that I only vaguely recall as stressful, his mother moved in to live with us when she became too sick to care for herself. Years later, after her passing, another hospital bed was delivered for one of his brothers who came to live with us when he succumbed to the deterioration of advanced diabetes.

At my father's seventieth birthday party, my sister, who lived in Atlanta, was unable to attend. She sent a taped message thanking him for being the man he was. As she spoke through tears, she told him how grateful she was that we never had those stories to tell like so many children unfortunately do – the ones about eating mayonnaise sandwiches because there wasn't any food in the house, or having to do their homework by candlelight because the electricity was turned off, or watching their mother go down to the local bar to drag their father out.

My father went home to be with the Lord in 1995. His funeral was a testament to the greatness of an "everyday" man. My brothers, sister and I were overwhelmed by the turnout of not only friends and neighbors, but also of township officials, former business associates and even the ninety-year-old doctor who had delivered all of us into the world.

Today's fathers could learn a lot from the lives of men like Tommy Brown. He stood only five feet two inches tall, but to me he was a giant.

Thank you, Daddy!

~Denise Jones

We Called Him "Pop"

I remember the day you left like it was yesterday. The call came to my classroom where I was teaching and all I heard was "He's gone." I remember not thinking or feeling, just trying to get myself together to get home to my mother who was there alone. I don't remember the drive at all. It seemed I got to the house sooner that I wanted to. Parking on the street because the morticians were there, I hoped no one would hit my car. Pop helped me buy it.

As I walked to the door, almost about to ring the bell, I almost forgot that I lived there, I dreaded turning the knob. I opened the door, entered the foyer and heard voices, not really sure what they were saying just knowing that they are discussing Pop. Pop is, I mean used to be, I mean was in the room to the left. I go right because, well just because. I walked into the family room looking for my mother who was seated at the table talking with Hospice. Mind you, I had not cried yet. At that point, I was still not really hearing words being spoken, just knowing that people are talking. Fast forward to them bringing in the stretcher and the black bag. I don't remember Pop going in because I could not watch. Last thing I remember was me trying to hold my mother up at the door as they drove off with Pop.

As I write this, it still hurts even though it was over ten years ago. It was January 11, 2001. I will remember that day forever only because my daughter's birthday is January 10th. I prayed to God that He would please not take him on that day. We all knew the end was near. You could just feel it in the air. I did not want to remember him leaving us on that day. Thank God for hearing my prayer.

Pop died from cancer that finally reached his lymph nodes. We found out that he had found out years before and never did or said anything about it. He never got any treatment besides pain control. I guess he figured if he did not talk about it, it would go away. You know how some of us were raised. The only reason we found out was because the pain got so bad. I remember my mom having to give him shots for pain-migraines was what we were told. Well, one night, I remember him lying on the floor in pain. Mom and Pop used to argue at times. I thought originally that Mom got one in. He lay there, and no pain medicine we had in the house helped. He begged us not to take him to the hospital. My mother insisted and did not take 'no' for answer. They went on without me because I had my three-year-old daughter and we knew having her in the hospital was sure disaster. I remember my Mom saying they would be back. Hours later when she got back alone, I saw the look on her face and knew it was not good. She said the doctor was going to talk to her. Patient/doctor privilege kicked in and he had to talk with Pop before he could share the news with my mother. The next day, they gave him six months to live. He lived for eight. At the very young age of 48, Kenneth Alexander Mays left us here. That's how I felt, how my sister felt, how his brothers felt, how my mother felt.

My reason for writing this submission was to purge, share, and encourage those whose *Man of Honor* is gone on or still here. Cherish all the moments and start over again everyday with fresh one. I dedicate this to my mother, Juliet Wring Mays, whose due diligence as a wife was unsurpassed. I dedicate this to my sister who is still waiting for Pop to walk through that door. To his grandchildren, Alexandria and Lauryn, who had the opportunity to meet him and Jonathan, Mariah and Mark Jr., who never will.

Men, take care of yourselves. Get tested, follow-up and find a support system to help you. One that understands, loves and supports you. Sometimes I wonder if Pop had gotten the right medical attention, if he would still be here.

~Wanda Mays Noel

Robert Pinkney: My Grandfather, My Sage

One day, my dad was rambling. The only thing I recall from his drunken tirade was, "I'm the seventh-son of a seventh-son..." Although I've never done the proper research to verify the validity of that claim, the man of whom he spoke stays in my heart long after his death - my father's father, Robert Pinkney.

Born August 6, 1922, in Montgomery County, Mississippi, my grandfather, Robert Pinkney, was a different person to different people. To his wife, he was a provider, the father of her fourteen children, a hard worker and a wild rapscallion. My estimation is that he passed on the trait of alcoholism and the sobering redemption that comes decades later to my father, if not to any one of his other sons. That, however, is another story, and another subject...

To his children, Robert Pinkney was enigmatic. The calm, statuesque man sitting motionless in the living room was an ominous trap. Once in his presence, the tension could easily be likened to that moment the lion and gazelle lock gazes. The state of mind brought on by cheap whiskey all but affected his children in various ways.

By the time I came around, Robert Pinkney was a sober and funny man. Although I dreaded spending my summers away from Memphis, Tennessee and my parents, I really enjoyed the precious moments he gave me in Winona, Mississippi. We would joke, run around, watch Westerns, and listen to Country music.

The summer that stands out in particular is the Summer of 1989. I was about fourteen-years-old, going to ninth grade after summer break, and sprung on some random girl that I had maybe one class with at *Snowden Middle School.*

With my hormones totally out of whack, I was struggling to keep my sanity in the middle of the small town of Winona, when all of my friends were riding bikes and playing basketball and buying candy from the corner stores all over my beloved North Memphis neighborhood.

One evening, after his routine walk, Granddaddy sat me down and had a heart-to-heart as the muggy sun went down and the crickets got louder. Although he was talking to a child, his words were meant for the adult that I would later become. He gave me sage advice like some of our African cultures mandate: from grandfather to grandson.

He told me not to let people hop in my car and slam the doors. At the time, I was still *jones-ing* for the bike I left behind in Memphis. Car ownership was beyond my realm of existence. The lesson came into play in college and the years beyond. It let me know that it's reasonable to deny another person free reign over my possessions for the sake of feigning coolness. "You don't have to slam my door that hard," and that's that!

I remember his pointing out an old, heavy metal box. At the time he told me about it, I was not very impressed with the awkward cube. He told me about his past as a welder at a company called *Screw Conveyor* and how he made that box from scratch.

I remember sitting there and smiling at him because he was smiling; my granddad's grin was always comical to me in light of his otherwise menacing straight face.

He looked me dead in the eye with a wry smile and a quick nod, telling me about taking pride in whatever I choose to do regardless of how others perceive it. The words were over my head, but they stayed in my heart. I took ownership of that metal box much later in my life. As ugly as it is, it's a testament of that conversation and the lesson it bore.

During my stay in Winona that summer, my parents came down. I was so happy to see them. I rushed to get my stuff together, only to be told that I had two more weeks there before I was coming home. I could have fainted with sheer devastation. I was so ready to go back home that I had the audacity and confidence to assert my opinion to an abusive father.

It worked, and I went home...

Later that same night, while in the comfort of my own bed, in my own room, with my own set of ghosts that kept me under my covers in fear, the phone rang. All I could hear was my heart pumping and my dad say, "Hello?" I can't remember if he cried or not; I just remember the shock of discerning that my Grandfather was dead. I felt so selfish, especially when my parents and I attended my grandfather's funeral.

I benefited from that chance evening many, many years after experiencing it. In reality, at my age and level of immaturity, I can't really say that I could have taken that learning session seriously, even if he told me he was going to die in a couple of weeks.

I was blessed by what he shared with me. It taught me to talk "adult talk" to my children as early as I can communicate ideas to them, just in case there's a chance that my *tomorrow* may never come. I have been cautioned against doing this, but my grandfather's words made parts of my journey through adulthood a little more bearable. I hope my words to my children do the same.

~Joey Pinkney

10th Anniversary Edition

Life with Father

My mother left the three of us, when we were infants. My father took on the awesome responsibility of rearing us with help from his mother. My grandmother died after eight years and my father continued raising us alone.

During my childhood, my father instilled values and principles in us which have had a lasting effect for me. These values included to stand alone if necessary, and never be a follower. I could have succumbed to the many temptations of the inner city neighborhood where I grew up, but instead I always chose to make my own decisions thereby diverting gangs, drug and alcohol abuse and many other societal ills.

Another sound principle he taught us was to save money and buy only what you can afford with cash. In these times where so many people are in debt and overwhelmed with bills, it is a great feeling to be debt-free. He insisted that we become well learned and always keep abreast of the current news. He made sure that we read the newspaper daily and subscribed to cultural magazines to heighten our awareness.

One of the greatest lessons my father taught was to value people. He never allowed us to call anyone ugly, often reminding us that we don't make ourselves and if we did, we would probably all look alike. In the same vein, he would lecture us on never teasing or criticizing another child regardless of the country they were from because we also have no choice in where we are born. This has helped me to appreciate cultural differences and to learn from others of diverse backgrounds.

My fondest memories of my father during childhood include his love for music. He loves jazz and always had music playing including the oldies but goodies. Henceforth, I have acquired this same passion which has expanded to all types of music including gospel, classical and smooth music. He would often watch old movies giving us the history of the movie and the actors. Today some of my favorite movies include classics such as *Imitation of Life* and *It's a Wonderful Life*. An avid sports fan, he always stood by his favorite team, The *New York Mets*, whether they were in the cellar or winning the pennant. I have also acquired a love for watching baseball, along with basketball, tennis, ice skating and other sports.

I could probably go on and on with this list, but in a day and age where values don't appear to have preeminence, it's good to pay tribute to such a principled man as my father. My dad was a fighter who survived many challenges in life, so I was believed when he was diagnosed with prostate cancer that he would beat it and he did. But it was extremely difficult when my father was diagnosed with dementia. I understood the process and what would happen as time went on. Although my sister and brother are his primary caregivers it gives me great pleasure to see that my father still remembers some of the things he taught, he still loves music and remembers his favorite jazz artists. Many of my friends grew up with fathers, but I am so glad and blessed to have had a life with Father!

~Rolanda T. Pyle

10th Anniversary Edition

"Grind like a bull that charges through a crowd,
utterly
impervious to what's in front of it."
~Unknown

Legend of Honor

Lowell W. Perry Sr.

Lowell W. Perry Sr.: The Gentle Lion, King of Kindness, Fruit Bearer

"You shall know them by their fruits...wherefore; by their fruits ye shall know them." Matthew 7:16 & 20

"Glory, honor & peace to all men who worketh good." Romans 2:10

Those are two scriptures that come to mind when I think of "Uncle Lodi." Lowell W. Perry, Sr. made his transition just a week into the year 2001. He was my uncle by marriage, and I felt I knew more about how life because of the fruit he yielded in his life.

He had a marvelous spirit that oozed with kindness, generosity and gentleness. You could see the favor of God on his life. He was an All-American star for the University of Michigan in the 1950's. His career began as a football player with the *Pittsburgh Steelers* after completing

Military Officer training in D.C. He was recognized as an outstanding player in the service and ending up a first lieutenant. Before that, he met and married the love of his life, the beautiful Maxine Perry (Lewis).

A man of character and commitment, Uncle Lodi knew God was in control of his life and would work all things together for good. (Romans 8:28) So in his first year when *New York Giants'* Rosie Grier crunched Perry fracturing his pelvis and dislocating his hip, Uncle Lodi didn't give up. Had he not suffered a career-ending injury, he was destined to be "Rookie of the year."

He took that thirteen-week hospital stay in traction to seek God. He'd often said that was a "turning point in his life." With complete trust in God, Uncle Lodi girded up and sought another direction for his life: Law school. God gave him a better plan for his life and he joyfully submitted. Uncle Lodi was a humble man; that's why the grace of God rested on him so greatly.

After his short playing career was over, the *Steelers* provided him with the opportunity to coach in the national football league while he attended Law school in the evening. When a man knows their purpose, God will give you the power to complete the mission. It's also ironic that we celebrated Rev. Dr. Martin Luther King, Jr.'s birthday the same day of Uncle Lodi's funeral. Both men paved the way for all of us. I realized we had a real "trail blazer" in our midst.

Perry's life was a litany of many accomplishments:

- He was the first Black legal counsel for the *National Labor Relations Board*.
- First black executive at *Chrysler Corporation* in 1963 and later became Director of Personnel.
- First black *NFL* broadcaster when *CBS* hired him as a game analyst in 1996.
- First black auto plant manager in charge of 3,800 employees in 1973.
- First black appointed by U.S. president to head a major government agency.
- Chairman of the *Equal Employment Opportunity Commission/EEOC* (a position Supreme Court Justice, Clarence Thomas also served as chair following Perry.)
- First black automotive manufacturer in the country.
- Director of community relations at *Michigan Bell*.

- Retired in 1999 as Director of the *Michigan Department of Labor* (One of few Black appointees of the Governor).

Uncle Lodi was always one to race towards a goal line and tackle the work. We can measure our lives based on our bank accounts, possessions, fame and reputation. But the only thing that really matters in the end is what matters to God. He's looking for how we planted our "seeds" and what difference we made in the lives of others.

He bore much fruit and received many honors.

FRUIT is an indicator of what you have been filling your life with. If you feed your life with selfishness, greed and pride, you produce rotten fruit. But if you are a person who is aware of who you are and what God has planned for you; you produce good fruit and create a harvest of blessings for others.

That's what the fruit is for! Trees don't partake of their own fruit Apple trees give apples for others not for itself. That's what uncle Lodi was about. Whatever experiences he had, he shared. He was like a big, strong apple tree that took pleasure in providing shade and nourishing fruit for others. (1Timothy 6:18).

Even in circumstances that were beyond his control, he was always able to rise above them and glean wisdom to share with others. I remember a time in my career when I even sought his wise counsel and he always had time to listen and give good advice.

Just like the late Rev. Dr. Martin Luther King, Jr., Uncle Lodi's life will continually affect many for generations to come. He was an authentic man of great magnitude, not because of what he did in his career, but for what he did for others. The Bible says, "whoever is greatest among you will be your servant." Uncle Lodi was a great helper, supporter, ally, and friend to many.

Despite his notable positions, he remained humble. He was just as comfortable talking with the President of the United States as he was talking with a group of inner-city kids; and he loved kids. His own children were fine products of the harvested life of Lowell Jr., Scott and Meredith. All of his children are parents as well and have made their dad proud.

Uncle Lodi's spiritual fruit production says a lot about his relationship to the will of God. "...the fruit of the spirit is: love, joy, peace, patience, kindness, goodness, faithfulness, meekness, and self-control." Galatians 5:22.

10th Anniversary Edition

Looking at the life of Lowell W. Perry we see the fruit of the spirit rich and ripe. He served others with love without thought of return. We saw joy by his hearty laugh, quick wit and humor. We saw peace; because he was a peacemaker. We saw patience; because he remained constant despite circumstances. We saw kindness and tenderness apparent with his family. We see goodness; because he gave freely and generously. We see faithfulness in his career; because he was committed to the cause. We see humility; that caused the favor of God to operate in his life. He was determined to give God the glory and others the credit. We saw discipline exhibited in his sports career making him a star athlete.

He reaped what he sowed. A great harvest. His actions spoke louder than his words. We should all want to plant seeds and cultivate our lives as Uncle Lodi did. He didn't put his light under a bushel; he let his light shine before men. (Mathew 5:16). He was a testimony of God's grace wherever he went. But mostly he was successful because he walked in love. He garnered his talents, flowed in his purpose and accomplished the goal set for him by God. He fulfilled his assignment. He completed the race and finished the course. He fought the good fight of faith. (2 Timothy 4:7).

We all want God, our Father, to say at the end of our lives, "Well done, my good and faithful servant...enter into the joy of the Lord." (Matthew 25:21). Uncle Lodi was an inspiration. We will miss him and always honor him for the legacy he left.

~Pam Perry

Gumbo For The Soul

10th Anniversary Edition

Clocks & Mirrors

When I graduated from elementary school (what now seems like ages ago), I was so excited that my Dad was going to come to my school. I was especially excited that my beloved homeroom teacher, Mrs. Hemmans, would finally get to meet him. All week long, I kept telling her how big and strong and handsome he was. I was so disappointed at what she told me after she finally met him. She said that from the way I described him she was expecting some *"Great big ole man"*. To her he was just an average sized guy, but to me he was still a giant of a man.

To me, my Dad was truly a *MAN* in every sense of the word. Recently, I have observed that most of the *"Men"* of my generation don't seem to have that same appearance of *"Grown Man"*liness that men of my Dad's generation had. There was a certain unmistakable maturity and masculinity about the way he walked, talked and carried himself. When my Dad was my age there was no mistaking it, he was a **Grown Man.**

Of course I'm aware that the labor-leisure opportunities were not the same for Black men back in his day. My Dad was certainly, to some degree, hardened by the demands of working the kind of back-breaking job that I have never had to work. Nevertheless, I can't picture my Dad playing with a video gaming system, going to the latest Pop-Idol's concert, watching comic book Superhero movies in a theatre, or wearing some teenaged athletes college throwback jersey as many men in their 30s, 40s and 50s or older do these days.

My Dad had a bearing and countenance about him such that no teenager today would dare to address him as "Player" or "Pimp" or "G". Nowadays, some young people are accustomed to greeting "mature" men that they don't even know using such titles. However, the current state of affairs is not just an issue of young people respecting their elders. It's more an issue of the elders being worthy of the youngsters' respect.

Men of a certain age used to take pride in the responsibility of teaching young men respect, wisdom and the other various life lessons of being a man. I have observed that, these same men now take pride in the fact that younger men see them as a peer, a buddy, or a "homey". They would be more apt to smoke a blunt with "kids" or drink a beer with them or even tag along to "hook up" with some young girls. They would prefer this type of relationship, rather than teach young men the lessons of respecting young ladies, saying no to the various vices of life and mentoring them through the frontiers of getting an education, planning a career or starting a family.

I must admit that as a member of the current generation of "middle-aged" men, I don't really feel like an "adult" myself some times. I have not always felt possessed of that natural *"Grown Man"* gravitas, despite the responsibilities of a high pressured career, business ownership, home ownership or even being in a position of mentoring younger people. I think this is partially a sign of the times of our youth obsessed culture. Yet, it is also a larger symptom of my generation's conscious aversion to taking on the family, community and organizational responsibilities that used to guide men and women through the maturation process.

It used to be absolutely necessary for men to "put away childish things". Honoring serious commitments and responsibilities like those made to their Mother, fighting for their country or fighting for "the Struggle" simply could not be avoided. When my father was just a teenager, he came to the "big city' to start earning money to send back home. Nevertheless, it seems nowadays that people have been taught that their one and only responsibility is to self fulfillment, self gratification and self satisfaction. We (me included) seem to be in a never ending pursuit of pleasure and living the "good life" rather than any other higher pursuits whatsoever.

I still want to fulfill certain personal aspirations. Looking young, being healthy and satisfying my various appetites are still priorities. If this is somewhat selfish, then so be it. However, I feel like it is time now that my generation also put away some childish things and take responsibility for building the next generation of MEN. I want to be able to appear to be an example of maturity and masculinity for young people that need guidance.

10th Anniversary Edition

We can no longer afford to just be some old dudes that they think are still "Cool".

Personally, I want to be able to accept maturing as a blessing not a curse. I want to graciously embrace all of the forthcoming stages of life, not run away from them. I want to be a person that younger people look to for wise counsel and sound guidance. I do not need to aspire to be somebody they can "kick it" or "hang out" with. I want to be the same great guiding presence that my father was for me. I want to be a MAN.

~Vince Rogers

Roscoe Samuel Strother
6/19/19 - 05/10/02

What My Father Did For Me
... in memory of my loving father, Roscoe Samuel Strother

He taught me how to ride a bike
He showed me how to drive,
He gave the advice I'd need someday
to achieve, to succeed, to survive.

He fought in wars, broke down barriers
By those who clearly hated,
To see him achieving his high set goals
He never slowed nor compensated.

He expressed the importance of dignity
At first, I did not understand,

I observed him with friends and family
I saw grace engulf this black man.

He always said, "Give it your best...
...stand tall when faced with strife,"
He succeeded and overcame colorful hate
to give me a boundless life.

He expressed to me that I must overcome
All obstacles which will arise,
He could never hide his humbled heart
'Cause you could see it in his eyes.

So now my time has come to pass
The love he gave freely,
By doing for my children
What my father did for me.

~Kathie Strother-Scholl

Gumbo For The Soul

This One's For My Father

How does a strong Black man make his way in this world?
Bringing up four boys and one slightly spoiled girl?
What kind of man improves on all that he touches?
Yet takes great care in his work,
Deliberate and thoughtful-not one who rushes,
Who is this man with the blessed gift of song?
Joyfully praising his savior his whole life long?

Who is this man with the silky-tenor voice?
Who chose heaven, not this world, when given a choice?
What kind of man still gives of himself?
Always providing for family,
Before fleeting fame and earthly wealth?

Who came into manhood amidst turbulent times?
When being Black and proud was an American crime?
Who stood-up for his people and expressed what he felt?
Who made a royal flush out of the crooked hand he was dealt?

Such a man is alive and well,
Those who have ears-listen,
I have a story to tell,
About a living example for all of his days,
About a righteous man of God who always:
Showed up, stood up, but never cut up,
A man who wouldn't be silent,
When racists told him to shut up.

This one's for my father,
Some men wouldn't bother,
To teach his sons and daughter what it means to be a man,
In this afflicted and often bitter land,
For those like us with a permanent tan,
See, I don't think y'all truly understand-

10th Anniversary Edition

The severity of the need
For a Black man to pass on dignity to his seed-
God, not greed,
Was his sole motivation, his inspiration.
Few words but deeds and perspiration,
Anything that he did,
Everything that he does,
It's blessed from a heavenly perspective,
I seek truth in my life so,
I'm contemplative and reflective-
I ponder the myriad qualities
That makes a man great-
One thing's not open to debate,
Surely, it's God in him-
It wasn't by chance or on a mere whim-
That He chose this man, in this place,
In that time, in his prime-
He did so many things,
If you want to know a man,
Look into his face,
Look for a sign…of God's Grace,
On that man, in his life,
His love for his children,
His relationship with my mother, his wife,
Has always been exemplary,

But in this contemporary world
It's not always so,
Some men might look at you crazy,
As if they don't know,
The difference between a man who makes babies,
And a bona fide Dad,
Lots of bruthas I know never had…
A real role model,
Someone to lead, not follow…
The next man… the wrong way…
So many bruthas are led astray…
From their true purpose,

Gumbo For The Soul

From their own vision,
From their lifelong dream,
Lights years away from a love supreme,
Tough love, yes, yet not to an extreme,
Someone to teach,
We all know he's the Lord's minister,
Though he may not preach.
Leading by his good deeds,
Someone who's known for helping those in need,
Be it spiritual or otherwise,
It didn't take long for me to realize,
The proof was staring me straight in my eyes,
That I was blessed with a father who cares,
Who loved deeply in his own way,
Who provided, who shares,
He was given great gifts-to laugh and to sing-
And a heart that yearns to remains faithful,
Each day the Lord brings,
Through him God provided a breathing illustration,
The truth that he lives,
The songs that he sings,
Serves as a witness of the Lord's promise,
By faith we can do all things.

This one's for my father,
Some men wouldn't (even) bother,
To teach his sons and daughter what it means to be a man,
In this bitter, cruel and afflicted land,
For those like us with a permanent tan,
See, I don't think y'all truly understand-
The severity of the need,
For a Black man to pass on dignity to his seed.
This one's for my father.

~Anthony D. Spires aka Phruishun

There Are Great Men of Honor – This I Can Attest

A phenomenal women before conception
I learned major lessons through the male connection
I never had a full time, or a part time father in my life
Too often I had intimate male partners who did not practice mutual love and support,
instead they often gave me strife with their lies, games, neglect and abuse
I made efforts to minimize attachment to the heart burns I experienced
that almost shattered my belief about there being Men of Honor
I met a few Great Men of Honor in this life time - this I can attest
They were not my father, grandfather, brother, cousin, nor my lover
 instead two friends-like-brothas and a mentor
They did not expect me to be their freaky sex toy, sugar momma, nor surrogate mother
These men of higher intentions and a heart of light shined in my life
They have and still are unknowingly helping me to transmute and
heal old wounds of relational pain
These men are fathers to children, husbands to their wife, brothers to sisters and other brothas,
and leaders in the community and in their family
S.E.X.Y (**S**ophisticated, **E**difying. **X**traordinary & **Y**oung at heart) when they speak about love
family, relationships, community, politics and even their feelings
They have enriched me with a sweet knowing that there is pure love from a man like natural honey
These men of virtue bare life on their shoulders and back just as I do,
yet they had time for me and gave without expecting something in return
They wear and live life well.
Why would I not want to write about such great essence walking the earth?
I honor thee Dr. Uric Johnson, Haji Sheare and Joel Mackall
You confirmed my belief that there are Great Men in my life
Peace, love and gratitude my brothas. Namaste.

~Christine Vaughan aka Solmantress

Taking the Step Out of Stepdad

I don't recall if it was winter, spring, summer or fall when the man I would call stepfather walked into my life. In truth, we actually walked into his. But little did we know that we would be the ones who would forever be changed. I was not much more than six years old when I first met him. He was a kind man who was always in good spirits. He loved to laugh. It seemed to be his favorite pastime. While far from an old Saint Nick image, he brought with him the personality of a jolly fellow, always humorous and lifting the spirits of everyone he met. From the first day I saw him, I knew something had come to stay. That thing was a lifetime of laughter and a father who was unlike any father I'd seen via the many media images--images that painted stepfathers as something less than, people who weren't worthy to be claimed as part of the family. My stepfather filled the foreground and all the empty spaces of my life, those spaces that sometimes were not filled by the father who gave life to me.

My life with him began not unlike that of any other young girl child. Enter, a man. This man knew my mother and she knew him. There is no need to taint this telling with the biblical sense of knowing. The knowing was a story of love that would span a score and ten plus. It's a tall tale to be told on short paper, with limits only created by time and space. I've imagined what their first meeting must have been like. In the end, the truth was simply that a hard working Registered Nurse met and fell in love with a determined and diligent Electrician whose hobby was reading and jazz. The street was Bell Avenue in the North Bronx, New York about five minutes outside of Mount Vernon. Bell Avenue was a quiet street in a quiet neighborhood. Nothing terribly exciting happened there. No gunfire, no wild children, no cars speeding up and down the road. It was a simple block, with a simple set of folks who enjoyed a simple life.

On our left was the home of a Spanish family who had a dog named King. In truth, King was the most excitement we had in those days. While the early seventies were coming down off the high of the Civil Rights movement, Bell Avenue was coming down off the echoes of King who insisted on barking at everything that moved within his line of sight and not infrequently in earshot. King was the real leader of his household--he commanded attention when anyone passed by the small quaint home on that narrow street. To our right was another home, set a bit back, with a front yard filled with running vines. As a child, although I thought the dark strong green of the vines were beautiful, they were also very frightening. I imagined that lurking beneath them was a monster of some sort, waiting to claim anyone who would dare set foot in the large bed of ominous greenery. Further down the street were a couple of homes that had grape vines growing all along the brick exterior. I still recall that they were the best grapes I'd ever tasted. Sweet did not begin to describe them.

As I remember my stepdad, I realize now that it is the memory of him that jars the memory for all those fun and delicious things that made my childhood special. As the years walked on, he would be there. He was unmoved in his determination to love us all. My mother brought into the relationship me and my oldest sister. My youngest sister, the child between them, would be the bond that tied my stepdad to us. There was never a day when he acted as though he were tied, however, inescapably bound by two young girls that were not of his loins. He would remind us always that we were his daughters and he would treat us equally. He never broke his promise. There was not a day when I felt as though my youngest sister, due to her being his blood child, was treated more special than me and my older sister. He was a man of his word, a true man of honor.

I wish I could say that I understand the many television shows, books and experiences of so many who have lived the sometimes sad life of a stepchild. Or maybe I should express that I am glad I don't understand. I am glad I never felt neglected or second to mother or sister. I am glad I had a father there for me, every day and every night to guide my steps as a young woman. Having a father figure in the home made a huge difference in my life. Were it not for him, I can't say I would be the woman I am today. He helped to mold me. He was never afraid to tell me when I wasn't behaving like a lady. Or when I was being inconsiderate to my mother.

As the one who would prepare most of our meals, I would learn how to cook from him. He was our resident chef, always creating ever new and interesting foods for us to try. I recall there was always playing in the background songs from some of the great musicians whom he enjoyed-- Thelonious Monk, John Coltrane, Miles Davis, Donald Byrd, Lou Donaldson, Stanley Turrentine, Greg Osby and many more. He was a jazz man. Not your fly by night jazz man, a real jazz man. He was the kind of jazz man who knew that good jazz could only be played on good equipment. So he shelled out for top of the line. When he'd sit to listen, it was like watching one entranced. He sank into the music and allowed it to transport him. Jazz lived in him. Through him, I learned jazz over dinner. Over dinner, I learned bits and pieces of history. He was well read, a man who knew about the days of Truman, Kennedy and Kissinger. He understood in fairly intricate detail why every war on American soil was fought. He was acutely aware of the affect that America had on other cultures, on wars they'd precipitated off land, in distant countries. He would speak of many things in terms that made it seem as though nothing had changed in the world. But something had changed. I had changed. I became more aware of the world around me. I was a blind person who had suddenly regained vision. Everything looked brighter, sounded louder, and smelled stronger. My stepfather was and always will be one of my greatest teachers.

As the years rolled by, I would lean more on him for thoughts about various things. When I wasn't asking questions, I was carefully listening, often pretending that I wasn't. But I heard him, loud and clear. His voice was gentle, but his wisdom was like a tornado blazing through a once quiet town. It sounded off, a sonic boom, and filled my mind with ideas unimagined. He was never at a loss for a well-reasoned and logical response to anything presented to him. He was a man among men. He had everything going for him, and through the years he fulfilled all that he could and would ultimately be. I would never know if he wanted more, but I knew he always lived with a high level of outward contentment--he looked happy with his life.

I will never forget the morning he left us. He had been sick. But not so sick that we would have expected anything out of the ordinary. When my sister called to tell me that her daddy died, all I could do was pause and allow a numbness to flow through me. He wasn't just her daddy, he was my daddy. In fact, he was the daddy every young girl would want. He was the daddy so many were jealous they couldn't have. He was certainly my daddy.

I walked to where he was and looked down at the man I had called father for many years. He lay seeming to be asleep. My mother cried a heavy cry that broke my heart. The man who held the glue of our family together was gone. Gone. He would never return. There would be no more days of walking through the house in dusty work jeans. There would be no more pork dinners or curry anything. It was a loss that permeated both houses, our family and his. But something else happened that in many ways surprised no one. When it came time to say our final good-byes, there was no "his" family and "our" family. We were all one big family, no matter how we viewed our position. That is the way he lived. He didn't hold grudges. He didn't say a foul word to anyone. He was the peace keeper, the balancer. Everyone was equal and dealt with based on who they were. Even infractions were met with kindness and forgiveness. To upset him meant one had to work at it, daily doing things intentionally to create friction. I cannot recall a time when he would permanently succumb to the madness of anyone and completely disown them. He was a good man.

Was he perfect? Who is? Like most mortals, he had his flaws. But they were overshadowed by the goodness in him, the kindness in him, the everything in him that made him able to mend things. He made forgiveness easy. He made life an amazing adventure. Had I the chance, I would gladly be daughter to him again. He did not like everyone, but he loved everyone in an unexplainable way at times. He was a caregiver in his own way and a confidant to many.

Dad, I miss you. I have not met another one like you. And I should be so lucky to meet someone as amazing as you again who could be father to me. I hope that wherever you are, the jerk pork is cooked the way you like, the jazz beats can be heard out through the kitchen window and the stories you tell are over a glass of rum and coke. Send another round on the house for all those you left behind. We were the better for knowing you.

~Zaji

"I often accompanied my father. I really liked riding with him on his bicycle on Saturdays. He was very fond of fishing. I don't think I liked fishing.
I mean, you had to sit quietly and still, but I enjoyed the ride. And it was fun, it was fun. I mean, as I say, you didn't go around lugging a deep sense of resentment. We knew, yes, we were deprived.
It wasn't the same thing for white kids, but it was as full a life as you could make it. I mean, we made toys for ourselves with wires, making cars, and you really were exploding with joy!"
~Desmond Tutu - June 12, 2004

10th Anniversary Edition

Lifetime Legendary Man of Honor

Bishop Desmond Tutu
Archbishop Desmond Tutu:

Firebrand Lighting the Way

The Archbishop Desmond Tutu has long been a beacon for those of us who may feel torn between fear and faith. He speaks his truth as he sees it, no matter who might be offended or what consequences might follow. He provides living testimony that faith can overcome fear, and that no one can put out our light if our spiritual connection is sufficiently strong. . .

I felt privileged to make contact with the Archbishop when my writing partner Askhari and I sought to keep alive the sayings of our African ancestors. Our editor asked us whom we wanted to write the foreword of our book, *Lifelines: The Black Book of Proverbs*. We immediately said "Archbishop Desmond Tutu." Our editor suggested a famous person whom he had started to approach through a maze of intermediaries. "Not that person", we said, "Archbishop Desmond Tutu."

"That might be a stretch," our editor said. It might indeed have been a stretch, as we had never met the Archbishop. He lives in South Africa, Askhari is in the Deep South of the US, and I am in Jamaica. Further, our names would have meant nothing to him, even though we love him deeply and follow his career closely. We were drawn, then as now, by the fierceness of his spirit, the joyousness of this smile, the mischievous twinkle in his eyes, and a directness of expression that seems to arise from his heart.

"Give me a list of three persons ranked in the order of preference." our editor continued, "and we will see what we can do."

We submitted a list that said: number one: Archbishop Desmond Tutu; number two: Archbishop Desmond Tutu. We managed to list someone else as number three.

Less than a week later, our faith or our stubbornness was rewarded. Our editor was able to make direct contact with the Archbishop about three days after our conversation. As a tribute to his humility, the Archbishop had communicated without intermediaries, and his response came within 24 hours of our editor's e-mail to him. He consented so graciously that it seemed we were the ones doing him the honor!

We felt blessed to have this connection with a living legend. According to an African proverb, "the fire burns because of the wood gatherers." The Archbishop says he is retired now, but there is no doubt that the fire of justice continues to burn because of the Archbishop's lifetime of activism. Even while enjoying the leisure of chatting to his wife and playing with his grandchildren on his patio, he will no doubt be thinking about causes to which he can lend his name, his faith, and his energy. In a most recent photograph, for example, he was doing push-ups with Michelle Obama in support of an event to raise awareness about HIV/AIDS and teach children the importance of physical activity.

His passion for rights and justice is phenomenal. He is quoted as saying," If you are neutral in situations of injustice, you have chosen the side of the oppressor. If an elephant has its foot on the tail of a mouse and you say that you are neutral, the mouse will not appreciate your neutrality."

Neutrality therefore has no place in the Archbishop's advocacy. The apartheid government arrested him several times for being forthright in his criticism of the oppressive system. For example, he said apartheid was against the will of God; he demanded the repeal of the oppressive passport laws, and an end to forced relocation. The Archbishop could have chosen the route of cooperating with the apartheid government; he could have opted to be "safe", like a well-behaved house slave, while others suffered.

With his typical courage, he risked house arrest and a ban from public speaking – the penalties for speaking out against the apartheid regime. He was repeatedly arrested, but could never be silenced.

The Archbishop did not give easy passage to his allies in the anti-apartheid campaign. For example, he voiced strong objections to the violent tactics of some anti-apartheid groups. Further, he has been forthright in condemning South Africa's Black rulers for corruption, continued poverty, and violence against foreigners in parts of South Africa. In his view, "What is black empowerment when it seems to benefit not the vast majority but an elite that tends to be recycled?"

He has been equally outspoken to world leaders. The Archbishop has chided Tony Blair for joining the US in going to war on Iraq, and George Bush for detaining terrorist suspects in Guantanamo Bay. He denounced Zimbabwe President Robert Mugabe as "a cartoon figure of an archetypal African dictator." He has accused Israel of practicing apartheid in relation to Palestinians, and has consequently been labeled "anti-Semitic." He has risked a pro-terrorist label by calling on U.S. President Barack Obama to apologize to the world, and especially to Iraqis, for the invasion of Iraq. He has not been deterred by the possibility that he could be called socialist or communist for demanding that world leaders narrow gaps between rich and poor. At the same time, some socialists have criticized him for defending capitalism and opposing social revolution.

Accepted concepts of God have come in for his scrutiny and comment. The Archbishop has described communion with God in terms of a fire in winter: the fire will warm anyone who sits close to it, whether or not the person happens to be smart. .He recently stirred indignation among some Christians by pointing out that God is not a Christian. He stated in his recently published book, *God is not a Christian: And Other Provocations:*

... what we call the Spirit of God is not a Christian preserve, for the Spirit of God existed long before there were Christians, inspiring and nurturing women and men

in the ways of holiness, bringing them to fruition, bringing to fruition what was best in all.

To the consternation of his fellow Christians, he asserted that God therefore belongs equally to Jews, Muslims, Buddhists and other religions.

The Archbishop has stood apart from the Catholic Church and fellow Anglican clergy in matters of human sexuality. He criticized the Catholic Church for its disapproval of condoms as a way of preventing HIV/AIDS. He was uncompromising in his criticism of his colleagues in the Anglican Church for focusing on sexual orientation of consenting adults, rather than seeking to address the world's social problems. In a 2007 *BBC* interview he said, "If God, as they say, is homophobic, I wouldn't worship that God." He also wrote, in a new book:

Every human being is precious. We are all — all of us — part of God's family. We all must be allowed to love each other with honor. Yet all over the world, lesbian, gay, bisexual, and transgender people are persecuted. We treat them as pariahs and push them outside our communities. We make them doubt that they too are children of God. This must be nearly the ultimate blasphemy.

He has consistently defended those infected and affected by HIV/AIDS. This disease took the lives of 330,000 to 340,000 South Africans and infected one in ten persons, while the then South African president denied the science behind HIV/AIDS. Archbishop used his global stature to call on the call on the international community "which was so tremendous in its fight against another epidemic, apartheid, to show the same commitment to deal with TB and HIV/AIDS." In addition, he established an HIV centre to enable the needy to access antiretroviral treatment and receive testing, support, education, and voluntary counseling.

The Archbishop's status as winner of a Nobel Peace Prize has given him a platform for his advocacy. His focus seems to remain constant no matter the praise or the criticism that comes his way. For example, he seems unperturbed when his critics term him a "loose cannon" and a "scandalous man." Being labeled "naïve" or "irritating" may indeed have served to strengthen his commitment to shining his light on solutions to human problems.

Personal challenges, like criticism, seem like fuel for his passion to help others. He contracted tuberculosis when he was 14 years old, and he is an unceasing advocate for tuberculosis research, treatment and prevention. "TB is the child of poverty," he said, "but also its parent and provider." He is therefore patron of TB Alert (a UK organization working internationally); and lends his name and support to the Desmond Tutu TB Centre at *Stellenbosch University*.

When he was diagnosed with prostate cancer, he took every opportunity to share his struggle with an illness that can be fatal. He encouraged men, especially Black men to consider a prostate examination as the best gift they can give to their families. The Archbishop is quoted as saying:

When you hit 50, men should have the prostate examination annually. If there is a history of prostate cancer in your family, then start earlier. My wife and I decided to go public because cancer gets bad press. People assume it's [always] terminal...I appeal to our people that the rectal examination is not as bad as people make it out to be. It may be slightly uncomfortable, but no more than going to the dentist for an examination.

He later became the patron of South African Prostate Cancer Foundation.

Since "one piece of wood doesn't keep the fire alight during the night," the Archbishop has brought together a group of world leaders, the Council of Elders, to tackle some of the world's toughest problems. He chairs this body. In addition, following his experience as chairman of *South Africa's Truth and Reconciliation Commission*, he has helped to spread the model to about twenty countries.

As the Archbishop approaches his eightieth birthday, his achievements challenge us to exercise our faith. If he ever feels fear, he does allow it to deter him. Indeed, seeming roadblocks seem only to spur him on to greater service to humanity. He is the firebrand: his legacy is in lighting fires from which we can take live coals.

~Yvonne McCalla Sobers

Gumbo For The Soul

10th Anniversary Edition

"…for I only make company with the noteworthy
forces of change
and those with high range
I guess it's a yin and yang thing
with a young, gifted and black swing
but forgive me if I choose to not sing
but take notes…"
~Bruce George

Helpful Resources Section

American Cancer Society:
Dedicated to helping persons who face *cancer*. Supports research, patient services, early detection, treatment and education.www.cancer.org

Association of Cancer Online Resources: cancer information system currently offers access to 99 electronic mailing lists and a variety of unique websites. www.acor.org. Includes search options on types of cancer and treatment options.

Men's Guide to Test and Screenings for Good Health

Type of test: Blood Glucose
Purpose: To screen for diabetes
Age group and recommended screening schedule:
18 – 44: If you are overweight or have other risk factors, as directed by doctor.
45 & over: Every three years if test results are normal, or as directed by doctor.

Type of test: Blood Pressure Reading
Purpose: To detect high blood pressure or hypertension – a risk factor for heart disease, strokes and other problems
Age group and recommended screening schedule:
20 & over: Every 1-2 years, more frequently if over 140/90, or as directed by doctor.

Type of test: Bone Density Test
Purpose: To test for osteoporosis, a disease in which bones become fragile and are more likely to break.
Age group and recommended screening schedule:
50-69: For men with risk factors, rheumatoid arthritis or other conditions associated with bone loss-initial test, then as needed.
70 & over: One time, or as directed by doctor.

Type of test: Cholesterol

Purpose: To check if cholesterol content of blood is too high – a major factor in heart disease.
Age group and recommended screening schedule:
20 & over: Every 5 years or as directed by doctor.

Type of test: Colorectal Screening
Purpose: To screen for colorectal cancer, which is highly treatable with early detection.
Age group and recommended screening schedule:
50 & over: There are several tests that find polyps and cancer and others that mainly find cancer. Talk to your doctor about which test is best for you.

Type of test: Dental Exams
Purpose: To check for cavities, early signs of gum disease and other oral problems.
Age group and recommended screening schedule: Every six months

Type of test: Eye Exam
Purpose: To check for problems including cataracts and glaucoma.
Age group and recommended screening schedule:
20-29: At least once, **30-39:** At least twice.
40: Baseline eye disease screening.
40 – 64: As directed by doctor.
65 & over: Every 1-2 years.

Type of test: Prostate Specific Antigen Test
Purpose: To detect prostate cancer; a digital rectal exam is recommended at the same time.
Age group and recommended screening schedule:
50 & over: Consult your doctor about annual screenings, (African Americans and others at high risk should begin testing at age 45.)

Type of test: Skin Cancer Exam
Purpose: To detect new skin growths, spots, bumps, patches and misshapen moles that may indicate cancer.
Age group and recommended screening schedule:
18 & over: Self-exam (entire body): monthly. Clinical exam: annually.

Type of test: Testicular Exam
Purpose: Self-exam: To check for painless lumps that could indicate testicular cancer. Clinical exam: To check for testicular cancer.
Age group and recommended screening schedule:
15 & over: Self exam: monthly. Clinical exam: When you have a complete physical exam or upon early detection of lumps.

Type of test: Thyroid Screening
Purpose: To check proper functioning of the thyroid gland.
Age group and recommended screening schedule:
35 & over: Every 5 years or as indicated by doctor.
Source: Guide card © Positive Promotions, Inc. Rev. 11/09. Reviewed by: Pam Taxal, M.D.

Note: If you are at high risk for certain diseases or conditions, ask your doctor about the need for more frequent test or screenings.

10th Anniversary Edition

Additional Servings of Gumbo

The 4th YOUnity Reviewers Guild of America awarded the "Most Outstanding Anthology of the Year!" to 'Gumbo for the Soul: The Recipe for Literacy in the Black Community' which was also named by Blackrefer.com 3rd Annual Reviewer's Choice Awards, "Best Anthology of 2007!"

Gumbo for the Soul: The Recipe for Literacy in the Black Community

'Gumbo for the Soul: The Recipe for Literacy in the Black Community' anthology, served by over 100 generous contributors offering accounts of educational, occupational and personal experiences dealing with adversity, obstacles, perseverance and determination eloquently portrayed in the form of poetry, personal stories, quotes & reflections.

Book cover ©1990 "With Honors" by Synthia SAINT JAMES
Foreword by Heather Covington, author of Literary Divas: The Top 100+ Most Admired African American Women in Literature and NAACP Image Award Nominee.

"Gumbo for the Soul" dares to call it like it is. This serving of Gumbo is a must-read for every parent, teacher, mentor and all who believe it is important that our children can read and comprehend the English language."
~Tavis Smiley, Author, Television and Radio Host

"GUMBO FOR THE SOUL tells African-Americans exactly what the recipe for a good life is. It is inspirational, uplifting, and recommended for people of all ages, colors and aspirations." ~ Alice Holman
Rawsistaz Reviewer Alice Holman rates Gumbo 5 out of 5

ISBN: 0-595-42907-6

2007© Gumbo for the Soul Publications.

Gumbo for the Soul: "Here's Our Child, Where's The Village?"

"Here's Our Child, Where's The Village?" conveys that every child deserves the opportunity to flourish as happy, thriving and free spirited people regardless of race and the displacement factors governing their lives. The question isn't "Here's Our Child, Where's The Village?" The question is whose village will you be?

~Beverly Black Johnson

Book cover: Grandmother Spirit© Synthia SAINT JAMES Foreword by Tee C. Royal founder of Rawsistaz Literary Group.

"We must bear each other's burdens. Though the village has been replaced by concrete and Roe v. Wade, there remains innocent children deserving of love and a safe haven. They may be parentless, but they are not Godless…"
~Bruce George, Co-Founder of Def Poetry Jam

"Connecting kids to permanency is paramount."
~Stacia C. Hammond- Executive Director/Founder
Adoption Support & Consultation Services of Florida, Inc. (ASCS)
Rawsistaz Reviewer Dawn Reeves rates Gumbo 4.5 out of 5
ISBN: 978-1-4401-0126
2008© Gumbo for the Soul Publications.

10th Anniversary Edition

Gumbo for the Soul: Women of Honor
~Special Pink Edition~

"I am utterly ecstatic to read about all of the strong, loving, creative, and determined women who are being honored in this book. Each story, poem and quote is an inspiration, and reminds me how incredibly indomitable we women are. Congratulations to all the COMBAT DIVAS – mothers, grandmothers, daughters, sisters and girlfriends – to whom tribute is being paid."

Gail D. Bishop, Sisters Network, Inc. San Francisco Chapter president, breast cancer survivor and recent recipient of the San Francisco Chapter Susan G. Komen 2010 Hope and Inspiration Award, is lovingly pictured on the book's back cove

COMPILED by Beverly Black Johnson
Gumbo for the Soul Publications, Oct. 2010
ISBN: 978-0-9790479-1-6
Paperback, 140 pp, $11.95 U.S.
GENRE: Inspiration/Self Help
A Bruce George Media vision
BOOK COVER: "Sisters of Courage"© by Synthia SAINT JAMES, celebrated artist, author, architectural designer and Kwanzaa postage stamp illustrator
FOREWORD by Synthia SAINT JAMES

This publication is made possible, in part, by the following supporters. We, the Gumbo family, thank you for your generosity.

PR, et Cetera, Inc.

PR, et Cetera, Inc. congratulates GUMBO founder and cancer education advocate Beverly Black Johnson, and visionary Bruce George on this, the fourth in the enthralling "Gumbo for the Soul" anthology series that honors extraordinary men for unselfishly imparting courage, love, inspiration and wisdom in both joyous and difficult times.

Toni Beckham
President & CEO
PR, et Cetera, Inc.
TONI@PRETCETERA.COM
WWW.PRETCETERA.COM

10ᵗʰ Anniversary Edition

The Bandana Republic

The Bandana Republic, **A Literary Anthology by Gang Members and Their Affiliates**, edited by Louis Reyes Rivera and Bruce George
with a foreword by Jim Brown
http://www.myspace.com/thebandanarepublic

Sister to Sister: One in the Spirit

www.sistersoneinthespirit.org

10th Anniversary Edition

Patricia Bridewell presents "A Generation of Curses"

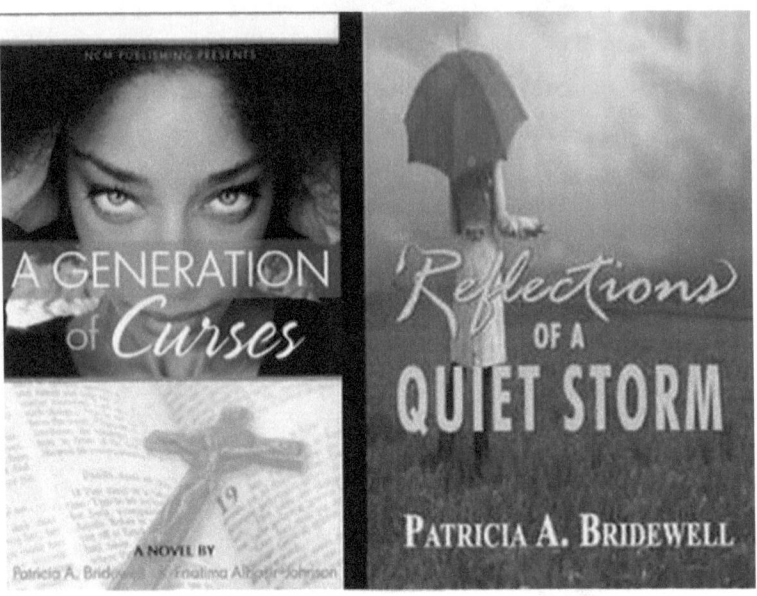

and "Reflections of a Quiet Storm"
www.patriciabridewell.com

Gumbo For The Soul

www.loritawrites4u.com

10th Anniversary Edition

A Slip In The Right Direction, a coming-of-age story for tweens & teens. The story of life, puppy love, and lessons, as seen through the eyes of a fourteen-year-old young man coming of age in Chicago.

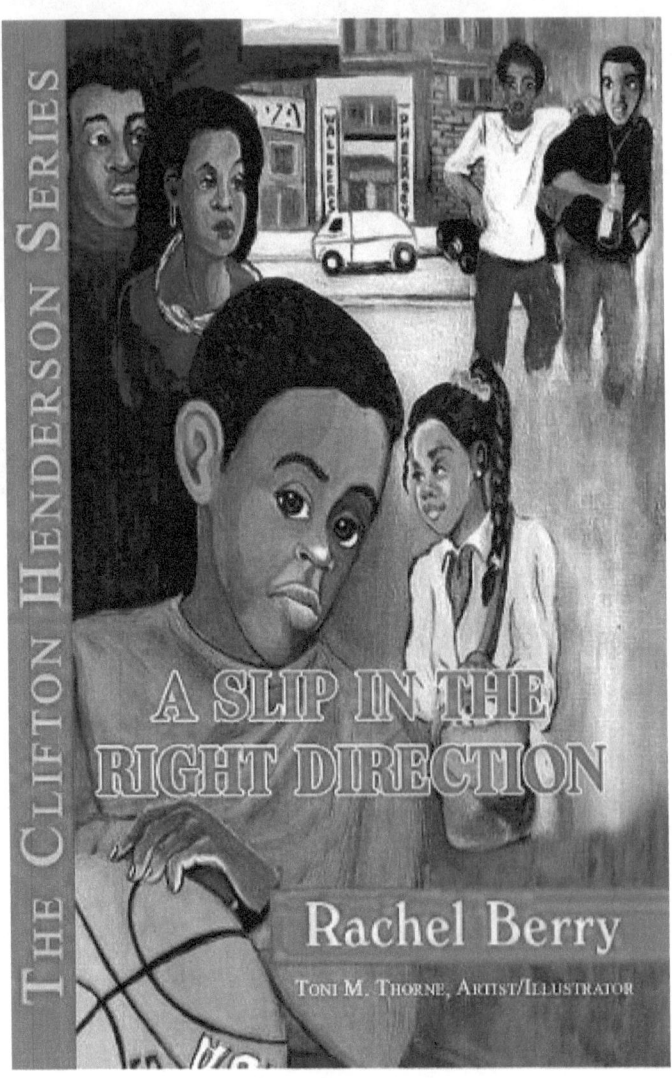

http://rachelberry.webs.com

10th Anniversary Edition

WWW.AMBERBOOKS.COM
The Nation's Largest African American Publisher of
Self-Help Books & Celebrity Biographies

WWW.QUALITYPRESS.INFO
The #1 African American
Self-Publishing Book House

10th Anniversary Edition

Gumbo for the Soul Radio - Soul Brother Circle

Gumbo for the Soul Radio presents in honor of
Dr. Hershel Swinger, a soulful brother circle of spectacular Men of Honor. Tony Rose **(TR)**, CEO of Amber Communications Group Inc., Co-founder of the African American Pavilion, takes a seat at the table of **Gumbo for the Soul Radio - Soul Brother Circle*** with Lady Serenity aka Rachel Berry **(RB)**. Excerpt from June 16, 2011 broadcast.

(RB) Welcome to the show, before we start I want to say Happy Father's Day to you. Good evening. How are you?

(TR) I'm fine and glad to be here with you.

(RB) For the first time you're telling your cancer story, what was your first reaction when you learned of your diagnosis? Tell us about those first feelings?

(TR) You know, when you find out anything that's perilous in your life, or when you're in danger, it's always sudden, you don't expect it…you're hearing the words-you have tumors and they're cancerous…so the first reaction was panic! Where am I going? What am I doing? I was told this on the morning I was leaving for the African American Pavilion at Book Expo America. I had had a PSA test two weeks before…when the doctors said you have cancer, tumors, basically, from that point on I went into work mode. I didn't tell Yvonne for a week…the whole month of June was dealing with a lot of testing and decisions to be made. You have to basically now begin to save your life. It's as simple as that. You have cancer…the cancer can spread to your bones. What can you do? Who do you trust? What doctors can you go to? Luckily, I had an uncle that had gone through prostate cancer for years and he reached out to me. By August, I found a doctor and began the process of radiation, chemotherapy, hormone shots and all that went along with that.

(RB) Now that you are cancer-free, and we are so very thankful to the creator for that, what would you say about your journey that has made you vigilant about your health, and keeping it intact, and also proclaiming to others to do the same?

(TR) You know, I was always vigilant about my health. I loved walking, bicycling, running, and the outdoors…What this did was make me aware that life is a blessing and every morning when you get up, every time you go out and there's no pain, and you're not on morphine, every day is a Blessing. I watched Montel enough and I said; let me buy that blender Montel's selling. I'm blending my fresh fruits and vegetables more...we live putting a lot of wrong things in our body for years...we came up project-strong...so we as a people have absorbed so much that it doesn't bother us, until it does. But when you're young, strong and beautiful you feel you can do anything...

(TR) (Closing remarks re: On making health changes)...you hear a voice say start taking care of yourself now because later you will have to.

(TR) (Closing remarks re: message to other brothers) We need help...we were born in turmoil...we live in turmoil. We have to reach one, each one, teach one...be a blessing to one another...respect one another...and love one another.

*Listen to the entire one-hour show by visiting
http://www.gumboforthesoul.net/11.html

10th Anniversary Edition

Contributing Authors

Khaliid R. Bean - A native Californian, loves classic cars, amateur photography and commands respect on the Chess board. Khaliid is the first-born son of *Gumbo for the Soul* creator, Beverly Black Johnson.

Marvin Bean - A God fearing man. Marvin resides in California with his family.

Donna Ford - A freelance clothing designer, also specializing in one-of-kind wearable artistic apparel. Aspires to design a line with Bob Mackie.

George C. Fraser - Author of *Success Runs In Our Race, Click,* and *Race for Success.*

Bruce George - Entrepreneur, activist, Co-founder of *Russell Simmons' Def Poetry Jam* on HBO.

Gerald Green - a retired mechanical engineer, lives in Oakland with his wife Monica and teenage son Charles. He attended numerous workshops that led to a writer's fellowship at Stanford University. His writings reflect the importance of early cancer detection, good medical insurance, and the necessity of a loving supportive family.

He released *Life Constricted: To Love, Hugs and Laugher,* a memoir, in 2010 which chronicles his and his family's saga and victories over tongue cancer in 1995, neck cancer in 1997 and prostate cancer in 2008. His chapter, *Fatherhood Love,* appears in the second edition of *Black Fathers an Invisible Presence in America* published by Routledge in 2011. Gerald's poetry appears in the Healing Journey an on-line publication and The Monthly, a premier magazine of culture and commerce, recently published one of his essays.

You may order his book at lifeconstricted.com.

Sylvia Larane Green is a poet/author of the inspirational collections of poems, *Gift of Life* and *Songs for the Single,* has been composing inspiring verse for family, friends, and others for about twenty years. She began writing poetry in her late teens when she accepted Christ into her life and made a conversion over from creating secular rap lyrics. Her books, *Gift of Life* and *Songs for the Single*, are available at

www.amazon.com and her official website, www.sylvialaranegreen.com.

Linda A. Haywood is the author of *Does God Really Hear Me When I Cry? A Life Transformed*, which is her autobiography. She has also written for a number of newsletters and received Honorable mention in *Writers Digest* in 2008. Linda is also a Licensed Minister and Social Worker in the State of Michigan. She may be reached by email at lhaywood45@yahoo.com or her website at

www.thecalledandreadywriters.org

Beverly Black Johnson is the creator of *Gumbo for the Soul* Publications.

Wanda Mays Noel is an innovator, speaker, marketing strategist and serial entrepreneur. Born in Fort Myers, Florida, and raised in Tampa, Florida, she knew very early her destiny was to design and create successful projects. She is an Alumni of *Florida A & M University*, member of *Delta Sigma Theta Sorority Inc.* and a proud mother of 2 beautiful children.

Ms. Noel is the proud Founder/CEO/President of *La'John Media, LLC*. Her area of expertise includes public relations, marketing, promotions, publicists, entertainment management, business consulting, and training. *La'John Media, L.L.C* also focuses on advertising, image management, event planning and encouragement to the professional and urban markets.

Ms. Noel has recently expanded with the development of *La'John Media Publishing Group*. Author of *How I Failed Up To Doing Good Business*, July 2011; co-author of *Victorious Living for Moms*, April 2011, and *99 Business Tips for Women*, available in bookstores now.

Pearl Jr. is CEO of *Elbow Grease Productions*, a full-service production company that focuses on activism via the media. EGP was the ONLY Black-owned media credentialed to cover the Michael Jackson Trial, produced the DVD, "Michael Jackson - The Trial and Triumph of the

King of Pop" from their first documentary, "Behind the Scenes at the Michael Jackson Trial". It's the documentary that tells the truth about the trial featuring FACTS! EGP produced the DVD, "Barack Obama The Power of Change" All their products are available on amazon.com Pearl Jr. is the author of three books, including, "Black Women Need Love Too!"

Pam Perry is a PR Coach & social media strategist delivering online branding and marketing solutions for best-selling authors, nonprofits and entrepreneurs/authorpreneurs. Her company is *Social Media PR Solutions, LLC.* (www.socialmediaprsolutions.com)

Joey Pinkney - Author, book reviewer. http://joeypinkney.com

Rolanda T. Pyle published her first book entitled *FINALLY,* a collection of her poems in 2004. She published her second book, an anthology, "Beneath His Everlasting Wings" in 2009 . Rolanda is a certified social worker and has worked in the aging field for more than fifteen years. She is a frequent contributor to the *Gumbo for the Soul* series. Her website is www.rorosrainbowcommunications.com.

Yvonne McCalla Sobers is a former educator who studied at the University of the West Indies, is currently a human and community development consultant,. She is also a human rights activist and researcher. Yvonne writes fiction and non-fiction, and is also the author of "Delicious Jamaica!: Vegetarian Cuisine". Apart from a decade spent in Ghana and England, Yvonne has lived all her life in Kingston, Jamaica. She and Askhari Johnson Hodari, Ph.D., co-authored, LIFELINES: The Black Book of Proverbs. Foreword by Bishop Desmond Tutu. (Random House 2009). Inspired by the biblical Book of Proverbs, a wondrously illustrated collection of aphorisms, witticisms, and sayings from Africa and the African Diaspora that will entrance, entertain, and enlighten readers of all ages.

Birth and Parenting: "When a yam does not grow well, do not blame the yam; it is because of the soil." (Ghana)

Marriage: "Getting married is nothing: it is assuming the responsibility of marriage that counts."(Haiti)

Money Problems: "The poor person does not experience poverty all the time." (Ghana)

Peace and War: "To engage in conflict, one does not bring a knife that cuts but a needle that sews. (Kiswahili)

This book of proverbs is uniquely arranged by life cycle themes from birth to death and speaks to the tragedy and triumph in between. Unforgettable vignettes showing how African proverbs comfort, inspire, and instruct during different phases of life.

LIFELINES sharpens understanding of how traditions, civilization, and spirit survive and thrive, despite centuries of loss of freedom, family, identity, language, land, and wealth.

More about Lifelines:

www.lifelinesproverbs.com

Kathie Strother-Scholl is a wife, mother of 2, and a children's book fanatic. She is the recipient of several awards for her children's literature and was named one of Auburn California's most creative in 2007 and 2008. She holds an AA Degree in Television/ Video Production and a BA in Behavioral Science. She wrote and co-produced the television show, PM Magazine, and wrote for the Superior Courts in San Diego and Ventura County. She is a published poet and a past contributor to Gumbo for the Soul: The Recipe for Literacy in the Black Community (2007). Additionally, she wrote the introduction and back cover for Bridge To Triumph (2007). She is a 6 year member of the Society of Children's Book Writers and Illustrators (SCBWI) and is currently working to publish the 6 completed children's book manuscripts she's written. Her goal is, and has always been, to inspire reading by creating characters in which children can laugh, learn and identify.

Anthony Spires - A graduate of San Francisco State University, Tony Spires is a filmmaker, longtime theatre artist, poet, award-winning playwright, critically acclaimed director and co-writer of the NAACP Award nominated, "Ali: The Man, The Myth, The Peoples' Champion. Tony's feature films include: The Pan African Film Festival's Best Feature nominated "Tears Of A Clown," starring Don "D.C." Curry and the gritty, urban crime drama "Two Degrees." He's the Founder/Executive Producer of The Bay Area Black Comedy Competition & Festival and Founder/creative force behind Oakland, CA-based youth performing arts organization, Full Vision Arts Foundation. He is active as the performing and recording, spoken word artist "Phruishun." His poetry has been published nationally and has been performed in numerous professional stage plays and musical productions. He's a self-taught musician and a long-time live event producer and personal manager to some of comedy's brightest talents. He's also the featured columnist for Humor Mill Magazine.

Christine Vaughan **aka Solmantress** is a soul led writer, author, poet, spoken word artist and motivational speaker. She wrote two books of poetry, "Epiphany ~ Third Eye Poetry and He Raised the World From My Shoulders ~ Poetry In Motion", creates framed affirmations. She is co-founder of the Nubian Writers Group in Boston.

Marvin Winans, Jr. is an award winning gospel recording artist, entrepreneur, and actor..

Zaji is a published freelance writer, journalist, speechwriter, copywriter and copyeditor. She enjoys writing, reading, listening to music, playing piano, singing, traveling and skating. She has published her first novel, When We Were One; a book of poetry, Words…Loving Emotions; two short stories, The letters published through Amazon Shorts and Lights on a Cave Wall published in the anthology, *Making the Hookup*. She is currently working on her second novel and an anthology of short stories.

About the compilers:

"And so he bequeath, a necktie to me, symbolic to honor our continued legacy."
~Beverly Black Johnson

Beverly Black Johnson hails from the San Francisco Bay Area, born in the liberal city of San Francisco, raised in East Palo Alto from the age of six. The youngest of four, if asked to define her child hood she would say in one word, "lonely."

By age seventeen, Beverly would experience the death of her stepfather, the suicide of her closest friend and only brother, and would barely graduate high school. Between 1977 and 1980 she made several attempts to attend college only to drop out, yielding her destiny to a booming electronics industry. She would learn the trade from laser's to electrodes and everything in between. This trade would prove valuable for over twenty years with bouts of drug and alcohol abuse intertwined. In 1982, she gave birth to her first child, a very healthy baby boy. In 1984 Beverly, after falling deep into the crack epidemic, gave birth to an underweight, crack addicted baby girl. By the ages of three and five, the kids were brought into the "system" by her father, who also arranged for Beverly to deal with her warrants, vowing not to lose another child. While her mother and sisters fought tirelessly to keep the kids together, Beverly's bout with drugs continued, save for a few breaks in jail or treatment programs. Years later after going in and out of drug programs, jail and the streets, Beverly moved to Oakland to assist in her father's general contracting business and to "get clean." Beverly became active in the reunification process to have her children returned to her as she began to clean up her life. That was short lived because Beverly would be forced by a child welfare system to move back to San Mateo County or risk her children being moved to a foster home in the county of Oakland.

10th Anniversary Edition

To prevent the uprooting of her children, Beverly hesitantly moved back to East Palo Alto, "the old hood and the old friends," only for the drug cycle to begin again. Not more than a year later she gave birth to a baby boy who tested positive for crack and wasn't allowed to leave the hospital with her. A change would come that would allow her to make a vow to turn her life around. She never looked back.

Beverly did complete the reunification process and did regain custody of her children. She was told she would never get her baby boy that tested positive. She regained custody of him when he was eighteen months old. Her story will be told in autobiography of her life's trials and tribulations, "A Wretch Like Me."

Beverly has been "crack free" since February 24, 1992 and eventually returned to her first love, poetry. She is the publisher of the award-winning anthology, *Gumbo for the Soul: The Recipe for Literacy in the Black Community*. She continues her advocacy for literacy with the *Gumbo for the Soul* series anthologies. ,

Life has been no cake walk but now that Beverly has turned hers around she has much to be thankful for.

Her testimony bears truth that All Things are possible through Christ Jesus.

About Gumbo for the Soul:

Gumbo for the Soul is a savory blend of anthologies that focuses on humanitarian issues effecting communities worldwide. We address health, education, wellness and spirituality while offering philanthropy with inspirational and informative publications. The subjects we address can't be discussed enough. Statistics convey too many disparities in this highly advanced and technologically driven world of failing, and all too often relied upon, broken systems. The media report's one thing, the look in a person's eyes, and the writing on the wall, paints a completely different view. We are in a world that cries for help. As part of our mission, we will continue to spark change, heighten awareness, and offer resources for resolutions about the issues we outline. *Gumbo for the Soul Publications* has been able to give away hundreds of books since our inception through our *Gumbo for the Soul Literacy Program*.

10th Anniversary Edition

Bruce George is an entrepreneur, speaker, author, poet, panelist, executive producer, consultant, social activist, and Director of Business Development for Gumbo for the Soul. He was born and raised in New York City and has written poetry/prose & articles for over thirty-seven years. His work has been published in major magazines, anthologies, and literary publications. He has written testimonials from the likes of *Essence Magazine, Emerge Magazine, Class Magazine, Harlem River Press* etc...

Bruce has won multiple poetry & talent contests. He has won several awards such as a "Peabody Award" for "Russell Simmons Presents, Def Poetry (HBO)," a "Miky Award" for "Russell Simmons Presents, Def Poetry Jam (HBO)," an "Upscale Showcase Award," a "Trail Blazer Award" etc...for his outstanding vision, production, writing and performance.

Bruce is the Co-founder of the critically acclaimed award winning, "Russell Simmons's Def Poetry Jam." He's also the Founder/Managing Editor of "The Bandana Republic, an Anthology of Poetry & Prose by Gang Members & Their Affiliates."

As an activist Bruce has been and currently is associated with major grassroots organizations that fosters and uplifts people in struggle.

A Bruce George Media vision and Gumbo for the Soul publication

BRUCE GEORGE MEDIA

www.brucegeorgemedia.com
"Power belongs to the People"
www.thepeoplepowernetwork.ning.com/

~ Shedding Light On Life ~
www.gumboforthesoul.com

© 2011 Gumbo for the Soul Publications
Inspiration | Self-Help
Gumbo for the Soul
Men of Honor
-Special Cancer Awareness Edition-

10th Anniversary Edition

In honor of Homer Joe Black Sr.
April 22, 1931 – July 22, 2009
"Just like his golf swing, Daddy strove at the art of taking his best shot at life!"
~Beverly Black Johnson

"Marvin Winans Sr. is a Man of Honor in my life. I honor him because he represents Godliness and boldness in a time where both are rare commodities. He is never afraid to stand up for what is righteous...more importantly, he is never afraid to stand up!"

-Marvin Winans Jr.

www.ingramcontent.com/pod-product-compliance
Lightning Source LLC
Chambersburg PA
CBHW021348290426
44108CB00010B/152